FIRST THROUGH GRAND CANYON

BOOKS by Michael P. Ghiglieri

The Chimpanzees of Kibale Forest

East of the Mountains of the Moon: Chimpanzee Society in the African Rainforest

Canyon

The Dark Side of Man: Tracing the Origins of Male Violence

Over the Edge: Death in Grand Canyon (with Thomas M. Myers)

First Through Grand Canyon: The Secret Journals and Letters of the 1869 Crew Who Explored the Green and Colorado Rivers

Off the Wall: Death in Yosemite (with Charles R. "Butch" Farabee, Jr.)

Boatman: Lessons on Survival in the Back of Beyond (forthcoming)

Into the Great Unknown (fiction, forthcoming)

FIRST THROUGH GRAND CANYON

Michael P. Ghiglieri

FIRST THROUGH
GRAND CANYON

The Secret Journals and Letters of the 1869 Crew Who Explored the Green and Colorado Rivers

Michael P. Ghiglieri

With writings by

George Young Bradley
Andrew Hall
William Robert Wesley Hawkins
Oramel G. Howland
John Wesley Powell
Walter H. Powell
John Colton Sumner

With Foreword by

Richard D. Quartaroli

PUMA PRESS

Flagstaff

SECOND, REVISED EDITION
2010

ISBN: 978-0-9700973-2-3
LCCN: 00-2002114638

Book cover design by Michael P. Ghiglieri & Bronze Black
Cover photos by Michael P. Ghiglieri & E.O. Beaman
Author photo by Conan Michael Ghiglieri
Rear cover photograph by Bronze Black
Rear cover etching by A. Muller from Canyons of the Colorado
Editing by Thomas M. Myers
Book production by Positive Impressions, LLC

The author is grateful for permission to reprint the following copyrighted material:
pages 17, 18, 19: photos of Frank Goodman, Andy Hall & William Hawkins courtesy of the Huntington Library.
pages 22 & 23: photos of Oramel G. Howland and Seneca B. Howland courtesy of the Howland Society.
page 38: photo of Walter Powell courtesy of Special Collections, Univ. of Arizona Library.
page 66: Imax photo of Powell reconstruction boats at River Mile 34 courtesy of Imax.
pages 48 & 49 : transcribed copy of "The Agreement" between J.W. Powell and J. Sumner, O.G. Howland, and W. H. Dunn courtesy of Special Collections, Univ. of Arizona Library.
page 76: Map of the Green and Colorado rivers, from *Powell of the Colorado* by W. C. Darrah, copyright 1951 by Princeton University Press.
pages 223, 226, 231: photos of Separation Rapid and Lava Cliff Rapid by the Kolb Brothers.
multiple pages : 1947. *Utah Historical Quarterly* Vol. 15, pp. 73-88, 90-92, 95-105, 113-124, and the 1948-49 *Utah Historical Quarterly* Vols. 16-17, pp. 506-508, & 1969, Vol. 37, pp. 173-189.
pages 281, 282: autobiography of James Leithead courtesy of L. Tom Perry Special Collections, Harold B. Lee Library, Brigham Young University.

DEDICATION

In recognition of the first professional Colorado River boatmen:

George Young Bradley

William H. Dunn

Andrew Hall

William Robert Wesley Hawkins

Oramel G. Howland

Seneca B. Howland

Walter Henry Powell

John Colton Sumner

And in memory of the 1869 Powell Expedition historians who never lived to see their hard work published as books:

Robert Brewster Stanton

Otis "Dock" Marston

Martin J. Anderson

And dedicated to every river runner and adventurer — armchair or in the wild back of beyond — who has wondered: "Hey, what really *did* happen on that 1869 expedition, anyway?"

TABLE OF CONTENTS

FOREWORD

August 28, 2002. One hundred thirty-three years ago today, three men walked away from the Colorado River and out of the Grand Canyon. The conjecture as to the experiences of John Wesley Powell and his 1869 expedition members, and to the events leading to the split of the party at Separation Rapid, are still passionately argued. Beginning with some of the remaining six participants, seemingly all Canyon and River historians consider the details and state their interpretations of one of the most important Colorado River controversies imaginable.

In the 1930s and '40s, Utah State Historical Society published much of the primary source material from the men on Powell's Green and Colorado River expeditions of 1869 and 1871-72. For members of the Society and interested others, this significantly increased the readily available knowledge of this portion of the "unexplored" territory of the Colorado Plateau.

However, researchers with access to the original records in the archives and repositories realized that the published transcriptions varied in accuracy. Dock Marston and his protégé Marty Anderson met on an early 1970s Grand Canyon Expeditions river trip, one with a historical emphasis. Interpreter Marston on the west coast enlisted Anderson on the east coast to do some "sleuthing" for him. Of course, one of the main subjects of investigation was John Wesley Powell.

Anderson would travel from his home in New Jersey to the New York Public Library and spend many hours with the Robert Brewster Stanton Collection, transcribing journals by hand, typing them at home, double-checking against the originals, correcting, re-typing, and then sharing his work with Marston. In addition, Anderson discussed the finer points of Powell with William Culp Darrah, whose published transcriptions in the Utah Historical Quarterly he had now scrupulously corrected.

Although Anderson wrote some journal articles, he never published the newer transcriptions. Thus, in 1988, he, I, and many others with Colorado River history fascination looked forward to a book purporting to have "assembled for the first time ... all the surviving journals, accounts, and letters left behind by Powell and his [1869] crew." Its failure to do so made me believe the title should have been, instead of *The Great Unknown, The Great Disappointment*. A reasonably priced compilation such as this would have been a welcome addition to those collections lacking copies of the hard to find and pricey, though flawed, volumes of the *Utah Historical Quarterly*.

Which brings us to the justification for Michael Ghiglieri to write and publish, in this centennial year of the founding of the Reclamation Service and the death of John Wesley Powell, what may seem at first glance merely another book about Powell and the Colorado River. Earle E. Spamer's *Bibliography of the Grand Canyon and Lower Colorado River* now has over 27,000 citations, several hundred with either Powell as author or subject. With the flurry of recent publications on Powell, is there room on the shelves for a book solely focusing on the hard-core adventure during the 1869 first descent and the critical roles that its crew played? To hardcore collectors and bibliophiles, the answer might always be yes. Perhaps the question should be not one of quantity, but instead of quality. Does this work have value, not only to the collector, but also to the armchair traveler and the consummate researcher?

As a person who might fit into most, if not all, of the above categories, I must reply with absolute affirmation. Herein lies the most complete, the most accurate of transcriptions, with the accounts, particularly Powell's, stripped of their romanticism. Michael has returned to the originals, in as many instances as possible, and painstakingly read and deciphered faded, scribbled, and wrong-handedly written thoughts and feelings, most often penciled within hours or days of occurring. Having worked with many of these primary sources, I know the effort required. In doing so, he has now provided a reference source of inestimable value regarding the 1869 Powell exploration of the Colorado River and its tributaries as well as a long overdue saga that finally gives us a blow by blow account of the heroic efforts and harrowing experiences of the 1869 crew, thus far sadly overlooked by most writers, including Powell himself.

In text proceeding and following the transcriptions, Michael has introduced new research material by himself and others, particularly Don Lago, adding greatly to the story and understanding of the events of 1869 and providing corroboration and opinion concerning answers to speculative questions. Debate on these and other points will continue, of course, as there are enough "river historians" concerned with the picayune details willing to discuss them at any gathering, both on the river and off.

Michael supplied me with several preliminary drafts of this work, which has already become indispensable in my research. Luckily, it should also become so to those who have been waiting to vicariously travel, as Powell wrote, that "unknown river to explore."

Richard D. Quartaroli
The Special Collections Librarian
Northern Arizona University Cline Library
Special Collections and Archives
2001-02 President, Grand Canyon River Guides, Flagstaff, Arizona

ACKNOWLEDGEMENTS

No historical work such as this can be accomplished in a vacuum. While the writing itself is normally a lonely business, the quest for reliable source materials is, by its nature, a very social one in which the graciousness and generosity of people who rarely receive adequate recognition is indispensable. I owe several people who were in the right place at the right time debts of gratitude. Even more, I owe a debt to several Powell historians for their work, their passion, and, in some cases, their mistakes.

My greatest debt is owed to Martin J. Anderson, a protégé of Otis "Dock" Marston. Marty amassed a big collection of Colorado River documents, in folder after folder. These were donated posthumously to the Cline Library Special Collections. Anderson not only helped me selflessly when he was alive, his collection continued onward in the same spirit after he had moved on to that great river run into infinity. The Anderson collection included copies of many vital original documents but, in some cases even more importantly, it also contained several, some never published, that Anderson himself had written which critically analyzed the 1869 expedition and the writings and actions of John Wesley Powell himself.

The NAU Cline Library Special Collections also hosted a copy of Robert Brewster Stanton's monumental and indispensable magnum opus, "The River and the Cañon: The Colorado River of the West, and the Exploration, Navigation, and Survey of its Canons, from the Standpoint of an Engineer." A document better researched and more analytical of Powell's 1869 trip in detail would be tough to conceive of. Thank you, Mr. Stanton, for your obsession.

Librarian Richard Quartaroli was consistently instrumental in steering me on the shortest roads to these vital materials of Anderson and Stanton and many others, including Powell's 1869 Journal #2 and his puzzling astronomical observations. Richard navigates the rock garden of the special collections — which is riddled with the idiosyncratic holes and reversals of its now deceased contributors — with the same precision and flair with which he dazzled clients while piloting the major rapids in Grand Canyon as a professional guide. Richard also painstakingly combed two versions of the manuscript for errors – and found them in both. Thank you, Richard, for your diligence and generous spirit.

Over more years than I care to contemplate, fellow Flagstaff writer and historian Scott Thybony has shared with me, in truly selfless generosity, many of his discoveries and insights on Canyon history. These include, but are not restricted to, information about the fates of William Dunn, Seneca Howland, and Oramel G. Howland. Scott's help has been instrumental in making *First Through Grand Canyon* as complete and fascinating as it is. Thank you, Scott.

In the same vein I owe a large debt to Wesley P. Larsen, whose curiosity, energy, and courage uncovered not only the enigmatic letter written by William Leany, but whose sense of justice also spurred him to pick up the stone cold trails to and from this letter and follow them. My debt — and our debt — to this courageous man may never be possible to pay in full.

While seeking out lost histories of the more recondite among Powell's crew members, historian Don Lago probed into some thus far unplumbed sources and found a few missing pieces of George Y. Bradley's post-1869 life and travels. Don also made two fairly major discoveries — Sumner's letter to Lewis Keplinger and Bishop James Leithead's autobiography — that had eluded previous Powell historians for nearly a century. On top of these, Don also found photos of the Howland brothers and cleared up several of William Culp Darrah's errors by clarifying who William Hawkins really was and also what sort of man Seneca Howland was as well. We all owe Don a debt for his enthusiasm, energy, and insights in following leads that other historians have overlooked and for his faith and perseverance to discover heretofore unknown records of what transpired when the survivors of the 1869 expedition reached the Virgin. More personally, I owe Don thanks for sharing these hard won discoveries with me so unselfishly and so early in the game.

Others who took up the banner for me in regard to locating rare materials include AzRA boatman and river historian Drifter Smith. Drifter went beyond the calls of friendship and enthusiasm by not only personally delivering to me W. W. Bass' book (containing William Hawkins' 1919 letter) plus other information in various media, but also doing so almost as fast as Scotty could have beamed it to me. Drifter also nipped a few of my errors in the bud. Thanks, Drifter, for your passion for the Canyon's past.

On the eve of print-setting, fellow Grand Canyon Boatman Rick DuCharme sent me from Fairplay, Colorado, copies of John Wesley Powell's military records. These cleared up a few murky points. Thank you, Rick.

While rowing with OARS guides Dennis Smoldt and Robert Garrett in Dinosaur National Monument, they were helpful in revealing Denis Julien's most upstream and recent inscription and in sharing what they knew of his history. I owe them thanks for this help — and more.

Special thanks also go to Karen Greig for proof-reading what I considered the final typeset draft of this manuscript. Her work saved me from many mistakes.

I also have to admit that I pushed my friendship to the limit with Mark J. Davis of Newburyport. I asked him to prowl the entire Bridge Street

Cemetery in search of George Y. Bradley's grave (no known photo of Bradley has been found despite 55 years of searching, but I figured he must at least have a grave marker). And while I did not ask Mark to dig up Bradley's corpse (I was tempted), I did make a plea for Mark to dig up whatever he could of records relating to Bradley, who has been one of the most mysterious of the 1869 crew while simultaneously being its prime chronicler.

Yet another friend who slipped me paydirt that he likely did not even know existed was Daniel Graber. Thanks, Daniel, for Joseph Christmas Ives' 1861 *Report*. It's amazing what previous historians failed to see in it.

While writing his own book on the 1869 expedition, writer Ed Dolnick, at intervals, sent me his chapter installments in seeking my critiques on factual aspects of river running and my interpretations of parts of the 1869 journals. His questions to me included interpreting what the crew members might have meant when they wrote this or that seemingly enigmatic entry in their journals during the expedition. Other questions concerned Powell himself. Ed was haunted by confusion over several nitty gritty river-running realities. Beyond these, he was also curious as to what I had dug up on the fates of the Howland brothers and Dunn while I had worked on two of my other books, *Canyon* and *Over the Edge: Death in Grand Canyon*. An unforeseen — and, for Ed, likely undesired — byproduct of his having revealed his work in progress to me chapter by chapter was the kindling in me of the desire to write this book containing everything that the 1869 crew had written from the river, unabridged and unsanitized, along with my own interpretations in this book's front and back ends of what this expedition was really like, both physically and socially. So, thank you, Ed, for inspiring me to do something that you may well wish I had never thought of. Thanks too for some of the source materials that helped in this.

As to further source materials, Jennifer and other librarians of the Denver Public Library and Carol Kasel of the *Rocky Mountain News* helped me procure copies of Oramel G. Howland's two published letters from the 1869 Powell expedition (on July 19 and August 18, 1869) and Sumner's obituary on July 10, 1907 — now all in public domain and for clearing my permission to reproduce them in full, respectively. Sandy of the *Chicago Tribune* cleared my permission to reproduce six of John Wesley Powell's letters published by the *Tribune* on May 29, July 19, July 20, and August 20, 1869 (now also in the public domain). The Flagstaff Public Library also assisted me assiduously with awkward interlibrary loans of rare microfilms of all the other crew letters published in 1869 newspapers. Stanley Layton of the immensely valuable *Utah Historical Quarterly* also granted me permission to reprint the published versions of John Colton Sumner's journal and Andy Hall's letters provided by Otis "Dock" Marston and William Culp Darrah, respectively. I owe thanks to all of these helpful people and institutions.

Again, every item other than Sumner's and Hall's writings that is reproduced verbatim here now resides in the public domain.

I also owe thanks to Bernie Schnerr and Robert Perkins for permission to use the IMAX photo of the Powell reconstruction boats at River Mile 34.

Finally, as every author knows all too well, one of the by-products of writing books is a degree of suspicion by one's family that the writer has become obsessed. If not unbalanced. If not demented. Well, worse yet, I dragged my 15-year-old daughter, Crystal, into this project. I owe a debt of thanks to Crystal Ghiglieri for reading aloud to me my entire computer transcription of Bradley's journal while I simultaneously read his hand-written original to insure that no errors of my transcription would find their way into this book. Thank you, Crystal.

"Head of Grand Canyon" (etching from *Canyons of the Colorado*).

INTRODUCTION

WHY SPEND YOUR HARD-EARNED MONEY ON THIS BOOK?

Have been working like galley-slaves all day. Have lowered the boats all the way with ropes and once unloaded and carried the goods arround [sic] *one very bad place. The rapid is still continuous and not improving. Where we are tonight it roars and foams like a wild beast.*

The Major as usual has chosen the worst camping-ground possible. If I had a dog that would lie where my bed is made tonight I would kill him and burn his collar and swear I never owned him. —
George Young Bradley, June 11, 1869.

In May of 1869, eleven men in Wyoming stood beside four moored boats on the Green River where, seven months earlier, the Union Pacific Railroad had bridged it. These men's mission, their goal, and their fates hung on their intent to navigate those four boats down the Green River and through the unexplored canyons of the Colorado River downstream a thousand miles to, through, and beyond Grand Canyon. As fortune would have it, 98 days later, only six of those eleven men and only two of those four boats would ride the Colorado past the Grand Wash Cliffs at the foot of Grand Canyon. The story of these brave — maybe too brave — men and their harrowing accomplishments forms one of the most astonishing epics in the entire exploration history of North America.

Arguably John Wesley Powell's 1869, thousand-mile descent of the canyons of the Green and Colorado rivers — mostly terra incognita even to Indians — ranks at the top of America's exploration list in audacity and romance. "Powell's journey down the legendary river of the West," concludes historian Donald Worster, "was one of the greatest events in the history of exploration. Only the travels of Meriwether Lewis and William Clark some six decades earlier compare in significance or drama."

Here, for the first time ever, this gripping saga of extreme adventure, optimism, courage, fear, heroism, humor, triumph, treachery, and tragedy is told in full by the men themselves via their unabridged journals and letters — in newly transcribed and accurate transcriptions — written *during* the expedition.

Surprisingly, despite 133 years and scores of enthusiastic writers who have tackled the "John Wesley Powell Story" — including Powell himself — none of them attempting to describe the 1869 expedition has managed to get it right or even complete. Containing several never before published letters and journal entries — indeed all known journals and letters — that help clear up century-old mysteries, *First Through Grand Canyon* is the definitive history of this amazing journey. If you have ever felt the lure of exploration tug at your heart, then *First Through Grand Canyon* will become a treasure.

Indeed, it also can be argued that the 1869 exploration, by traversing the heart of the last Great Unknown, slammed shut the era of major North American discoveries. During this odyssey, the pencils of Powell and his men filled in the last large blank area on the map of the continental United States. Powell *and* his men. I emphasize this plurality of effort because, as you will discover, Powell could have done none of this on his own.

How Powell and his crew fared against such a vexing array of unknown dangers while burdened with inappropriate equipment and with naive leadership challenging a landscape so inhospitable that even Indians avoided it, forms the core of this quintessential American saga. To tell this story in full requires using not only the crew's 1869 writings but also those from the years after the last two surviving boats had been tied to the sun-blasted shoreline of the lower Colorado. This is because unraveling the fates of Powell's crew members in this book's final chapter (and introducing them to begin with) demands use of these later writings.

Perhaps surprisingly — in view of the hoopla Major John Wesley Powell received for his published "journal" — only one man, Sergeant George Young Bradley, actually wrote a truly coherent, detailed, and candid journal of the entire expedition. Powell biographer William Culp Darrah wrote in 1947 of Bradley: "Indeed, Bradley is harshest when he speaks of the Major. He appears to have been somewhat sentimental, somewhat lonely, something of a scholar. Largely self-taught, he was nonetheless an intelligent observer, an expressive diarist, and an honest critic." Bradley's journal — the Rosetta Stone for the 1869 expedition — doubled what we knew. In this we are one-up on Powell; he never even knew Bradley had written a journal.

Bradley's talents become abundantly clear in the 22,000 words of his journal. Whether he is discussing the painful labor of lining a boat around a bad rapid, or instead describing the adrenaline-soaked joy of running big whitewater, or recounting how to choose a camp, escape a raging inferno, catch a three-foot fish on a thin silk line, track a bighorn ram up a cliff, collect fossils, repair a battered boat, or is depicting the vast aridity and expanse of a Southwestern landscape utterly foreign to an Easterner's eye — and depicting it while experiencing the anxious uncertainty of being trapped in the middle of it without enough rations to survive — Bradley offers us an insider's insights into the ultimate Western adventure. His journal is a gem: self-revealing and self-effacing, sensitive, humorous, evocative, critical, optimistic, determined, inspiring, descriptive of the Southwestern desert, and amazingly true to the essentials of what every boatman faces: the terror of what nasty rapids can do, a terror which paradoxically metamorphoses into an addiction to run the great rivers funneling through the canyons that flow into the best known of the World's Seven Natural Wonders. Fellow boatman William Hawkins wrote that Bradley was "a man of nerve and staying qualities, as he proved later on." Hawkins also noted that after they launched downriver: "We were all green at the business [of rowing]. Bradley was the only one that had any experience."

Major Powell's head boatman, John Colton Sumner, also kept a journal — at Powell's behest. A bit more than half the length of Bradley's, Sumner offers additional details and perspectives on the chancy enterprise upon which the "Ten Who Dared" had embarked. At times the prickly little (5 and 1/2-foot) Sumner is poignant, objective, indignant, then heroic with a charming modesty rarely displayed today. Sumner's journal of the first half of the expedition often pendulums from philosophical ruminations to wry humor that cuts like a Bowie knife. Typical of Sumner is the following view on how to grease the wheels of society: "When I see how drink shows the true colors so plainly, I sometimes wish the whole world could be drunk for a short time, that the scoundrels might be all killed off through their own meanness." Typical too is Sumner's later entry revealing his suspicion that those wheels were currently being greased by the wrong men: "Passed the mouth of a small stream coming in from the west, which we named King Fisher Creek, as there was a bird of that species perched on the branch of a dead willow, watching the finny tribe with the determination of purpose that we often see exhibited by politicians, while watching for the spoils of office."

Unfortunately, as the expedition faced ever more exhausting dangers in Grand Canyon, Sumner's daily entries (and Major Powell's as well) became mere abbreviated summaries. Meanwhile Bradley continued his chronicle in full.

Beyond Sumner's 13,300 words, we also have a pair of long letters (5,600 words) that Oramel G. Howland, Powell's cartographer, wrote to the *Rocky Mountain News*. Howland, an optimist by nature, provides additional descriptions of the early part of the expedition that bring several details to vibrant life. Even Walter Henry Powell, the Major's mentally unstable brother, wrote a touching, 1,300 word letter to the *Chicago Evening Journal* and *The Chicago Tribune*. It conveys yet more of the beauty of the upper canyons of the Green River, now drowned behind Flaming Gorge Dam.

In 1947, many of these letters and journals were published by one of the best journals of Western history, the *Utah Historical Quarterly*, volume 15. This is now a rare book, selling today for as much as $300. This volume, though one I personally treasure, unfortunately has its serious shortcomings. For one thing, it includes only half of Sumner's journal and none of Andy Hall's letters. Second, as I found to my shock, it contains platoons of errors in basic research and transcription — nearly a thousand of them — from Powell's, Bradley's, Sumner's, and Howland's original writings.

Some errors are understandable. Powell wrote his 2,922-word journal #1, relating general details, and his 2,714-word Journal #2, strictly devoted to geology, left-handedly, but he was a right-handed man. His penmanship was atrocious. And Bradley's was nearly microscopic. Hence the transcriptions by the *Utah Historical Quarterly's* volume 15 editor, William Culp Darrah, are fraught with errors. Some are ludicrous. When, after blasting through the standing waves of terrifying Sockdolager Rapid, for example, Bradley writes " — we are a lucky set," Darrah misread him and transcribed this as " — we are a lusty set." Beyond Darrah's many errors of transcription from script are his several additional errors of transcription of the men's letters printed in the 1869 newspapers mentioned above. In several cases these consist of innocent but complete changes of words, from Powell's "grand," for example, to Darrah's "beautiful," or from Powell's "exhilaration" to Darrah's "exaltations." In other cases, Darrah lost a few words — one or two or even ten — from sentences in the men's accounts. Far more serious, in repeated cases, Darrah lost Powell's entire paragraphs — of 122, 160, and even 388 words in length — being present in Powell's original *Chicago Tribune* letter from the river but absent from Darrah's *Utah Historical Quarterly* transcription of that letter. More important, as you will see later in this book, Darrah may have purposely rewritten the history of the 1869 crew to paint a set of pro-Powell impressions that he favored more than he did the apparent truth.

Despite these published writings, most people interested in the history of the Colorado River know nothing of this valuable *Utah Historical Quarterly* volume. Instead they know only that Major John Wesley Powell wrote a 400-page book in 1895, *Canyons of the Colorado* — an expansion of his 1875 report to congress, *Exploration of the Colorado River of the West and its Tributaries,* discussed below — purported to be his journals of the 1869 expedition and of his later journeys into the West. *Canyons* was published by

Flood and Vincent. It has become the standard history (interestingly, the mere 1,000 copies printed never sold out, and Flood and Vincent went bankrupt). Yet Major Powell's *Canyons of the Colorado* (reprinted later as *The Exploration of the Colorado River and its Canyons*) is problematic. Powell's biographer, Darrah, admits of *Canyons*, "the account given by the Major is a literary composition rather than a scientific document."

Even this vastly understates the liberties with fact that Powell took when he wrote this book. Powell had been spurred to write by political ambition — specifically by Ohio Representative James A. Garfield, Chairman of the House of Representatives Appropriations Committee who told Powell that funds for his explorations would be granted only on his promise to publish an account of his 1869 expedition.

To meet this obligation Powell recycled the series of four adventure-oriented articles he had written for *Scribner's Magazine*, combining them into a predominantly self-serving account which he then presented to congress as his 1875 report of the 1869 expedition, (in 1895 he expanded this to his book, *Canyons*). Sadly, this facile but colorful document left much of the truth — and the legacies of his crew — standing marooned and forgotten on the banks of the Colorado.

Again, Powell presented his *Report* as if it were a transcription of his journal. In reality, it not only failed most of the time to resemble his journal entries, far more serious, it also failed to recount what actually happened during the 1869 expedition. Powell, for example, added to his account of the 1869 expedition episodes and accomplishments which instead occurred in 1871 and 1872 with men other than his original 1869 crew. He attributed these later episodes fictionally as if they had occurred in 1869 to his original crew, for example, boating and hiking upstream on the Yampa, which did not occur in 1869, but instead in 1871. Powell also changed the dates, physical locations, and crew participation of adventures from that first expedition to enhance, one supposes, their dramatic impacts. Further, Powell altered geography and history so rampantly that his report and subsequent book, *Canyons*, are sadly inaccurate. On top of Powell's deliberate inaccuracies, from the onset of the expedition Powell was a half-hearted note taker with a poor memory for facts. Hence he got several details wrong from the start. Beyond Powell's deliberate and accidental inaccuracies are his more serious omissions: he ignored important — even death-defying — accomplishments of his crew. Bear in mind here that Powell was submitting his report as a scientifically accurate document of exploration written specifically for the readership of U.S. Congress and to be printed with federal funds by the Government Printing Office. Unlike many other explorers who endeavored to provide Congress with "truth" as they knew it, Powell gave Congress an extended, poetic but semi-fictional magazine treatment of the 1869 expedition nearly devoid of science and unreliable even as "history." Many historians of this expedition have concluded that Powell must have believed no one would ever repeat his voyage or examine his veracity.

These many problems make it truly impossible to know from Powell's writings what actually happened on that epic 1869 expedition. Indeed, Powell's fictions have made fools and liars of dozens of writers who have taken Powell at his word and then written effusively and enthusiastically — but inaccurately — of the experiences of Powell and his crew on the Green and Colorado. If, by chance, you may doubt that my allegations are as serious as stated, read this book — then read Powell's.

Perhaps worse yet for posterity, Powell made his "history" in his 1875 report (and in *Canyons*) even more fictional by deciding to grossly exaggerate some of the dangers that the 1869 expedition faced. For example, in the now famous first run of Sockdolager Rapid, a rip-roaring wave-slammer in Grand Canyon flanked by nearly sheer banks of steep Precambrian schist offering no foothold for lining boats, Major Powell wrote in his book: " — at last we find ourselves above a low, broken fall, with ledges and pinnacles of rock obstructing the river. There is a descent of, perhaps, seventy-five or eighty feet in a third of a mile, and the rushing waters break into great waves on the rocks, and lash themselves to a mad, white foam....and we must run the rapid or abandon the river. There is no hesitation. We step into our boats, push off, and away we go...."

Heroic prose alright. But what did Powell actually write in his brief journal that day (August 14) about this same event? "Must run it or abandon the enterprise. Good Luck! Little boat fills with water twice. Chute 1/2 mile long, fall 30 ft., probably. Huge waves."

Somehow, to Powell, the chance that a mere 30-foot drop (Sockdolager actually drops something like 19 feet) might seem tame to a fickle public prompted him to nearly triple it to 75 or 80 feet. Powell's literary excesses were so glaring that Powell's head boatman, John Sumner, would finally, twenty years after the expedition, spill the beans to Robert Brewster Stanton. As Stanton wrote in his river diary:

"Friday, December 13, 1889

— At about 2 PM was hailed by a man on shore asking us for tobacco...found it was old Jack Sumner, Major Powell's right hand man in 1869. I had a half hour's talk with him and he gave us encouragement & good cheer and advice. Simply to go slow & carefully & we would be alright....

I asked Jack many questions about the river below, particularly about the Catarect [sic] where the three men left the party and had gone out and were killed by the Indians, telling him that was the one rapid & one place on the whole river from Maj. Powell's acct. that I was afraid of. He assured me there was no such awful difficulties [sic] at that point and encouraged us in every way. But I said, 'Jack, Major gives a long detailed account of your experiences at that rapid,' & read it to him from the copy we had. Sumner turned away with an air of resentment and said, 'There's lots in that book besides the truth.'

I don't understand this, but Sumner wouldn't tell anymore about it."

Stanton was the expedition leader first to replicate Powell's Colorado River expedition (but by beginning at Green River, Utah, not Wyoming) in 1889-1890. He became obsessed with Grand Canyon and with Powell. Tellingly, Stanton originally idolized Powell's 1875 report. "To John Wesley Powell belongs all the glory and renown possible for his first trip through the unknown canyons of the wonderful river." Stanton writes, adding: "Major Powell's work and that of his companions in 1869, to my mind, stands [sic] out as one of the bravest exploits ever known anywhere....When I first became acquainted with Major Powell's *Report* giving his account of that first exploration, it was to me the most fascinating story I had ever read....I first read the document as I would the Gospel of St. John, with an almost worshipful reverence."

But after Sumner hissed to Stanton his brief opinion of Powell's 1875 report, Stanton, in his apostasy, gnawed through Powell's writings like an angry wolverine trapped in a log cabin. He ripped apart one after another of Powell's gratuitous distortions or fictionalizations. It took Stanton 40 pages in his *Colorado River Controversies* to exorcise the demons of his lost faith in Powell.

Stanton's ferocity was triggered, at least in part, by Powell's having claimed to Stanton — in person, face to face, and with no hesitation or corrections — that Powell's 1875 *Exploration of the Colorado River of the West and its Tributaries* was indeed his "diary written on the spot [on the river expedition]." But, on the contrary, Stanton's assiduous research later revealed Powell's claim to be an out and out mendacity.

Powell's true and original diary — relocated by a *very* determined Stanton after Powell's death — is, despite sloppy errors, otherwise fairly accurate with regard to the river canyons. But Powell's published report and 1895 book instead "are," Stanton discovered, "in many instances distorted and exaggerated.... demonstrably inaccurate and, it would seem, deliberately misleading on a number of counts....[showing] that the Major was undoubtedly guilty of suppression of the truth and unblushing exaggeration...."

Hence, while historian Wallace Stegner praised Powell's *Canyons of the Colorado* as "probably the finest narrative of exploration in all of American literature," biographer William Culp Darrah begrudgingly admitted of the same book: "The Major was not blameless when it comes to deliberate inaccuracy." Meanwhile Stanton, as we've seen, was far less complimentary about Powell's "deliberate inaccuracy."

This "inaccuracy," however, has misled Powell fans and frustrated careful historians to the point of profanity. Indeed, until now, the only solution to the problem of reading Powell while still not knowing what actually happened during one of the most important explorations of the American West was to find that inaccurate *Utah Historical Quarterly* then go fish for additional tidbits in far-flung old letters — and then end up pulling one's hair out while trying to reconcile these conflicting and incomplete reports.

Partly in response to this frustration — but unfortunately more, it seems, out of awe of Major Powell and the Colorado than of the expedition itself — historian John Cooley edited a book of journals and letters, et cetera. His goal in this promising book, *The Great Unknown: The Journals of the Historic First Expedition Down the Colorado River*, was to combine the "best" parts of all accounts of the 1869 expedition. These include portions of Powell's *Canyons of the Colorado* excerpted more or less as if they were journal entries, but called by Cooley "accounts." Cooley also added partial accounts by other crew members — William Hawkins and John Sumner — written decades after the expedition but presented much as if they too were journal entries. Cooley guessed as to the actual time and place during the expedition where these accounts might best fit to insert them as journal-type entries. Sadly, Cooley also *deleted* "about five percent of the original text...to avoid excessive duplication," thus leaving historians frustrated yet again and leaving river-runners wondering.

Worse, Cooley wrote a surprising number of misleading inaccuracies due to his own facile errors, careless approach, and misquotes. Some of these are hard to forgive. For instance, in discussing the fateful events at Separation Canyon, Cooley writes that, ironically, "Separation was the last of the river's great rapids." In fact, Bradley and several other river runners since consider the worst rapid of the entire trip to be Lava Cliff Rapid. Lava Cliff still awaited the expeditionaries six miles farther downstream from Separation. Another error by Cooley was his assuming that the photos of Powell's 1871-72 boats with stern-mounted steering oars and triple compartments depicted his 1869 boats, which had neither ruddering devices nor compartments amidships (see section on boats below).

Compounding these shortcomings, it also seems that Cooley failed to transcribe directly from Bradley's and Powell's original journals in script or from the original letters as published in 1869 newspapers. Instead, Cooley avoided the toils of research and simply copied Darrah's transcriptions from the 1947 *Utah Historical Quarterly*, complete with those hundreds of errors, gross omissions, weird substitutions, and other shortcomings. Even more difficult to understand, Cooley left out of his book all of the words of original observations written by Walter H. Powell and Andy Hall during the expedition. Cooley also failed to include one of Oramel G. Howland's two detailed letters to the *Rocky Mountain News*. The letter omitted? Howland's description of the early part of the expedition, including his full description of the dramatic — and ultimately fatal — wreck of the *No Name*. Cooley's editorial decisions, one guesses, seem to have been made for a similar reason as Major Powell's own literary fudging: to compose a quick and favorable narrative, not an accurate history.

Frustration and confusion is the end result for anyone who wants to know what actually happened on the fateful 1869 trip and how the minds of its crew worked and why some of the men did not survive. Colorado River historians I know speak unfondly of Cooley's book.

Both Powell's and Cooley's books vastly downplay the vital roles that Powell's crew played in his success, both scientifically and as an explorer. Both books also sap the vitality of these men's honest accounts of extreme adventure in the unknown.

A partial antidote to the gap in understanding that exists in the written histories of this expedition is given by Ed Dolnick's 2001 book *Down the Great Unknown*. Dolnick tried to remedy two main failings in previous books: their tendencies to gloss over the level of dangers that the 1869 crew faced, and these books' repetitions of inaccuracies faithfully transcribed from Powell's own many errors and fictionalizations. Dolnick did a fair job at the former but was less successful at the latter, despite his enthusiasm. The many problems his book leaves for river runners, armchair adventurers, and certainly historians emerge from Dolnick being, metaphorically speaking, a virgin writing at length and authoritatively on sex — and often getting it wrong. Some of the problems I see in Dolnick's well-intended book emerged from his decision to include in his narrative a never-ending, almost frenetic flow of forced similes and analogies of dubious application borrowed from the late twentieth century — from airports and freeways and cars — to try to explain what Powell and his crew experienced on the river in 1869, instead of simply recounting what they actually *did* experience. Also disappointing (to me) are Dolnick's errors of fact regarding who did what and where during the expedition and the conditions under which they did it. For example, Dolnick has Hawkins and Hall travel together to the Gulf of California (an error many historians have made), whereas in reality Hawkins never made it below Fort Yuma. It was Sumner and Hall who rowed to the Gulf. Surprisingly, Dolnick even fell prey to many of Cooley's mistakes. For example, after the men ran Sockdolager, Dolnick has Bradley write, an error of transcription by Darrah, "We are a lusty set..." But, again, Bradley, of all the men on the crew, not only would never have characterized himself as being a regular partaker of one of the seven deadly sins, what Bradley actually wrote (legibly) was: "we are a lucky set and our good luck did not go back on us then." Also disappointing, as Cooley had done so confusingly before him, Dolnick included uncritically entry after entry from Powell's 1895 *Canyons'* revisionist prose for *Scribners*, not only as if those words were river journal entries but also as if they possessed equal weight against the true 1869 journal accounts written while on the river.

Even if Dolnick's book possessed no errors or misleading prose the final — and to me fatal — shortcoming in his book is his omission of the vast majority of what the men themselves wrote while they worked their way downriver into and beyond the Great Unknown.

If you scent here an air of messianic perfectionism on my part with regard to what should be written as the best, most entertaining, and absolutely reliable book on the 1869 Expedition, then, yes, I do admit that I am guilty as charged. In fact, it was my reading of Dolnick's book, chapter by chapter as it was written, that became the final straw that forced my decision to write *First Through Grand Canyon*. With this book I aimed at several goals: to set the record straight; to give the 1869 crew the full recognition they deserve; to provide absolutely accurate, reliable transcriptions of their thus far much mangled journals and letters; to add several newly discovered writings that shed significant light on the world's most famous river run; and, above all, to write what I consider to be the most intense true North American adventure story of the second half of the 19th century. As hinted at above, I was shocked several times by newly discovered, unpublished materials which shed some highly controversial light on many of the most mysterious and misunderstood events on this expedition. These, I guarantee, will rattle even the most jaded Powell fan.

To sum up, Powell's 1869 crew of free-thinking mountain men labored as hard for Major Powell as any slave ever did while shackled to the pyramid building of an Egyptian pharaoh. Yet these brave men also worked smart to overcome the many lethal risks of running whitewater in their inadequate boats and without the protection of life jackets. Moreover, Powell's crew toiled week after week on starvation rations. They did all of this faithfully and in good humor during an expedition of such high adventure that some of us now would be tempted to sell our souls to have accompanied it. Even more important — and again this is *the* prime reason for publishing *First Through Grand Canyon* — some of these men wrote captivating accounts of their amazing experiences that surpass Powell's own writings and those of all subsequent historians as well. These accounts do not deserve to be deleted or abridged or "improved."

For anyone who ever imagined being a crew member on the exploration of a major unknown river in the middle of a very inhospitable nowhere flanked by immense arid landscapes which could have been lifted from the planet Mars, *First Through Grand Canyon* will be a feast.

But before we look at what this crew had to say about their experiences — and each other — let's look at who they themselves were, at the task they set themselves to accomplish, and at the resources they possessed which somehow convinced them to stick their necks out just far enough to tempt Mother Nature to lop off their heads.

THE EXPEDITIONARIES

"I fell to day while trying to save my boat from a rock and have a bad cut over the left eye which I fear will make an ugly scar. But what odds, it can't disfigure my ugly mug and it may improve it, who knows?" **George Y. Bradley, June 14, 1869**

George Young Bradley. Born in October, most likely in the year 1836, in Newberry, Massachusetts, Bradley, at 32, was one of the oldest men on Powell's 1869 expedition. At five feet, nine inches tall and weighing 150 pounds — at the onset of the expedition — Bradley was also one of Powell's tallest crew members. John Colton Sumner, Powell's next in command, described Bradley thus: "He was something of a geologist and, in my eyes far more important, he had been raised in the Maine codfishery school, and was a good boatman, and a brave man, not very strong but tough as a badger."

Prior to the Civil War, however, Bradley worked as a shoemaker in West Newbury. He apparently also worked at sea for an unknown span. As with two-thirds of Powell's 1869 crew, Bradley was a Union Civil War veteran. He enlisted in the army on August 12, 1862, and received orders to report to Company A, 19th Regiment, Massachusetts Volunteer Infantry Battalion. Bradley eventually attained the rank of lieutenant. His unit soon marched in Virginia. During the bloody river crossing at Fredericksburg, on December 13, 1862, Bradley was hit by enemy fire in the thigh. His wound proved slow to heal. Bradley was transferred to Company H, 12th Regiment, 2nd Battalion Veteran Reserve Corps. On July 28, 1864, he was retired from active duty.

Bradley traveled and worked in Florida and the surrounding region, then he returned to Boston. But Massachusetts had shrunk for Bradley. On January 16, 1867, he re-enlisted in the Army as a private, giving his profession as "druggist." The military assigned the dark complected, hazel-eyed, mustached, brown-haired Bradley to Company B, 36th Infantry Regiment at Fort Kearney in Nebraska Territory. As the Union Pacific threw track down in a frenzy to span North America, the U.S. Army trotted ahead to defend the route from Plains Indians who saw all too clearly that the iron horse was their public enemy number one.

Bradley was transferred from Fort Kearney to Fort Sedgwick. Then transferred to Lodge Pole Creek. Then to Fort Sanders, Dakota Territory. Then to Fort Bridger, near Green River City, Wyoming. By November 1, 1868, Bradley was promoted to First Sergeant, but not back up to lieutenant. Soon Bradley's 36th Infantry merged with the 7th Infantry.

Chasing Indians away from the advance workers on the rails, however, had paled for Bradley. Perhaps he sympathized with the plight of Plains dwellers. Either way, Bradley was finding the fossil-hunting in this rich region of Wyoming — a veritable graveyard of dinosaurs — to be a far more engaging pastime than skirmishing with the Sioux and Cheyenne. At any rate, in 1868, John Wesley Powell arrived at Fort Bridger to make arrangements for his exploration of the Green and Colorado rivers to begin the following spring. Powell's arrival would change the course of Bradley's life.

Once Powell discovered Bradley's talents in studying western geology, running boats, and surviving the rigors of the West, Powell invited him to join the expedition as boatman and geologist. Bradley agreed to Powell's proposal — *if* Powell could get Bradley discharged from the Army at the onset of the expedition. Bradley was sick of the Army, which, as many historians agree, was composed during this post-Civil-War era of recruits from the lowest rung of the human ladder. As a far more gaunt Bradley would write later, after about 80 days on the river (August 11, 1869): "Thank God the trip is nearly ended for it is no place for a man in my circumstances, but it will let me out of the Army and for that I would almost agree to explore the River Styx."

To attach Bradley to his expedition, Powell inveigled the Secretary of War, General Ulysses S. Grant. Grant issued a special order facilitating First Sergeant Bradley's honorable discharge on May 14, 1869.

Almost immediately Bradley was put to work instructing the rest of Powell's crew assembled on the bank of the Green River — mountain men except for Powell's brother, Walter — in how to calk and paint the four boats so that they would not sink or deteriorate prematurely.

Ten days later the expedition launched those boats on the spring spate of the Green and were swept downriver to their diverse fates. Bradley next had to instruct the men, as boatman William Robert Wesley Hawkins admits, in how to row Powell's four Whitehall boats.

As will be clear from Bradley's journal, he was a hard worker; he found beauty and joy in the great canyons; he saw irony and sometimes incompetence in the antics of his fellow expeditionaries; and he perceived an enigmatic self-absorption in his leader, Major John Wesley Powell. Bradley possessed only a sixth-grade education formally, but he had educated himself well beyond that level during his years after school.

Bradley retained his sense of humor throughout the expedition, often, as the example heading this section illustrates, poking fun at himself. Powell wrote of Bradley: "He is scrupulously careful, and a little mishap works him into a passion, but when labor is needed he has a ready hand and powerful arm, and in danger, rapid judgement and unerring skill. A great difficulty or peril changes the petulant spirit into a brave, generous soul."

Bizarrely, many Powell historians up to and including those in 2001 characterize Bradley as a complainer, or as an "inveterate worrier" and, aping Powell, as a "petulant" man. I dispute such characterizations not just as inaccurate, but ignorant. The problem with most of these historians — Darrah, Stegner, Worster, and Dolnick, for example — is their real world experience. Few Powell historians, until now, are, or were, men of action. Nor were any professional whitewater boatmen. None had run first descent expeditions on uncharted rivers tearing through unknown canyons. None had faced the hardships that such expeditions can offer in spades: the uncertainty of living to see the next sunrise, a fear of drowning in whitewater due to inappropriate boats or a lack of life jackets, a regimen of brutally difficult labor, a subsistence on starvation rations, being plagued by cumulative injuries and debilitating illnesses in the wilds, and being haunted by a growing awareness that the expedition leader does not know enough to be doing what he is doing. Indeed, neither Darrah, nor Stegner, nor Worster ever boated Grand Canyon. A fair question here might be: Does it take experience to convey that experience accurately? The answer lies in the following questions: Does it take a surgeon to accurately write of the challenges of surgery, or a fighter pilot to explain air-to-air combat? I am convinced that "insiders" do know more than tourists. Whether or not insiders are great communicators is a separate issue. At any rate, previous Powell historians neither knew nor understood the true nature of the 1869 expedition and thus, in my opinion, they were incapable of putting themselves into the waterlogged, rotting boots of those who did. Hence their taking Powell's "petulant" Bradley seriously was probably easy, but, as often has been the case with taking Powell at his word, precarious with regard to accuracy. Having myself experienced hundreds of river expeditions as a professional boatman and trip leader, including all of the above travails of a first descent on an unknown river, I can assert that Bradley's writings capture the joys and the pains of a first descent river expedition with clarity, accuracy, exuberance, optimism, wry humor, and a self-effacing modesty seldom seen today. If Bradley sinned at all in his attitude, he sinned in his secret journal only in not worshiping John Wesley Powell.

An unequivocal example of Bradley's positive and irrepressible spirit is evident in his journal entry for July 14, in Labyrinth Canyon, roughly halfway through the journey:

> "As we float along on a muddy stream walled in by huge sandstone bluffs that echo back the slightest sound, hardly a bird save the ill-omened raven or an occasional eagle screaming over us, one feels a sence [sic] of loneliness as he looks on the little party, only three boats and nine men, hundreds of miles from civilization bound on an errand the issue of which everybody declares must be disastrous. Yet if

he could enter our camp at night or our boats by day he could read the cool deliberate determination to persevere that possesses every man of the party and would at once predict that the issue of all would be success."

If these are the writings of a petulant, inveterate worrier, one wonders how optimism and determination to succeed might read.

For this book I transcribed Bradley's journal from a photocopy of the original donated by Charles H. Morss in 1915 to the Library of Congress. Bradley wrote his notes furtively as opportunity allowed during the work day then stuffed them in his hat for safe-keeping. He later, as opportunity permitted in camp (often while fishing) transcribed his notes into his journal. The following photographic copy of a typical journal entry reveals Bradley's consistent style and microscopic penmanship.

George Y. Bradley's journal entry for July 14, actual size.

William H. Dunn. Little to nothing is known of William H. Dunn's origin. Powell met Dunn in 1868 as he worked along side John Colton Sumner, William Robert Wesley Hawkins, and Oramel G. Howland as packers and guides for Powell in his student-oriented expeditions in the Colorado Rockies. Dunn was about as close to a classical "mountain man" as any man could be in this era. He wore buckskins and a beard and his hair flowed nearly as long as an Indian's. Dunn made his living as a trapper, hunter, and muleskinner. He was intelligent enough, however, for Powell to have hired him for specific technical duties (see section, "THE AGREEMENT," below). Powell spelled out Dunn's assignment: "W. H. Dunn to make barometrical observations night and morning of each day when required, also to make observations when needed for determining altitude of walls of the cañon, also to make not more than sixteen-hourly series of not more than eight days each, to have the air of an assistant for the last two mentioned classes of observations."

What this implies is that, despite Dunn's buckskins and long black mane, he was technically competent. All the more tragic, one concludes, considering Dunn's ultimate fate (explored in the final chapter). If Dunn kept a journal or personal notes, they did not survive the expedition.

Dunn, as William R. W. Hawkins would note years later, was the best swimmer among the crew. This was no small consideration on a 1,000-mile, whitewater river trip possessing only one life jacket, John Wesley Powell's.

On Dunn's courage, Hawkins wrote: "The state of Ohio never turned out a man that had more nerve than William Dunn."

Frank Valentine Goodman. Born on February 2, 1844, in England, Goodman sailed to America at age 17 and soon joined the New Jersey Volunteers and fought for the Union. In 1869, Goodman was wandering in search of adventure in the Wild West. By chance, it seems, he found Major Powell at Green River City and propositioned him. With Powell's expedition, however, Goodman found more adventure than he could comfortably digest. Rumors that Goodman offered Powell money to be allowed to accompany the expedition remain rumors. Powell's subsequent explorations (all more tame) indicate that Powell was constantly interested in increasing his "soft money" cash flow via adjunct payments.

Historian Vince Welch quotes E.G. Evans, a friend of Goodman, describing him: "height, about 5' 9", weight about 180, fairly good-looking, very healthy and strong, most always wore a beard which was red-brown in color—had a sunny disposition, loved the out-of-doors, did not care for hard work, made friends with most people he met, was a deep thinker and a great reader, quite a talker." Welch notes that before 1869 Goodman joined the Hudson Bay Company as a trapper in British Columbia and went down the Columbia River to Washington territory, becoming a boatman en route.

Sumner mentioned years later that Goodman was "a fine singer of sea songs" around the campfire. But the journals say little else positive about Goodman. Obliquely, it appears that Goodman's skill level was low and that his level of industriousness may have been a match for his level of skill. Whether or not Goodman's energy and skill as a boatman may have played a tragic role in the loss of the *No Name*, which he and Seneca Howland were rowing, will likely never be known (more on this in the final chapter).

As the journals indicate, Goodman quit the expedition at the Uinta Indian Agency, relatively early in the expedition. No scholar thus far has discovered any writings of the expedition penned by Goodman.

After quitting the 1869 expedition Goodman eventually settled and married in Vernal, Utah, and raised his family not far from the scenes of adventure that he experienced during its first 250 miles. He died around 1914.

Frank Valentine Goodman

Andrew Hall. As with Goodman, Hall too was a last minute recruit. The reason why openings still existed in Powell's crew as late as the eve of departure is discussed below in the sections, "W. H. Bishop" and "The Missing Tenderfoot." Powell spotted Andy sitting at the oars of a homemade boat at Green River City. Hall had been using this boat for hauling firewood. Hall was the antithesis of Goodman. True, Hall was an immigrant; he was born at Rocksfordshire, Scotland, and had immigrated to America with his widowed mother, brother, and sister when he was seven years old.

Even so, Hall seemed more American than most men who were born here. He left home at age 14 to work as a bullwhacker, mule driver, Indian scout, and a guard on wagons hauling freight on the prairie. This on-the-job

Andrew Hall

education made him fit to survive in the Wild West, but perhaps less fit for fitting in back East.

At 19 years old, Andy Hall was the youngest member of the expedition. And, as with William Dunn, he looked the part of a Wild Westerner; he wore his hair long and wild, Buffalo Bill style, and seems to have possessed an irrepressible zest for life and an ebullience that bubbled to the surface even when the expedition was under duress. Sumner later called him a "rollicking young Scotch boy." Bradley notes in his journal on July 24, for example, that while everyone else was dead tired from portaging boats in the lower half of Cataract Canyon, Andy spent the evening throwing rocks across the Colorado.

Major Powell wrote, Hall "is nineteen years old, with what seems to us a 'secondhand head,' which doubtless came down to him from some knight who wore it during the Border Wars. It looks a very old head indeed, with deep-set blue eyes and beaked nose. Young as he is, Hall has had experience in hunting, trapping, and fighting Indians, and he makes the most of it, for he can tell a good story, and is never encumbered by unnecessary scruples in giving to his narratives those embellishments which help make a story complete. He is always ready for work or play and is a good hand at either."

At the end of the expedition, Hall, with Sumner, rowed *Kitty Clyde's Sister* all the way to the Gulf of California and then *sailed* it back upstream to Fort Yuma by rigging a wagon sheet as a sail. Hall — and Hawkins — both settled in Arizona. They were the only two members of the expedition to do so. Of the two men, one flourished beyond all reasonable expectations while the other died in what many might think of as the worst of all possible fates.

Hall wrote very little regarding this expedition. What he did write consists of three very brief, poorly written, God-awful letters that he sent home, all of which are included in this volume, reprinted from the 1948-49 *Utah Historical Quarterly*.

William Robert Wesley (a.k.a. "Missouri Rhodes") Hawkins.

Yet another colorful character on the 1869 expedition — arguably *the* most colorful character — was Hawkins. Powell had met Hawkins at John Sumner's trading post/cabin at Hot Sulphur Spring, Colorado, in 1868. Hawkins at that time was part of the Sumner-Howland-Hawkins-Dunn association who guided, hunted, trapped, and ran mule-train services in the Rockies. Only Hawkins was not Hawkins then. Instead he was going by the moniker "Missouri Rhodes." This Missouri Rhodes alias threw historian William Culp Darrah off the track so far that previously published descriptions of Hawkins' early life — virtually all of which come from Darrah's *Utah Historical Quarterly* profile — have been in error until historian Don Lago tracked down the real Hawkins.

William Robert Wesley Hawkins

Born in July 1848, in Gentry County, Missouri, Hawkins was 20, then 21 years old during the 1869 expedition. As was the case with Bradley, Sumner, Seneca Howland, and both Powell brothers, Hawkins was a veteran of the U.S. Army during the Civil War.

Hawkins, at 5 feet 5 inches tall and fifteen years old, had enlisted in late 1863, and likely had lied about his age to do so. He joined his older brother's regiment, the 15th Cavalry of the Missouri State Militia. He brought his own horse into battle, valued at $110. After serving more than a year, however, Hawkins missed muster in his unit and, as Don Lago notes, was listed instead as being under arrest for an unspecified offense connected with failure to obey orders, or "mutiny." After 18 days of arrest, he was back with the cavalry.

Some time during Hawkins' twenty months of service, which included several skirmishes with Confederate troops and one major cavalry charge against a Confederate force twice as strong as the Union army, Hawkins was disabled. Possibly his horse fell on him. Unhelpfully, records do not explain the nature of his injury. Hawkins was discharged from the Union Army on July 1, 1865, still owing the Army $1.61 for, as Lago discovered, "One waist belt, one gun sling, one shoulder sling and plate." And with this trivial debt to the Union Army hanging over him, "Missouri Rhodes" was reborn (the original Missouri Rhodes had recently died), a free trapper ranging in the wild Colorado Rockies.

In the summer of 1868, Hawkins was encamped at John C. Sumner's trading post at Hot Sulphur Spring in Middle Park. This was when John Wesley Powell's pack outfit arrived. "I found the Major a very pleasant gentleman," the buckskin-clad, long-haired Hawkins would later write, "and very easy to get acquainted with." Part of this getting acquainted included Major Powell informing Hawkins that Powell was planning an exploring expedition down the Colorado, including Grand Canyon.

Hawkins replied:

> "I told him that would be an interesting trip, that I had been to some parts of it, and it was rough enough for any use. That some of my neighbors, the Ute Indians, said the river in places ran under the ground. Powell said it was his intention to find out, and that he was acting in the interests of the Smithsonian Institution....Sumner, Bill Dunn, and I had been talking for some time past of building us some boats and starting down through the canyons to trap....Next morning Sumner and Major Powell came over to my camp, where Dunn had spent the night with me, and Sumner spoke up and said that the Major would like us (Dunn and me) to join his party for the winter, as also for the trip down the canyons of the Colorado. I told the Major that Sumner was thinking of selling his trading post, and in company with Dunn and myself, we were going to try the canyons as far as Cottonwood Island. That I had already packed my year's supplies in from Denver, to which the Major replied, 'Those things are just what I want, also your mules and horses, I will buy them and pay you just that you can sell them for elsewhere.'"

By the time the 1869 expedition was in the preparation stage, Hawkins still evinced nervousness at any manifestations of the law, especially in the form of an approaching sheriff. While on the expedition, Hawkins was not only a hard worker, he was also the camp cook and a part-time hunter. Hawkins prepared three meals per day on just about every day that the expedition was on the river. He reported later that Major Powell had promised him a wage of $1.50 per day for these services — as well as for rowing, et cetera. Hawkins rowed, with Andy Hall on the second pair of oars, the 21-foot "freight" boat, *Kitty Clyde's Sister.*

Hawkins, again like Hall, also possessed an irrepressible spirit. Highly energetic, Hawkins was seemingly indefatigable, intolerant of unfairness, and possessed by the imp of humor. Hawkins played a pivotal role on this expedition, being one of the three or four key personnel whose steadfastness made Powell's major gambit a success.

Powell described Hawkins as "an athlete and a jovial good fellow, who hardly seems to know his own strength." Powell, in his journal for July 22, in Cataract Canyon, also remarked on Hawkins' sense of the absurd: "Supper poor. Rhodes [Hawkins] takes instruments to determine the lat. & long. of the nearest pie."

Unfortunately for us, Hawkins did not keep a journal. After the Major and his brother had caught the Union Pacific back east, Hawkins, Bradley, Hall, and Sumner continued downriver, with instruments, apparently to continue surveying downstream of the most-upriver point reached by Lieutenant Joseph Christmas Ives in 1857-58. Hawkins and Bradley then rowed at least to Ehrenberg, Arizona, downstream of Fort Mojave.

Hawkins was years later interviewed by letter extensively (in 1907 by Robert Brewster Stanton regarding the specifics of the 1869 expedition, and then, in 1919, yet again on the same subject by William Wallace Bass). Hawkins' letter to Stanton resides in the latter's unpublished magnum opus, "The River and the Cañon: The Colorado River of the West, and the Exploration, Navigation, and Survey of its Cañons, from the Standpoint of an Engineer." Hawkins' interview with William Wallace Bass is published in Stanton's *Colorado River Controversies* and in W. W. Bass's *Adventures in the Canyons of the Colorado By two of its earliest explorers, James White and W. W. Hawkins with introduction and notes.*

What Hawkins had to say about Powell and his brother and about the expedition itself were so unflattering to the Major that many pro-Powell historians have squirmed mightily in their efforts to discount Hawkins' words as bitter grapes and exaggerations. The problem with discounting Hawkins' report, however, is that, in January of 1907, John Sumner said nearly identical things about Powell and the expedition, and he said these things independently of Hawkins. In fact, historian Martin J. Anderson spelled this out: "It is important to note that there was no collusion between Sumner and Hawkins. They wrote their versions at different times from different places." Neither Hawkins' nor Sumner's account appears in the main part of this book because they were penned after the expedition ended. You will see them in detail though in the final chapter, which attempts to unravel the fates of the men.

Hawkins not only outlived every other member of the expedition, he made the greatest turnabout becoming, of all things, a Justice of the Peace.

Oramel G. Howland

Oramel G. Howland. Unlike most of Powell's American crew members of 1869, Oramel G. Howland had remained a civilian in Denver during the Civil War and had worked as a printer and editor for the *Rocky Mountain News.* This is despite Major Powell referring to him as "Captain" Howland. Howland — a descendant of Pilgrim John Howland who came to North America in 1620 on the *Mayflower* — remained a very busy man up until the expedition shoved its boats off the cobbled beach at Green River City. In addition to working on the *News* and to working in the mountains as a guide, he also worked on three other periodical publications as a business agent. In 1867, O. G. Howland was also Vice President of Typographical Union Local No. 49. He was also Secretary and Trustee Board Member of the Nonpareil Prospecting & Mining Company.

Born in 1833, a year before Major Powell, Howland was 36 years old during the expedition. His age and his many social ties within Denver society and his advanced education placed him in the position of being the only widely experienced *and* well-educated man on the expedition besides Major Powell himself. One byproduct of this "equality of maturity" with Powell may have been that Howland might have identified himself as Powell's equal (or more) when it came to analyzing the best course of action during pivotal points during the expedition. In short, O. G. Howland might have been the only man who felt well justified in challenging Powell on Powell's decisions.

The Major hired Howland — as stated in "THE AGREEMENT"

(provided below) — for the expressed role: "to make a topographical drawing of the course of the rivers." Howland may have kept a journal, but, if he did, nothing of it has survived beyond his pair of letters to the *Rocky Mountain News*. It is very possible that he made few to no journal entries. His cartographical duties, and the repeated demands of re-drawing of maps and survey records due to losses of much of his work may have monopolized his time and precluded faithful journal writing. Again, Howland did manage to write a pair of polished and entertaining letters in journal format while on the expedition. He sent these to the *Rocky Mountain News*, which published them on July 17 and August 18, 1869. They are included as journal-type entries in this book, since they were written on the river en route and in more or less journal format.

Seneca B. Howland. Very little is known of Oramel Howland's younger, half-brother, Seneca. At 5 feet, 9 1/2 inches tall, the grey-eyed, light-haired Seneca was one of the tallest men on the 1869 expedition. He was 26 years old during the expedition. During the Civil War, Seneca enlisted at age 20, on September 4, 1862 (he was born in 1842), for a nine month hitch. On October 23, Seneca was mustered into Company G, 16th Regiment, Vermont Infantry. Of Seneca Howland's combat experience Powell biographer William Culp Darrah notes only that Seneca "suffered a minor wound at the battle at Gettysburg and was temporarily incapacitated for further action."

Seneca B. Howland

As mentioned earlier, Darrah, a faculty member of Gettysburg College, was a Powell admirer as well as his biographer. I've also tried to convey how my retranscriptions of the original writings have shown Darrah to be a relatively sloppy historian, if not biased, at least as far as Powell is concerned.

The problem with Darrah's wounded-at-Gettysburg scenario, discovered historian Don Lago, is that there exists no evidence that Seneca was wounded. Not only did Seneca's "wound" not correspond with an early discharge from the infantry — Seneca served closer to ten months, not the nine of his enlistment, and was mustered out of the Army with an honorable discharge on August 10, 1863 — not even in the immense William Culp Darrah Collection housed at the Utah State Historical Society did Darrah leave a military report or even a scrap of paper supporting his notion that Seneca had been wounded at Gettysburg — or anyplace else. Nor do U.S. military records record that Seneca was wounded. Nor do battlefield records mention such a wound. The Howland Family records also fail to list any such wound, although they do note that Seneca was there at Gettysburg and that Seneca's brother John was at Gettysburg too, but was ill. Why then would Darrah comment that Seneca was wounded yet then otherwise say nothing about Seneca's contribution to the war?

What contribution?

Not only was Seneca B. Howland there at Gettysburg, notes Lago, he was a pivotal player in the Civil War's most important battle, the one that shifted the balance to power forever to the Union Army.

Here's how that happened. On July 1, 1863, James J. Pettigrew's Confederate brigade detached from Robert E. Lee's Army to steal a supply of shoes from Gettysburg. But Pettigrew's men collided unexpectedly with John Buford's Union cavalry division. Within hours, Lee, who was making a desperate bid to attack and occupy Washington, D.C. from the west with his nearly 70,000-man Confederate Army, had arrayed his forces through the town of Gettysburg to face the Union's 4-mile-long "inverted fishhook" line stretching from the "barb" at *Culp's Hill*, along the shank of Cemetery Hill and Cemetery Ridge to the "eye" at the Round Tops. Hence, more or less by accident, Lee's army had run head-to-head at Gettysburg into General George G. Meade's 88,000-man Union Army. Tactically unfortunate for Lee, those 88,000 Union troops occupied the high ground.

Lee's units attacked Meade's flanks, including the position on Culp's Hill, but failed to overrun Union positions. The next day, against the protest of his own General James Longstreet, Lee ordered a frontal assault on Meade's center with 13,500 men — a tactic, again unfortunately for Lee, that Meade had anticipated.

After two hours of artillery barrages, Lee's troops emerged from Cemetery Woods and, as if on a parade ground, advanced uphill onto Cemetery Ridge and into withering fire. General George E. Pickett commanded the largest of Lee's divisions in this charge. In forty minutes of blistering, brutal defensive fire by entrenched Union forces, Pickett's Charge actually reached the Union positions. It now seemed possible that Pickett's Charge might overrun them and win a true invasion for the Confederacy.

At this point two regiments of Vermont troops, the 13th and 16th infantries, charged over the wall and into the open field. The Vermonters aggressively assaulted Pickett's right flank with gun fire, bayonets, and sabers. This surprise counterassault not only stopped Pickett's Charge, it helped annihilate it. It even captured one entire Confederate brigade nearly intact. Pickett's Charge had cost him, in just one unit alone, 3,393 men killed out of 4,800.

Upon seeing this, Union General Abner Doubleday shouted, "Glory to God! See the Vermonters go [to] it!" As historian George R. Stewart summarizes in *Pickett's Charge*, "these raw troops from the far northern hills were to be granted, and were to seize, a military opportunity such as a professional soldier might dream about during a lifetime of fighting and never realize." This flank attack by Vermont's 13th and 16th became "the pivotal movement of the pivotal battle of the war."

On July 5, the remnants of Lee's battered army retreated south across the Potomac River, having suffered 30,000 casualties killed, wounded, or missing in action. The North lost 23,000 men. Although President Abraham Lincoln was appalled that Meade had allowed Lee to retreat, not only did Confederate forces *never* return to the north again, this pivotal battle inspired Lincoln to pen the most famous words ever spoken by an American President (on November 19, at Gettysburg):

"Fourscore and seven years ago our fathers brought forth, on this continent, a new nation, conceived in liberty, and dedicated to the proposition that all men are created equal.

Now we are engaged in a great civil war, testing whether that nation, or any nation so conceived, and so dedicated, can long endure. We are met on a great battlefield of that war. We have come to dedicate a portion of that field, as a final resting place for those who here gave their lives, that that nation might live. It is altogether fitting and proper that we do this.

But, in a larger sense, we can not now dedicate — we can not consecrate — we can not hallow — this ground. The brave men, living and dead, who struggled here, have consecrated it far above our poor power to add or detract. The world will little note, nor long remember what we say here, but it can never forget what they did here. It is for us the living, rather, to be dedicated here to the unfinished work which they who fought here have thus far so nobly advanced. It is rather for us to be here dedicated to the great task remaining before us — that from these honored dead we take increased devotion to that cause for which they here gave the last full measure of devotion — that we here highly resolve that these dead shall not have died in vain — that this nation, under God, shall have a new birth of freedom — and that the government of the people, by the people, and for the people, shall not perish from the earth."

In short, the Union soldiers who fought at Gettysburg were heroes. And those soldiers of the Vermont Infantry who leaped into hand-to-combat to turn the tide of Pickett's Charge, and thus turn the tide of battle, and thus turn the tide of the entire Civil War itself in favor of the Union, were heroes among heroes.

But what does this pivotal moment in American history have to do with Seneca B. Howland and/or Powell biographer William Culp Darrah? As historian Don Lago notes, William Culp Darrah, a geologist and a medically handicapped one at that, adored John Wesley Powell, also a medically handicapped geologist. Indeed, as Darrah's daughter writes: "Major Powell was truly the young [as a Boy Scout] Darrah's hero, a role model for outstanding accomplishment in the face of adversity and great obstacles." As Lago notes further, *Culp's Hill* was owned by William Culp Darrah's grand uncle Henry Culp. Darrah had played on this hill as a child. Note, too, Lago points out, that William Culp Darrah regularly used his middle name with pride. As an adult Darrah knew the history of Culp's Hill during the turning point of the Civil War. Darrah also knew that another of his relatives, Wesley Culp, fought for the Confederacy and was killed while assaulting Culp's Hill.

Again, so what? Well, here it is. Seneca B. Howland was one of those daring infantrymen in Company G, 16th Regiment Vermont Military Infantry who leaped over that wall and, exhibiting tremendous courage, helped carve Pickett's Charge into mincemeat — and, by the way, save the nation that our forefathers had risked everything to create.

So why not, in Darrah's role as Powell historian, note that one of Powell's 1869 boatmen was not merely a Civil War veteran, someone who simply showed up, but was in fact a Civil War hero? After all, it would be very hard for Darrah to have missed Gettysburg's prominent monument to Seneca's 16th Vermont Infantry.

Because, Lago explains, Darrah, as did Wallace Stegner, not only idolized Powell, both men endeavored to keep him squeaky clean. To do so, however, Darrah apparently took a visible step beyond Stegner. To preserve Powell's image, Darrah seemed willing to resort to subterfuge.

Did Darrah have such an agenda?

The most damning incident during the 1869 expedition — and during Powell's life as a whole — was the defection and fates of three of his crew members at Separation Rapid. Here William Dunn and both Howland brothers decided to hike north and separate from the river expedition.

Why?

This incident has been mired in controversy for 133 years. And clearing away the murk had been made far more problematic due to one after another Powell biographer having whitewashed Powell's significant role in this tragedy by suppressing the reports of the men who survived the expedition.

For example, Darrah notes in the *Utah Historical Quarterly*: "The three diaries which are preserved, those by Major Powell, Sumner, and Bradley, agree that the trio refused to go further. There is no hint of dissension or serious disagreement which might have induced the men to leave. Certainly there is no suggestion that they had been ordered to do so."

Au contraire, as will become clear in the final chapter, there exist more than hints. Instead there exist full disclosures by both William Hawkins and John Sumner of Major Powell ordering Dunn to leave. And worse.

Darrah, however, goes further than merely misleading us about reports not existing that "hint" at dissension, serious disagreements, and/or Powell ordering any of the men to leave. In his book, *Powell of the Colorado*, Darrah states (in a footnote on page 141): "Yet the simple fact is they [the Howlands and Dunn] were afraid to go farther and deserted."

Darrah's allegation of cowardice could not be in greater conflict with William Hawkins' eye-witness testimony regarding this incident: "Of course we knew what was the reason Dunn left: as for fear, he did not possess it. As for the other two boys [Seneca and Oramel], they never showed any signs of fear. The older of the Howlands was in the boat with me since his boat was wrecked." No surprise, Darrah does not quote Hawkins, he simply discounts Hawkins' first-hand experience as of no consequence.

While conspiracy theories are appealing when the data lean heavily in their direction, this one, Don Lago's interpretation (one he sat on for a year and then finally released after he took the time to plow through the entire Darrah Collection at the Utah State Historical Society), as you will see before this book ends, is plausible. But what all of this implies, notes Lago, is that William Culp Darrah so badly wanted his readers to believe that Major Powell was utterly blameless and that, instead, William H. Dunn, Oramel G. Howland, and Seneca B. Howland had abandoned Powell out of cowardice that he not only ignored eye-witness accounts, he deliberately painted Seneca Howland as a plausible coward. To do so, Darrah could not reveal Seneca's heroism in the face of violent death at Gettysburg. To do so, Darrah had to suppress significant information. To do so, in essence, Darrah himself had to mislead us — by omission — in print.

Thus, much like his childhood — and adult — idol, Powell the prevaricator, Darrah apparently became entrapped in manufacturing an alternate reality for Powell.

After Seneca Howland was mustered out of the infantry, his older brother Oramel urged Seneca to join him in Colorado. Seneca did so in 1868, taking a job in the office of the *Rocky Mountain News*. Little is known about Seneca from records, and very little was written of him in any of the expedition's journals or letters. John Colton Sumner, however, does write very well of Seneca, describing him as: "as good and true a man as can be found in any place."

Otherwise, Seneca Howland seems to have been almost the invisible man on the expedition, never doing anything remarkably wrong (with the exceptions, perhaps, of his rowing the *No Name* into Disaster Falls and, later, his sticking with Oramel against his better judgement during the Separation incident) nor, on the other hand, accomplishing anything again that was notably heroic.

As far as anyone knows, Seneca Howland kept no journal. Nor has anyone reported thus far that he wrote letters from the river at the Uinta as some of the other men did. He may well have kept a journal and hiked out from Separation Rapid with it on his person. If so, Fate has stolen it from posterity.

Major John Wesley Powell at age 40.

Major John Wesley Powell.

As hinted earlier, Powell was interesting, controversial — and tragic — enough to have spurred a covey of biographies. Several authors over the past century have found in Powell an irresistible biographical target; at least one author decided that Powell was only one halo short of being a saint. One of the most readable of these works was William Culp Darrah's 1951 *Powell of the Colorado*. Another, even more famous and respected but more poorly informed and less accurate, is Wallace Stegner's glowing 1953 *Beyond the Hundredth Meridian: John Wesley Powell and the Second Opening of the West*. This is the biography that canonizes Powell. The most recent and perhaps most objective and well-researched — though sadly still rife with errors of fact concerning the 1869 expedition and with an incongruent defensiveness in excusing Powell's poor decisions — is Donald Worster's 2001 *A River Running West: The Life of John*

Wesley Powell. Despite all of this hoopla and good press on Major Powell over several decades, however, once you read the journals and letters of the six members of the expedition your own personal assessment may yield a different judgement.

Not that Major Powell was not interesting. He was. Very. But as with President William Jefferson Clinton, it is a trick to separate the man, the means, and the legacy without entering some dark closets jumbled with a heap of the by-products of the unsavory side of human nature.

Bearing in mind that the famous Major John Wesley Powell has been "biographied" in thousands of pages, while the nine crew members who worked like slaves to make his 1869 expedition a success — and to earn for Powell his main claim to fame — have received only a few pages of attention, I will try to be brief on who Powell was, and why he might have been that way. Even so, "brief" for Powell will still require nearly ten pages. Consider these pages an antidote to the prevailing literary myth about the man.

John Wesley Powell was born in Mount Morrie, New York, the fourth child of eight and the eldest son of Joseph Powell and his wife Mary on March 24, 1834. Joseph Powell frequently moved his family, making yet more money with each sale of property. J. W. Powell spent much of his teenage years on one, then another, family farm in Wisconsin and Illinois. Later he briefly attended several schools — Illinois College, Oberlin College, and Illinois (Wheaton) Institute — dropping out quickly from each one as his desire to learn natural science was met instead with theological lessons. Yet while he never graduated, he did learn enough, often as an autodidact, to become a school teacher by age 18. Later he was hired as a principal.

As William Culp Darrah writes in his biography of Powell, John Wesley Powell proved to be not at all the ideal son of a Methodist Episcopal Missionary. Young Powell was more interested in the natural sciences and the outdoors than in becoming a preacher. Nor did young Powell seem attracted by the prospect of remaining the senior Powell farmer (a role he had assumed as early as age twelve) on any of his often-absent father's farms.

One significant spin-off of J. W. Powell's desire to be a naturalist was his surprising — and disappointing to his father — journeys by oarboat or skiff during the 1850s down the Illinois, Mississippi, Missouri, and Ohio rivers to collect biological specimens, mostly freshwater mollusks.

Powell biographers often refer to these early river journeys made to collect specimens to reveal how Powell was at heart a scientist. Indeed, Powell thought of himself as a naturalist, and he was interested in science. But in all my readings by and about Powell I have been unable to locate even one instance where Powell employed the scientific method to examine any phenomenon in nature, be it geological, biological, or anthropological. Powell did read science, but he was incredibly facile in explaining the origins of interesting phenomena that he encountered in the West. Typically, Major Powell would see an interesting landscape or other phenomenon, ponder it a bit, then make a snap judgement on some mechanism of nature that explained how it came to be as it was. He rarely, if ever, proposed his explanations of the real world as *hypotheses that might be tested for their accuracy or lack of it via the scientific method of carefully designed research and appropriate data collection capable of falsifying those hypotheses.* Instead, he seemed to consider his intuition and snap judgements infallible. In his own way, Powell had traded the dogma of Methodism for the dogma of science, but he never truly adopted the rigorous thinking processes of the scientific method. In short, Major Powell, the scientist, wasn't. Powell, the naturalist, was.

Important insights as to Major Powell's psychological modus operandi in the canyons of the Colorado — and later beyond them — may reside in the example set by his father. After leaving New York, the reverend Joseph Powell bought farm land in Ohio. He improved this land and sold it at a profit. Next he moved his family to Wisconsin and bought yet more land. Even at age twelve, John Wesley, as the eldest son, was impressed into land improvement work and basic farm management while his father traveled away from home to preach Methodism. The Reverend Joseph Powell then sold this farm too at a profit. He next moved the Powells to Illinois and bought yet more land. And, you guessed it, he depended on young John Wesley to improve and manage this also. Thus, yet again, young J. W. Powell helped earn a hefty profit for his often absent father while also developing a firm revulsion for farm labor. Joseph Powell's inculcation into John Wesley Powell the pragmatic goal of always turning a profit by using the labor of other people who are not in a position to refuse helps explain Major Powell's later relationships with his own underlings, including those in 1869.

Added to Joseph Powell's lessons on the profitability of using other people is John Wesley Powell's own tendency to be fickle — with his schooling and then later with his many brief teaching and professorial positions (discussed below). On the Colorado River Exploring Expedition of 1869, at the least, Powell's opportunism, combined with his weak loyalty to those who greased the hinges of the doors that opened opportunities for him, would manifest themselves fatally.

But I am getting ahead of myself. Another major influence on Powell was the horror of war. He and his family believed firmly in the abolitionist cause. John Wesley Powell himself believed in even bigger issues. Consider, for example, Powell's assessment of the significance of the Civil War:

"It was a great thing to destroy slavery, but the integrity of the Union was of no less importance: and on and beyond it all, was to be counted the result of the war as an influence which should extend far into the history of the future, not only establishing in North America a great predominating nation, with a popular and powerful government, but also as securing the ascendancy of the Anglo-Saxon branch of the Aryan family, and the ultimate spread of Anglo-Saxon civilization over the globe. Perhaps it is only a dreamer's vision wherein I see the English language become the language of the world; of science, the institutions, and the arts of the world; and the nations integrated as congeries of republican states."

At age 27, on October 8, 1861, the five foot, six-and-one-half-inch, sandy-haired, grey-eyed Powell enlisted for three years in Company H of the 20th Illinois Infantry. Powell had been quickly shunted into the engineering of fortifications. This was no random military assignment. Powell had furiously studied all he could of army physical infrastructure. Despite his last minute cramming, soon, by December 1861, Powell was commissioned Captain of Battery F, 2nd Illinois Light Artillery Regiment. He now commanded 24-pounder cannons instead of bridges. Soon Powell received permission from General Grant to take a short leave to marry. To his parents' disappointment he chose his second cousin, Emma Dean, as his bride. She accompanied him back to his unit at Cape Girardeau, Missouri.

Not long afterward, in April of 1862, Grant's army stood arrayed in Tennessee around a small Methodist church built of logs and named Shiloh. On April 5, General Albert Johnston's Confederate troops launched an aggressive surprise attack that nearly over-ran several of Grant's units.

On April 6, John Wesley Powell, on his own initiative because he was lacking orders to join the defense, finally ordered his own artillery unit to advance. In the confusion, he advanced beyond the Union lines into Confederate deployments.

Most of Powell's unit recovered, reversed, and re-joined Grant's pinned-down forces who had held firm under generals Benjamin Prentiss and Will Wallace. After hours of thunderous defense, however, the tide still favored the Confederates. As Powell wrote:

"About four o'clock, as I have always remembered the time, Gen. Wallace asked me if I could not plant a section to his left in advance of the line where there were some trees near the corner of the Peach Orchard fields. This I did and the section was immediately engaged. Soon I discovered that there was a line of men concealing themselves in the fence and I dismounted and pointed one of the pieces along the fence loaded with solid shell. As I raised my hand for a signal to the gunners to stand clear of the recoil a musket ball stuck my arm above the wrist which I scarcely noticed until I attempted to mount my horse. Looking about I found that the infantry which had also moved with me into this position were running away as I thought from the line. I stood by a tree and tried to examine my arm, and looking about the field and at the running men, I was more angry than I remember ever to have been at any other time, but this was very quickly explained when I saw in the distance a Confederate force coming down in double quick time, and that my supporters were engaged in repelling them. At about this juncture a medical officer rode up to me and commenced to cut my sleeve for the purpose of examining the wound; but immediately Gen. Wallace himself rode up and dismounted picking me up, for he was a tall athletic man, and put me on my horse and directed the sergeant to take me back to the landing."

Two days later a Union sawbones amputated Powell's right arm below the elbow. This was bad luck for Powell, whose stump would trouble him for life. But Powell's luck was not nearly as bad as that of the twenty thousand other troops who died among the one hundred thousand who engaged in this battle — including both General Will Wallace himself and Confederate commander General Albert Johnston — in this incredibly bloody melee which, ironically, ended in a stalemate.

Powell remained in the Army. After several months of convalescing, General Grant assigned Captain John W. Powell to recruiting duty, a billet which lasted until nearly the one-year anniversary of his wound at Shiloh. He returned to his artillery unit as chief, eventually receiving more specialized organizational assignments. Powell was finally promoted to the rank of Major on September 1, 1864; he became Inspector of Artillery for "the Department and Army of the Tennessee." Upon being honorably discharged on January 4, 1865, Powell retained the "title" of Major. He applied for his disablement pension in May of 1865.

The now mutilated Major Powell soon gained a professorship in geology at Illinois Wesleyan College. This was facilitated by an honorary master's degree conferred on Powell by this same institute during the war. This professorship lasted barely more than a year before Powell engineered for himself a new position elsewhere. In 1867, Powell moved to Illinois State Normal University as the curator of its newly expanded museum. Almost instantly he began his fateful field trip of a dozen members to the

Colorado Rockies to collect specimens and to climb Pike's Peak. This same year the seed was planted, perhaps by Powell himself, perhaps by ex-Colorado Governor William Gilpin, or perhaps instead by John Colton Sumner — whom Powell had met late in 1867 at Middle Park — to explore the heretofore unknown canyons of the Colorado and Green rivers.

Powell's original plan, Sumner says, was to travel *upstream* on the Colorado from Callville into Grand Canyon and beyond, much as Lieutenant Joseph Christmas Ives had done in 1857-58 up to the Rio Virgin. This soon changed to the more fundamental downstream plan from Green River City. After extensive local study of the region of the upper canyon of the Green during 1868 and a bit during early 1869, Powell traveled to Washington, D.C. to request support for a party of twelve men to explore the river. There Powell was granted no money but was given authorization to draw supplies for twenty-five men — or cash for unused rations — from any western Army post. The Illinois State Natural History Society offered the Powell Expedition its auspices. Illinois State Normal University granted him $500. Illinois Industrial University also granted $500. The Chicago Academy of Sciences gave him $100. The Smithsonian loaned Powell several instruments. Powell also apparently provided $2,000 of his own salary from Illinois Normal University as museum curator. The Union Pacific and Burlington railroads provided passage for Powell's men, boats, and equipment from the East to Green River City.

Equipped on not much more than a shoestring, Powell mustered the bulk of his small crew and pioneering gear in the spring of 1869 and rode the iron horse to Green River City.

Andy Hall, Powell's last minute recruit at Green River glowed effusively: "The major is from Bloomington, Ill. I suppose you never herd [sic] of him and he is a Bully fellow you bett."

But Powell was not always bully. Describing Powell's tendency to be oblivious to inconvenient realities Frederick S. Dellenbaugh wrote up an episode from 1871:

> "We had a fine lot of men on that expedition and every one of them did his best at all times without any 'kicking.' Steward, who was sick, did object the morning the Major and two or three others of us, started to climb Navajo Mountain, saying: 'Major, you have no right to keep us here any longer.' 'Why?' said the Major. -- 'Because we have nothing to eat.' Examinations of the larder proved this to be true, so we went on reaching our next supply station late the next day and finding the supplies there."

What were the other men's opinions of Powell during the expedition?

Hawkins noted more than thirty years after the trip: "I can say one thing truthfully about the Major — that no man living was ever thought more of by his men up to the time he wanted to drive Bill Dunn from the party."

On July 29, 1869, Bradley wrote of Powell in Glen Canyon after Powell had decided to name a major tributary from the north the "Dirty Devil." In this naming, Powell was apparently also aiming a slight at *Emma Dean* boatman William Dunn, whom Powell had allegedly also called a "dirty devil." "Major named the new stream 'Dirty Devil Creek,'" wrote Bradley, "and as we are the only white men who have seen it, I for one feel quite highly complimented by the name, yet it is in keeping with his [Powell's] whole character, which needs only a short study to be read like a book."

John Sumner noted of Powell: "As I shared the blankets with Major J. W. Powell for two years, I believe I knew him — perhaps not....He was a man of many traits, good, bad and indifferent — vastly over estimated *as a man*, (underlining/italics are Sumner's) as so many others have been, though as a scholar and scientist he was worthy of all praise."

A careful reading of Powell — and of his biographies — reveal his strengths to be numerous. Major John Wesley Powell was curious, energetic, optimistic, physically courageous, visionary, enthusiastic, insightful, fairly astute politically, a charismatic schmoozer, and ambitious. On the other side of the coin, Powell was stubborn, demanding, self-serving, facile, opportunistic, perhaps over-ambitious, and he evinced amazingly little loyalty to those who assisted him (this list includes entities from universities to boatmen). And, yes, Powell regularly stretched the truth beyond its breaking point when it might benefit him to do so. In short, Powell exhibited diagnostic signs of a narcissistic personality disorder.

Additional critical insights into Powell's character — helping to explain what went right and what went wrong on the 1869 expedition — come from his brother-in-law, Almon Harris Thompson, husband of Nellie (Ellen) Powell. Thompson was Powell's key man on his 1871-1872 expedition. Thompson led and managed much of Powell's survey work, often in Powell's absence, and generally made the right things happen, often under harsh conditions. On October 23, 1902, after working for and under and despite Major Powell for thirty years, Thompson wrote to Frederick Dellenbaugh, Powell's 18-year-old boatman on the 1871-72 aborted Colorado River trip. Dellenbaugh — a sleep-walker who went for his gun so often during his dreams that the rest of the 1871-72 crew had to disarm him at night — was working on his own history of this latter Colorado expedition and seeking the journals of his fellow expeditionaries to supplement his own meager notes. Thompson wrote back to warn Dellenbaugh, who idolized Powell as a father figure, that he should be honest about Powell and Powell's strong talents as an organizer, but also about his lack of talent as an investigator, despite such honesty placing

Powell in an unfavorable light — or else, Thompson warned further, Dellenbaugh should not bother to write a "history" at all. Thompson spelled out to Dellenbaugh what he considered Powell's shortcomings:

> "The second expedition is completely ignored though liberal use is made of its incidents and labors in the text of the so-called narrative of the first expedition. I think it would be just and appropriate that you speak plainly of this. The phase of the Major's character which led him to ignore the second expedition is no mystery to me. He had no fine sense of justice, no exacted loyalty to a high ideal and honor and so far as his subordinates were concerned did not know the meaning of noblesse oblige. He was generous, sympathetic and possessed all the estimable qualities you and I assign him but you will notice neither you nor I speak of his justice or loyalty. He was sadly deficient in these....He wasn't all Saint. He could lie on occasion — be generous one minute and contemptible the next."

Thompson's advice to Dellenbaugh, however, went for naught. Dellenbaugh idolized Powell to the point of near blindness despite being troubled by Powell's unjust track record even with Dellenbaugh himself. The starry-eyed Dellenbaugh not only canonized Powell much as Stegner would do, he also perversely did his best to destroy the reputations of the Howland brothers and William Dunn. For example, Dellenbaugh lobbied successfully – and vindictively – to keep Dunn's and the Howlands' names off the Powell Memorial Plaque on the Canyon's South Rim.

Interestingly, Major Powell's nephew, Walter Clement Powell, in his expedition journal on November 12, 1871, would comment in concert with Thompson on the Major's leadership after 164 days:

> "The whole party is disgusted with the way the expedition is run. Bish [Bishop] is going to leave, Steward has left, Jones will leave if he has any spirit in him. Being called a baby and a calf would be enough to send any ordinary fool out of the party. It will take mighty little to send Fred [Dellenbaugh] and I home; even Prof. [A. H. Thompson] said if things don't go differently he would leave....The expedition is a farce [November 16]....The Maj. thinks he can do anything with us because he has us out here [January 15, 1872].

Yet another crew member of Powell's 1871-72 attempt on the

Colorado, John F. Steward, irritated with Powell for "appropriating" Steward's geological discoveries in Cataract Canyon *and* his hypotheses for their genesis, both without credit, would later note: "I cannot say I am pleased that in Major Powell's reports all credit is given to the miners and trappers who took the preliminary trip with him, and almost none to our party for the geological, topographical, and photographic work accomplished. Why such a course was taken I will not explain, but merely say for myself, that no business motive should lead a man to be unjust..."

An insight into Powell's loyalty to his loyal men of 1869 is revealed by his river journal. Powell explored downriver with George Y. Bradley for 99 days in terra incognita. Bradley personally rescued Powell from death twice, possibly three times. Yet Powell could never even correctly remember Bradley's name. Powell consistently wrote "Bradey" in his journal when referring to Sergeant Bradley. Other expedition members, however, somehow did manage to get Bradley's name right.

Another often misunderstood point, Major Powell religiously wore an inflatable rubber, "horse-collar" life jacket in 1869 while running rapids. This compensated for the loss of his right arm. This was the only life jacket on the expedition. Robert Brewster Stanton researched this issue and concluded that Powell never admitted, publicly or otherwise, to having possessed this life jacket even to the day he died. His later crew of 1871-72, for example, was certain that Powell had *not* possessed a life jacket in 1869. After Separation Rapid, Powell allegedly presented this life jacket to Hawkins, who, years later, at Stanton's suggestion, donated it to the Smithsonian. Indeed Hawkins reported, "Major Powell said he was dressed when he had his life preserver on, and he always had it on when the water was bad."

For this book Powell's on-river writings come from three sources. The first is newspapers from 1869. Powell's "journal-like" letters describing the expedition's experiences from Green River City, Wyoming, to the Uinta River are transcribed into this book from the *Chicago Tribune* on May 29, July 19 & 20, and August 20, 1869, and yet another letter published in *The Missouri Republican-St. Louis* on July 22, 1869. Powell's original hand-written copies of these letters covering the expedition upstream of the Uinta are not known to have survived. On the other hand, Powell's hand-written journal #1 covering the portion of the expedition occurring downstream of the Uinta — the second major source from Powell — is transcribed here from a photocopy of the original residing in the National Anthropological Archives of the Smithsonian Institution. The third source is Powell's on-river geological notes beginning below the Uinta River written in his journal #2, also at the Smithsonian. Strangely, Powell wrote two versions of these in his journal, an original but partial version on pages 2 to 11 (the Uinta to the Colorado), then, later, he rewrote an expanded and more complete

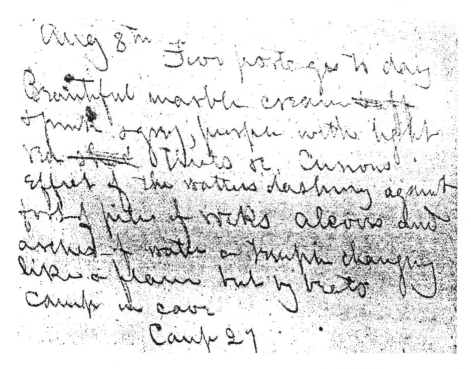

John Wesley Powell's Journal entry for August 8th

version, still in his Journal #2, on pages 62 and 43 to 70, with a second page 62. In Powell's expanded version one of his estimates grows bigger (one cliff grew from 600 feet high to 750 feet high). Hence, in this book I have transcribed and used the first, but incomplete, version, followed by that portion of the expanded version which covers the canyons not described in that first, partial version. Lastly, in the Appendix of this book resides Powell's original 1869 astronomical observations as transcribed by Richard D. Quartaroli from copies of the original housed in the Smithsonian's National Anthropological Archives.

A major question regarding the 1869 expedition is: would it ever have launched without John Wesley Powell to ramrod it? Hawkins and Sumner both say that, even before Powell appeared on the scene, they intended — with Dunn — to explore the upper canyons of the Green for the purpose of trapping and prospecting. Sumner not only wrote of himself as a "free trapper," he also stipulated to Powell in their "AGREEMENT" that he and Dunn (and likely Hawkins as well) should be guaranteed time for multiple days of trapping and prospecting during the expedition. Sumner also told Stanton that exploring the unknown Green and Colorado rivers by traveling *downstream* — in 1867 Powell was entertaining the idea of traveling the river *upstream* — became the reality due, in part, to Sumner's suggestion that downstream travel was the best bet. It remains indisputably true (as you will discover) that these men — along with Bradley — were indispensable to Powell's success during this expedition. The question, however, remains: would a *full* traverse of the canyons of the Green and Colorado rivers have been successful during this era without Major Powell at the helm?

Historian Don Lago offers a twist to this question by noting how the only thread connecting the Howlands, Bill Dunn, Hawkins, and Sumner was the organization, skill, and experience of Oramel Howland who began helping Powell in 1867 in full connection with William Byers, editor of the *Rocky Mountain News*. Byers was the major bankroller for Powell's 1867 and 1868 expeditions. Byers held greater wilderness experience than Powell and planned to accompany and possibly lead the 1869 river exploration with the above five men. Why didn't he? Byers' time constraints and a falling out with Powell, Lago suggests, changed his mind — and history.

Walter Henry Powell

Walter Henry Powell. Walter Powell's story is not a happy one. He was born in 1842 in Jackson, Ohio, and educated at Illinois Institute. He became a school teacher at age 16.

In 1862, Walter joined his older brother's Battery F, 2nd Regiment, Illinois Light Artillery, and became a second lieutenant. He served at Shiloh, where John Wesley lost his arm. Lt. Walter Powell served in Vicksburg and the Battle of Atlanta.

During the latter conflict, Confederate troops captured Lt. Powell and most of his troops and incarcerated them in the prisoner of war stockade, Camp Sorghum (a.k.a. Camp Asylum) near Charleston, South Carolina. Here Lt. Powell faced very short rations and strange Southern fevers that racked him unmercifully while being crowded into an open pen with hundreds of other POWs and their unburied excrement.

Lt. Powell managed an escape. But too late. He was recaptured several days later in a state of insanity. After hospitalization, Lt. Walter Powell was returned to the North during an exchange of prisoners on March 1, 1865.

After the war, Walter Powell was never the same. He had apparently suffered irreparable brain damage. He was emotionally unstable in much the same way as later Vietnam War veterans suffering post-traumatic stress disorder and, beyond this, was subject to uncontrollable fits of deep anger. Unfit now for teaching school, he joined Major Powell in 1868 in Colorado and then again in 1869 for the Colorado River Exploring Expedition.

Much has been made of Powell's men dubbing Walter Powell "Old Shady" because of his deep bass voice and his predilection for frequently singing this dismal, even macabre tune. Powell made much of this nickname in his book, *Canyons.* Yet as you will read in the journals, no one, not even John Wesley Powell himself, ever refers to Walter as "Old Shady" in their on-river writings. This seems to be yet a fiction fabricated by — or at least an affectation of — Major Powell that struck him while dictating his 1875 report in Washington. In 1907, however, Sumner, after having read Powell's report, does refer to Walter Powell as "Old Shady."

Very telling is Bradley's account of Walter Powell. There isn't one. This is despite Bradley and Walter having shared the same boat, the *Maid of the Cañon*, each sitting at his own set of oars (and hopefully coordinating their strokes), for three months: from Green River City to the mouth of the Virgin River. Bradley did write in his journal faithfully each day. But what did he say about Walter Powell in those 22,000 words he penned so minutely? Almost nothing. For starters, Bradley never wrote the name "Walter" (nor "Old Shady") in his journal *ever.* Nor did he talk about Walter at all unless it was a rare and oblique reference such as "Major & brother are gone ahead *to see what comes next*" (underlining/italics by Bradley) or the even rarer type of entry, the most intimate entry Bradley writes of Walter Powell: "the first wave dashed partly over us with fearful force striking one oar from the hand of Major's brother but did not fill the boat."

As far as Bradley lets us know, he might as well have been sharing the *Maid* with a male mannikin.

Yet while Bradley may have been charitable — or perhaps instead interested in saving his own sanity — by ignoring the reality of sharing a boat for three months with Walter Powell, when Sumner later spoke of Walter, his choice of words was anything but charitable. "Captain Walter Powell was about as worthless a piece of furniture as could be found in a day's journey," Sumner noted. "O. G. Howland was far his superior physically and morally and, God knows, away above him mentally."

Hawkins would later sum up the pleasures of traveling with Walter Powell thus: "None of the party except the Major liked Capt. Powell. He had a bull-dozing way that was not then practiced in the West. He threatened to slap me several times for trying to sing like he did, but he never did slap anyone in the party."

The bottom line? Walter Powell was no one's pleasantly memorable character during the 1869 expedition. And as we will see in the final chapter, Walter was apparently fortunate indeed at having arrived at the Rio Virgin without one of the other expeditionaries, particularly Andy Hall, having yielded to the hot desire, to "blow the top of his damn head off."

Despite Walter's tragic handicaps, he did pen one letter while on the upper reaches of the Green, a rather charming letter describing in evocative language some of the beauties of the upper river that was published in the *Chicago Evening Journal* on July 19, 1869. It is included here not just because it was written while on the river, but also because it is worth reading.

John Colton Sumner

John Colton Sumner. In hindsight it is clear that Sumner, Bradley, and Hawkins — in that order — were Major Powell's keys to success. Sumner, more than anyone else, acted consistently as *the* key. Most historians refer to Jack Sumner as Powell's "head boatman." Indeed, Sumner, along with William Dunn, did row Major Powell in his little, lead, scout boat, the *Emma Dean*, until the Major abandoned it at the mouth of Separation Canyon on day #97. As stated explicitly in "THE AGREEMENT," however, there is no talk of Sumner being head boatman. Instead: "J. C. Sumner agrees to do all necessary work required with the sextant....also agreeing [along with Dunn and O. G. Howland] to do a fair proportion of the work necessary in getting supplies and boats safely through the channels of the aforementioned rivers, for use of the expedition; and also agreeing to save for specimens for stuffing, for the party of the first part [Powell], all suitable skins of animals which they may collect while engaging in the above exploration of the Green and Colorado rivers."

Who was this man — who, at five feet, five and three-quarter inches tall, apparently the smallest man on the trip — that he became the most critical to Powell's success?

Born on May 16, 1840, in Newton, Indiana, John Colton Sumner grew up on a farm along the Cedar River in northeastern Iowa. Thus Sumner was the closest thing to a "born Westerner" on the expedition. Sumner learned to trap, hunt and shoot, and run an oarboat as a boy; he also attended a local academy. As with most of Powell's crew, the Civil War caught up Sumner too. On August 8, 1862, he enlisted in Company E, 32nd Regiment, Iowa Volunteer Infantry (a.k.a. the Bolton Rangers). The light-complected, auburn-haired Sumner saw frequent action, which he often volunteered for, during his three-year hitch. He re-enlisted and continued to perform as a sharpshooter and scout. He was promoted to corporal. He was finally mustered out, apparently uninjured, on May 22, 1865.

In 1854, Sumner's sister, Elizabeth, had married William N. Byers. Later the couple moved to Denver where Byers soon became proprietor and editor of the *Rocky Mountain News* and also guided professionally. Sumner followed them to Denver in June 1866, shortly after doffing his Army uniform — hence Sumner's early association with guiding and with Oramel G. Howland, who worked for Byers. Soon Sumner built a trading post at Hot Sulphur Springs in Middle Park, with the local Utes and a few mountain men. He also trapped and professionally guided. In short, Sumner worked as a wilderness jack-of-all-trades, his outdoor training as a boy on the Cedar River coming to the fore.

An episode which provides an insight as to Sumner's presence of mind under fire in this wild country is given by Robert Brewster Stanton in his *Colorado River Controversies*. It occurred during Sumner's early days as an Indian trader.

> "At one time while crossing the range for supplies, he was fired upon and promptly returned the shots. Next day two Indians were found dead by their companions. Soon Sumner's cabin was filled with angry savages bent on vengeance. He explained the facts to the Indians, but they were not appeased. With a coolness that excited their wonder, for there was not a white man within fifty miles of him, Sumner drew his revolver. Pointing it at a couple of boxes of powder that he had on hand, he told them the sooner they departed the better, as he would blow cabin and all to pieces. The Indians were impressed by his nerve, and at once left."

When asked later if he really would have fired, Sumner responded, "Of course, I would. It would have been better than death at the hands of the Indians, and then we all would have gone to hell together."

Robert Brewster Stanton described Sumner as "a true frontiersman, with a kind, gentle, loving heart, and yet with a temper and a spirit that knew no bounds when he was treated unjustly by others. A true friend, a faithful companion, a man in the true sense of the word. As every strong man has, he had his faults, but they were not of the heart. Brave to the last degree...[yet] knowing and recognizing what fear and danger were. A man of indomitable will — of the kind that has built up our western empire — ever ready, even after a failure, to take up some new work and battle bravely to the end."

Major Powell heard of Sumner's good reputation. Byers helped Powell seek him out as a guide in 1867 to assist with Powell's Illinois Wesleyan University field trips with students. A year later, when Powell returned to the Rockies, Sumner closed his trading business to guide again for Powell, this time enlisting William R. Hawkins, O. G. Howland, and William H. Dunn to assist. This was how the latter two men made their fatal acquaintance with the one-armed Major.

As Sumner tells it in 1907, when Powell asked him in 1867 to accompany him on a field trip to the Badlands of the Dakotas in 1868, Sumner says:

> "[I] fired back at him the counter-proposition — *the exploration of the Colorado River of the West*, from the junction of the Green and Grand Rivers to the Gulf of California. He at first scouted the idea as foolhardy and impossible. I urged on him the importance of the work and what a big feather it would be in our hats if we succeeded. After several windy fights around the campfire, I finally outwinded him, and it was agreed that we should come out the following spring and we should make the attempt. I believe Major Powell states in his report that the exploration of the Colorado River had been in his mind for years. He mentioned nothing of the kind to me previous to our discussion of and agreement to do it, and the idea was certainly not his own."

Indeed, on page *ix* of Powell's 1875 *Exploration of the Colorado River of the West and Its Tributaries Explored in 1869, 1870, 1871, and 1872*, he admits:

> "In the summer of 1867, with a small party of naturalists, students, and amateurs like myself, I visited the mountain region of Colorado Territory. While in Middle

Park, I explored a little cañon, through which the Grand River runs, immediately below the watering-place, "Middle Park Hot Springs." Later in the fall I passed through Cedar Cañon, the gorge by which the Grand leaves the park. The result of the summer's study was to kindle a desire to explore the cañons of the Grand, Green, and Colorado Rivers, and the next summer I organized an expedition with the intention of penetrating still farther into that cañon country."

Powell does not mention any role played by Sumner, or Hawkins, or anyone else in this process of "kindling."

In character — as will be clear well before the final page of this book — Sumner embodied a very strong code of the West, that of fierce loyalty, integrity, self-sufficiency, and trustworthiness. Indeed, as the journals will reveal, Sumner was even more heroic than Bradley, who twice quietly rescued Powell from death. At significant risk to himself, Sumner, to name but two of several examples you will read, rescued both Howland brothers and Frank Goodman at Disaster Falls in Lodore, and later, rescued William H. Dunn from a nasty capsize and near drowning near the foot of Desolation Canyon. Powell not only benefited from all of Sumner's capabilities and his competence, a case can be made that Powell owed his life to them. But, as we shall see, Powell did not reciprocate Sumner's actions or spirit in kind — at least to the degree that Sumner expected.

Major Powell asked Sumner to keep a journal during the 1869 expedition. Sumner did so, though often highly descriptive and punctuated with wry humor, it was not quite to the level of prose and introspection that Bradley provided. Still, Sumner's was the only other consistent journal of the trip and offers us several fascinating insights into the expedition that otherwise would have been lost forever. Sumner was so modest — or at least so concerned that no one label him a braggart — that during his heroic rescue of the Howlands and Goodman, he referred to himself in the third person as "the Trapper." The May 24 to June 28, 1869, portion of Sumner's journal — which he fluffed up with additional details at the Uinta River — was published by the *Missouri Democrat* on August 24 & 25, 1869, as "A Daily Journal of the Colorado Exploring Expedition." It was reprinted faithfully by Otis "Dock" Marston in the 1969 *Utah Historical Quarterly*. The version in this book is transcribed from the original *Missouri Democrat*. Interestingly, Major Powell submitted Sumner's journal almost apologetically, as if half embarrassed that he could be associated with, and also be sponsoring, the inferior writings of a backwoodsman possessing no college education. Powell's letter of submission to the *Missouri Democrat* was published as follows, after the *Democrat's* headline:

FROM COL. POWELL.

Interesting Memoranda.

Daily Record of the Expedition.

Latest Dates Published

**Journal of Jack Summers, a Free Trapper
in the Expedition,
up to June 28th Inclusive.**

We are indebted to Colonel J. W. Powell, in charge of the Colorado River Exploring expedition for the complete journal of one of the party up to the 28th of June, when all were well, and in camp. The journal is best introduced with a note from Colonel Powell, and will be read with interest. The Colonel's note is as follows:

Mouth of Uinta River, July 6, 1869.

Editors Missouri Democrat:

I send manuscript journal of one of the trappers connected with the Colorado River Exploring Expedition. I think you will find them somewhat lively, and may be able to use them. Of course they will need "fixing" a little, maybe toning somewhat. Jack Sumners [sic], the writer, has seen much wild life and read extensively. He has prepared the manuscript at my request. Should you conclude to publish he will send more.
Yours, &c.

J. W. Powell
In charge Colorado Ex. Ex.

A DAILY JOURNAL OF THE
COLORADO RIVER EXPLORING EXPEDITION.

What followed was Sumner's journal down to the Uinta. Notable here, not only did the *Missouri Democrat* spell Sumner's name incorrectly, so, apparently, did Major J. W. Powell.

The rest of John Colton Sumner's journal — from July 6 to August 31 — which describes the remaining three-quarters of the river expedition,

Sumner expanded into a more fleshed-out version then turned over to Powell. The Major used it as his guidebook for the second, aborted river expedition in 1871-1872. Major Powell's brother-in-law, A. H. Thompson, de facto expedition leader for a great portion of that trip, and his crew perused Sumner's journal for previews of what they should expect to find beyond each bend. As Crew Number Two poured over it, Sumner's words became ever more faded. Many of them apparently vanished, erased by handling. When Major Powell decided to rewrite his 1875 report into his 1895 book, *Canyons of the Colorado*, Thompson returned Sumner's journal to Powell. Afterward no one was ever able to locate these original words that Sumner had written on the river. The only extant copy was obviously a copy, transcribed at the Smithsonian by a scribe who seems to have been an immigrant from Germany, and later published in the 1947 *Utah Historical Quarterly* edited by William Culp Darrah. For years, this was the only version describing the second portion of the expedition known to have survived. Three pages of Sumner's first, original journal, however, did survive the years and abuse. These pages, scrawled in what appear to be Sumner's very faded original handwriting, were found torn from a journal and shoved between the pages of Powell's own writings. They are housed and listed in the National Anthropological Archives of the Smithsonian as document BAE #4419. As will be seen in Sumner's entries for August 17th to the 27th (the eleven days between Silver Creek [a.k.a. Bright Angel] and Lava Cliff Rapid), Sumner's original, first version was a terse listing of the work load the crew accomplished and the miles they traversed. Only in his expanded copy do we learn actual details of how that work progressed and how the 1869 crew muscled those miles.

In addition to both sections and both versions of his journal, Sumner's later letter to Stanton was transcribed into his unpublished "The River and the Cañon: The Colorado River of the West, and the Exploration, Navigation, and Survey of its Cañons, from the Standpoint of an Engineer." This fascinating letter is quoted here in the final chapter of *First Through Grand Canyon*. So too is Sumner's previously unknown, blockbuster letter written to L. W. Keplinger, Paradox, Colorado, on September 14, 1906.

At the conclusion of the 1869 expedition, Sumner, even more than Bradley, seemed unable to avoid imparting his true feelings as to what the exploration meant in the final analysis. The apparent lack of gratitude — or even concern — by Major Powell for his crew at this juncture apparently seemed too callus to Sumner to have been real.

The missing tenderfoot. Major Powell wrote in December of 1869, in W. A. Bell's 1870 *New tracks in North America*: "Of my party, I should like to say that some left me at the start, cutting the number down to ten, including myself."

Who *were* these mysterious expeditionaries who got cold feet before the expedition launched? Major Powell was referring to W. H. Bishop (see below) and to yet another young man, unnamed, who almost made history. Hawkins explains who this final, pre-trip defector was:

> "While we were camped at Green River, something happened which may be worth telling. The Major brought from the east a young man who some friends of the Major's sent out west to see the sights and join our expedition down the unknown regions of the Great Colorado of the West. We boys noticed this young man did not seem to like our bill of fare. I was the cook and the boys, particularly Sumner, bragged on my cooking and said I could make the best coffee in the world and a pie that would last a man a week. But it did not exactly suit the young tenderfoot. So, the third day, Captain [Walter] Powell, had bought him a new pair of boots and wanted to wash his socks. I gave him a small camp kettle and he put them to soak.
>
> At noon I had the coffee in a large camp kettle, and the small one the Captain's socks were in was hid from the boys behind the large one. When we all sat down on the ground to eat our dinner — and I had done my level best that day to please our new comer — and I had dished up the coffee and they were all drinking it and feeling fine — Sumner said there was something mighty peculiar about the coffee, and asked me what was the matter with it. I took my bowie knife and stuck it in one of the Captain's socks and held it up over the kettle just back of the coffee, and the red, brown water running off it, looked just as though I had taken it out of the coffee kettle. I said, 'Who in H— put their socks in the coffee?' All said that they had not, except the young man, who did not answer. When I asked him if he had, he said very politely that he had not, but he was getting up and leaving at the time. That was the last we ever saw of him.
>
> When the Major got his mail at the Virgin [100 days later], he heard that the young man had gone home and said our grub did not suit him, and that he thought the Major had a hard crowd with him."

So Walter's old sock dripping mud off Hawkins' bowie knife was the "final straw" that prevented this unknown young man from making history. On the other hand, maybe it saved his life....

W. H. Bishop (Who dared not). W. H. Bishop was, as Donald Worster tells it, a college student and an Illinois farm boy who had become Major Powell's main mule packer in 1868. Powell and his party of that year decided in October to abandon their Summer camp at Middle Park and move south to winter on the lower grasslands along the White River. Bishop, however, was away at the town of Empire and engaged in mailing Powell's updated report back east.

When Bishop returned to Middle Park all he found was a note pinned to a tree and a rugged landscape buried by a new, two-foot blanket of snow that now obliterated any trail Powell's party may have left for Bishop to follow.

But at least the note instructed Bishop:

> "We have moved camp to a point on White River, 50 miles distant. General directions South of West. You will find provisions cached in the rocks 20 steps North. Come along as fast as you can."

Ravens, Bishop now found, had sawed through the cached provisions and liberated them for a higher purpose. Bishop stared at the rifled stores in dismay. At least he had those directions. But, assuming that the White River was the drainage whose headwaters he was now on, Bishop headed downstream. Unfortunately, he was following a tributary of the Yampa, not the White River. As this route was not southerly enough, Bishop covered many miles of snow-covered paths used by Indians before he knew something was very wrong. For one thing, he had found no signs that Powell's party had ever passed this way.

Feeling increasingly uneasy about this lack, Bishop turned around and headed back up to the site of the note, hoping for inspiration — and for food. He was now subsisting on low rations in a very cold, deserted country. Rethinking the note, he struck off again, this time on a more southerly bearing. Living off the fruits of his rifle, he kept starvation at bay.

Bishop and his trusty rifle spent thirty-three days alone in the winter-clad Rockies in his search for Powell's winter camp. During his entire odyssey "he had not seen a living soul, white man nor red." The worst part, he noted, was neither hunger, nor cold, nor grizzlies, nor Indians, nor solitude. Instead it was the uncertainty of not knowing whether he was on the right track.

Bishop, being fairly self-reliant, did finally make it to Powell's camp. Then, months later, in 1869, Powell invited Bishop to accompany the Colorado River Exploring Expedition. Bishop pondered how well Major Powell had managed the expedition thus far, over the past months. Then he made his decision.

Bishop, who might have been immortalized on some bronze monument (and in this book), decided that his certainty of life deserved a higher priority than did spending yet another questionable year with the Major in unknown terrain.

THE AGREEMENT

Before the expedition ever got its boats to Green River City, Powell had worked out his contractual relationship with at least some of the members of his crew. Although I know of no copy of Powell's contract with William Hawkins, the expedition cook who prepared all three meals per day while on the river — for a reported $1.50 pay per day promised by Powell (but not paid) — a hand-written copy does exist of an unpublished "agreement" between J. W. Powell, party of the first part and parties of the second part: John C. Sumner, William H. Dunn, and Oramel G. Howland. Apparently this was ordered to be hand-copied from the original by/for Frederick S. Dellenbaugh.

> "This *agreement* made this twenty-fifth day of February, eighteen hundred and sixty-nine, between *J. Powell, party* of the first part, *and J. C. Sumner*, W. H. Dunn, and O. G. Howland, parties of the second part, witnesseth, that the said party of the second part agree to do the following work respectively, for the party of the first part, namely: J. C. Sumner agrees to do all necessary work required with the sextant; W. H. Dunn to make barometrical observations night and morning of each day when required, also to make observations when needed for determining altitude of walls of the cañon, also to make not more than sixteen-hourly series of not more than eight days each, to have the air of an assistant for the last two mentioned classes of observations; O. G. Howland to make a topographical drawing of the course of the rivers. The above and foregoing work to be performed during the proposed exploration of the Green River from Green River City, Wyoming territory, to the Colorado River, and of the Colorado River from that Point to Callville,   [sic]; the parties of the second part to perform the foregoing work to the best of their ability; the party of the second part also agreeing to do a fair proportion of the work necessary in getting supplies and boats safely through the channels of the aforementioned rivers, for use of the expedition; and

also agreeing to save for specimens for stuffing, for the party of the first part, all suitable skins of animals which they may collect while engaging in the above exploration of the Green and Colorado rivers. J. W. Powell, party of the first part, agreeing to allow the party of the second part five days at one time for prospecting for gold and silver, if not too often, also to allow thirty days to the party of the second part for hunting and trapping between the first day of September and the first day of December, eighteen hundred and sixty-nine, and sixty days between the first day of January and the first day of June, eighteen hundred and seventy; the party of the first part also agreeing to pay to the party of the second part, respectively, twenty-five dollars each per month for the time employed in all such service, and also agreeing to pay in addition the annexei [sic] prices for all skins procured for him by the party of the second part, J. W. Powell, the party of the first part, to furnish boats, supplies, ammunition, etc., sufficient for the use of the expedition. This agreement to go into effect the first day of June, eighteen hundred and sixty-nine, and not to continue over one year. Should it be necessary to proceed on the journey without delay on account of disaster to boats or loss of rations, then the time specified for hunting may not be required for hunting by either party, nor shall it be deemed a failure of contract to furnish supplies should such supplies be lost in transit.

J. C. Sumner   J. W. Powell
William H. Dunn   In Charge of Col. River Exp. Ex.
O. G. Howland

Deer	$1.25 each	Otter	$3.50 cash	Bear (grown grizzly) $10.00
Sheep	1.25 "	Beaver	1.00 "	" Cub " 1.00
Antelope	1.25 "	Wildcat	.50 "	" grown cinnamon 5.00
Elk	2.00 "	Porcupine	.50 "	" cub " 1.00
Wolf (grey)	1.00 "	Squirrel	.35 "	" grown black 3.00
" Coyote	.50 "	Rabbit	.35 "	" cub " 1.00
Fox (cross)	1.50 "	Woodchuck	.35 "	
Fox red	.75 "	Badger	.50 "	
Mink	1.50 "	Weasel	.35 "	
Martin	1.50 "			

And all other skins at proportionate rates

Again, William Hawkins likely had some sort of contract as expedition cook with Major Powell. Powell did pay him $60 for 99 days of work, less than half the $1.50 per day that Hawkins said Powell had promised. Even Bradley was paid something at the Rio Virgin, but the details of what his original arrangements might have been with Powell are now lost. Whether Seneca Howland or Andy Hall were promised some sort of wages remains unclear.

A very important point here, one missed or glossed over by many Powell historians, is that, for Powell, the purpose of this expedition was the exploration of an unknown region of the planet. Powell's aim was to discover and to perform what he envisioned as "science." To be a true exploration in the scientific sense this exploration required barometrical measurements and compass sightings and astronomical observations on nearly a daily basis to record the geographical character of the canyon country that the expedition — and the river — traversed. Various members of the expedition climbed cliffs and mountains thousands of feet above the river to make geological sense of this labyrinthine land and to determine elevations, general topography and so on. As the "Agreement" above notes, the men, several of whom were hunters and trappers, were also supposed to collect the skins and skulls of birds and animals encountered, up to and including grizzly bears, for the sponsoring museums. Bradley, as a geologist, was likely expected to work in concert with the Major in collecting fossils and geological specimens for the same institutions. In short, these men not only worked to survive, they also worked very hard to advance the state of human knowledge of an unknown region bigger than several Eastern states combined.

THE BOATS VERSUS THE RIVER

*"The **Emma** being very light is tossed about in a way that threatens to shake her to pieces, and is nearly as hard to ride as a Mexican pony. We plunge along, singing, yelling, like drunken sailors, all feeling that such rides do not come every day. It was like sparking a black eyed girl — just dangerous enough to be exciting."* **John C. Sumner, June 2, 1869**

No known photos, drawings, etchings, or any other sort of picture of Powell's 1869 boats survive. Indeed none may ever have existed. Hence we have only verbal descriptions of the boats and sketchy accounts of how these boats were manned and maneuvered to figure out their exact design and to visualize the crew's techniques for navigating, lining, or portaging them over rapids. The boats that Powell described in his report and *Canyons of the Colorado* were not his 1869 boats. Instead they were the boats he used in 1871-72. The journals and letters of the 1869 crew, however, do provide a few descriptions and tantalizing asides as to how these men rowed, steered, bailed, lined, portaged, and so on. Yet despite the dearth of detail, one unarguable certainty in all of this is that Powell's 1869 boats were not well-suited for maneuvering in rapids rated today as Class IV or above. Even Class III rapids were potentially lethal to these boats.

Perhaps surprisingly, Powell's "plan A" for equipping the expedition was to tote tools to the river and construct boats on the bank from locally available materials. But, as William Culp Darrah noted, upon seeing the swiftness of the White River in 1868, Powell reconsidered in favor of professionally built craft.

As Hawkins notes, Powell chose for his boat design Whitehall haulers. These boats, however, were not designed for river running. Their sleek and eye-pleasing design originated in New York City around 1820, being built first on Whitehall Street as a harbor boat used to haul passengers and/or gear back and forth from the dock to large, ocean-going square-riggers. These "water taxis" were usually painted white, often well-cared for, and were immensely popular for more than sixty years coast to coast. Sometimes they were even fitted with a centerboard so that they could be sailed. Whitehall boats were built as short as 12 feet long. Yet some were 40 feet or longer. The "average" Whitehall was about 16 to 22 feet long. By one report, eighteen-footers were equipped with multiple pairs of 11.5-foot oars, although these seem to me to be at least two feet too long. Dellenbaugh would write later that, during the 1871-72 expedition, they sawed their oars down to eight feet long to row their 22-foot Whitehalls. The first expedition may have done likewise; and, when they were later forced to hew new oars from driftwood, they too may have sized them for

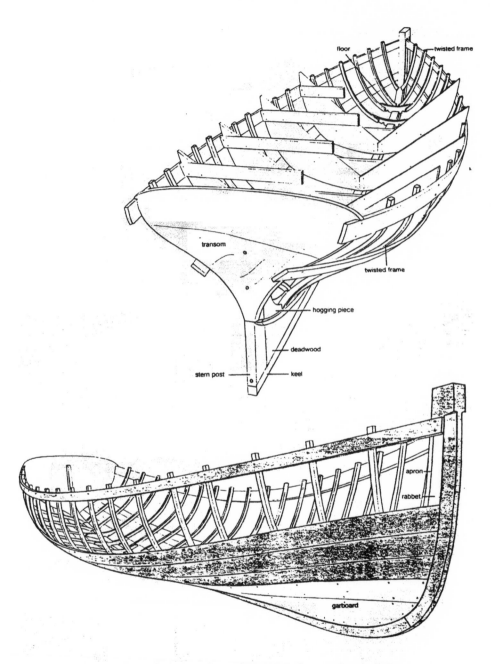

General hull design and configuration for a Whitehall Boat.

leverage. For steering, Whitehalls were normally built with a squared stern and transom equipped with a fixed rudder. On bays and harbors these boats — built with carefully steamed frames to achieve a wineglass stem, keel, and transom that reduced drag — performed smoothly, easily, dryly, elegantly, and were fast. They also tracked well in choppy water.

But, again, they were not in the least whitewater river boats. Powell tried to remedy this design flaw by asking the boatbuilder, Thomas Bagley, located at the north end of the old Clark Street Bridge in Chicago, to modify the standard Whitehall model by adding double ribbing and oak planking for added strength. Powell apparently also instructed Bagley to build all four boats with double stern and stem posts. This modification retained the wineglass transom but eliminated the rudder. (Powell's 1871-72, teenage boatman Frederick Dellenbaugh would agree with Powell that a rudder would have been useless in rapids.) These boats, which were difficult to steer without a rudder even on a bay, would now become alarmingly unresponsive to efforts to steer them in fast moving whitewater. And being round-bottomed, Powell's Whitehalls possessed the additional flaw of lacking the lateral stability now so taken for granted in modern, rocker-floored whitewater dories and inflatable river boats. In short, Whitehalls were hard to steer but easy to capsize.

Worse, Powell compounded these problems by further instructing Bagley to add bulkheads and decking over the bows and sterns to create sealable five-foot-long compartments fore and aft for buoyancy and storage. These compartments were intended to help prevent the boats from sinking. While this may have seemed a good idea on dry land, additional problems arose when these compartments were loaded so heavily — 7,000 pounds for the expedition, or about 2,000 pounds per boat. The problem lay in basic Newtonian physics that Powell should have understood — from his engineering education if nothing else.

Powell's bow and stern compartments dictated positioning their heavy loads a maximum distance from the boat's center of mass. This "end-loading" was the worst possible arrangement because it forced the oarsmen to combat a maximum load leverage — or maximum angle of moment — working against him every time he tried to turn, pivot, or steer the boat. Center-loading — had a waterproof center compartment been built instead — could have helped to cure this.

Powell's 1869 Whitehalls possessed yet one more fatal flaw — that of taking on tons of water in the eleven-foot-long open bilge while running rapids. The sheer mass of so much total weight (up to 4,000 pounds) added yet more difficulty to the pre-existing challenge of getting the boat to change direction in fast water. Indeed, when these boats swamped, they nearly sank, despite the air-tight compartments fore and aft.

Hence, some of Powell's modifications would convert these already unsuitable, round-bottomed, very difficult to steer boats into almost unsteerable craft nearly impossible to maneuver in complicated rapids. The essential Whitehall design did, however, retain an elegant ability to track on a straight line through big waves. And when the men ran "straight-shot," wave-train rapids, they were euphoric over the boats' performances. As Oramel Howland put it:

> "When we have to run the rapids, nothing is more exhilarating; it keeps in play a rapid train of thought and action, equalled only by the river's progress; and as a breaker dashes over us as we shoot out from one side or the other, after having run the fall, one feels like hurrahing. It must be something like the excitement of battle at the point of victory, or much more agreeable, perhaps. Much to produce this effect, I conceive, is to be attributed to the purity of the atmosphere, cleansed as it is by the spray dashed through it by the rushing river, of which one gets beautiful draughts as he goes plunging down the tide with all the senses in active play. A calm, smooth stream, running only at the rate of five or six miles per hour, is a horror we all detest now, although we make more distance in the same length of time; but the trouble is, we don't get wet, nor have the slightest sense of danger. Danger is our life, it seems now, almost."

Unfortunately, one hundred of the rapids that the men and boats would face were more complicated than merely a straight wave train. This is because rapids emerge in a river due to four main factors affecting its bed: gradient, constriction, bed topography, and the volume of the river flow itself. The first factor is simple. If a river descends at an increased gradient, it will flow faster and hence be more "rapid." Second, if, other things being equal, the river is constricted into a channel of reduced cross-section, it also speeds up. The third factor, bed topography, is complicated. This topography is created by curves, by boulders strewn across the river and/or by bedrock ledges over which it tumbles and/or by the alluvial gradient from one *side* of the river to the other. Bed topography is not only what makes many rapids unique; it also turns many of them into technically challenging minefields of boulders, holes, lateral waves, reversals, falls — a maze of implacable currents flowing in *every* direction, including straight up, straight down, upstream, laterally, and downstream — where split-second boating maneuvers spell success or failure, perhaps disaster. Add to the unique combinations of gradient, constriction, and bed topography the fourth and final factor of specific *flow* of river, and the rapid will then assume its character. If the river multiplies its flow by ten times more, or instead shrinks it to ten times less, the resulting rapid will not only be different, it will be so drastically different as to be a new rapid. It will also sound different. As the flows of big rapids increase, their roars leap in decibels to become unnerving thunderous deafening gut-quivering vibrations. Or, as their flows ebb, their roars dwindle to the white noise of mountain brooks.

So much for theory. The reality of rapids that Powell's men faced on the Green and Colorado rivers was a series of pool-drop phenomena constructed in a consistent way due to the depth of the canyon system itself. The rivers here in canyon country have, over millions of years, carved very deep canyons whose beds change in shape and width, mile after mile, mainly due to slicing through different types of bedrock possessing differential resistance to erosion. Hard rock, such as the Precambrian schists and gneisses in Grand Canyon's Upper Granite Gorge, for example, yields narrow canyons. Easily eroded rock, such as the Dox Sandstone upstream of Upper Granite Gorge, yields wide canyons, even valleys. But the rapids themselves on this river system emerge not from something created by the main river itself, but instead as "gifts" of its tributary canyons.

The critical reality here is that the canyons of the Colorado and Green are so deeply incised into the high Colorado Plateau that they have fostered the deep and lengthy erosion of hundreds of tributary canyons. Some of these tributaries are dozens of miles long and thousands of feet deep and drain a hundred square miles. Some drain closer to a thousand square miles. When massive monsoonal or winter storms are forced higher to glide over the upper elevations of the huge Colorado Plateau, the world's second largest and highest plateau after that of Tibet, these storms often drop their moisture as rain that is violent, abrupt, and copious. Because these patterns of rainfall are so sporadic and punctuated by dry spells, much of the canyon region is desert that lacks enough soil to soak up precipitation. Hence, much of the violent rain here hits, splashes, and obeys the dictates of gravity to flow downhill. Or it roars downhill in debris-flow flash floods that carry boulders bigger than the Conestoga wagons used by American pioneers.

In canyon country these flows funnel down canyons. Indeed, not only do the famous "slot" canyons of the Southwest act as charmingly narrow funnels for these violent storms, these canyons are the stone children of these storms. And when these stone children disgorge their guts via semi-liquid debris flow — the same flows that are responsible for carving these canyons like some gargantuan stone mason seized by a berserker rage — they disgorge them into the main channel of the Colorado or Green rivers. The greater these flows, the larger the boulders they transport slamming and banging down the canyon. As the speed of these tributary flows doubles, the size of the particles — or boulders — they carry increases in a cubed relationship. Put another way, double the flow rate while it is already transporting a two-pound rock and now it can carry an eight-pound rock. Double that same flow again and it can carry a 512-pound boulder (8 x 8 x 8 = 512). Double that flow yet again and, well, you get the point. In a huge enough flash flood debris flow in the Southwest, the Washington Monument would *float* downstream.

Once these flash floods hit the main channel, their momentum diminishes enough to drop their heaviest burdens first. These heaviest of burdens are those biggest of boulders, which in some places jam together to dam the main river.

Before the late twentieth century, the Colorado River experienced rare peak flows of 300,000 and even 500,000 cubic feet per second roaring out of the major portion of its 242,000-square-mile drainage. This is roughly half of what the huge Congo River often flows. These big flows slammed into these natural alluvial dams that form rapids and scatter and slowly pulverize the boulders of which they were formed. Despite these episodic poundings, however, nearly every steep tributary canyon draining into the Colorado and Green rivers still hosts at its mouth a rapid flowing — for a mere 100 yards or up to half a mile — over the submerged portion of its alluvial fan. These fans increase the gradient of the river, constrict its flow, and complicate its bed topography.

An aerial view of the river corridor reveals these rapids to look surprisingly alike: at the mouth of the tributary there usually exists a large deltaic fan of alluvium bulging into the mainstream of the river. This pinches and constricts its flow, shoving it hard into a curve against the shore opposite the major tributary. Because many of these tributaries form and flow along fault lines crossing the river, often one big tributary may disgorge right cross the river from yet another tributary. These "double whammy" tributary pairs often create humdinger rapids, like today's Crystal Rapid and Powell's Separation Rapid in Grand Canyon. Depending on the flow of the river, these rapids often present themselves as frothing boulder fields that offer no straight shot to the boatman.

Instead, navigating such rapids demands one or several technical rowing moves to avoid those boat-crunching boulders. To make these moves the boatman must power his or her craft laterally in the flow from one side of the river toward the other. Often the boatman must accomplish this in a mere second or two. In some rapids the only feasible runs demand a complicated zig-zag course. The rub here is that, for each zig and each zag, the boat must be pivoted, steered, and powered into new "ferry angles" across the current — with split second timing.

But with Powell's Whitehall boats, such timely steering into tight zig-zag combinations of ferry angles was not just dicey or difficult, it was impossible. No one is certain exactly how the 1869 crew actually rowed their boats through these rapids when they did row them. Indeed their technique has long been assumed — due to the presence of stern-mounted steering oars on the 1871-72 boats — to simply consist of aiming the boat bow-first in the right direction and then the oarsmen rowing with pull strokes for all they were worth, their backs aimed downstream, thus speeding downstream faster than the current. This sort of tactic certainly must have been used here and there on the river in 1869. Yet entries in the men's journals suggest that these willy-nilly dashes were not the only navigation trick in their bag. One hint is found in Powell, who explains: "When we approach a rapid, or what on other rivers would often be called a fall, I stand on the deck to examine it, *while the oarsmen back water, and we drift on as slowly as possible* [italics mine]. If I can see a clear chute between the rocks, away we go; but if the channel is beset entirely across, we signal the other boats, pull to land, and I walk along the shore for closer examination."

The tactic or technique of rowing back water (rowing upstream), by using an upstream ferry angle, is commonly assumed to be an invention of boatman Nathaniel Galloway in the 1890s. I suspect, however, that Powell's 1869 crew already had figured out this technique and used it here and there as early as the Canyon of Lodore. The journals of the 1871-72 crew mention using this technique at the heads of rapids, in spite of their steering oars. With no steering apparatus at all mounted on the boats' sterns in 1869, the oarsmen would often have been even more tempted — if not convinced by fright — to run stern-first. But, again, the Whitehalls' keeled hull design did not allow for the quick changes of ferry angle needed to make technical maneuvering reliable. Hence, all too often, no matter which direction the men faced while rowing, they could not row through the rapids in safety.

So the crew devised alternate approaches. None was fun. The first, of course, was simply to portage everything, including the waterlogged boats, around the rapid. When I say, "simply," I mean conceptually. In the doing of the thing, a portage was almost always brutally punishing labor. Like dragging one of those slabs of stone to build the great pyramids of Egypt, but dragging it over a boulder field.

Hence it did not take long for the 1869 crew to devise an easier technique. Not easy. Just easier than the hell of a portage.

This was called "lining" the boat. This technique was also simple in concept: first the crew portaged the boats' several thousand pounds of contents. Next they fixed a 130-foot rope to the bow of the boat and a second rope to the stern. Then they assigned some men to ease the boat out into the current and down the shoreline of the rapid by paying out that bowline. Meanwhile the one or two men positioned farther downstream were assigned to the sternline, which might be tied to a rock. These lower men would reel in their slack to snug the boat close to shore again, safe from the brute force of midstream collisions with boulders. In between the men manning the ropes might be another crew member or two positioned strategically in shallow water with an oar in hand to shove the boat away from problem boulders or to ease the rope over obstructing rocks. Sometimes a man carrying a loose oar might ride inside the boat to fend it away from big rocks. And sometimes the men were forced to swim downstream through the swift shallows to expedite all this.

While this suite of techniques may sound fairly slick, the process of lining in whitewater can mimic flying a 1,000-pound kite during a typhoon. Worse, the shorelines of these rapids were boulder fields offering even worse passage than midstream. But at least the river near shore flowed slower and shallower. This was important not only for controlling the boats in the squirrelly currents, but also because it offered a much safer location for men possessing no life jackets.

Even so, this "safety" for boats and crew also exacted a hefty price in pain, yet still entailed human risk. That's because lining a boat, even when things go well, can be tough work. And normally things do not go well. Instead the boat hits a boulder, or a cluster of them. These deflect the boat sideways and broach it against them where the boat is pinned immobile by the powerful current, and perhaps submerged. All of these things happened to Powell's crew while lining. Extracting a boat from such predicaments is hellish work. Yet failing to extract the boat can spell disaster. Other expeditions down the Colorado following Powell's, including Robert Brewster Stanton's 1890 trip and Clyde Eddy's 1927 trip, for example, did pin and destroy their boats while trying to line them.

It is no small feat that Powell's 1869 crew managed this process at about one hundred rapids without destroying a boat.

But their success came at a price. The men were frequently forced to wade deep into the river. Their rotting boots consistently slid on the silt-lubricated boulders hidden under the muddy surface of the roiling flow. Bruises due to lost footing were common. So were palms burned raw by the sudden friction of the hemp rope as boats surged in the current. So were cuts due to skin softened by immersion and dried by the salty water (the Colorado River becomes progressively saltier as desert tributaries join it). So were backs strained with lifting the waterlogged boats over boulders in channels too shallow to float them. Meanwhile every crew member who stumbled into the muddy river ("too thick to drink and too thin to plow") when yanked forward by a runaway boat also risked augering in, face-first, into a field of boulders. In short, all too often, lining was punishment. Ed Dolnick notes too that the men may have faced the additional danger of foot entrapment — Dolnick had heard of a fellow tourist who drowned this way. Foot entrapment, while a horrible way to die, is also such an obvious yet controllable hazard that veteran boatmen, while forced to line, vigilantly process the possibility in the back of their minds with virtually every step they take in the river, much like a house painter's constant awareness of

An 1871 photo of Powell's crew lining, rather pleasantly, it might appear, around Ashley Falls. Photo by E.O. Beaman.

where his bucket is so he does not kick it over. The 1869 crew became such veterans quickly. Quickly enough that Bradley confided to his journal a terse summation: "They [the rapids] don't interest me much unless we can run them. That I like, but portage don't agree with my constitution."

As Walter Clement Powell would confide to his journal on September 21, 1871 (during Major Powell's second river expedition), four months after shoving off from Green River City:

> "The boat at times will be wedged in between the rocks while we are tugging and pulling away; suddenly away she will go, dragging us after her, holding on for dear life, and woe to the unlucky one who does not keep his legs in his pockets at such a time. 'Tis a wonder that some of us have not had a leg or two broken. All of us wear horrible scars from our knees downward to remind us of the days when we made portages."

On top of all these punishing injuries, the sheer work of lining was exhausting. Worse yet, during the last month of the 1869 trip, rations had dwindled to starvation level, making the work yet more draining.

Most galling in this process of serving Powell's repeated decisions to be conservative was the men's knowledge during dozens of these episodes of lining — which could entail one to several hours of work — that the rapid could instead be run in the boats at an exhilarating 15 to 20 miles per hour in a mere 30 seconds.

So, while Powell's Whitehalls were not the right boats for the job, they were the only game in town for this first expedition. Bagley built Powell's three "freight" Whitehalls 22 inches deep, and 21 feet long (fifty years later, Hawkins remembers the boats, inaccurately, as 22 feet long), and somewhere between 4 to a bit more than 5 feet wide (no one is sure on this; Sumner, decades later, recalls the boats at 6 feet wide). Bagley built Powell's 16-foot, sleek scoutboat of light white pine. All four boats were equipped with rowing benches and iron oarlocks for two sets of oars.

Powell paid Bagley with money from Illinois Industrial University, from the Chicago Academy of Sciences, from private pledges, and probably from his own funds as well.

The ten men set off from Green River on May 24, 1869, in these four boats. Powell's 16-foot scoutboat, named the *Emma Dean* (after his wife) was intended to be the lead, or signal boat. The other three 21-footers hauled rations and gear. Named by their crews, they were the *Maid of the Cañon*, *Kitty Clyde's Sister*, and the *No Name*. The reasons for the names of these boats have often pricked the curiosity of fans of this expedition. The origin of *Emma Dean* is obvious. *Maid of the Cañon* seems a reasonable name for a boat carrying two bachelors who are about to plunge into a series of unknown canyons. At first glance, however, the Howlands' *No Name* seems the product of either a congenital lack of imagination or else a downright dislike of the boat itself. Neither is accurate.

As historian Don Lago discovered, the *No Name* was a "ghost" of particular interest to the Howland family and also a boat infamous to millions at the close of the Civil War.

Here's the short version. Two Quaker brothers, Matthew and George Howland, Jr. — both being relatives of Oramel and Seneca — were masters of a fine whaling fleet harbored in New Bedford, Massachusetts. Ships of the Howland fleet floated at considerable risk from Confederate pirates. Of forty-six northern ships sent to Davy Jones' locker by the Confederate warship *Alabama*, notes Lago as an example, more than half (twenty-five) were New Bedford craft. Compounding this danger, Confederate Captain John Taylor Wood commanded the British built CSS *Tallahassee*, faster than any Union ship, on a daring raid up the coast to New England. He sank 32 Northern ships, thus earning the everlasting enmity of every New England seaman from fleet owners to the lowest scullery hands.

When the Confederacy disintegrated, John Taylor Wood fled the North American continent with Confederate Secretary of War John C. Breckinridge and four other men in a Union lifeboat. They shoved off from a Florida swamp. At first they headed toward the Bahamas against unfavorable winds. Blown off course, they encountered a sloop, unnamed but manned by what seemed to be Union Army deserters, also trying to escape. Wood's crew closed on them by rowing madly. Then they hijacked the sloop at gunpoint. After successfully trading boats, Wood and company headed for Cuba. They successfully fought off small-time pirates with small arms fire. And they endured a very nasty squall en route. Barely alive and suffering from exposure, hunger, and thirst, they sailed their lucky sloop into the harbor at Cuba.

"What is the name of your sloop?" the Cuban customs agent asked, pen in hand.

"The *No Name*," Wood answered, possibly christening the means of his salvation from pirates and fierce storms right there on the spot.

Soon after his arrival, American reporters interviewed Wood. Hence the details of this story of escape and its publication in the *New York Herald*. Yankees, Lago suggests, loved this tale of high adventure because in it the hated Confederate Captain John Taylor Wood had been reduced from top predator to a lowly criminal who had been deeply humiliated by fleeing ignobly and by resorting to petty piracy to save his skin.

As you will read in Sumner's first journal entry, he parenthetically provides the critical hint as to the origin of the Howlands' name choice: "The last to leave the miserable adobe village [Green River City] was the

"No Name" (piratic craft) manned by O. G. Howland, Seneca Howland, and Frank Goodman."

Wood's infamous *No Name* was the little pirate boat that could. Likely Oramel and Seneca reckoned that there could be few better names for their own small boat as they rowed it into dangers that no one had ever successfully navigated. If so, then, as you will also read, they were proven incorrect.

Yet another 1869 boat name that has tormented historians into pulling their hair out is *Kitty Clyde's Sister*. *Who* was Kitty Clyde's Sister? Was she some pined-for lover of Hawkins or Hall, who had named the Whitehall? Or was she some astonishingly beautiful young woman whose image refused to vacate one of these two men's smitten mind?

After giving this boat name considerable thought, historian Martin J. Anderson suspected that Hall and Hawkins' had named the Whitehall after a popular song. But search as he might, Anderson never found a song of that title. After Anderson died, however, river historian Ardian Gill cleared up this long-standing mystery via a computer search.

It turns out that "*Kitty Clyde's Sister*" was the refrain in a popular song of that era, but one titled "Minnie Clyde, Kitty Clyde's Sister" and penned by L. V. H. Crosby. The chorus of this light-hearted tune goes:

> "Oh, Minnie Clyde, she is my pride,
> And sure I am no jester;
> For if ever I loved a girl in my life,
> 'Tis Minnie, Kitty Clyde's sister."

Timeless lyrics aside, Powell's modified Whitehalls were, again, reasonable boats for navigating a lake or bay but horrible in complicated whitewater. No crew member mentions it, but, due to the narrowness of the boats, the leverage that the oars offered to the oarsman — with a very short length of shaft inside the boat from the oarlock but a great length outside it extending into the river — was far from ideal for ease of transferring power in long strokes. Thus even the mere act of rowing must have proved disappointing, especially when struggling to pivot the boat so as to maneuver. Still, the double ribbing of oak made them pretty tough. As Sumner would write on June 7, 1869, "Rhodes [Hawkins] [is] brushing up *Kitty's Sister*, swearing all the time that she can stand more thumps than Kitty ever could."

Because Powell reported in error which crew members rowed and were responsible for each boat, and because most previous Powell historians (Marty Anderson and Dock Marston being notable exceptions) have been almost uniformly too careless to recognize his errors and thus correct them in their own writings, and because who rowed which boat as which crew may have played a significant and formative role in the lethal social dynamics of the expedition, I will now report these crews accurately. Powell commanded the expedition and the *Emma Dean*, crewed by John Sumner and William Dunn. George Y. Bradley commanded the *Maid of the Cañon*, with Walter Powell as his crew. William Hawkins and Andy Hall ran *Kitty Clyde's Sister*. Oramel and Seneca Howland and Frank Goodman crewed the *No Name*, with Oramel in charge but normally engaged in cartography rather than rowing. Once the *No Name* was scattered downriver in splinters, Oramel rode on *Kitty Clyde's Sister* with Hall and Hawkins. Seneca rode aboard the *Maid*. Goodman hitched a ride on one boat or the other for the next two weeks before he quit the expedition. No personnel changes occurred aboard the *Emma Dean*. These were the true crews for the 1869 expedition's Whitehalls.

It is important to note again that all published etchings and photos of Powell's boats are not of the above mentioned boats of 1869 but instead of those from his 1871-72 trip. Powell's 1869 boats possessed neither a compartment amidships nor a chair mounted amidships for Powell himself. Powell's original boats also possessed neither a steering oar nor a sweep mounted off the stern as most illustrations depict. As historian Martin J. Anderson explained, the arithmetic on this makes the reason for this "lack" obvious. With only nine able-bodied men to row eight pairs of oars, there remained only one man who might have used a steering oar, yet four boats to steer. This one man was Oramel G. Howland who, instead of rowing or steering, drew maps and took bearings all day from the boat's deck. Hence there would have been no able-bodied man available to steer any of the boats. All of these additions — steering oars, amidship bulkheads, a captain's chair — Powell would make later for his 1871 boats.

What about the possibility of having retrofitted one or more of the boats with a steering oar later during the 1869 trip, specifically after the wreck of the *No Name*, when more hands became available per boat? Two testimonials make this seem unlikely. The first is Sumner's journal description of the men racing in their three surviving boats toward the Uinta River confluence on the Green on June 26:

> " — all at once the great Uinta Valley spread out before us as far as the eye could reach. It was a welcome sight to us after two weeks of the hardest kind of work, in a canyon where we could not see half a mile, very often, in any direction except straight up. All hands pull with a will, except the Professor and Mr. Howland. The Professor being a one-armed man, he was set to watching the geese, while Howland was perched on a sack of flour in the middle of one of the large boats, mapping the river as we

rowed along. Our sentinel soon signaled a flock of geese
ahead, when we gave chase, and soon had ten of them in
the boats."

Here Sumner tells us that eight men were "pulling with a will" on three
boats — each equipped with two pairs of oars — while two men were
occupied with non-boating chores. Hence, again, at least one of these boats
had no able hand to steer it. Therefore, one might reasonably suspect,
steering oars had not been retrofitted onto all of these boats at this point.
    Earlier (on June 22, in Whirlpool Canyon), after the wreck of the *No
Name*, O. G. Howland explains how the third able-bodied man in each of
the large boats was instead well-occupied while running swift water:

"From this time on to camp our ride was fine, just current
enough to glide along swiftly, and not breakers enough to
necessitate stopping to bail, one of the crew being
employed in that capacity while running down."

Hence, between Disaster Falls and the Uinta, eight men rowed three
boats, yet one or more of them also had to bail them. Below the Uinta for
the next seven hundred miles or so, seven men rowed these same three
boats. This arithmetic too — six pairs of oars but only seven able-bodied
men available for rowing — left but one man free to steer all three boats —
and also to bail them. Ergo, it appears likely that no steering oars were
mounted on these boats. This is not to pooh-pooh the idea that, had the
arithmetic granted to each boat three available boatmen, a steering oar
would have been useful. It would have been very useful at times. But
steering oars and 1869 seem mutually exclusive, unless, during various times
or places during the trip, an oarsman had developed the habit of
abandoning one of his running oars to then shift himself to the stern deck
and use the other oar, freed from its lock and held as a paddle, employed as
a rudder braced against the gunwale. None of the journals mention such a
tactic as having been adopted, but 38 and 50 years later, Hawkins does
mention doing this. He wrote in 1919 to William Wallace Bass about day #1
of the 1869 trip, "I remember our first camp that evening for the night and
as I was steering the boat with one oar behind and standing up I could see
what was in front of us. " Hawkins and Hall still failed to get their Whitehall
to shore until 400 yards below camp, but therein lies the can of worms
regarding steering oars.
    Perhaps tellingly, depictions in Powell's *Canyons of the Colorado* (p. 162) of
the boats in Lodore during the 1869 fire storm reveal them unmistakably to
be Whitehalls (with, however, the center compartments of the 1871-72
boats) and with wineglass transoms that completely lack steering apparatus;

neither rudder nor a steering sweep oar. Whether Powell, knowing, or the artist, unknowing, left these sterns naked is unknown. Etchings, however, taken from photos of the 1871-72 boats do reveal steering sweeps.

The single most revealing journal entry regarding steering oars — or their lack — comes from Bradley's entry for August 28. On day #97, during a terrifying and unexpected run through Lava Cliff Rapid, the last and arguably the worst rapid on the entire river, Bradley is forced to steer *Maid of the Cañon* on his own. How does he do it? Not with a stern-mounted steering oar: "By putting an oar first on one side then on the other," Bradley writes, "I could swing her round and guide her very well."

Yet the 1869 "steering oar" controversy continually is reborn, Hindu-fashion. This is because each time another documentary filmmaker gets his hands on replicas of Powell's boats — say, for the IMAX film, *Grand Canyon, The Hidden Secrets*, the American Experience *Lost in the Grand Canyon*, or the German *"Journeys through Hell"* series, or the recent National Geographic Society Powell film — the producers use photos from Powell's *Canyons* book as a blueprint for 1869 and then normally hire modern Grand Canyon Dories' boatmen or their ilk to act the roles of Major Powell's men. These guides universally find the Powell reconstruction boats about as maneuverable as a dugout canoe. Appalled at these boats' lack of steerability with only their running oars, these boatmen insist that they need a steering oar mounted on the stern — just like Powell's men had....

In 1871 and 1872, not in 1869. This lack of steerability in 1869 was one big reason why the *No Name* was dashed to splinters. It also explains why the men had to line with ropes or portage approximately 100 rapids during their nearly 1,000-mile trip. They could not reliably steer these boats around boulders in anything like a "tight" channel. Indeed, this many portages and linings explain how Powell's original crew did manage to work their way downriver without a steering oar mounted astern; they simply did not run rapids unless they were straight shots or during the very few places where they had no choice, for example, at Sockdolager and Separation rapids. Hence, if not running the rapids (as today's better trained boatmen of course *do*), they did not really "need" steering oars to have traversed these canyons as they did.

Interestingly, Powell's crew and boats of the 1871-72 trip, even though equipped with "necessary" stern sweeps, performed worse than those in 1869. Before even entering Grand Canyon, in Flaming Gorge, even before the Canyon of Lodore, in 1871, both the 22-foot *Emma Dean* (#II) and *Nellie Powell* had capsized upside down. By the time Powell's second crew reached the Paria at the head of Grand Canyon they had staved in their boats five times, fully portaged seven times, and lined these bigger boats 86 times. Below the Paria this crew stove yet more holes in the *Cañonita* and *Emma Dean* (#II), then capsized the latter yet again. In contrast, the men of

Reconstructions of Powell's 1871-72 boats equipped with long stern sweeps, at River Mile 34, used in the IMAX production of Powell's 1869 expedition (photo used by courtesy of IMAX).

the 1869 crew ran more rapids yet never capsized any of their 21-foot boats, despite having no stern sweeps. Whether this worse boating record by the 1871-72 crew, who gladly aborted the expedition at River Mile 144 in Grand Canyon, is due more to the subtle differences in the boats or to the more major differences in the crews themselves is open to debate. Powell deliberately chose for his second crew relatives, in-laws, and friends who were Midwesterners or Easterners. This is in stark contrast to his more capable but independently-minded 1869 crew, who were almost uniformly Civil War combat veterans and self-made men already living and working in the Western wilderness.

A final word may embody the sum of the 1869 boats' maneuverability. Sumner reported that young Andy Hall, bullwhacker by trade, complained that *Kitty Clyde's Sister* would "neither gee nor haw nor whoa worth a damn — in fact, it wasn't *broke* at all!"

THE CHALLENGE, THE STAKES, AND THE PRIZE

"Think it will not be many years before these green hills will be covered with cattle and dotted here and there with the homes of ranchmen, for the hillsides are green and watered with little mountain torrents that seem to leap and laugh down the hillsides in wild delight. Can stand on almost any eminence and overlook thousands and thousands of acres of most excellent grazing land, and we have lowered our altitude and latitude until it is warm enough to raise almost any kind of vegetables that will grow in northern New England. Think it would pay well to buy cattle in Texas and bring them here to fatten and then send them to market, but it would not pay to raise horses for the Indians (Utes) would steal too many of them to make it profitable." — **George Y. Bradley, June 3, 1869**

"Not the least of the objects in view [of the Colorado River Exploring Expedition] *is to add a mite to the great sum of human knowledge. Science has its devotees in the laboratory; peering into the infinitesimal; on the observatory, keeping an outlook into the universe, and it has its laborers searching and exploring all over the earth for more facts, these characters in which the truth is written. Now if we can record a few more facts, and from them learn a lesson, we shall feel repaid for toil, privations and peril."* — **John Wesley Powell, May 24, 1869**

Why did Powell's Colorado River Exploring Expedition take place in 1869? What historical, political, or economic forces favored or opposed such an expedition at this time? And just how difficult and dangerous was Powell's river expedition? And what, on the flip side of the coin, was at stake as the rewards of success?

The year 1869 obviously fell within the immediate post-Civil War era. Hundreds of thousands of former soldiers, wounded or otherwise, had recently returned to civilian life with a very different perspective of the meaning — and the value — of life. Many of these combat veterans naturally gravitated toward the West. They were now willing to take risks in a high-stakes game of fortune hunting in a stupendously beautiful landscape free of government meddling and innocent of the political sophistries that conclude to solve disputes in political affairs by means of lining up a million patriotic men and ordering them to shoot each other.

Hence the as-yet-unspoiled West was an escape from the insanity of internecine war and from certain dubious "blessings" of "civilization." The West was also a balm for the war-tarnished soul and a beautiful land promising potential fortunes. Much of the Wild West remained unexplored.

A lot of it seemed empty, even of Indians. It was a place that fired the romantic dreams of all boys and most men. And as we've seen, nearly every man on Powell's 1869 crew not bearing the surname "Powell" had decided years earlier that the rigors and risks of the Wild West were a fair trade for its rewards. In short, Powell's 1869 crew was made up of men accustomed to danger and also to taking individual responsibility for their own decisions about how to contend with it.

The one big stumbling block to making most men's dreams of the West a reality was the hardships of traveling west of the Hundredth Meridian. Only the most hardy — and frequently the most foolish or desperate — of men made their way west before 1869.

The year 1869 was not just a pivotal one, it was *the* pivotal year. Before 1869, the West was a vast wilderness visited only by the bold. But in 1869, as the iron horse chugged to Promontory Point, Utah, it carried a death sentence to the Wild West. As historian Stephen Ambrose recounts in his history of the transcontinental railway, *Nothing Like It in the World: The Men Who Built the Transcontinental Railroad 1863-1869*, the existence of this railway rang a swift death knell to the Western Indians by delivering an ever swelling river of Eastern immigrants eager to homestead the Indians' "empty lands."

The Union Pacific had been in its building process even during the Civil War, but by late 1868 it had finally crossed the Green River in Wyoming. On May 10, 1869, top-ranking dignitaries of the Union Pacific and the Central Pacific carefully inserted (not hammered) the famous 5 5/8 inch long, 13.4 ounce, 17.6 carat gold spike — the ceremonial Hewes Spike — into an auger hole on a tie linking the rails of the two railways. This, in turn, now linked the entire continent of North America by rail from the Atlantic to the Pacific oceans. This was Thomas Jefferson's dream and Lewis' and Clark's epic feat done in iron, wood, and a few ounces of gold and silver.

And while the combined promise and tragedy of the iron horse could fill shelves of history books, the single most important reality of the iron horse for Major John Wesley Powell was that the Union Pacific could deliver him, his brother, his equipment, and his four boats from Bagley's boatyard in Chicago to the Green River with incredible ease. Better yet, not only would the Union Pacific transport the expedition with ease, for Powell, they would do it for free.

Clearly, that Powell's expedition launched from Green River City, Wyoming, on May 24, 1869, only two weeks after completion of the transcontinental railroad was no coincidence. The railroad actually dictated the location and timing of such a launch even while also making it easy. So easy that Powell himself likely worried that someone else might beat him to the punch by executing his exploration plans before him and thus scoop *the* epic expedition of the post-Civil War West.

In the same vein, it was due just as little to coincidence and just as much to the transcontinental railway that Dr. Ferdinand V. Hayden, a former U.S. Army surgeon and now a naturalist and explorer eerily similar to Powell, launched his own ambitious expedition months later to explore Yellowstone — then known as "Colter's Hell." Hayden took with him the accomplished painter Thomas Moran. Moran's art would put Hayden, Moran himself, and Yellowstone on the national map. So much so that Congress would gazette Yellowstone as the nation's first national park and would later buy Moran's beautiful "Grand Canyon of the Yellowstone" painting for an astounding $10,000 — more money than Powell had at his disposal from all sources for his entire expedition. Indeed, Powell would soon learn this lesson so acutely that Moran would be instrumental in creating the art for, and enhancing the visual appeal of, Powell's Scribner's articles of the early 1870s describing his 1869 expedition and later of his *Canyons of the Colorado* as well (and of this book too).

Yet while Yellowstone was such an amazing natural wonderland that Congress would gazette it as the nation's first national park, the thousand-mile mystery of the courses of the Green and Colorado rivers was a far more vast and even nationally embarrassing blank on the map of the continental United States. Here was a hundred thousand square miles of absolute mystery, multiple Eastern states' worth of territory about which darned little was known. Hence the prize for succeeding in unveiling this vast region was fame and, very likely, fortune — not to mention a guaranteed launch pad for a career. Powell was unaware, however, that several sections of the first few hundred miles below Green River, Wyoming, had already been run and "explored."

In 1825, fur-trapper William H. Ashley and seven other trappers set off down the Green River in bull boats of bison hides stretched over willow frames. These boats proved less than safe. After several nonfatal mishaps involving the loss of most of their food and equipment, Ashley and his fellow mountain men abandoned the river upstream of Lodore to rendezvous with one of Ashley's other groups. Later, in 1849, Captain William L. Manly and six companions impatient to reach the gold fields of California defected from a plodding wagon train at Green River Crossing late in the year to set off downriver in a twelve-foot ferry boat. They expected the boating route to afford far quicker progress. Manly's crew pinned then destroyed their boat in Ashley Falls, but continued downriver in hastily constructed dugout canoes. Eventually, when the whitewater became too daunting, Manly's group decided that the overland route was the only survivable one. They defected from their river trip and continued overland on an ever more hellish journey. In addition to Ashley and Manly, H. M. Hook had boated sections of the upper Green River.

Beyond these naive, early challengers on the Green, downstream in

Labyrinth and Stillwater canyons, in the 1830s, French trapper Denis Julien made an extended trapping expedition along the lower Green River by boat, often, apparently, by rigging a sail. His petroglyph markings dated from 1831 to 1838 are unequivocal in multiple locations in Labyrinth, Stillwater, and Cataract canyons, and also upstream of them in Whirlpool Canyon, at the foot of Lodore, where I saw the wall on which Julien had etched his initials and "1838." The one in the Hell Roaring Canyon tributary depicts his boat with mast erect and spells out "D. Julien 1836 3 mai." Little to nothing is known about the extent of Julien's apparently solo river travels and trapping expeditions, except that dates suggest that he, at least at times, was sailing *upstream* and that he was in his sixties when doing so. Why was he there on those isolated rivers?

Julien's 1831 inscription along the Uinta River matches Antoine Robidoux's 1831 establishment of a trapper's post in the Uintah Basin. Julien may have been Robidoux's guide. Julien, historian Charles Kelly found, was a French Canadian resident of St. Louis before the turn of the century where as early as 1807 he had received several licenses to trade with tribes to the west. Some additional "1837" inscriptions are known from Glen Canyon but are not signed "D. Julien." Perhaps he was getting tired of signings. If they are Julien's, then it may just be possible that he navigated (or lined or ghost-boated) much of Cataract Canyon. Kelly even speculated that he eventually died while running the river. If Julien did drown in Cataract, or even Grand Canyon, he would have gone several hundred miles out of his way to do so — his 1838 inscription in upper Whirlpool Canyon implies that he had returned safely well upstream. All in all, Julien must have navigated roughly 400 miles of the thousand that Powell and his crew ran. Strangely, none of the 1869 crew noted having spotted any of Julien's inscriptions.

The upshot? Most of the first seven hundred miles of river that the 1869 expedition tackled had already been boated to some extent. Exactly how many hundreds likely will remain a mystery.

Nor has the possibility been put to rest that the 1869 crew was not the first to float Grand Canyon either. On September 8, 1867, at Callville, Nevada, two men waded out and rescued an emaciated, bruised, half-naked, severely sunburned wreck of a 30-year-old human being who gave his name as James White. White's story of how he came to be where he was — and in the state he was — has been disputed and debated ever since he told it.

After prospecting about 200 miles downstream along the San Juan River, White and George Strole and Captain Baker crossed over to the Colorado River (likely in Glen Canyon). The canyon proved so inhospitable that they retraced their route. On August 24, while ascending the tributary out of the canyon, 15 to 20 Indians attacked them, killing Baker almost immediately. White and Strole gathered their guns, four ropes off their horses, and a sack of flour. Then they fled on foot fifteen miles downcanyon back to the Colorado. Reaching it at night, they built a driftwood raft in the dark. They launched and had smooth floating for three days. On the fourth, however, Strole fell overboard in a rapid and drowned in a whirlpool.

White pulled off his own boots and pants (so he could swim) and tied himself by his waist to the raft by a fifty-foot rope. His raft floated over 10- or 15-foot falls and flipped upside down three or four times per day. Seeing no sign of civilization, White stayed on the river. For seven days he ate nothing. He finally ate his rawhide knife scabbard. After eight days, he found some honey mesquite beans and ate them. On days nine and eleven he had to rebuild his raft. On day twelve, he saw about 75 friendly looking Hualapais. A squaw gave him a bit of honey mesquite loaf. Meanwhile other Indians stole one of his revolvers and a hand axe. When they would give him nothing more, he paddled onto the river again. The next day he traded his last revolver to another group of Indians for the hind quarters of a dog that they had butchered. He lost half of these accidentally. The following day the men at Callville grabbed his raft.

Critics — Stanton and Dellenbaugh among them — insist that instead of floating 500 miles of the Colorado, White had been seriously lost before that Indian attack and he had floated only 60 miles from Grapevine Wash near the Grand Wash Cliffs (Mile 277 from Lee's Ferry, 330 miles from the San Juan River) to Callville. Powell too discounted White's story. Yet Powell was not really in a position of knowledge that would allow him to discount White based on facts. Powell, I suspect, was instead indulging in wishful thinking by stating that the Colorado River remained unrun in its big canyons. Indeed, it may well have been James White's inadvertent claim of having gobbled up the whole enchilada that forced Powell's hand: to out-do White, the Major had to plan a "full" Green and Colorado exploration instead of carry out his previous intent, apparently originally conceived of by or before November of 1867 (as noted by William Culp Darrah), to launch a journey down the Grand River in Colorado ending "prematurely" at its confluence with the Green in Utah.

Yet, while Powell knew about White, he apparently knew nothing about the other previous "explorers" upstream of Grand Canyon except for what Ashley's petroglyph would reveal to him at Ashley Falls. The 1869 crew did know that the Green, down to the Uinta had been visited and crossed by white men. Downstream of the Uinta, the crew presumed, they were rowing into an unknown maze where no man had gone before. In truth, despite all trapping expeditions on the river before Powell's, the vast majority of the course of the Colorado River canyon system did remain terra incognita to the world in general and to Washington, D.C. in particular. And it remained a very forbidding, very large, middle of nowhere terra incognita at that.

Whoever showed the audacity to reveal it to the American public could not help but make extremely significant discoveries.

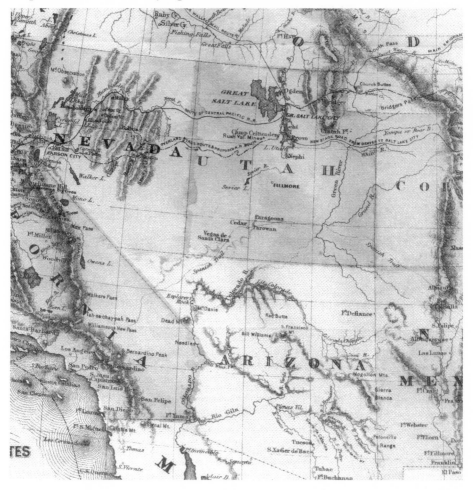

1865 map of the western United States. The dotted line just right of center, on the Colorado River, was Powell's terra incognita.

How risky was Powell's 1869 expedition? The Green River at Green River City, Wyoming, flows at elevation 6,100 feet. Almost 500 miles downstream it becomes the Colorado and, after another 500+ miles, it flows past the mouth of the Rio Virgin in Nevada, having dropped more than a mile in elevation. These thousand miles cut through what was, in 1869, a mysterious maze of dizzying canyon country isolated from civilization and most Indian villages by potentially lethal distances and seemingly impossible ramparts of cliffs. One critical sub-mystery that the crew faced was whether, in this vertical mile of drop, the descent was gradual, intermittent, or episodic, punctuated by huge, unrunnable waterfalls impossible to portage. With no way for the expedition to retreat, one impassible, unportageable waterfall could assassinate the entire crew. The strong possibility exists that Powell secretly believed that James White *did* raft through Grand Canyon, however, and thus anticipated that his own Whitehall boats could more or less safely follow.

Waterfalls or not, most of the region the river traversed was inhospitable, untracked desert offering extremely limited resources for living off the land in the event that a few of the right things went wrong. Hence the absence even of Indians. The region's vast inhospitality was in fact why so much of the river remained "The Great Unknown."

And as the crew would discover, many sections of this Great Unknown *were* in fact nearly impassable to the expedition, equipped as it was with inappropriate Whitehalls — except by portaging or lining them. While no one knows the flow levels that the 1869 expedition faced, we do know they hit Grand Canyon on August 5, during the onset of active monsoons. The river level climbed almost daily during at least the first half of the trip. My guess is the crew floated past the Paria at the head of Grand Canyon on about 10,000 to 15,000 cubic feet per second (cfs) but may have seen as high as 30,000 cfs or more at times before passing the Grand Wash Cliffs.

The dangers faced in this thousand-mile gambit were legion: starvation, drowning, lethal falls, incapacitating injuries during the brutal labor of lining or portaging, hostile Indians, and loss or destruction of the boats compelling an attempt to escape the canyons by hiking overland across a high desert labyrinth of unmapped and unknown canyons thus risking dehydration and heat stroke.

To romantically say that Powell's 1869 crew was willing to risk their lives for the sake of adventure, fame, and/or fortune misses the point that none of them, Powell included, understood the true nature of the trap they were entering. Yes, they knew they were risking their lives but they did not know that they were entering an unfamiliar gauntlet of severe physical challenges that could easily prove lethal if just a few big things went wrong.

The boys of the 1869 expedition were optimists, one and all.

What resources did the men possess to combat this gauntlet? The food started out lousy then deteriorated to starvation rations. Bradley, for example, described the expedition's situation after 79 days: " — we have had no meat for several days and not one sixth of a ration for more than a month. Yet we are willing to do all that we can to make the trip a success."

Powell's boatmen not only lacked life jackets, they also lacked the whitewater experience that safety would demand. These latter two details would dictate not only a difficult expedition, but a lethal one.

An important point here, the risk that the 1869 crew faced solely due to their lack of life jackets is often underestimated. In fact, the risk the men faced was immense. In the analysis that Thomas M. Myers and I conducted in our book *Over The Edge: Death in Grand Canyon* of the 82 drownings we researched, about 85 percent occurred to victims not wearing life jackets (most of the other victims were over 50 years old and drowned as part of a "cold shock" syndrome). Dozens of additional victims have drowned in the canyons upstream of Grand Canyon. Many of these victims were better equipped than the 1869 crew. To reiterate, the risks of drowning during this expedition were extremely high.

Despite the expedition's shortcomings in equipment and the crew's shortfalls in preparation, as one reads the accounts of these men, it remains all too easy to miss or gloss over the many hardships that these men did surmount in their quest for scientific knowledge — and for beaver pelts, gold, and adventure. This is because they were not complainers. Whining for rewards is more a symptom of today's America, not America of the 1860s. For perspective, if Powell's trip had happened in the year 2000 instead of in 1869, each surviving member of it would have been offered book and movie contracts exceeding half a million dollars.

But in 1869, experiencing uncertainty, terror, and brutally difficult and exhausting labor while lining and portaging the boats past chains of roaring cataracts in an unmapped, endless, middle-of-nowhere, abysmal canyon system while being led by a man who knew far too little to be safely doing what he was doing was par for the course in the unexplored West. In short, the survival of this epic expedition pivoted on the fierce determination of many of the men, their competence, their good humor in the face of lethal dangers, their camaraderie, their bone-bruising labor, their savvy of the West, and, to no small extent, on their luck.

Okay; at last, the moment for which you have patiently waited: the put-in at Green River, Wyoming, on May 24, 1869. Fasten your seatbelt; this time machine is about to rock and roll into one of the most amazing North American expeditions ever launched.

"Noonday rest in Marble Canyon" revealing Powell's 1871-1872 Whitehall
modifications (etching by Thomas Moran from *Canyons of the Colorado*).

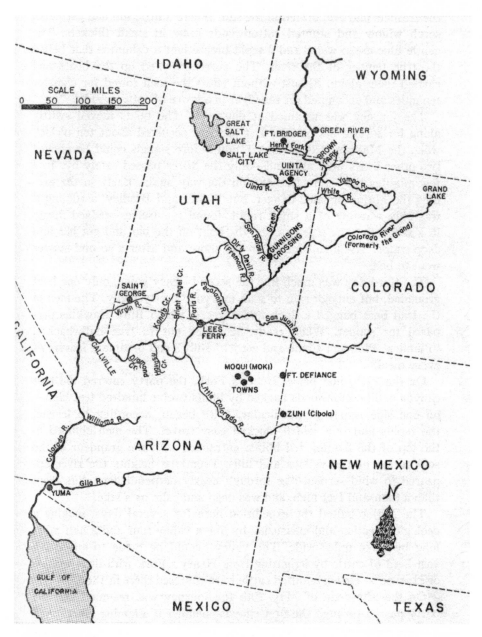

The drainage of the Green and Colorado rivers, courtesy of Princeton University Press, from W. C. Darrah, 1951. *Powell of the Colorado.*

THE ORIGINAL WRITINGS

By

George Young Bradley
Andrew Hall
Oramel G. Howland
John Wesley Powell
Walter Henry Powell
John Colton Sumner

As promised, what follows are the original writings of the 1869 crew penned while they were on the expedition. Their words came from the sources mentioned above and as noted below. Every word that follows is reproduced faithfully. None have been omitted. If Bradley, the Powells, Sumner, Howland, or Hall misspelled a word, it will appear that way here. Here also, appearing apparently for the first time ever, is printed the *original* journal written by John Sumner for the dates between August 17 and the 27th; these are from original pages torn from a journal and found in Powell's collection. These entries are printed herein immediately after Sumner's more expanded — and transcribed by a mystery scribe — journal entries.

One of the problems with both Bradley's and Powell's journals is their original pencil or ink writing has faded over the past 133 years. And the first things to vanish are small punctuation marks. Either commas were written by these two in invisible ink, or else both men considered them to be a hex. Bradley wrote in mile-long sentences. Far worse, Powell often did not write in sentences at all. He wrote in murky penmanship and obscure abbreviations. He often eschewed periods to end his sentences and then forgot to use capital letters to hint that he was beginning a new one. Powell's verbs often lack subjects. Powell's nearly 5,600 words in Journals #1 and #2 often, at first, seem like shorthand notes to himself.

Hence, to make Bradley's journal a bit easier to read — and to make Powell's writings possible to read at all — I have inserted a few commas, semicolons, periods, and capital letters. Other than these punctuational additions, however, everything is identical to the original writings.

Despite less than perfect prose written over the roar of rapids, these men's writings, when combined, narrate very well one of the greatest adventures in the history of exploration. Please note that readers familiar with Powell's *Canyons* or William Culp Darrah's transcriptions of the 1869 writings may discover many discrepancies between either and the following writings. Again, this is just one more added value to this book.

Powell's 1871 boats on the bank of the Green River at put in. Photo by E.O. Beaman.

Chapter 1.

AN OUTDOOR FROLIC FROM GREEN RIVER, WYOMING, TO BEE-HIVE POINT, May 24 - 30

As the 1869 expedition shoves its boats onto the current of the Green, its members likely feel trepidation. But the feelings they impart to their journals smack more of suppressed excitement. Like city kids going to camp for the first time, the crew feels exuberance bordering on manic. Despite their vast experiences with wilderness and the potential dangers they know it can pose, the crew during this first week seems to feel that whatever lays ahead on the river will be fun and, either way, harmless. This holiday euphoria offers time for philosophy and lasts for two weeks — after all, several of the crew have already scouted parts of the river's course here in 1868. If the journey were to be marred at all during this early phase, it seems, it would be marred only by a few cold, soggy rain storms. Despite this apparent harmlessness, Bradley does manage to strand himself atop a cliff for an afternoon. And several men manage to ground their boats on mid-river sandbars and suffer dunkings trying to shove them off. During week number one, the expedition begins its orgy of assigning a name to every notable piece of landscape.

Day #1 [BRADLEY] May 24. 69. Left Green River, Wyoming, with four boats. (The "Emma Dean," "Maid of the Cañon," "Kitty Clide's [sic] Sister" & "No Name.") And ten men (Prof. Powell's Brother, The Howland brothers, Wm. Dunn, Wm. Rhodes [Hawkins], Andy Hall, Frank Goodman, Jack Sumner & myself) at about one o'clock, P.M. for the purpose of exploring the Green and Colorado rivers. Passed rapidly down with the tide almost without effort for about 8 or 10 miles when we encamped for the night in a cottonwood grove. The night was pleasant with indications of approaching rain. Made geological survey, found nothing worthy of note.

[HALL, May, 1869]
Dear Mother,
    It is a long time since I wrote you but I want you to know I am still alive and well and hope you are the same.

I can not write you any news at present for I have not time to write to you now.

I am going down the Colorado River to explore that river in boats with Major Powell, the professor of the Normal college [sic] in Illinois.

You need not expect to hear from me for some time ten or twelve months at least. You can write to me at Collvile [sic], Arizona give my love to all.

Yours til death

Andrew Hall

[J. W. POWELL/*Chicago Tribune***, published May 29, 1869/ written at Green River]** Green River, Wyoming Territory, May 24. Permit me, through your paper, to explain the purposes for which this expedition is made, and its organization, as statements have been made in the public press that are somewhat inaccurate. The expedition is under the auspices of the Illinois Natural History Society — its chief is the Secretary of that Society.

About a year ago Congress passed a law authorizing the Secretary of War to issue rations to the party. I send herewith a copy of the law and the order of the General of the Army relating hereto:

Headquarters of the Army

Adjutant General's Office

Washington, June 13, 1868

Special Orders No. 140

(*extract*)

5. By a joint resolution, authorizing the Secretary of War to furnish supplies to an exploring expedition, approved June 11, 1868, it is provided, "That the Secretary of War be, and he is hereby, authorized and empowered to issue rations for twenty-five men of the expedition engaged in the exploration of the River Colorado, under direction of Professor Powell, while engaged in that work: *Provided* That [sic] such issue is not detrimental to the interests of the military service.

The Secretary of War accordingly directs that the Commissary General of Subsistence give the necessary detailed instructions for making the authorized issues from the commissary stores at posts most convenient to the route of the designed expedition, the ration to embrace all the articles of the full authorized army ration, or, in lieu thereof, the prescribed equivalents of other articles, with the privilege to Professor Powell of dropping any undesired articles and receiving in lieu thereof an equivalent in value of any other article that may be on hand for issue, and preferred by him; also, with the privilege, when the desired stores are not on hand for issue, or when, from peculiar circumstances, as from inability to receive, carry, or utilize rations, or any portion thereof, then the proper local commutation value of such rations or parts of rations as shall be undrawn in kind may be paid to Professor Powell in money.

By command of General Grant:

E. D. Townsend
Assistant Adjutant General

It will be seen that permission is given to commute a part of the ration. This gives a fund sufficient to employ four men, who hunt and fish, and thus supply the party with meat. The principal saving is in the meat ration, and, of course, we prefer wild meat to army bacon.

The Illinois Industrial University, for the two years past, has made a small appropriation [for] the enterprise — $1,100 in all. The Smithsonian Institution and the Chicago Academy of Sciences have granted us some favors.

The funds of the Illinois Natural History Society devoted to this work, amount to less than $1,000 annually. The amount from all these sources will not quite furnish the instruments and supplies, the balance coming from private sources.

The railroads have shown great liberality, giving transportation to the party. The hunters managed the pack train last year, and will largely man the boats this. As we float down a rapid river there is not much labor of rowing, add [and?] all help when there is need, as over rapids, portages, &c., the other members of the party give their time, feeling remunerated by the opportunity for study.

The object is to make collections in geology, natural history, antiquities and ethnology for the institutions assisting the work. Not the least of the objects in view is to add a mite to the great sum of human knowledge. Science has its devotees in the laboratory; peering into the infinitesimal; on the observatory, keeping an outlook into the universe, and it has its laborers searching and exploring all over the earth for more facts, these characters in which the truth is written. Now if we can record a few more facts, and from them learn a lesson, we shall feel repaid for toil, privations and peril.

This summer's work will be devoted chiefly to the study of the geography and geology of the Valley of the Colorado, the great cañon district, the chief of which is the "Grand Cañon" yet unexplored. We are provided with instruments for determining latitude, longitude and altitude, and for making observations of the climate.

May be that I shall find opportunity to send you an account, from time to time, of our progress, by hunters or Indians, though through a large part of the country where we expect to see no human being. After a three years' study of the matter, I think it doubtful whether these cañons have ever been seen by man. The Indians never go into them, and there is little game on the cliffs to tempt them. They tell me they never climb the peaks of the higher ranges, and never clamber over the cliffs of these awful cañons. Some day I will tell you their traditions concerning them.

Our boats are launched, and we are ready to start. Yesterday we had a merry time naming them. The flag-boat, which is smaller than others, and is to be the pioneer, being made for fast rowing, is called the "Emma Dean"; the others, "Maid of the Cañon," "No Name," and "Kitty Clyde's Sister."

They are all decked forward and aft, making a little, tight cabin at each end. Should it be necessary to run them over falls — making a portage of the rations — these cabins will act as buoys. The three large boats are made of oak, the small one of pine — the large ones having a capacity of forty-five hundred pounds, though they will not be loaded quite that heavily.

We feel quite proud of our little fleet as it lies in the river waiting for us to embark; the stars and stripes, spread by a stiff breeze, over the Emma Dean: the waves rocking the little vessels, and the current of the Green, swollen, mad and seeming eager to bear us down through its mysterious cañons. And we are just as eager to start. — J. W. Powell

Green River City in 1871. Photo courtesy of Arizona Historical Society, Tucson.

[J. W. POWELL, *Chicago Tribune*, **published July 19, 1869/ written in Flaming Gorge, on Green River, June 2, 1869]** On the 24th of May, at half past 1, we started from Green River City. The rations, instruments, &c., were so divided among the boats as to have a fair proportion of the several articles on each. This precaution was taken that we might not be seriously crippled by the loss of a boat. The good people of the city turned out to see us off. This does not indicate that a great crowd came out, as the cities here lack people to make them densely crowded. But there are plenty of vacant lots yet.

We dropped down the river about seven miles, and went into camp, satisfied that our boats were quite manageable and not overloaded, as we feared they would be.

"The Start from Green River Station" (Thomas Moran etching from *Canyons of the Colorado*).

[W. H. POWELL, the *Chicago Evening Journal*, July 19, 1869]

Colorado River Exploring Expedition
Camp by Red Cañon, July [June] 3, 1869

To the Editor of the *Chicago Evening Journal*:

The object of the expedition of which I am a member is well known to the readers of your paper, and anything in regard to it is unnecessary at this time. Our boats having arrived at Green River City, on the Union Pacific Railroad, were launched on the 24th of May and loaded with the freight, consisting of the instruments necessary for the scientific work of the expedition, and provisions, chiefly flour, bacon, coffee, and sugar, with such other creature comforts as the nature of the voyage and the capacity of the boats would allow.

We were thoroughly tired of our sojourn at Green River City, which is situated in a desolate region, surrounded by sandy barren bluffs, and at 1 o'clock in the afternoon of the 24th we rowed into the stream and were soon out of sight of the town. Dropping down the river ten or twelve miles, we landed and camped in a cotton-wood grove, well satisfied with the trial trip of our little fleet of four boats, which were built with all the "logic" displayed in the construction of the "wonderful one-hoss shay."

[SUMNER] May 24, 1869. — After many weeks of weary waiting, to-day sees us all ready for the adventures of an unknown country. Heretofore all attempts in exploring the Colorado of the West, throughout its entire course, have been miserable failures. Whether our attempt will turn out the same time alone can show. If we fail it will not be for the want of a complete outfit of material and men used to hardships. After much blowing off of gas and the fumes of bad whiskey, we were all ready by two o'clock and pulled out into the swift stream. The Emma Dean, a light four-oared shell, lightly loaded, carrying as crew Professor J. W. Powell, W. H. Dunn, and a trapper [John Colton Sumner himself], designed as a scouting party, taking the lead. The "Maid of the Cañon" followed close in her wake, manned by Walter H. Powell and George Y. Bradley, carrying two thousand pounds of freight. Next on the way was "Kitty Clyde's Sister," manned by as jolly a brace of boys as ever swung a whip over a lazy ox, W. H. Rhodes [Hawkins], of Missouri, and Andrew Hall, of Fort Laramie, carrying the same amount of freight. The last to leave the miserable adobe village was the "No Name" (piratic craft) manned by O. G. Howland, Seneca Howland, and Frank Goodman. We make a pretty show as we float down the swift, glossy river. As *Kitty*'s crew have been using the whip more of late years than the oars, she ran on a sand-bar in the middle of the river, got off of that, and ran shore on the east side, near the mouth of Bitter's creek, but finally got off and came down to the rest of the fleet in gallant style, her crew swearing she would not "gee" or "haw" a "cuss." We moved down about 7 miles and camped for the night on the eastern shore, where there is a large quantity of cord wood. As it was a cold, raw night, we stole a lot of it to cook with. Proff., Walter, and Bradley spent a couple of hours geologising on the east side. Howland and Dunn went hunting down the river; returned at dark with a small-sized rabbit. Rather slim rations for ten hungry men. The balance of the party stopped in camp, and exchanged tough stories at a fearful rate. We turned in early, as most of the men had been up for several preceding nights, taking leave of their many friends, "a la Muscovite." The natural consequence were fogy [foggy?] ideas and snarly hair.

How strange it is that adopting foreign ways will so change us in many respects. If there is any meanness in a man, get him drunk and you will soon see the Devil's claws, if not the whole of the traditional "Auld Cootie." If he is a goodhearted man when sober, he will be willing to sell his only shirt to help his friend. When I see how drink shows the true colors so plainly, I sometimes wish the whole world could be drunk for a short time, that the scoundrels might be all killed off through their own meanness.

☀ Day #2

[BRADLEY] May 25. 69. Started little after 6 o'clock and passed on rapidly as ever until about 9 1/2 A.M. when the leading boat grounded and before the signal of danger could be obeyed two other boats were aground. I had just time to go to the right of the leading boat and passed without touching. Landed and in a few moments all were clear. Only two men were wet by pushing off the boats. Went down a few miles farther and landed at 10 1/2 A.M. to allow the two men to dry clothing. Bill Rhodes [Hawkins] caught a young mountain sheep which afforded an excellent dinner.

About noon started again and passed on without accident until about 3 P.M., when landed for "refreshments." Rain commences falling little after noon. After supper entered boats and took a long run down. Just before 7 p.m. the leading boat signalled danger but supposing it to be only a small rapid, did not obey immediately and in consequence was caught on a shoal and for the first time get a wetting, but by both getting out we succeeded with a great deal of tall lifting and tugging in getting the boat into deep water, and the party having just landed we went into camp for the night. Got dry clothing and after a second supper went to bed. Rained some during the night but not enough to wet us badly.

[J. W. POWELL/*Chicago Tribune***, published July 19, 1869/ written in Flaming Gorge, on Green River, June 2, 1869]** Next morning [May 25] we got an early start and ran along at a good rate until about 9 o'clock when we ran aground on a gravelly bar. All jumped up and helped the boats over by main strength. Then came on a rain, and river and cloud seemed to conspire to give us a thorough drenching. Wet, chilled and tired almost to exhaustion, we stopped at a cottonwood grove on the bank and built a huge fire, then made a kettle of coffee, and were soon refreshed and quite merry.

When the clouds got out of our sunshine, on we started again. A few miles further down, a flock of mountain sheep was seen on a cliff on the right. The boats were quickly tied up, and three or four men went after them. In the course of a couple of hours they came straggling in again. The cook only had been successful in bringing in a fine fat lamb. The other men taunted him with finding it dead, but it was soon dressed, cooked, and eaten, making a hearty 4 o'clock dinner. Then "all aboard," and down the river for another dozen miles. On the way down we passed the mouth of Smith's Fork, a dirty little river that seemed somewhat swollen.

[W. H. POWELL, the *Chicago Evening Journal***, published July 19, 1869]** Continuing on our voyage the next morning, we made a distance of seventy-five miles during the 25th and 26th, and on the 27th [of May] passed the mouth of Henry's Fork — a small stream flowing into Green River from the west — when the vertical walls of "Flaming Gorge," the entrance to the upper cañon of the Green, came in view, but a few miles distant. As we entered the narrow cañon the walls of brilliant red sandstone, rising to a height of 1,200 feet, looked threatening and ominous. The low, narrow banks between the river and the walls were covered with cotton-wood and box elder.

[SUMNER] May 25th. — Pulled out early, and dropped down to an old cabin, where I stole two bread pans for the cook's use. Moved about eight miles, and camped in the willows, as it was raining hard; stopped two hours; made some coffee, and cooked some villainous bacon to warm us up a little. Then pulled out again, as it showed some signs of clearing off. Went another five or six mile stretch, when we saw five mountain sheep on a cliff; stopped to give chase, but they proved to be too nimble for us. Rhodes, however, found a lamb asleep on the cliff, caught it by the heels and threw it off toward camp. The Professor and Bradley climbed a black looking cliff on the west side to see how it was made. All into camp by 3 o'clock, when we had our young sheep for dinner. Packed up the cooking utensils, and pulled out again, and moved down through a rather monotonous country for six or eight miles further. Saw several wild geese and four beavers, but failed to get any. While rounding to on the west side, all the boats except *Kitty's Sister* got fast on a sand bar — the *Maid* so fast that she had to be pried off with oars. Camped on the west side, in the willow brush. While we were gathering drift-wood for camp fires, two mountain sheep ran out of the willows and up the side of the bluff. Two of the boys followed, but failed to get either of them. Rained all day and most of the night.

☀ Day #3

[BRADLEY] **May 26. '69.** Got breakfast and entered boats at 8 A.M. Shortly after it commenced raining and kept it up all day. Stopped for dinner at 12 M. and then passed on, crossed the largest and most difficult rapid yet seen. Only one boat grounded and no injury done except *one man took a bath*. The leading boat having shot a Duck and Goose, we went on shore at about 4 P.M. and had an excellent supper. Prepared a bed of willows with great care expecting that, as it had rained all day, it would be fair at night, but soon after bed-time it commenced to rain and kept it up all night. Got pretty wet but expect to be wetter before we reach our destination.

[J. W. POWELL, *Chicago Tribune*, published July 19, 1869/ written in Flaming Gorge, on Green River, June 2, 1869] On the 26th [actually this happened on May 27] we ran down to a point about two miles from the mouth of Henry's Fork, where a *cache* of rations and instruments had been made last spring. When we landed it was cold and stormy, a brisk wind blowing from the mountains. The *cache* had been made under an overhanging rock near the river, where it was safe from the elements and wild beasts, but not safe from man; and as we had learned that a party of Indians had camped near it for several weeks, we had some anxiety for its safety. That was soon allayed; it was all right, and chronometer wheels were not taken for Ute hair ornaments, barometer tubes for beads, and sextant thrown into the river for "bad medicine," as had been prophesied. Taking up our *cache* for the next day, we went down to the foot of the mountain and made this camp.

At a distance of from one to twenty miles from this point a brilliant red gorge is seen, the red being surrounded by broad bands of mottled buff and gray at the summit of the cliffs, and curving down to the water's edge on the nearer slope of the mountain. This is where the river enters the mountain range — this head of the first cañon we are to explore, or, rather, an introductory cañon to a series made by the river through the range. We have named it Flaming Gorge. The cliffs or walls we found to be twelve hundred feet high. You must not think of a mountain range as a line of peaks standing up out of the plains, but as a broad platform, fifty or sixty miles wide, from which the mountains have been carved by the waters. You must conceive, too, that this plateau has been cut up by gulches, ravines and cañons in a multitude of directions, and that beautiful valleys are scattered about at varying altitudes. A mountain range is a mountain region, not a line of mountains, though such a region is much greater in length than width in most cases.

This first series of cañons we are about to explore is a river channel cut through such a range of mountains. The Uintah Mountains here have an easterly and westerly direction. The cañon cuts nearly halfway across the range, then turns to the east and runs along the central line, slowly crossing it to the south, keeping this direction more than fifty miles, and then turns to the southwest and cuts diagonally through the southern half of the range. This much we know before entering the cañon, as we made a partial exploration of the region last fall, and climbed many of its peaks, and, in a few places, reached the river walls and looked over precipices of many hundred feet to the water below. Now and then the walls are broken down by lateral cañons, the channels of little streams entering the river. Through two or three of these I found my way down to the water's edge in early winter, and walked along the low water beach for several miles, at the foot of the cliffs. Where the river has this easterly direction, there is a cañon only on the western half. Along the eastern half, a broad valley has been made by the river. This has received the name Brown's Hole, in honor of an old-time trapper, who once had his cabin there, and caught beaver and killed deer.

[SUMNER] May 26th. — All afloat early; went about three miles, when we came to our first rapid. It cannot be navigated by any boat with safety, in the main channel, but the river being pretty high, it made a narrow channel under the overhanging willows on the west shore, so that we were not delayed more than twenty minutes, all the boats but *Kitty's Sister* getting through easily. She getting on a rock, compelled Rhodes to get overboard and pry her off. About 4 o'clock, came to a meadow of about a thousand acres, lying between Green River and Henry's Fork. Camped for the night on the east shore, about a mile above the mouth of Henry's Fork. Passed the mouth of Black's Fork of the Green River today; it is but little wider at the mouth than at Fort Bridger, but deep. Henry's Fork is a stream about thirty ft. wide, and is fed by the snows of the Uinta mountains [sic], about seventy-five miles northwest of this camp; it has some good pasturage on it, but no farming land, as it is at too great an altitude. At the mouth is a good place for one or two ranches. There are about three hundred acres of good land, but is inundated nearly every spring by freshets. There is a large stack of hay standing in the meadow, that has been left over from last year's crop.

☀ Day #4

[BRADLEY] May 27. '69. Started late this morning as we intended to go only a few miles down to the first cañon at Henries Fork. Landed about two miles below starting point and took in some goods which had been cached since early spring; found everything safe, and we passed on and soon passed a ranch at the mouth of Henries' Fork now occupied by a Mormon family. Just below this fork we entered the mouth of the first cañon, and encamped amid the cottonwood trees surrounded by bluffs 1200 ft high and on one side nearly perpendicular. It is the grandest scenery I have found in the mountains and I am delighted with it. I went out to see the country this morning and found it grand beyond conception. The river winds like [a] serpent through between nearly perpendicular cliffs 1200 ft. high but instead of rapids it is deep and calm as a lake. It is the most safe of any part we have yet seen for navigation. Found some marine focils [sic] in hard limestone — first yet found.

[J. W. POWELL, no entry specified for May 27]

[SUMNER] May 27th. — Raised a cache that we made two months since, and found everything safe; moved down to head of a canyon and camped on the east side, under a grove of cottonwood trees. Proff., Walter, and Bradley went geologising. Tramped around most of the day in the mud and rain to get a few fossils. Distance from Green River City to mouth of Henry's Fork sixty miles; general course, 30° E. of S.; estimated land distance forty miles. Country worthless. Grease wood and alkali on the river bottom; on the hills sparse bunch grass. Artemissia [sic] and a few stunted cedars. At intervals of four or five miles on the river there are a few scrubby cottonwoods, but none large enough for anything but fuel. Rained most of the day.

☀ Day #5

[BRADLEY] May 28. '69. Started alone this morning to explore the clift [sic] on N.E. side of the river. Went out at 8:20 A.M. and having traveled without being able to find foccils [sic] or to get down the clift to the river, I got *mad* and resolved to get down if possible, but having climbed and walked until 2 1/2 P.M., gave it up and set out for home and having walked as fast as possible against a driving rain with an empty stomach until 7 1/4 P.M., I arrived opposite camp, and the boat took me to camp as tired and hungry and mad as a bear.

[J. W. POWELL, *Chicago Tribune*, **published July 19, 1869/ written in Flaming Gorge, on Green River, June 2, 1869]** The second day in this camp it rained, and we employed the time in repairing one of our barometers, that had been broken on the way from New York. A new tube had to be put in; that is, a long glass tube had to be filled with mercury, four or five inches at a time, and each installment boiled over an alcohol lamp. 'Tis a delicate task to boil the mercury without breaking the glass, but we had success, and were ready to climb and measure mountains once more. So the day following we went to the summit of the cliff on the left, and took an observation.

[W. H. POWELL, the *Chicago Evening Journal*, **July 19, 1869]** We remained at this place during the 28th and 29th [of May], engaged in measuring the height of the walls of the cañon, collecting fossils, mending broken instruments, &c., and resumed our voyage again on the 30th. Through this cañon the river has cut a narrow channel a distance of 50 miles, with often just sufficient room for the water to flow between the walls, leaving no bank of dirt or rock on either side. Sometimes, at irregular intervals, are low, narrow banks of sandy soil, dotted with small groves of cottonwood trees, with an undergrowth of box elder. Wild grape vines trail on the ground, or festoon the undergrowth of the groves. Flocks of wild geese paddle in the shoal water along the banks or hurry across the rapid current in front of our boats as we pass. The stream is comparatively sluggish for some distance from the entrance, and then rapidly increases in speed till it becomes a mountain torrent, with often a succession of rapids and cataracts, where the bed of the river is encumbered with large rocks, that sometimes rise a number of feet above the water.

[SUMNER] May 28th. — Still in camp. Proff. and the "Trapper" repaired a broken barometer. Walter and Bradley went geologizing [sic] on the west side. Bradley did not get into camp till night, having lost his way, and had a long, weary tramp through the mud and rain.

☀ Day #6

[BRADLEY] May 29. 69. Rained all last night and is still (10:15 A.M.). Can't go out at all but if it rains only till noon shall take a geological section this P.M. The Major is mending two barometers which have become broken. Nothing of importance occurred. Rain ceased at night.

[J. W. POWELL, *Chicago Tribune*, **published July 19, 1869/ written in Flaming Gorge, on Green River, June 2, 1869]** Another day has been spent in geological and topographical work, and we are ready to enter the mysterious cañon. With some anxiety we start, for the old mountaineers tell us it cannot be run. The Indians say, "Water heap ketch 'em." But all are eager for the trial, and off we go.

[SUMNER] May 29th. — Proff. climbed the hill on the east side of the canyon and measured it with a barometer; hight [sic] above the river 1140 feet, not perpendicular. There is a cliff on the west side that is fifty feet higher, and perpendicular. The rock is hard, fiery-red sandstone. It has been named Flaming Gorge.

☀ Day #7

[BRADLEY] May 30. 69. Went out this morning and took a section. Measured by line a valley 4 1/2 miles long by about three miles wide. It could be made to support a vast herd of cattle by irrigating from Henries' Fork with little trouble and expence [sic] — 1100 cattle wintered in this valley last year. Got on board this P.M. and passed down through the cañon about 7 miles. Named the first cañon "Flaming Goarge," [sic] the second "Cañon of the Rappid" [sic] for we found in it a roaring rapid with a fall of several feet but there being plenty of water we passed it with little difficulty though we took off boots and coats and prepared for a swim. My boat went over next to the little boat [the *Emma Dean*] and took in but little water. All passed in safety. Next passed through another cañon which we named "Kingfisher Cañon" and, at the upper end, a stream which we called Kingfisher Fork, from a kingfisher we saw at the mouth of fork. Camped in this cañon for the night just above another rapid which I think we can pass with safety if we keep on the other side of the river. The bluff opposite our camp we call "Beehive Point" from its resemblance in shape to a straw beehive. Pleasant all night. Shot two geese and a bever [sic] but the latter sank before we could get it.

[O. G. HOWLAND, *ROCKY MOUNTAIN NEWS*, July 17, 1869, written in camp at Mouth of Bear River on the Green, June 19, 1869] [May 24-30] Dear *News*: — As I wrote you [original hand-written letter not located], we started the twenty-fourth ultimo from Green River City and got along rapidly to the mouth of Henry's Fork, sixty miles by river, in about ten hour's [sic] time without rowing a stroke. Here we camped until the thirtieth and then ran down Flaming Gorge in flaming style, then through the Cañon of the Rapids and Kingfisher Cañon to Beehive Point, ten miles by river, in a short hour. Next day we made a mile and a half and entered Red Cañon with a rush. In this cañon we would run a bend in the river and prospect ahead with our light boat, and signal the large boats to come on if all was right. The river here has some very heavy rapids, and our boats had to be bailed at almost every one we ran. This cañon is about thirty-five miles by river, and the average fall will exceed fifteen feet to the mile; perhaps twenty feet would be a nearer estimate. When in the rapids, we ran with the speed of the wind. We ran an estimated distance in a rapid of three quarters of a mile in two minutes. At another time, where the current was more confined and the rapids were swifter, we passed the flagboat, which had hauled in shore, and those in her said we passed them as rapidly as a railway train at its highest speed — sixty miles an hour. However, this was slow to some rapids we have run since. At the tail of these rapids, on either side, usually, occurs a calm or nearly calm cove, into which we could run to bail our boats if we shipped more water than we could conveniently carry through the next rapids.

[J. W. POWELL, *Chicago Tribune*, **published July 19, 1869/ written in Flaming Gorge, on Green River, June 6, 1869]** [May 30]. We left camp at Flaming Gorge on the 30th of May, and quickly ran through the gorge; then wheeled to the left on the swiftly gliding current into another cañon with a direct run of nearly a mile; then the river turned sharply around the point of a narrow cliff to the right, about fifteen hundred feet high, and rolled in great waves back again to the west ford another mile; then became a quiet stream in a little valley. As this was our first experience with cañon rapids, we called it Cañon of the Rapids. Soon we entered another Cañon in the gray rocks, and made a ride to the point where the river makes its grand turn to the east, and camped for the night. This camp was on the south side of the river, just opposite a dome-shaped mountain, around which the Green makes its turn, and we called it Beehive Point. Down the river the mountains were of red sandstone, and the evening sun played in roseate flashes from the rocks and shimmering green from the cedar spray and shimmered and flashed along the dancing waves away down the river. The landscape revelled in beautiful sunshine.

[W. H. POWELL, the *Chicago Evening Journal*, **July 19, 1869]** On the night of the 30th [of May] we camped at a bend in the river, which we called Bee Hive Point, for the appearance of a cliff, on the left side of the river, rounded to the shape of a dome at the top, and covered with cells carved by the action of the water during some past age, in which hundreds of swallows have built their nests of clay. As the swallows flit about the cliff they look like swarms of bees, and the cliff has the appearance of a colossal bee-hive. Opposite this cliff, and where we camped, is a vast amphitheatre, composed of a succession of terraces, rising to a height of 1,500 feet; each platform or terrace is built of red sandstone, and the space between them is a gentle slope clothed in green verdure, and on which a row of pine trees grow in the arc of a circle, and the amphitheatre is painted with alternate bands of green and red. As we near this marvelous work of nature in our little boats, a herd of mountain sheep are [sic] seen standing in a line on a terrace two or three hundred feet above the river, and as they remain motionless, watching our approach, they look like statues exquisitely chiseled by some master artist, and we are half surprised to see them suddenly wheel around like a platoon of well-drilled soldiers, and leaping gracefully to a platform above, file again into line and eye us with suspicion as we land our boats. This animal is much larger than the domestic sheep, and is pursued with the greatest persistency by hunters on account of the fine flavor of the meat, but is less frequently secured than other game, because of the ease and rapidity with which he climbs the highest cliffs and most precipitous peaks, of which he is sovereign and sole inheritor.

[SUMNER] May 30th. — Professor, Bradley, Senica [sic] and Hall went up the river five miles, measuring a geological section. All in camp by three o'clock, when we loaded up and pulled on again into a channel as crooked as a street in Boston. Passed out of Flaming Gorge into Horseshoe Cañon, out of Horseshoe Cañon into Kingfisher Cañon. While rounding a bend we came on a herd of mountain sheep, that scampered up the steep, rocky side of the cañon at an astonishing rate. The crews of the freight boats opened a volley on them that made the wilderness ring, reminding us all of other scenes and times [during the Civil War and/or Indian skirmishes in the Rockies], when we were the scampering party. Passed the mouth of a small stream coming in from the west, which we named King Fisher Creek [now Sheep Creek], as there was a bird of that species perched on the branch of a dead willow, watching the finny tribe with the determination of purpose that we often see exhibited by politicians, while watching for the spoils of office. Killed two geese, and saw a great number of beavers to-day, but failed to get any of them. No sooner would we get within gun-shot, than down they would go with a plumping noise like dropping a heavy stone into the water. Made seven miles today and camped for the night on the west bank of the river, opposite a huge grayish white sandstone that loomed up a thousand feet from the water's edge, very much the shape of an old-fashioned straw bee-hive, and we named it "Beehive Point." Saw the tracks of elk, deer and sheep on the sand. Near our camp Goodman saw one elk, but missed it.

Powell's 1871 boats below Ashley Falls. Photo by E.O. Beaman.

Chapter 2.

"Roll out! Roll out! Bulls in the corral! Chain up the gap! Roll out!"

BEE-HIVE POINT TO THE CANYON OF LODORE, *May 31 - June 7*

During the second week of the expedition the idyll continues, marred only by being forced to learn how to line their boats as a team and, next, to line them and also make an onerous portage over the rough terrain flanking Ashley Falls. Here too a beam of disillusionment forces itself through a crack in Bradley's armor of optimism regarding the hunting prowess of the men whom Major Powell has hired as hunters by having taken money from the army post to pay them in lieu of loading the boats with more Army bacon. For now, Bradley's fishing skill fills the gap, but here the first inkling creeps in that the expedition's rations might prove to be less than optimal. The crew also learns, as all new boatmen do, how upstream wind can convert a hitchhiker's drifting — or speeding at near "railroad speed" — into a draft horse's slog. This, the expedition's second week, will prove to be the last innocent and naive one. The men camp at the head of Lodore Canyon and feel only the faintest of premonitions that their wilderness holiday is about to metamorphose into a protracted war against whitewater.

Day #8 [BRADLEY] May 31. 69. Have been passing rapids all day. Have once had to let the boats down with ropes [this process is called "lining"]. Have worked very hard to pass about 10 miles and have encamped in the midst of a very bad rapid which we must pass with ropes in the morning. Went out at night with Bill R. [Hawkins] and saw a deer. Shot at it but could not get it.

[J. W. POWELL, *Chicago Tribune,* **published July 19, 1869/ written in Flaming Gorge, on Green River, June 6, 1869]** The next day [May 31] we started down through what we called Red Cañon, and soon came to the rapids, which were made dangerous by huge rocks lying in the channel. So we ran ashore and let our boats down with lines. In the afternoon we came to more dangerous rapids and stopped to examine them, and found that we had to let down with lines and were on the wrong side of the river, but must first cross. No easy manner in such a current with dangerous rocks below and rapids above. First I sent the pioneer boat, "Emma Dean," over to unload on the opposite bank; then she returned to get another load, and running back and forth, she soon had nearly half the freight over. Then one of the large boats was manned and taken across, but carried down almost to the rocks, in spite of hard rowing. The other boats soon followed, and we went into camp for the night.

At the foot of the cliff on this side, there was a long slope covered with pines. Under these pines we made our beds, and soon after sunset were seeking rest and sleep. The cliffs on either side were of rich, red sandstone, and stretched up to the heavens two thousand five hundred feet. On this side, the long pine clad slope was surmounted by a perpendicular cliff with pines on its summit. The cliff on the other side was bare rock from the water's edge up to two thousand feet, and then sloped back, giving a footing to pines and cedars. As twilight deepened the rocks grew dark and somber. The threatening roar of the waters was loud and constant, and I laid awake with thoughts of the morrow and the cañons to come, interrupted now and then by characters in scenery that would attract my attention. And here I made a discovery that has been interesting and useful to me since. On looking at a mountain directly in front, the inclination of the slope to the horizon is greatly exaggerated, and the distance to its summit and its true altitude is correspondingly diminished. To judge of the slope of a mountain side you must see it in profile. Now, in coming down to this point in the afternoon, I had noticed the slope of a particular part of the cliff, and had made an estimate of its altitude. While at supper I had noticed the same cliff from a position facing it, and it seemed vertical but not half so high. But lying on my side and looking at the same, its true proportions appeared. This seemed a wonder, and I got up to take a view of it standing erect; 'twas the same cliff as at suppertime. Lying down again, it was the cliff as seen in profile in proportions, with the advantage of seeing the features of its full face. And musing on this I forgot the morrow and the cañons to come. I had found a way to judge of altitude and slope as I could of distance and trend along the horizontal. The reason, too, is simple: a reference to the stereoscope will suggest it at once. Since then I have often laid down on my side to search the cañon wall far away [for a way?] to its summit.

[W. H. POWELL, the *Chicago Evening Journal*, July 19, 1869]
Continuing our way from this place on the morning of the 31st [of May], it became necessary to proceed with the greatest caution, as the rapids became more and more dangerous; and the most skillful handling of the oars was required to prevent the boats from being hurled by the water against the

rocks that strewed the bed of the river, and dashed to pieces. Finding now only a succession of rapids, many of which we had to let the boats over with ropes, we proceeded in this manner. The light boat, carrying no freight, and manned by two oarsmen and a pilot, the commander of the expedition, took the lead. The pilot closely observing the best course to take to avoid rocks, ran the boat ashore as soon as possible after running the rapids, and then signalled the direction, with a red flag, to the other boats. After bailing the water from the boats, which were often half-filled by the waves and breakers of the rapids, and if the next rapid was thought to be practicable, we rowed into the stream, and the current soon carried us to the next Signal Station. In this manner 25 or 30 miles were made during the 31st of May and the 1st day of June, and....

[SUMNER] **May 31st.** — This morning Professor, Bradley, and Dunn went up the river two miles to examine some rocks and look for a lost blank book. Howland and Goodman climbed a high mountain on the west side to get a good view of the country at large, and so draw a good map. All ready by ten o'clock, when we pull out and are off like the wind; ran about two miles through a rapid and into still water for half an hour, then to a bad rapid through which no boat can run; full of sunken rocks, and having a fall of about ten feet in two hundred yards. We were compelled to let our boats down along the west side with ropes from men holding the line, two men with oars keeping them off the rocks; made the passage in about two hours, and ran a large number of them in ten miles travel.

About 5 o'clock, we came to the worst place we had seen yet; a narrow gorge full of sunken rock for 300 yards, though which the water ran with a speed that threatened to smash everything to pieces that would get into it. All the boats were landed as quick as possible on the east side of the river, when we got out to examine the best point to get through, found ourselves on the wrong side of the river, and how to cross it was the next question. We all plainly saw that it would be no child's play. Dunn and the trapper finally decided to take the small boat across or smash her to pieces; made the passage safe, unloaded and returned to relieve the freight boats, they taking out half their loads by making two trips with the freight boats and five with the small; we got everything safely across where we wanted it by sunset. Had supper, turned in, and in two minutes all were in dreamland.

☀ Day #9

[BRADLEY] **June 1st. 69**. Let the boats down a little way this morning and then got in and went down like lightning for a very long distance until we came again to so bad a place we had to let down again after which we passed on for many miles sometimes going like a racehorse until near night when we when we came upon a place where the red sandstone from the mountain had fallen into and blocked up the river making a heavy fall. Have unloaded and taken one boat down with ropes but, night coming on, we shall wait until morning before we take the rest down the fall.

We unload them and, attaching a strong rope to each end, we let them down without much injury to the boats, but we have to carry the rations arround [sic] on our backs, and the shore is filled with huge bowlders [sic] recently fallen from the mountain. We shall have a hard day's work to get all arround tomorrow for each of the three large boats has over 2000 lbs baggage. The river looks smoothe [sic] below and as the mountains begin to slope more, we feel certain that we are getting out of this succession of rappids.

Weather has been pleasant for the past two days but threatens rain tonight. Named the falls "Ashley Falls" for we found his name on the rocks beside them. Named the cañon "Red Cañon" for it is chiefly red sand-stone.

[O. G. HOWLAND, *ROCKY MOUNTAIN NEWS,* July 17, 1869, written in camp at Mouth of Bear River on the Green, June 19, 1869] [June 1] We had to let our boats down past some bad rocks once in this cañon, and made a portage of 200 yards past Ashley Falls — so named by us from finding on the rock there, this: "Ashley, 1825."

[J. W. POWELL, *Chicago Tribune*, published July 19, 1869/ written in Flaming Gorge, on Green River, June 6, 1869] The day following [June 1] we had an exciting ride. The river glided and rolled down the cañon at a wonderful rate. No rocks in the way to stop us, we made almost railroad speed. Here and there the water would rush into a narrow gorge, the rocks at the side rolling it to the centre in great waves, and the boats would go leaping and bounding over these like things of life. They reminded me of scenes I had witnessed in Middle Park. Herds of startled deer bounded though forests beset with fallen timber. I mentioned the resemblance to some of the hunters, and so striking was it that it came to be a common expression, "See the blacktails jumping the logs." Sometimes these waves would break, and their waters roll over the boats, which necessitated much bailing, and sometimes we had to stop for that purpose. It was thought by members of the party that at some points we ran at the rate of a mile per minute [60 miles per hour].

I estimated that we ran twelve miles in one hour, stoppages included. The distance was thought to be much more by others of the party. Last spring I had a conversation with an old Indian who told me of one of his tribe making the attempt to run this cañon in a canoe with his wife and little boy. "The rocks," he said, holding his hands above his head, his arms vertical, and looking between them to the heavens, "the rocks h-e-a-p h-e-a-p high! The water hoo-woogh, hoo-woogh, hoo-woogh! Water pony (the boat) heap buck! Water ketch 'em! No see 'em Ingin any more! No see 'em papoose any more!" Those who have seen these wild Indian ponies rear alternately before and behind, or "buck," as it is called in the vernacular, will appreciate his description.

At last turning a point we came to calm water, but with a threatening roar in the distance. Gradually approaching this roar, we came to falls and tied up just above them on the left bank. Here we had to make a portage. We unloaded the boats; then fastening a long line to the bow and another to the stern of one we moored it close to the edge of the falls. The stern line was taken below the falls and made fast, the bow line was taken by five or six men and the boat let down as long as they could hold it; then, letting go, the boat ran over and was caught by the lower rope. Getting one boat over that night we rested until morning;

[W. H. POWELL, the *Chicago Evening Journal*, **July 19, 1869]** ....on the afternoon of the latter day [June 1] we came to a direct fall of 12 or 14 feet. The current is scarcely perceptible for some distance above the falls, and we ran our boats ashore, without danger, within but a few feet of where the water makes a perpendicular descent, and is beaten into foam on the rocks below.

[SUMNER] June 1st. — After an early breakfast, all hands went to work letting the boats down with ropes, made the passage in three hours, when we jumped aboard again, and off we go like a shot; ran through about a dozen rapids in the course of ten miles, when we came to some signs of the country opening out. The walls were getting lower and not so rough, and the current gradually slackened till it almost ceases. As the roaring of the rapids dies away above us, a new cause of alarm breaks in upon us from below. We ran along on the still water, with a vague feeling of trouble ahead, for about two miles, when, turning an abrupt corner, we came in sight of the first fall, about three hundred yards below us. Signalled the freight boats to land, when the *Emma* was run down within a rod of the fall and landed on the east side. Her crew then got out to reconnoitre; found a fall of about ten feet in twenty-five. There is a nearly square rock in the middle of the stream about twenty-five by thirty feet, the top fifteen feet above the water. There are many smaller ones all the way across, placed in such a manner that the fall is broken into steps, two on the east side, three on the west. We all saw that a portage would have to be made here. Without any loss of time the *Emma Dean* was unloaded and pushed into the stream, four men holding the line, the remainder of the party stationed on the rocks, each with oar, to keep her from being driven on some sharp corners and smashed into pieces. Got her under the fall in fifteen minutes, when we returned, unloaded *Kitty's Sister*, had supper and went to sleep on the sand. There is not much of a canyon at the falls. Three hundred yards from the east side there is a cliff about 450 feet high, from whence the rocks have fallen to make the dam.

☀ Day #10

[BRADLEY] June 2nd. 69. Had the boats all over the fall and loaded at 11 A.M. and were onboard and away again immediately after dinner. Have run over 15 miles and camped at 3 P.M. in what hunters call "Little Brown's Hole." The camp is green and grassy and our beds are made beneath two noble pines. The hills arround seem low after passing such huge mountains as we have had for several days. The rapids have been more noisy today than yesterday but the bowlders have not been so thick as usual, and a general improvement in the water as the hills grow lower. The men are out hunting and have not yet come in, but if they have their usual luck, *we shall have bacon for breakfast.* I am too tired to go out for specimens today. Think the hills are too much covered with earth to be good ground for foccils. The hunters have come in as usual without game. But the Major has brought in two grouce [sic] which will make a nice breakfast. The sky is clear — weather warm and delightful.

[J. W. POWELL, *Chicago Tribune*, published July 19, 1869/ written in Flaming Gorge, on Green River, June 6, 1869] [T]hen [June 2] [we] made a trail among the rocks, packed the cargoes to a point below the falls, ran over the remaining boats, and were ready to start before noon.

On a rock, by which our trail ran, was written "Ashley," with a date, one figure of which was obscure — some thinking it was 1825, others, 1855. I had been told by old mountaineers of a party of men starting down the river, and Ashley was mentioned as one; and the story runs that the boat was swamped, and some of the party drowned in the cañon below. This word "Ashley" is a warning to us and we resolve on great caution. "Ashley Falls" is the name we have given the cataract. The river is very narrow here; the right wall vertical; the left towering to a great height, but a vast pile of broken rocks between it and the river; and some of the rocks, broken from the ledge, have rolled out into the channel, and caused the fall. One rock, "as large as a barn," stands in the middle of the stream, and the water breaks to either side. (Now, barns are of two sizes, large and small; take your choice.) The water plunges down about ten or twelve feet, and then is broken by rocks into a rapid below.

Near the lower end of Red Cañon there is a little valley where a stream comes down on either side from the mountain summits in the distance. Here we camped for the night under two beautiful pines.

[W. H. POWELL, the *Chicago Evening Journal*, July 19, 1869] On the morning of the 2d [of June] we unloaded our boats and let them over the falls by tying a rope to either end of a boat, and then fastening one of the ropes to a rock below the falls, held the boat with the other till taken from our hands by the force of the water, but held by the rope below; and by 11 o'clock in the morning the portage was made, and we continued down the stream. The velocity of the current now steadily increased till we attained a rate of almost railroad speed. The river, however, was comparatively free from rocks, and we stopped only to bail the water from the boats. And now, as we looked down the long vista of the narrow cañon, while we were sliding down an inclined plane, in fact "coasting," the walls seemed to meet where the river turned round a short bend; the water was lost from sight, and the earth had opened, we imagined, to gulp us down. The illusion is dispelled as we round the bend of the river, and dashing through a succession of breakers, we suddenly debouch into a beautiful valley. [This is the final known writing by W. H. Powell on this expedition.]

[SUMNER] June 2nd. — All out to breakfast: dispatched it, and let *Kitty's Sister* over the falls as we did the small boat. Then came the real hard work, carrying the freight a hundred yards or more over a mass of loose rocks, tumbled together like the ruins of some old fortress. Not a very good road to pack seven thousand pounds of freight. Got the loads of the two boats over, loaded them, and moved down three hundred yards to still water; tied up and returned to the other boats, to serve them the same; got everything around in still water by 11 o'clock; had dinner and smoked all around; distance from Bee-hive Point unknown; course east of south; continuous canyon of red sand-stone; estimated height one thousand feet; three highest perpendicular walls estimated at two thousand two hundred feet; named Red Canyon; on a rock the east side there is the name and date — "Ashley, 1825" — scratched on evidently by some trapper's knife; all aboard, and off we go down the river; beautiful river that increases its speed as we leave the fall [Ashley Falls], till it gets a perfect rapid all the way, but clear of sunken rocks; so we run through the waves at express speed; made seventeen miles through Red Stone canyon in less than an hour, running time, the boats bounding through the waves like a school of porpoise. The *Emma* being very light is tossed about in a way that threatens to shake her to pieces, and is nearly as hard to ride as a Mexican pony. We plunge along, singing, yelling, like drunken sailors, all feeling that such rides do not come every day. It was like sparking a black eyed girl — just dangerous enough to be exciting. About three o'clock we came suddenly out to a beautiful valley about two by five miles in extent. Camped about the middle of it, on the west side, under two large pine trees; spread our bedding out to dry, while we rested in the shade. Two of the party came in at sunset, empty handed except the Professor, he being fortunate enough to get a brace of grouse. Spread our blankets on the clean green grass, with no roof but the old pines above us, through which we could see the sentinel stars shining from the deep blue, pure sky, like happy spirits looking out from the blue eyes of a pure hearted woman.

As we are guided on this voyage by the star in the blue, so may it be on the next, by the *spirit* in the blue.

☀ Day #11

[BRADLEY] June 3rd. 69. After eating a hearty breakfast of fried grouce and hot biscuit went out to hunt for game and foccils. Found neither but found the country just as I expected, too much covered with trees and earth to be an interesting place to study geology. Think it will not be many years before these green hills will be covered with cattle and dotted here and there with the homes of ranchmen, for the hillsides are green and watered with little mountain torrents that seem to leap and laugh down the hillsides in wild delight. Can stand on almost any eminence and overlook thousands and thousands of acres of most excellent grazing land, and we have lowered our altitude and latitude until it is warm enough to raise almost any kind of vegetables that will grow in northern New England. Think it would pay well to buy cattle in Texas and bring them here to fatten and then send them to market, but it would not pay to raise horses for the Indians (Utes) would steal too many of them to make it profitable. Have not yet seen any Indians on our journey and if we do they will be Utes, and they are friendly and we are prepared to trade with them.

I returned to camp at 12 M., and found all the hunters in before me except one who is still out. Hope he may have better luck that the rest, for they, like me, could see no game, though the hills and ravines are covered with tracks of deer & mountain sheep. And yesterday just before we reached this place we saw three mountain sheep and fired at them from the boats, but the shot had no effect except to frighten them, and they ran up the almost perpendicular clifts as fast as a deer could run on level ground. They will scale any cragg [sic] however broken or giddy and seem to feel no fear except the single one of being shot.

Have just been fishing and have caught 12 of the finest whitefish I ever saw. The cook [Hawkins] has just taken them from my boat and it is about all he wants to carry. Some of them will weigh 4 lbs. They have been biting very fast while a shower has been coming on but it is over now and they seem to have left the ground. On account of showers we have just pitched the tents. There was a beautiful rainbow about sunset and it looks now like fair weather tomorrow. The last hunter is in, and if we were dependent on them for subsistence, we should be as fat as "Job's turkey" in a few weeks for they diddent [sic] bring in enough game to make a grease spot.

[J. W. POWELL, *Chicago Tribune***, published July 19, 1869/ written in Flaming Gorge, on Green River, June 6, 1869]** The next day [June 3] we spread our rations, clothes, &c., out to dry, and several went out for a hunt. I had a walk of five or six miles up a pine grove park, its grassy carpet bedecked with crimson velvet flowers, set in groups on the stems of a cactus that was like a huge pear; groups of painted cups were seen here and there, with yellow blossoms protruding through scarlet bracts. Little blue-eyed flowers were hid away in the grass, and the air was fragrant with a white flower of the family "Rosaccae." A mountain brook runs through the midst, which below was dammed by a beaver. 'Twas a quiet place for retirement from the raging waters of the cañon.

Well, I am only half way down to this camp, and my letter is now long; I'll write again. Good night. — J. W. Powell

[SUMNER] June 3d. — Laid over to-day to dry out, and take observations. Several of the party hunting, but killed nothing. In the evening some of the boys got out fishing tackle and soon had the bank covered with queer looking fish — two species of them — one a sort of mongrel of mackerel, sucker and white fish; the other an afflicted cross of white fish and lake trout. Take a piece of raw pork and a paper of pins, and make a sandwich, and you have the mongrels. Take out the pork and you have a fair sample of the edible qualities of the other kinds. From this camp to Beehive Point is called by the Professor, Red Canyon, not very appropriately, as there are two distinct and separate canyons. This park is the best land we have seen, so far; good land; season long enough to raise rye, barley and potatoes, and all kinds of vegetables that would mature in four months. Irrigation not necessary, but if it should be, there is a beautiful clear trout stream [Little Davenport Creek] running through the middle of it that can be thrown on almost any part of it at comparatively little cost. Counting agriculture out, there is money for whoever goes in there and settles, and raises stock. It is known by the frontiersmen as "Little Brown's Hole." Altitude 6,000 ft. Game in abundance in the mountains south of the park; good trail to Green River City, and there could be a good wagon road made without a great outlay of money. All turn in early, as we want an early start in the morning.

☀ Day #12

[BRADLEY] June 4th. 69. Made an early start and have run rapidly up to this time (12. M.) when stopped for dinner. Have had a very pleasant run of it, only few rappids and mostly deep water. Got wet once where the river was full of islands and all the boats grounded. But all were got off without injury. We find that the two men who started in a boat from the same point we did only a few days before we [sic] us have passed through safe and their boat lies where we are now lying. They are *prospectors*. The weather has been very fine this A.M. but it now threatens a shower. The light boat signals to move on so must stop writing until we camp for the night. Camped about two miles below the point at which we stopped for dinner and the Major made an ineffectual attempt to get an observation. Camped for the night.

[O. G. HOWLAND, *ROCKY MOUNTAIN NEWS*, July 17, 1869, written in camp at Mouth of Bear (Yampa) River on the Green, June 19, 1869] [June 3-7] We got through this cañon to Brown's Little Hole on the 2nd day of June. Here we lay until the morning of the fourth, and then went sweeping down through another cañon of about six miles length, past the mouth of Red creek, into the upper end of Brown's Hole, then through Swallow Cañon, which, by the way, is as smooth all the way — three miles — as a mirror, and camped in the Hole until the morning of the sixth, and ran down to the head of Ladore [sic] cañon at the lower end of Brown's Hole, passing the mouth of the Vermillion river five miles above. Here we stopped in camp to climb walls of cañon and take barometric observations for hight [sic]. The hight of Flaming Gorge we have calculated to be 1,200 feet above the river. The hight of Red Cañon walls from 1,500 to 3,000, estimated, not measured; at Ladore cañon head the walls measured by barometer 2,068 feet. Blacktail Cliff, near the middle of the cañon, measured 2,207 feet. There are some higher points than those measured; probably the highest standing four or five miles back from the river bed would come near to 3,000 feet.

[J. W. POWELL, *Chicago Tribune*, published July 19, 1869/ written in Flaming Gorge, on Green River, June 7, 1869] On the 4th of June we came down into Brown's Hole. Half way down the valley a spur of the Red Mountain stretches across the river, which cuts a cañon through it. Here the walls are comparatively low, but vertical, and vast multitudes of swallows have built their adobe houses on their sides. The waters are deep and quiet; but the swallows are swift and noisy enough, sweeping about in their curved paths through the air and chattering from the rocks, the young birds stretching their little heads on naked necks through the doorways of their mud nests and clamoring for food. They are a lively people.

So we called this Swallow Cañon. Stillwater Cañon was suggested as a name. Still down the quiet river we glide until an early hour in the afternoon, when we went into camp under a giant cottonwood tree, standing a little way back from the river, on the river bank. By night wild geese and ducks had been shot and a mess of good fish taken. We have a good supply of fish usually, and some birds, though the birds are not fine eating right now.

[SUMNER] June 4th. — All afloat early, feeling ready for anything after our rest. Had another splendid rapid ride of six or eight miles and came to the mouth of Red Fork, a most disgusting looking stream, coming in from the east, off the "Bitter Creek Desert." It is about ten feet wide, red as blood, smells horrible and tastes worse. Passed on through five miles more of canyon and came to "Brown's Hole," a large valley, about twenty miles long and five wide — splendid grass on it. Passed on about the middle of the valley and camped at the mouth of a small trout stream, coming in from the east, named on Fremont's map, "Tom Big Creek." Had dinner and moved down about two miles and camped on the west side of Green river, under a great cottonwood tree that would furnish shade and shelter for a camp of two hundred men. Hall killed several ducks in a lake near camp, and in the evening Bradley, Howland and Hall caught a large number of fish.

☀ Day #13

[BRADLEY] June 5. 69. Remained at same point all day but as usual could get no observations on account of clouds and rainy weather. Went acrost [sic] the river with two men to carry the line and measure out the bluffs a distance of 3 1/2 miles and it extends along the river for 15 or 20 miles affording excellent grazing land if anyone wishes to raise cattle here. Shot a rattlesnake but did not stop to count the rattles as the men were in haste to return. Saw many trout in a small brook about 3 miles from the river. Shot at them with my pistol but did not kill any. Returned to camp around noon and after dinner courted "Tired nature's sweet restorer" for a few hours and then went out and caught whitefish enough for supper and breakfast.

[J. W. POWELL, *Chicago Tribune*, published July 19, 1869/ written in Flaming Gorge, on Green River, June 7, 1869] The next day [June 5], with one of the men, I climbed a mountain off on the right. A long spur with broken ledges of rock, juts down nearly to the river. Along its crest, or up on the hogback, as it is called, I make the climb. Dunn, who was climbing to the same point, went up the gulch. Two hours of hard work brought us to the summit. These mountains are all verdure-clad, pine and cedar forests are set about green parks, and snow-clad mountains are seen in the distance to the west. The planes [sic] of the upper Green stretch out to the north until they are lost in the blue heavens, but the half of this river cleft range intervenes, and the river valley itself is at our feet. These mountains beyond the river are split into long ridges nearly parallel with the valley. On the farther ridge to the north four creeks are formed. These cut through the intervening ridges — one of which is much higher than that on which they head — by cañon gorges; then they run in gentle curves across the valley to the river, their banks set with willows, box elders and aspen groves. To the east you look up the Valley of the Vermilion [sic], up which Fremont found his path on his way to the great parks of the Colorado.

The reading of the barometer taken, we start down again, in company, and reach camp, tired and hungry, which does not abate one whit of our enthusiasm as we tell of the day's work with its glory of landscape.

That night my sleep was sweet, under the cottonwood tree.

At daybreak [of June 5] a chorus of birds awoke me. It seems as though all the birds of the region had come to the old tree — several species of warblers, and meadowlarks in great numbers, with woodpeckers and flickers, and wild geese on the river. I reclined on my elbow and watched a meadow-lark in the grass near by me for a time, and then woke my bed-fellow to listen to my Jenny Lind. A morning concert for me — none of your matinees. Our cook has been an ox-driver, or "bull-whacker," on the plains in one of those long trains now seen no more, and he has learned their ways. In the very midst of the concert his voice broke in: "Roll out! roll out! bulls in the corral! chain up the gap! roll out! roll out!" with a voice like that of a wagon-boss and night-herder combined and multiplied by two.

[SUMNER] June 5th. — This morning we were all awakened by the wild birds singing in the old tree above our heads. The sweet songs of birds, the fragrant odor of wild roses, the low, sweet rippling of the ever murmuring river at sunrise in the wilderness, made everything as lovely as a poet's dream. I was just wandering into paradise; could see the dim shadow of the dark-eyed houris, when I was startled by the cry, "Roll out; bulls in the corral; chain up the gaps" — our usual call to breakfast. The houris vanished, and I rolled out to fried fish and hot coffee. Professor and Dunn climbed the hill south of camp two miles from the river — hight, 2200 feet. Howland spent the day dressing up his maps; Bradley, Seneca and Hall crossed to the east side and measured off a geological section. The remainder of the party spent the day as best suited them. Measured the old tree; circumference 5 ft. from the ground, 23 1/2 ft.

☀ Day #14

[BRADLEY] June 6. 69. Started early this morning but have made only 15 miles. The river is so broad and still and the wind contrary that we have had to row all the way and I feel quite weary this night. We would rather have rappids than still water, but think I shall be accommodated for we have now reached the cañon at the lower end of "Brown's Hole" and have camped tonight at the mouth of the cañon. It looks like a rough one for the walls are very high and straight and the sides are of sand-stone much broken into seams but at the mouth nearly perpendicular; in such the worst boulders have been found, and I expect them below here.

[J. W. POWELL, *Chicago Tribune*, published July 19, 1869/ written in Flaming Gorge, on Green River, June 7, 1869] Our next day's journey [June 6] was to this point, the head of the cañon, made by the river where it turns to the southwest and cuts through the southern half of the range.

[SUMNER] June 6th. — Took our time in getting off, as we had but a short journey before us for the day; but it proved a pretty hard one before we got done with it. No sooner had we started than a strong head-wind sprung up directly in our faces. Rowed about twenty-five miles against it — no easy task, as the river is a hundred and fifty yards wide, with hardly any current. Saw thousands of ducks of various kinds; killed a few, and one goose. Camped at the head of a canyon at the southern end of the valley, on the east side of the river under a grove of box elder trees. The Professor and Hall caught another mess of fish.

☀ Day #15

[BRADLEY] June 7. 69. Have been lying in camp all day just where we came last night; have climbed the mountain and find it exactly 2085 ft. above the level of the river. The scenery from the summit is grand. We could see the river part of the way for 6 or 7 miles. It is very rapid and noisy but we hope not dangerous. Shall probably try it tomorrow. Nothing of interest has transpired.

[J. W. POWELL, *Chicago Tribune*, published July 19, 1869/ written in Flaming Gorge, on Green River, June 7, 1869] This morning

I climbed to the summit of the cliff on the left in one hour and thirteen minutes, and found it above camp two thousand and eighty-six feet. The rocks are split with fissures deep and narrow, sometimes a hundred feet to the bottom. A grove of lofty pines find root in fissures that are filled with loose earth and decayed vegetation. On a rock I found a pool of clear, cold water, caught from yesterday's shower. After a good drink, I walked out to the brink of the cliff and looked down into the waters below. I can do this now; but it has taken two years of mountain climbing to school my nerves to the state when I can sit with my feet over the brink and calmly look at the waters below. And yet I cannot look on quietly and see another do the same. I must either beg him to come away, or turn my back and leave.

The cañon walls are buttressed on a grand scale, and deep alcoves are cut out; ragged crags crown the cliffs, and there is the river roaring below. While I write, I am sitting on the same rock where I sat last spring, with Mrs. Powell, looking down into this cañon. When I came down, at noon, the sun shone in splendor on its vermilion walls shaded into green and gray when the rocks are lichened over. The river fills the channel from wall to wall. The cañon opened like a beautiful portal to a region of glory. Now, as I write, the sun is going down and the shadows are setting in the cañon. The vermilion gleams and rosy hues, the green and gray tints are changing to sombre brown above, and black shadows below. Now 'tis a black portal to a region of gloom.

And that is the gateway through which we enter our voyage [of?] exploration tomorrow — and what shall we find?

[SUMNER] June 7th. — Still in camp. Professor and Dunn measured the wall of the canyon on the east side; Bradley geologising; Howland and Goodman sketching; Rhodes brushing up *Kitty's Sister*, swearing all the time that she can stand more thumps than Kitty ever could. Professor and Dunn came in at noon and reported the wall 2086 ft. All the party in camp and rest of the day; wind and rain in the evening. Distance from the mouth of Henry's Fork 90 miles [more accurately 74]; general course of the river 25 degrees south of east. The valley called Brown's Hole is a pretty good piece of land; would make a splendid place to raise stock; it has been used for several years as a winter herding ground for the cattle trains. Last winter there about 4000 head of oxen pastured in it without an ounce of hay. I saw them in March and am willing to swear that half of them were in good enough order for beef.

1874 photo of the Gate of Lodore. Photo by James Pilling.

"Gate of Lodore" (Thomas Moran etching from *Canyons of the Colorado*).

Chapter 3.

DISASTERS IN THE CANYON OF LODORE, *June 8 - 18*

The 1869 crew's whitewater innocence is ground into dust and blown away in a hurricane of whitewater on the first day of what will prove to be a grueling ten-day struggle down the Canyon of Lodore's 18+ miles. This trial by fire will cost the expedition the destruction of the No Name, the near drownings of several crew members, the loss of one third of their rations, equipment, and personal gear, and, soon afterward, the loss of yet more equipment to fire. The crew's wrestling match with the river will also rack up for them uncounted bruises, cuts, and body slams during their protracted sessions of lining and portaging leaving them battered in their bodies and psyches. Far more serious, the episode at Disaster Falls will sow the fatal seeds of disintegration in the solidarity of the crew. This humbling experience prompts Bradley to note: "O how great is He who holds it in the hollow of his hand and what pygmies we who strive against it."

Day #16 [BRADLEY] June 8. 69. Started quite early this morning and find that what seemed comparatively easy rapids from the top of the mountains are quite bad ones, and as we advanced they grew worse until we came to the wildest rapid yet seen. I succeeded in making a landing in an eddy just above where the dangerous part begins. So did one of the other heavy boats.

But one (the "No Name") with three men in it [Oramel and Seneca Howland and Frank Goodman] with one third of our provisions, half our mess-kitt [sic], and all three of the barometers went over the rapid, and though the men escaped with their lives yet they lost all of their clothing, bedding, &c., everything except shirt and drawers, the uniform in which we all pass rapids. It is a serious loss to us and we are rather low spirited [sic] tonight for we must camp right at the head of a roaring rapid more than a mile in length and in which we have already lost one of our boats and nearly lost three of our number. Yet I trust the sun of another day will bring better cheer. "All's well that ends well," but the end is not yet.

[O. G. HOWLAND, *ROCKY MOUNTAIN NEWS*, July 17, 1869, written in camp at Mouth of Bear River on the Green, June 19, 1869]

We started down the cañon of Ladore [sic] the morning of the eighth [of June], dancing over the rapids at railroad speed until a foaming cataract ahead warned us to haul in and examine it. Had to let our boats down by ropes a few hundred yards past the worst of the rapids, and after dinner launched out again into the current and proceeded rapidly, only stopping to bail when breakers filled us too full to run; rapids coming in quick succession. About one o'clock the signal boat signals at the foot of a very bad rapid to go shore; boats nearly full of water — two were made fast, but owing to not understanding the signal, the crew of the "No Name" failed very effectually, owing in the main, to having so much water aboard as to make her nearly or quite unmanageable; otherwise, the mistake was seen by us in time to save her.

Our next move after failing to get in, was to run her as long as she would float, and gradually work her ashore on a bar below, where, from the spray and foam, showed shoal water. She sunk, however, striking rocks as she passed along, until she was stove up so bad that there was no use to stay by her any longer, so the crew all at the same time concluded quickly to strike for the bar. She had knocked two of us off twice, but we had clung to her and waited for another thump to spring for the bar or shoals, which we were rapidly nearing.

It came quickly. One of us, Frank Goodman, was swept over and immediately struck for the bar. I told my brother to jump, and I made a spring, getting quite an impetus from her deck, which was about six inches under water, striking among the rocks in about six feet of water; but by a stroke or two more in the lee of the rocks where the current was broke, I succeeded in anchoring myself safely on the shoal of the bar. My brother struck the shoal one hundred feet lower down, and Goodman was clinging for dear life to a boulder as big as a barrel fifty above and asking for assistance.

He had taken aboard a good deal of water, but we managed to get a root from some drift on the bar and reached it to him, to which he clung until we got him out. During this time, those on shore were rushing down to our help, but we so completely distanced them in our ride through the waves, that we were out of sight wholly before we struck the bar.

We did not any of us receive any serious injury, barely a few bumps on our shins as the waves dashed us against the rocks in the shoal. Our sand bar had a large line trunk drifted upon it, from the pitch of which, after drying our matches, we succeeded in starting a fire.

Our position on the bar soon began to look serious, as the water was rapidly rising, so much so, that what were boulders imbedded in the sand when we landed, was getting like the shoal above. However, Mr. Sumner, as soon as they could get the little boat down to us and dump her cargo, crossed the channel to where we could reach his boat. We then turned [towed?] the boat up among the shoals as far as we could stand, and wade, when three got in her and the other held her nose until they got their oars in position ready for a sharp venture.

Her nose was pushed into the current, the oars playing rapidly, struck one rock, tilting us up at an angle of of [sic] forty-five degrees; off in the foam below and struck shore twenty-five yards above a perfect hell of foam, safe and sound, barring a few bruises and a slight ducking.

With this boat we lost 2,000 pounds of provisions, besides the bedding and entire clothing of the crew of the three men, with the exception of a shirt and a pair of drawers apiece. We did not go thus scantily clad for comfort but for safety in case of any mishap. Any superfluous clothing is a hindrance in the water. We camped here until the morning of the tenth, having reclaimed from the wreck below a barometer and two or three thermometers, a blue keg and some wax candles, afloat. Nothing more has turned up since except a sack of flour, too far gone to be of use. Our three guns, ammunition, pistols, knives, belts, scabbards, &c. although we tried all kinds of methods, we could not find. My notes up that time were all lost, as also our topographical work, instruments, &c.

After finding it of no use to seek further over the lost cargo, we let our boats about three-fourths of a mile to the head of another fall, where we camped. On the eleventh we made a portage of provisions 100 yards and camped under the edge of overhanging rock 1,000 feet above us, with a beach of sand about 16 feet wide and 100 long.

[J. W. POWELL, *Chicago Tribune*, published August 20, 1869, written on June 18, 1869] On the 8th [June] our boats entered the Cañon of Lodore — a name suggested by one of the men [Andy Hall], and it has been adopted. We soon came to rapids, over which the boats had to be taken with lines. We had a succession of these until noon. I must explain the plan of running these places. The light boat, *Emma Dean*, with two good oarsmen and myself explore them, then with a flag I signal the boats to advance, and guide them by signals around dangerous rocks. When we come to rapids filled with boulders, I sometimes find it necessary to walk along the shore for examination. If 'tis thought possible to run, the light boat proceeds. If not, the others are flagged to come on to the head of the dangerous place, and we let down with lines, or make a portage.

At the foot of one of these runs, early in the afternoon, I found a place where it would be necessary to make a portage, and, signalling the boats to come down, I walked along the bank to examine the ground for the portage, and left one of the men [Dunn] of my boat to signal the others to land at the right point. I soon saw one of the boats land all right, and felt no more care about them. But five minutes after I heard a shout, and looking around, saw one of the boats coming over the falls. Captain Howland, of the *No Name*, had not seen the signal in time, and the swift current had carried him to the brink. I saw that his going over was inevitable, and turned to save the third boat. In two minutes more I saw that turn the point and head to shore, and so I went after the boat going over the falls. The first fall was not great, only two or three feet, and we had often run such, but below it continued to tumble down twenty or thirty feet more, in a channel filled with dangerous rocks that broke the waves into whirlpools and beat them into foam.

I turned just to see the boat strike a rock and throw the men and the cargo out. Still they clung to her sides and clambered in again and saved part of the oars, but she was full of water, and they could not manage her. Still down the river they went, two or three hundred yards to another rocky rapid just as bad, and the boat struck again amidships, and was dashed to pieces. The men were thrown into the river and carried beyond my sight. Very soon I turned the point, and could see a man's head above the waters seemingly washed about by a whirlpool below a rock. This was Frank Goodman clinging to the rock, with a grip on which life depended. As I came opposite I saw Howland trying to go to his aid from the island. He finally got near enough to Frank to reach him by the end of a pole, and letting go of the rock, he grasped it, and was pulled out. Seneca Howland, the Captain's brother, was washed farther down the island on to some rocks, and managed to get on shore in safety, excepting some bad bruises. This seemed a long time, but 'twas quickly done. And now the three men were on the island with a dangerous river on each side, and falls below.

The *Emma Dean* was soon got down, and Sumner, one of the men of my boat, started with it for the island. Right skilfully [sic] he played his oars, and a few strokes set him at the proper point, and back he brought his cargo of men. We were as glad to shake hands with them as if they had been on a voyage 'round the world and wrecked on a distant coast.

Down the river half a mile we found that the after-cabin of the boat, with part of the bottom ragged and splintered, had floated against a rock and stranded. There were valuable articles in the cabin, but on examination we concluded that life should not be risked to save them. Of course, the cargo of rations, instruments and clothing was gone. So we went up to the boats and made a camp for the night. No sleep would come to me in those dark hours before the day. Rations, instruments, &c., had been divided among the boats for safety, and we started with duplicates of everything that was a necessity to success; but in the distribution there was one exception, and the barometers were all lost. There was a possibility that the barometers were in the cabin lodged against a rock on the island — that was the cabin in which they had been kept. But then how to get to it? And the river was rising — would it be there tomorrow? Could I go out to Salt Lake and get barometers from New York? Well, I thought of many plans before morning, and determined to get them from the island, if they were there.

[SUMNER] June 8th. — Pulled out early and entered into as hard a day's work as I ever wish to see. Went about half a mile when we came to a terrible rapid, and had to let our boats down with ropes. Passed about a dozen bad rapids in the forenoon. Camped for dinner on the east side at the foot of a perpendicular rose-colored wall, about fifteen hundred feet; pulled out again at one o'clock; had proceeded about half a mile when the scouting boat came to a place where we could see nothing but spray and foam.

She was pulled ashore on the east side and the freight boats instantly signaled to land with us. The *Maid* and *Kitty's Sister* did so but the *No Name* being too far out in the current, and having shipped a quantity of water in the rapid above, could not be landed, though her crew did their best in trying to pull ashore at the head of the rapid; she struck a rock and swung into the waves sideways and instantly swamped. Her crew held to her while she drifted down with the speed of the wind; went perhaps 200 yards, when she struck another rock that stove her bow in; swung around again and drifted toward a small island in the middle of the river; here was a chance for her crew, though a very slim one. Goodman made a spring and disappeared; Howland followed next and made the best leap I ever saw made by a two-legged animal, and landed in water where he could touch the rocks on the bottom; a few vigorous strokes carried him safe to the island. Seneca was the last rat to leave the sinking ship, and made the leap for life barely in time; had he stayed aboard another second we would have lost as good and true a man as can be found in any place.

Our attention was now turned to Goodman, whose head we could see bobbing up and down in a way that might have provoked a hearty laugh had he been in a safe place. Howland got a pole that happened to be handy, reached one end to him and hauled him on the isle. Had they drifted fifty feet further down nothing could have saved them, as the river turned into a perfect hell of waters that nothing could enter and live.

The boat drifted into it and was instantly smashed to pieces. In half a second there was nothing but a dense foam, with a cloud of spray above it, to mark the spot.

The small boat was then unloaded and let down with ropes opposite the wrecked men on the island. The trapper crossed over and brought them safely ashore to the east side. She was then let down about a half a mile further, where we could see part of the stern cuddy of the wrecked boat on a rocky shoal in the middle of the river. Two of the boys proposed to take the small boat over and see how much of the lost notes could be recovered. The Professor looked ruefully across the foaming river but forbode the attempt.

All hands returned to the head of the rapids, feeling glad enough that there were no lives lost, a little sore at the loss of the boat and cargo of 2,000 pounds of provisions and ammunition, all the personal outfit of the crew, three rifles, one revolver, all the maps and most of the notes and many of the instruments that cannot be replaced in time to carry on the work this year, and do it right; ate supper of bread and bacon, and went to sleep under the scrubby cedars.

☀ Day #17

[BRADLEY] June 9. 69. Have lowered our boats and brought part of the baggage down with great labor, having first to clear an imperfect road through the broken rocks and stunted mountain cedars and have better luck with the wrecked boat than we anticipated for two of the men (Jack & Andy) with great risk have succeeded in getting a boat out to an island on which they found a small part of the boat and the barometers. They are what we cared the most about, after the men's outfit, for without them we should have to make the trip and never know the hight of the mountains which we pass through. We have plenty of rations left, much more than we care to carry arround the rappids. Especially when they are more than a mile long.

The scenery at this point is sublime. The red sand-stone rises on either side more than 2000 ft., shutting out the sun for much of the day while at our feet the river, lashed to a foam, rushes on with indescribable fury. O how great is He who holds it in the hollow of his hand and what pygmies we who strive against it. It will take us nearly or quite another day before we can start on again. Major & brother are gone ahead *to see what comes next.* Hope for a favorable report but can't rely on anything but actual tryal [sic] with the boats, for a man can't travel so far in a whole day in these cañons as we go in a single hour [by boat].

[J. W. POWELL, *Chicago Tribune*, published August 20, 1869, written on June 18, 1869] [June 9] After breakfast, the men started to make the portage, and I walked down to look at the wreck. There it was still on the island, only carried fifty or sixty feet farther on. A closer examination of the ground showed me it could easily be reached.

That afternoon Sumner and Hall volunteered to take the little boat and go to the wreck. They started, reached it and out came the barometers. Then the boys set up a shout; I joined them, pleased that they too should be so glad to save the instruments. When the boat landed on our side, I found that the only things saved from the wreck were the three barometers, the package of thermometers and a two-gallon keg of whiskey. This was what the men were shouting about. They had taken it on board, unknown to me,

"Wreck at Disaster Falls" drawn with a considerable injection of artist's license (Thomas Moran etching from *Canyons of the Colorado*).

and I am glad they did, for they think it does them good — as they are drenched every day by the melted snow that runs down this river from the summit of the Rocky Mountains — and that is a positive good itself.

Three or four days were spent in making this portage, nearly a mile long, and letting down the rapids that followed in quick succession.

[SUMNER] June 9th. — All up by sunrise and work at unloading the boats, ready for letting down with ropes. Got the boats and remaining cooking utensils over and opposite the wreck on shore. Had dinner, when Hall bantered one of the men [Sumner himself] to go over to the wreck and see what there was left. Away they went and got to it safely, after a few thumps on the rocks, and fished out three barometers, two thermometers, some spare barometer tubes, a pair of old boots, some sole leather, and a ten gallon cask of whiskey that had never been tapped. Not a sign of anything else. How to get back was the next question, it being impossible to go back over the route they came. A narrow, rocky race offered a chance to get through the island to the main channel. After half an hour's floundering in the water, among the rocks, they got through to the main channel, and dashing through some pretty rough passes, they reached the shore, where the rest of the party stood ready to catch the lines, their arms extended, like children reaching for their mother's apron strings.

The Professor was so much pleased about the recovery of the barometers that he looked as happy as a young girl with her first beau: tried to say something to raise a laugh, but couldn't. After taking a good drink of whiskey all around, we concluded to spend the remainder of the day as best suited. Some packed freight across the land for half a mile; some made moccasins for future use; the rest slept under the shade of the scrubby cedars.

☀ Day #18

[BRADLEY] June 10. 69. Brought down the rest of the stores and, having loaded the boats, we lowered them about a mile with ropes and crossed the river and camped for the night. The river in this cañon is not a succession of rappids — as we have found before — but a *continuous* rapid.

[J. W. POWELL, no entry for June 10]

[SUMNER] June 10th. — Out early again, and at work carrying the rest of our freight over the land. Had all done by noon; eat dinner, loaded up, and let down another two hundred yards with ropes, when we got aboard and rowed about half a mile. Crossed over to west side and let down another rapid through a narrow race. *Emma* and the *Maid* passed through safe but poor *Kitty's Sister* got a hole stove in her side. Camped for the night on the west side, on the sand.

 Day #19

Lining Hell's Half Mile in 1871. Photo by E.O. Beaman.

[BRADLEY] June 11. 69. Have been working like galley-slaves all day. Have lowered the boats all the way with ropes and once unloaded and carried the goods arround one very bad place. The rapid is still continuous and not improving. Where we are tonight it roars and foams like a wild beast.

The Major as usual has chosen the worst camping-ground possible. If I had a dog that would lie where my bed is made tonight I would kill him and burn his collar and swear I never owned him.

Have been wet all day and the water flies into the boats so badly that it is impossible to keep anything dry. The clothes in my valise are all wet and I have nothing dry to put on but fortunately it is not cold, for though I have only shirt and drawers on and they are only half dry yet I am not cold though the sun does not reach us more than 5 or 6 hours in the [day].

I fell to day while trying to save my boat from a rock and have a bad cut over the left eye which I fear will make an ugly scar. But what odds, it can't disfigure my ugly mug and it may improve it, who knows?

[J. W. POWELL, no entry for June 11]

[SUMNER] June 11th. — Rapids and portages all day. By hard work we made three miles. Passed the mouth of a small trout stream coming in from the west. Hall shot an osprey on her nest in the top of a dead pine, near the mouth of the creek. Camped for the night on the west side, under an overhanging cliff.

☀ Day #20

[BRADLEY] June 12. 69. Today has been the repetition of yesterday only more of it. We have carried the goods arround two bad places and run several others, one run of nearly or quite a mile is the largest for 4 days. We camp tonight in a fine spot on the east side of the cañon but below us about a stone's throw is another furious rapid near a mile long, past which we must take the goods tomorrow and if possible get our boats over, though the prospects of success are not bright. Still there is no retreat if we desired it. We must go on, and shall. And shall do doubt be successful — I am fishing while I write, but the fish in this cañon are scarce for the water is too swift for whitefish and too muddy for trout. The sun shone on us until nearly 5 o'clock this P.M. for we being on the east side and a notch on the bluff on the west afforded a clear space for it, and it was very fortunate for me as we landed here about 3 o'clock. I put out all my clothing, papers, &c., &c., and have got 2 hours good sun on them, which in this pure air will dry almost anything. My eye is very black today and, if is it not very *useful*, it is very ornimental [sic].

[O. G. HOWLAND, *ROCKY MOUNTAIN NEWS,* July 17, 1869, written in camp at Mouth of Bear River on the Green, June 19, 1869] On the twelfth we made a portage of 150 yards, loaded up, and ran down into smooth water just above heavy rapids, and camped. From the scene of the wreck to this point we have worked our way down over bad rapids and falls about four and a half miles.

[J. W. POWELL, *Chicago Tribune*, published August 20, 1869, written on June 18, 1869] On the night of the 12th, we camped in a beautiful grove of box elders on the left bank, and here we remained two days to dry out our rations, which were in a spoiling condition. A rest, too, was needed.

I must not forget to mention that we found the wreck of a boat near our own, that had been carried above high-water mark, and with it the lid of a bake oven, an old tin plate and other things, showing that some one else had been wrecked there and camped in the cañon after the disaster. This, I think, confirms the story of an attempt to run the cañon, some years ago, that has been mentioned before.

[SUMNER] June 12th. — More rapids that are impossible to run. Excessively hard work. Made three miles. Camped on the east side of the river in a grove of box elder trees, at the head of a long rapid. Will have to make another half mile cartage.

☀ Day #21

[BRADLEY] June 13. 69. We remain in camp today for we are tired out from the effects of constant hard labor and constant wetting. It is Sunday and the first one we have paid any attention to, and whether this is accident or design I can't tell but am inclined to believe it accidental for don't think anyone in the party except myself keeps any record of time or events [Jack Sumner and Major Powell *were* keeping journals though less detailed over time than Bradley's]. The sun reached our camp at 10 A.M. and will affoard [sic] us another excellent opportunity to dry clothing, &c. Our rations are getting very sour from constant wetting and exposure to a hot sun. I imagine we shall be sorry before the trip is up that we took no better care of them. It is none of my business, yet if we fail it will be want of judgment that will defeat it, and if we succeed, it will be *dumb luck*, not good judgment that will do it.

The men have all come in from hunting as ever without game. We frequently see mountain sheep as we pass along, and if we kept *still*, we might kill them. But as soon as we land, the men begin to shoot and make a great noise and the game for miles arround is allarmed [sic] and takes back from the river. This makes me think that these are not *hunters*, and I believe that if left to maintain themselves with their rifles they would feed worse than Job's turkey. They seem more like school boys on a holiday than men accustomed to live by the chase. But as I am no hunter myself I must not critisize [sic] others. Still as usual I have opinions.

[O. G. HOWLAND, *ROCKY MOUNTAIN NEWS*, July 17, 1869, written in camp at Mouth of Bear River on the Green, June 19, 1869] Here we stay in camp, night of the twelfth, the thirteenth, and fourteenth, to repair somewhat the raiment of the wrecked, and dry our cargoes, climb mountains, and to do what topographical work was lost as is fresh in memory.

[J. W. POWELL, no entry for June 13]

[SUMNER] June 13th. — Rested to-day, as we all need it very much. Three of the boys went hunting, but there is nothing in this part of the country but a few mountain sheep, and they stay where a squirrel could hardly climb. We are looking for better traveling pretty soon, as we have got to the point where the white sandstone caps the hard red, 2000 feet above our heads.

☀ Day #22

[BRADLEY] June 14. 69. Up to this hour (1 o'clock P.M.) we remain in camp. Have landed the provisions on the rocks above the rapid and spread them to dry. The weather is clear and while the sun reaches us, very warm. But our camp is finely shaded by box elder trees (a variety of the ash) that make it delightfully cool where our beds are made. Some of the men are making moccasins, some playing cards or reading, others mending clothing or sleeping, while I am lying flat on my back with a geology for a desk, writing. Major's brother lies beside me singing, "John Anderson, My Jo." The Major and Howland are fixing up as well as possible the map of the river over which we have passed, for all was lost in the lost boat and must be made again as correct as possible from memory.

I have been fixing my boat and calking [sic] the cubfins to keep my clothing dry while in the waves. Below each rapid there is a heavy sea and one would actually fancy himself in a gale at sea if he could not see the land so near him. Our boats being so heavily loaded ride the sea badly and that is the way we get so wet and get our clothing wet, for sometimes the boats will be nearly full before we can get through to smooth water again. We estimate that we have already come 15 miles in this cañon and it cannot be much longer unless it is longer than any we have seen. The longest before this was 25 miles. We are getting near the mouth of Bear [Yampa] River and hope for some favorable change after we reach it. If I knew I could keep them dry I would write a lot of letters but it is so uncertain that I must wait until we get into smoother water before I write for I think there will be no chance to send them for another month or more at this rate. Remained in camp all day.

[J. W. POWELL, *Chicago Tribune*, published August 20, 1869, written on June 18, 1869] On the 14th Howland and I climbed the walls of the cañon, on the west side, to an altitude of two thousand feet. On looking over to the west we saw a park five or six miles wide and twenty-five or thirty long. The cliff formed a wall between the cañon and the park, for it was eight hundred feet down the west side to the valley. A creek came winding down the park twelve hundred feet above the river and cutting the wall by a cañon; it at last plunged a thousand feet by a broken cascade into the river below.

[SUMNER] June 14th. — Still in camp; repaired a broken barometer and started our plunder over the Portage; Professor and Howland have been busy for two days restoring the lost maps.

☀ Day #23

[BRADLEY] June 15. 69. Another day finds us past that and at another five times as bad as the last. We have made a trail along the mountain side and think that from that point we can run it. We encamped for the night after making the trail. My boat was sunk while being lowered over the rapid this morning and all of my books and papers soaked with water and I fear both my albums and most of my photographs & tintypes spoiled. Some of them I value very highly for I can never replace them. My notes were soaked but I have dried them and since that have carried them in my *hat*. My clothing is of course all wet again but aside from the trouble of drying it, it is no matter for I need only shirt & drawers in this warm weather and lately have seldom worn anything else.

[O. G. HOWLAND, *ROCKY MOUNTAIN NEWS,* July 17, 1869, written in camp at Mouth of Bear River on the Green, June 19, 1869] The fifteenth of June we let down our boats a quarter of a mile, unloaded and made trail a quarter of a mile for tomorrow's portage.

[J. W. POWELL, *Chicago Tribune,* **published August 20, 1869, written on June 18, 1869]** The day after [June 15], while we made another portage, a peak on the east side was climbed by two of the men and found to be twenty-seven hundred feet high. On each side of the river, at this point, a vast amphitheatre has been cut out, with deep, dark alcoves and massive buttresses, and in these alcoves grow beautiful mosses and ferns.

[SUMNER] June 15th. — Made the Portage and ran a bad rapid at the lower end of the Portage and through half a mile of smooth water, when we came to another impassible rapid; unloaded boats and camped on the east side under some scrubby cedars. Rain at dark. Made a trail and turned in for the night.

☀ Day #24

[BRADLEY] June 16. 69. We labored hard all day and got all down. We shortened the distance somewhat by loading the boats and hauling them through a large eddy and then carrying the goods again acrost [sic] a point. We sank one boat today and another got away from us but we recovered both without serious dammage [sic]. We camp tonight on the top of a small rapid which we can run, and we hope and expect that the worst of this cañon is over for the softer rock is getting near the water, and the softer the rock the better the river generally. This cañon is mostly dark red sandstone containing much iron. What is coming is white sandstone containing lime and most of it is shaley. So we have the "testimony of the rocks" that the future is favorable.

[O. G. HOWLAND, *ROCKY MOUNTAIN NEWS,* **July 17, 1869, written in camp at Mouth of Bear River on the Green, June 19, 1869]** The sixteenth climbed Blacktail cliff, measured its hight with barometer, took the surrounding topography from its top, made portage of a quarter of a mile, and dropped down a mile to the Falls, and camped until the morning of the seventeenth.

[O. G. HOWLAND, *ROCKY MOUNTAIN NEWS*, **August 18, 1869, written in camp near mouths of Uinta and White rivers, on the Green, July 1, 1869.]** Another incident of interest I forgot to mention in my last letter, occurred on the sixteenth of June. Two of us had started out to climb Blacktail Cliff, for the purpose of measuring its hight by barometer, and to get the surrounding topography, while the rest made portage of provisions and let down boats. When we returned to camp it was deserted, and only one large boat was to be found. Soon, however, all appeared at camp and all were made aware of what had happened. After making the portage of provisions and letting down the little boat, they attempted to let down one of the large ones; but by paying out too much line to drop her around some big boulders, her nose got turned into the main current, into which she instantly shot so far that the combined strength of five men was unable to resist the action of the water, and she pulled away from them, shooting clear across the breakers to the opposite shore, into smoother water about a half mile below. The little boat was immediately manned and sent in pursuit. They overhauled her before she got into the next rapids, and tied her fast for the night. The next morning, taking her cargo and crew in the two boats, we ran down and across, loaded up and manned her with her usual cargo and crew, and went on our way rejoicing that we had not lost her entirely. She got one pretty severe thump in her stern, which stove a hole and made her leak badly; but at noon we repaired that, and she is now as good as ever.

At another time, prior to this, we were lucky enough to get our line snubbed around a rock about ten feet in diameter, when letting down past a similar place, which held her till she crossed the rapids twice and returned. On her second return we managed to get a bight of rope near her and pulled her in shore. She was in an awful fix though; full of water from stem to stern, and everything drenched to its fullest extent. Made portage of one-half mile the sixteenth, and let our boats down and loaded.

[J. W. POWELL, *Chicago Tribune*, published August 20, 1869, written on June 18, 1869] [June 16] While the men were letting the boats down the rapids, the *Maid of the Cañon* got her bow into the current too far and tore away from them, and the second boat was gone. So it seemed; but she stopped a couple of miles below in an eddy, and we followed close after. She was caught — damaged slightly by a thump or two on the rocks.

[SUMNER] June 16th. — Pulled out early and went to work with a will. While letting the *Maid* down with ropes she got crossways with the waves and broke loose from the five men holding the line, and was off like a frightened horse. In drifting down she struck a rock that knocked her stern part to pieces. Rhodes and the trapper jumped in the small boat and gave chase; caught her half a mile below. Got everything over by sunset and camped on the east side on a sand bar.

☀ **Day #25**

[BRADLEY] June 17. 69. Have had a little better running today. Have made over 5 miles. Ran many little rappids. Several times let down with ropes and once made a short portage. Have passed 5 or 6 whirlpools today, one so bad we had to take the boats around it with ropes. It whirled them around so fast we couldn't row them through it. One rapid we ran today was full of rocks and we all struck our boats and tonight they are leaking badly, but we can repair them with pitch from the mountain pine.

We camped for this night on a little point where the mountain pine and sage-brush was very thick, and the cook built his fire and had supper on the way when the fire spread to the pines. At first we took little notice of it but soon a whirlwind swept through the cañon and in a moment the whole point was one sheet of flames. We seized whatever we could and rushed for the boats and amid the rush of wind and flames we pushed out and dropped down the river a few rods. My handkerchief was burned that I had tied around my neck, and my *ears* and face badly scorched. We had hardly landed before the fire was again upon us and we were forced to run a bad rapid to escape it. We got through safely however and are alright tonight except that we lost most of our mess kit.

[O. G. HOWLAND, *ROCKY MOUNTAIN NEWS,* July 17, 1869, written in camp at Mouth of Bear River on the Green, June 19, 1869] [June 17] Morning of the seventeenth shouldered blankets, went down to the boats and let down loaded another half mile, then run half a mile, let down two hundred yards, make portage of forty yards, and then let down loaded two hundred yards more. Afterwards run down three and a quarter miles and camped. Morning of the eighteenth run down four a quarter miles to the mouth of Bear River, where we stay until the twenty-first.

"Fire in camp" (Coughlan S.C./W.V.S. etching in *Canyons of the Colorado*).

[O. G. HOWLAND, *ROCKY MOUNTAIN NEWS*, August 18, 1869, written in camp near mouths of Uinta and White rivers, on the Green, July 1, 1869.] Dear *News*: — My last letter gave you a hasty sketch of our trip from Green River City to the mouth of the Bear, and up to the eighteenth of June. I forgot to mention then a little incident in which the two elements — fire and water — played prominent parts. We had run in on smooth water, just above some falls, to camp for the night on a bench about fifty yards wide by a quarter mile in length, thickly overgrown by willows, cedar, sage and grass, so much so it was almost impossible to get through it; built a fire to cook grub by, and were unloading the boats to dry out things a little, when a heavy wind came sweeping up the river, scattering the fire in all directions over our small camp, and fanning into a blaze in a hundred different places the dry drift underneath the bushes. To beat a retreat to the rear was impossible, as the walls of the cañon rose perpendicular hundreds of feet above. Something must be done quickly — the boats were the only alternative — and a run over the falls. So tumbling in what little on shore could be reached, the boats were pulled out into the center of the river above the falls, the crew of each just having time to snatch off some of their clothing which was on fire, and smother the rest before the use of their oars was needed to engineer the boats down the fall. Luckily all three of the boats came in safe and sound. One of the crew came in hatless, another shirtless, a third without his pants, and a hole burned in the posterior portion of his drawers; another with nothing but drawers and shirt, and still another had to pull off his handkerchief from his neck, which was ablaze. With the loss of his eyelashes and brows, and a favorite mustache, and scorching of his ears [this victim was Bradley], no other harm was done. One of the party had gathered up our mess kit and started hastily for the boat, but the smoke and heat was [sic] so blinding that in his attempt to spring from the shore to the boat he lost his footing and fell, mess kit and all, in about ten feet of water, that put him out, (I mean the fire in his clothes,) and he crawled over the side of the boat as she was being pushed off, not worse, but better, if possible, for his ducking. Our mess kit, however, was lost, as also a number of other things, of which we felt the need quite often. We have since managed to raise up a sufficient number of bailing dishes to furnish one for every two of us, from which to drink our tea and coffee. The sum total of our mess kit for ten men, at the present time, is as follows:

One gold pan, used for making bread;
One bake-oven, with broken lid;
One camp kettle, for making tea or coffee;
One frying pan;

One large spoon and two tea spoons;
Three tin plates and five bailing cups;
One pickax and one shovel.

The last two articles we do not use on ordinary occasions, but when a pot of beans, which by the way is a luxury, is boiled in place of tea or coffee, our cook sometimes uses the latter article for a spoon, the former to clean his teeth after our repast is over.

[J. W. POWELL, *Chicago Tribune*, **published August 20, 1869, written on June 18, 1869]** Another day [June 17] was spent on the waves, among the rocks, and we came down to Alcove Creek, and made an early halt for the night. With Howland, I went to explore the stream, a little mountain brook, coming down from the heights into an alcove filled with luxuriant vegetation.

This camp was made by a group of cedars on one side and a mass of dead willows on the other.

While I was away, a whirlwind came and scattered the fire among the dead willows and cedar spray, and soon there was a conflagration. The men rushed for the boats, leaving all behind that they could not carry at first. Even then, they got their clothes burned and their hair singed, and Bradley got his ear scorched.

The cook [Hawkins] filled his arms with the mess kit, and, jumping on to the boat, stumbled and threw it overboard, and his load was lost. Our plates are gone, our spoons are gone, our knives and forks are gone: "Water ketch 'em," "H-e-ap ketch 'em." There are yet some tin cups, basins and camp kettles, and we do just as well as ever.

When on the boats the men had to cut loose, or the overhanging willows would have set the fleet on fire, and loose on the stream they had to go down, for they were just at the head of rapids that carried them nearly a mile while I found them. This morning we came down to this point. This had been a chapter of disasters and toils, but the Cañon of Lodore was not devoid of scenic interest. 'Twas grand beyond the power of pen to tell. Its waters poured unceasingly from the hour we entered it until we landed here. No quiet in all that time; but its walls and cliffs, its peaks and crags, it amphitheatres and alcoves told a story that I hear yet, and shall hear, and shall hear [sic], of beauty and grandeur.

[SUMNER, June 17th] Pulled out at seven o'clock, and ran a bad rapid the first half mile. The freight boats went through in good style, but the *Emma*, in running too near the east shore, got into a bad place and had a close collision, filling half full, but finally got out, all safe, baled out, and ran two miles through smooth water, when we came to another bad rapid and had to let down with ropes; tied up while we repaired the *Maid*; passed the rapid and on through two miles of smooth water, when we came to another rapid that has a fall of about twelve feet in one hundred and fifty, but clear of rock; the *Emma* ran through without shipping a drop, followed close by the *Maid*, she making the passage without shipping much, but poor *Kitty's Sister* ran on a rock near the east side and loosened her head block and came down to the other boats leaking badly. She was run ashore when [where?] Rhodes caulked her again with some oakum that would serve to keep her afloat for a while; when we pulled out again, run half a mile with the *Emma* and got into a complete nest of whirlpools, and got out of them by extreme hard work; decided that it was unsafe for the freight boats to attempt it; so we were compelled to let them down with ropes on the east side through a narrow channel.

Jumped aboard again and pulled down two miles further through smooth water, and camped for the night on the east side at the head of a rapid. While we were cooking supper a whirlwind came up the canyon, and in an instant the fire was running everywhere; threw what happened to be out on board again as quick as possible, and pulled out and ran the rapid and on down two miles further and camped again on the east side, and commenced anew our preparations for supper; had supper, and laughed for an hour over the ludicrous scenes at the fire. Went to bed and were lulled to sleep by the rain pattering on the tent.

☀ Day #26

[BRADLEY] June 18. 69. After a run of almost railroad speed for 5 miles we came to Bear River which comes into the Green from the East and at this season of the year has almost or quite as much water. What its effect on the future stream will be is uncertain. I predict that the river will improve from this point, for the more water there is the wider channel it will make for itself and the less liability will then be of its falling in and blocking up clear acrost, and if there is one side clear we can run it or at least have one good side to let down the boats with ropes.

I commenced fishing soon after we arrived but the fish were so large they broke four hooks and three lines for me in a few moments. I could haul them to the top of the water, great fellows, some of them quite a yard long. But the moment they saw me they were off and the hook or line must break. At last by twisting four silk lines together and putting on a hook two inches long, I managed to secure one that weighed 10 lbs. and will make a fine breakfast for all hands.

We intend to stay here several days and take a set of observations. Have named the cañon above this point Lodore Cañon for as the banks here are not more than 400 ft. high the Major thinks we better commence a new cañon at this point, but the cañon is realy [sic] continuous and has now reached 25 miles [actually 18 miles]. It has been the worst by far and I predict *the worst we shall ever meet.*

[O. G. HOWLAND, *ROCKY MOUNTAIN NEWS***, August 18, 1869, written in camp near mouths of Uinta and White rivers, on the Green, July 1, 1869.]** [June 18?] Our trip thus far has been pretty severe; still very exciting. When we have to run the rapids, nothing is more exhilarating; it keeps in play a rapid train of thought and action, equalled only by the river's progress; and as a breaker dashes over us as we shoot out from one side or the other, after having run the fall, one feels like hurrahing. It must be something like the excitement of battle at the point of victory, or much more agreeable, perhaps. Much to produce this effect, I conceive, is to be attributed to the purity of the atmosphere, cleansed as it is by the spray dashed through it by the rushing river, of which one gets beautiful draughts as he goes plunging down the tide with all the senses in active play. A calm, smooth stream, running only at the rate of five or six miles per hour, is a horror we all detest now, although we make more distance in the same length of time; but the trouble is, we don't get wet, nor have the slightest sense of danger. Danger is our life, it seems now, almost. As soon as the surface of the river looks smooth all is listlessness or grumbling at the sluggish current, unless some unlucky goose comes within range of our rifles. But just let a white foam show itself ahead and everything is as jolly and full of life as an Irish "wake" or merry-making, or anything of that sort. Jokes generate faster and thicker than mosquitoes from a bog, and everything is a merry as a marriage bell.

The scenery through the cañons we have passed thus far is truly wonderful. The river appears to run without design, starting into the highest mountain from out a broad valley, and cutting it down from dome to base, leaving on either side towering cliffs, massive buttresses, quaintly carved cornices and pillars, huge amphitheaters with numberless terraces, dotted with cedar and piñon trees, one above the other in wonderful order to the very top, immense gorges, deep chasms, curiously worn clefts, all worn sharp and clear as the finest masonry, and after having cut in twain one, going for another and serving it the same. The country we have passed though as yet, with the exception of Brown's Hole, for any useful purpose, is almost utterly worthless. That in the Hole, twenty-five or thirty miles in length and ten miles wide is good for grazing purposes. There is here and there a bottom of a few acres where could be cut some hay, but they are scarce. Game is plenty, in the hills, which are covered with cedar, piñon, sage and some bunches of grass, but is not suited to any domesticated animals.

[J. W. POWELL, *Chicago Tribune***, published August 20, 1869]**
[Sunday, June 20, 1869] At the point where the Bear, or with greater correctness the Yampa River enters the Green, the river runs along a rock about seven hundred feet high and a mile long, then turns sharply around to the right and runs back parallel to its former course for another mile, with the opposite sides of this long narrow rock for its bank. On the east side of the river, opposite the rock and below the Yampa, is a little park just large enough for a farm.

The river has worn out hollow domes in this sandstone rock, and standing opposite, your words are repeated with a strange clearness but softened, mellow tone. Conversation in a loud key is transformed into magical music. You can hardly believe that 'tis the echo of your own voice. In some places two or three echoes come back, in others the echoes themselves are repeated, passing forth and back across the river, for there is another rock making the eastern wall of the little park. To hear these echoes well, you must shout. Some thought they could count ten or twelve echoes. To me they seemed to rapidly vanish in multiplicity, auditory perspective, or *perauditory*, like the telegraph poles on an outstretched prairie. I observed this same phenomenon once before among the cliffs near Long's Peak, and was delighted to meet with it again.

[SUMNER] June 18th. — Repaired *Kitty' Sister* and pulled out again, and had a splendid ride of six miles, and came to the mouth of Bear river, a stream one hundred and twenty yards wide and ten feet deep; camped on a point of land between the two rivers, under some box elder trees. All hands went to work fishing, and soon had a good number of them. Bradley was much provoked by one large one that carried off three of his best hooks, but finally got him with a strong line got up for his especial benefit. He proved to be about thirty inches long and fifteen pounds weight. Opposite the mouth of Bear river there is the prettiest wall I have ever seen. It is about three miles long and five hundred feet high, composed of white sandstone, perpendicular and smooth, as if built by man. It has been christened Echo Rock [now Steamboat Rock], as it sends back the slightest and most varying sounds that we can produce.

Echo Park. Photo in 1871 by E. O. Beaman.

Chapter 4.

ECHO PARK, WHIRLPOOL CANYON, AND SPLIT MOUNTAIN TO THE UINTA, *June 19 - 28*

After surviving Lodore, the expedition arrives at the confluence of the Green and the Bear, also known as the Yampa River. The latter is somewhat better known territory for several of the crew, their having hiked parts of it during 1868. After two days spent drying out gear, climbing the 700-foot-high Echo Rock (now Steamboat Rock), fishing, repairing boats, and resting, the expedition shoves their boats onto the combined flow of two rivers and speeds down into Whirlpool Canyon. Although rapids force the men to line their boats again, the next few days reward the men with scenery that runs the gamut from sheer-walled sandstones and huge up- and downwarped anticlines to gorgeous open valleys populated with islands of cottonwoods. The joys of their river-running adventures upstream of Lodore resurge in the men, but now, after their chastisement in Lodore, more soberly. Finally, on June 28, five weeks after shoving off from Green River City, the 1869 crew proves many of those Green River citizens wrong by arriving alive and well at the mouth of the Uinta River.

Day #27 [BRADLEY] June 19. 69. Went out this morning to climb the rocks on the west side to ascertain the exact hight but, as it is quite perpendicular, we went up the river a mile or two where the red and white sandstone meet and thought to climb the red then work our way back onto the white and then onto the top of what we call "Echo Clift" [sic] opposite our camp. But what was our surprise to find on climbing a little over 800 ft. to come out right over the river. The crag on which we were fairly overhangs the water on the other side so much does the river fold back on itself. I could see two rappids but think we can run them both. The river looks much larger below than above Bear River and though it is quite noisy yet I think the increase of water will permit us to go safely.

[J. W. POWELL, no journal entry for June 19]

[SUMNER] June 19th. — Still in camp. Professor, Bradley and Hall climbed the northern end of Echo Wall. The remainder of the men in camp, fishing, washing, etc.

☀ Day #28

[BRADLEY] June 20. 69. Sunday again and we remain in camp. What is going to happen? I have kept my tintype album shut trying to save it whole but should have been more wise to have opened it at once for it fell to pieces anyway, and by lying wet so long shut up some of the pictures are spoiled. It is "painfully pleasing" to see what freaks the water has cut with the tintypes. Those on the first page are spoiled. Mother had but one eye, while all that is left of Aunt Marsh is just *the top of her* head. Eddie has his chin untouched while Henry looses [sic] nearly all his face. In short, they are all four spoiled. I have other pictures of all except Aunt Marsh, am sorry to lose that one. Two of Chas. Palmer, two of G. Marston's, Porter's, and several others are spoiled. One of Lucie's lost a nose but luckily it was the poorest one and I have a good one left yet. I count myself very lucky to save so many. The weather is delightful and we are in excellent spirrits --

[O. G. HOWLAND, *ROCKY MOUNTAIN NEWS*, August 18, 1869, written in camp near mouths of Uinta and White rivers, on the Green, July 1, 1869.] [June 20?] From our camp at the mouth of Bear River, on the west side of Green, is an overhanging cliff 500 feet in hight, and a mile in length, which has been named Echo Cliff. The echo is the most perfect and distinct I ever heard. The Green runs close to the base on its east side the whole length, then runs round back on the opposite side, so that at the upper end of the cliff the distance through the base is not over 200 yards. On the south side of Bear River is an elevated park, ten miles in length, and four or five wide, and standing back still farther south for a number of miles to an elevated plateau, 2,500 feet above the river bed, covered with sage and some cedar. The plateau is gently rolling, and game is plenty.

Bear River comes in here through a long cañon, for forty or fifty miles, with no valley of any size to be seen from any point of view near where we were in camp; there the water was apparently at its highest, and although quite small at its confluence with the Green, moved down with immense power. Before we left, however, it was gradually falling. The water is much clearer than that of Green river, and as they join below, the line of demarcation is clearly perceptible, the water of the Bear occupying the major part of the channel. We stayed in camp at the mouth of the Bear until the twenty-first.

[J. W. POWELL, no journal entry for June 20]

[SUMNER] June 20th. — All hands in camp to-day, taking a general rest. Wrote our names on Echo rocks opposite the camp. The entire distance from the southern end of the valley called Brown's Hole to the mouth of the Bear river is a canyon, except at two creeks on the west side, where there is a gorge cut through by the water of each. It has been named Ladore [sic] Canyon by the Professor, but the idea of diving into musty trash to find names for new discoveries on a new continent is un-American, to say the least. Distance through it, 25 miles [actually 18+ miles]; general course 25 degrees west of south; average hight on both sides about 1700 feet, highest cliff measured (Black Tail Cliff), 2307 feet. There are many still higher, but having enough other work on our hands to keep us busy, we did not attempt to measure them.

☀ Day #29

[BRADLEY] June 21. 69. Have made a good run today but have been obliged to make two portages on account of bad rappids. We could have run the last but for a whirlpool below which brought the small boat nearly back again into the worst of the waves. We camp tonight in a fine grove of cottonwoods through which a creek comes in clear and cold from the mountains full of fine trout. The boys are catching them while I write but I am too tired or too lazy to do anything except what I can't help. The river is very rappid but not dangerously so except in some short places. We are now out of the old red sandstone but I fear if we run west much farther we shall strike it again. Our first portage today was past a rapid in red sandstone. The second was in white but not so bad and but for a whirlpool below it we should have run it. The men (Andy & Howland) have just come in with 20 fine trout which will make a fine breakfast.

[O. G. HOWLAND, *ROCKY MOUNTAIN NEWS*, August 18, 1869, written in camp near mouths of Uinta and White rivers, on the Green, July 1, 1869.] On the morning of the 21st of June we again drifted out into the combined current of the two rivers and were borne down on a steady, powerful tide for about four miles toward a dark, towering cañon. As we gradually approached the cañon the channel narrowed, the current increased in rapidity, and the fall became greater. Soon the surface of the water became broken in places ahead of us indicating rapids. The walls of the cañon were quite smooth showing scarcely a rock on either side to which we could cling if necessary to haul inshore. The waves in the rapids, however, were quite large and our boats rode them like cork, so we were not compelled to bail, so ran on for nine miles in double quick time.

We had fairly got into one of the grandest cañons we had yet seen, when the thundering roar of the water ahead warned us to look for some place to stick to. The light boat was out of sight. One of the large boats took one side of the river and the other the opposite side, both seeking a landing place. At last a projecting cliff showed us on the right an eddy large enough for our boats to lay in comparative quiet, into which we pulled with all possible speed. Here we managed to cling until we could climb a cleft in the rock about fifty feet above water where was a narrow terrace a few feet wide running gradually down a couple of hundred yards to a bar on the right bank of the river. After several attempts we succeeded in getting our dropping line to the top of the rock and let our boat down to the bar below at the head of the fall; in the meantime the other large boat succeeded in finding a hold on the opposite wall above us. We then stood by to catch her line when she should cross to us. She came over and landed all right. The little boat had got too far down on the left shore to cross, so had to be dropped down a long distance before she could run with safety. The large boats had to make a portage of only a hundred yards, and then ran four miles further [sic] over a series of rapids and whirlpools, which were quite as bad, bailing at each, when we came to another fall.

Here we made another portage of one hundred yards and run two miles further to the mouth of a little creek coming down from the eastern end of the Uintah range of mountains, and camped for the night, having made 14 1/2 miles from the Bear. We caught a fine mess of mountain trout here, the first we had seen on the trip. The water of the creek is clear as crystal, and cool. From its locality we should judge it to be Brush creek, as laid down on a Government map we have with us. It may be Ashley's Fork, and the one four or five miles above Brush Creek. Both are laid down on the map in the last named order, and both are from the snow mountains.

[J. W. POWELL, *Chicago Tribune*, published August 20, 1869, written at Mouth of Winter [sic] River, Island Park, June 23, 1869]
When we left Echo Park on the 21st. [June], we soon ran into a cañon very narrow, with high vertical walls. Here and there huge rocks jutted into the water from the walls, and the cañon made frequent sharp curves. The waters of the Green are greatly increased since the Yampa came in, as that has more water than the Green above. All this volume of water, confined as it is in a narrow channel, is set eddying and spinning by the projecting rocks and points, and curves into whirlpools, and the waters waltz their way through the cañon, making their own rippling, rushing, roaring music. It was a difficult task to get our boats through here, as the whirlpools would set them spinning about the cañon, and we found it impossible to keep them headed down stream. At first this caused us great alarm, but we soon

found there was no danger, and that there was a motion of translation down the river, to which this whirling was but an adjunct. That 'twas the merry mood of the river to dance through this deep, narrow, dark gorge, and right gayly did we join in the dance. Soon our revel was interrupted by the view of a cataract, and its roaring command was heeded, with all our power at the oars as we pulled against the whirling current. The *Emma Dean* was landed against a rock, about fifty feet above the brink of the cataract. The boats following obeyed the signal to land. The *Maid of the Cañon* was pulled to the left wall where the cliff overhangs the water, and where, by constant rowing, they could hold her against the rock. The *Sister* was pulled into an alcove on the right. where an eddy was in a dance, and in this she joined.

I found that the portage could be made on the right bank. The little boat was on the left, and too near the fall to be taken across, but we thought it possible to take her down on the left. The *Maid of the Cañon* was under the cliff, out of sight. The roaring of the cataract would drown any human voice, and I must get them word what to do. By much search I found a way along the cliff to a point just over where the boat lay, and, by shouting loud and slow, made them understand. The portage was made before dinner.

Below the falls the cañon opens out, there is more or less space between the river and the walls, which is often covered by cottonwood and boulders; but the stream, though wide, is rapid, and rolls at a fearful rate among the rocks. But we proceeded with great caution, and ran the large boats altogether by the flag. We camp a night at the mouth of a small creek, which affords a good supper and breakfast of trout, and proceed again by stages of a half mile to a mile in length. While we are waiting for dinner today, I climb to a point that gives me a good view of the river for two or three miles, and think we can make a long run. So, after dinner, the large boats are to follow in fifteen minutes, and look out for the signal to land. Out into the middle of the stream we row, and down the rapid river we glide, making strokes enough only to guide the boat. What a headlong ride it is, shooting past rocks and islands! I was soon filled with exhilartions felt before only when riding a fleet horse over the broad prairie or outstretched plain.

One, two, three, four miles we go, rearing and plunging with the waves, and shoot out into a beautiful park filled with islands; Island Park, we call it, and the cañon above, Whirlpool Cañon. — J. W. Powell

[SUMNER] June 21st. — Off at seven o'clock and row down for one mile and a half along the base of Echo Wall, a nearly south course; passed the point of it, turned and ran due north for about five miles; back into the hard, red sandstone again, through a narrow, dangerous canyon full of whirlpools, through which it is very hard to keep a boat from being driven on the rock; if a boat should be wrecked in it her crew would have a rather slim chance to get out, as the walls are perpendicular on both sides and from 50 to 500 feet high. Made a portage at the lower end of it; had dinner and pulled out again, and went five miles further, making one short portage on the way; camped for the night on the west side, at the mouth of a clear, beautiful trout stream. Mr. Howland dropped his maps and pencils, rigged a line, and soon had a score of large trout, the first we have been able to catch so far. Made fifteen miles today, continuous canyon, named "White Pool [Whirlpool] Canyon;" trout stream named Brush Creek.

☀ Day #30

[BRADLEY] June 22. 69. Made a short and rapid run of about 5 miles and camped to allow the men to hunt. They *hunted* with the usual success. At 1 P.M. started again and after a run of about 5 miles more we came out into an exceedingly beautiful valley full of islands covered with grass and cottonwood. After passing so many days in the dark cañons where there is little but bare rocks we feel very much pleased when for a few days we enjoy the valley. I have found a lot of currants and have picked about four quarts which will make a fine mess for all hands. We intend to lay here tomorrow and allow the men a chance to *hunt*. Have spread the rations to dry and have found one sack of rice spoiled. We are glad to get rid of it for our boat is too much loaded to ride the waves nicely but is all the time growing lighter as we eat the provisions.

[O. G. HOWLAND, *ROCKY MOUNTAIN NEWS*, August 18, 1869, written in camp near mouths of Uinta and White rivers, on the Green, July 1, 1869.] On the morning of the 22nd of June we ran down about three miles, and were signalled by the light boat to head ashore. One of the boats in trying to make a landing could not be held when she touched, and the consequence was two of her crew had to run the unexplored rapid below stern down stream, dragging by her bow one hundred and twenty feet of line. She landed a half mile below the rapids, however, all sound, with the exception of being nearly full of water. The other boats let down past the worst of the rapids and then run out into the current again. From this time on to camp our ride was fine, just current enough to glide along swiftly, and not breakers enough to necessitate stopping to bail, one of the crew being employed in that capacity while running down. This day's run brought us out of the cañon into the upper end of a little Park. The river spreads out and runs in four or five different currents surrounding a number of islands, some of them a mile in extent. The cañon has been named Whirlpool Cañon, and the park Island Park. The entire distance through the cañon from Bear river mouth, by river, has been estimated at 25 miles.

[J. W. POWELL, no entry for June 22]

[SUMNER] June 22nd. — After a good breakfast of fried trout, we pulled out and made a splendid run of six miles through a continuous rapid and stopped to have a hunt, as we saw many tracks of deer and sheep on the sand. All ready by one o'clock, when the *Emma* started down a long rapid, which had a fall about thirty feet per mile. Went along in splendid style till she got to the lower end, where there is a place about a hundred yards long that had a dozen waves in it fully ten feet high. As she could not be pulled out of there her crew kept her straight on her course and let her ride it out. Went through them safe, but shipped nearly full and pulled ashore looking like drowned rats. Decided it unsafe for the freight boats to try it, so we were compelled to make a short portage and let down with ropes. Jumped aboard again and pulled out into more rapids, every one of which would thoroughly drench us and leave an extra barrel or two in the boats; but we kept bailing out without any unnecessary stoppages. Dancing over the waves that had never before been disturbed by any keel, the walls getting gradually lower, till about four o'clock, when we came suddenly out into a splendid park; the river widened out into a stream as large as the Missouri, with a number of islands in it covered with cottonwood trees. Camped on the first one we came to, and rolled out on the grass in the shade to rest. Distance from the mouth of Bear river 26 miles [actually 11 miles]. General course 20 degrees south of west from Brown's Hole to this point. The whole country is utterly worthless to anybody for any purpose whatever, unless it should be the artist in search of wildly grand scenery, or the geologist, as there is a great open book for him all the way.

☀ Day #31

[BRADLEY] June 23. 69. The men went hunting and wonderful to relate they have been successful for Bill R. [Hawkins] has brought in a deer. It is a fine large buck and is as fat as beef. He shot it on a mountain over 2,000 feet above the river and brought in both hindquarters himself. Frank brought in one forequarter but left the other hanging on a tree and as we are much in need of fresh provisions we have moved our camp around to the foot of this mountain, going 5 miles by the river, but if we could go straight it is less than one. The Major has been sick for two days and if he is well enough tomorrow, we shall go up to the top of the mountain and take observations and I will bring in the deer. The men are on tiptoe and each swears by everything he can name that some *little innocent* deer must die by his hand tomorrow. We shall see.

[O. G. HOWLAND, *ROCKY MOUNTAIN NEWS***, August 18, 1869, written in camp near mouths of Uinta and White rivers, on the Green, July 1, 1869.]** On the 23rd [of June] two of us attempted to climb a cliff on the left side of the river at the outlet of the cañon, for the purpose of making barometrical measurement of its hight, but failed in reaching the top after most of a day's hard climbing, only reaching a hight of about 2,000 feet. Two others climbed up, lower down, to the top of the mountain and killed a fine blacktail buck. We were all in camp about 1 o'clock and concluded to drop around a peninsula to a better camp, about three-fourths of a mile from this; so we loaded up and ran around a distance of four or five miles to the lower end of an island in the form of a crescent, a mile in length, where we camped until the 25th.

[J. W. POWELL, no entry for June 23]

[SUMNER] June 23d. — Unloaded the boats and spread our plunder out to dry. Rhodes, Dunn, Goodman harding [hunting], and Howland sketching; the others, in common, repairing boats and washing. Hunter came in about noon with a fine fat buck that Rhodes had killed, when we loaded up and moved down about five miles, and camped on the east side, at the lower end of a splendid island covered with a heavy growth of cottonwood. Our camp is within half a mile of the last one above, the river making an almost complete circle.

☀ **Day #32**

[BRADLEY] June 24. 69. Major is much better today but as he fancied that he wanted to explore the mountain to the south of here I left him to go his way and I went mine up to the top of the clift after the quarter of deer for I have no faith in the men finding another today and it will not do to leave a fine quarter of deer to the wolves while we live on bacon. I assended [sic] without much difficulty and found the meat untouched by wolves. I suppose they do not often climb quite so high for I found by the barometer that it is 2,800 ft. above the river, but I am so used to climbing them now that I hardly notice it. Yet it came very hard at first.

The river about four miles below here cuts this same mountain chain in two and comes out on the other side into delightful valleys like the one in which we now lie and which we have named "Island Park." The river is very rapid and we can see from the mountain that we must look to get through and shall go at it with a will for we can see for 50 or 60 miles that it is all valley and island covered with cottonwood groves and the cañon can't be very long.

[O. G. HOWLAND, *ROCKY MOUNTAIN NEWS*, August 18, 1869, written in camp near mouths of Uinta and White rivers, on the Green, July 1, 1869.] On the 24th [of June] we climbed a cliff about four miles south of here, at the head of our next cañon, and measured it by barometer. Its hight is 2,800 feet. Back east as far as the eye can compass, from the hights on our left, is an elevated plateau of rolling country, covered with artemisia, a fine pasturage for game of all kinds. The plateau averages about 2,500 feet above the river, with here and there a point as high as 3,000 feet. On our right is a various-colored broken country, running and rising gradually back to the Uintah range of mountains. It is cut by thousands of different water courses showing the strata, which has [sic] the appearance in color of a muddy looking rainbow.

[J. W. POWELL, no entry for June 24]

[SUMNER] June 24th. — The Professor and Howland climbed the mountain on the east side, with barometer and drawing materials; spent the greater part of the day sketching the park, which they have named "Island Park;" rain in the evening.

☀ Day #33

[BRADLEY] June 25. 69. Started this morning with the hope that we might get through the cañon today and possibly we could have done it but one of the men (Jack) was taken sick and as we came to a place about 11 A.M. where we had to make a portage we concluded to wait until tomorrow and let Jack have a chance to rest and sleep as he will take no medicine. We have carried the loads arround and lowered the boats so that we have only to load up and start. We shall have an easy run to get through tomorrow if we have no portages to make. Jack is better tonight and we shall probably start early in the morning.

[O. G. HOWLAND, *ROCKY MOUNTAIN NEWS*, August 18, 1869, written in camp near mouths of Uinta and White rivers, on the Green, July 1, 1869.] On the 25th [of June] we again started on our way, running down four miles and turning off in a tangent towards the east we entered the cañon. Soon began to appear rapids which followed, one upon the other, in rapid succession. To-day we made two portages and camped at the head of another rapid, where we shall have to make another portage to-morrow.

In my last letter to you I mentioned that the river appeared to run without any design. I have partially rejected that idea since leaving the mouth of Bear river. In Whirlpool Cañon, and also in this (Cleft Mountain Cañon) the river seems to go for the highest points within the range of vision, disemboweling first one and striking for the next and serving it the same, and so on, indefinitely. Here it turns short and sharp into the very center at the upper end of a long mountain, then turns again as sharply, and goes tearing down through it to almost the lower end, and shoots out to the left again into the prairie, whirling, splashing and foaming, as if in a fury to think so tiny an obstacle should tower 3,000 feet above it to check its progress. This makes me think it has designs on all mountains of any pretensions. Small ones are not considered worthy of its notice, it seems.

[J. W. POWELL, no entry for June 25]

[SUMNER] June 25th. — Pulled out at seven and moved down four miles, to the head of another canyon — cragged canyon — and into more rapids; made two portages and camped on the west side, at the head of another impassible rapid to loaded boats; one of the men sick [Sumner himself].

☀ Day #34

[BRADLEY] June 26. 69. Have made a pleasant run today of 30 miles. Made a short portage and have run a succession of rappids through the cañon, which lengthened out beyond our expectation. We have reached the valley this P.M. Found great numbers of geese, brought in 10 tonight but they are very poor at this season. Passed several old lodges where the Indians live at other seasons of the year. There are none living in them now. Jack is much better tonight and we anticipate a fine run tomorrow. Found a fine lot of foccils in the last cañon and have added three new varieties to our number and found them in great abundance.

[O. G. HOWLAND, *ROCKY MOUNTAIN NEWS*, August 18, 1869, written in camp near mouths of Uinta and White rivers, on the Green, July 1, 1869.] June 26th — We made our portage of provisions, let down out boats and pulled them out upon the rocks on the beach, last night. If we had not done so the waves would have rolled them about on the rocks so much as to have worn them badly. This morning we landed our boats, loaded up, ran down six miles to the head of the falls and made portage of a hundred yards. From here we ran with a good many short twists and whirls out into the valley. On our right, left and in front is an almost endless looking prairie country. The channel of the river widens from 200 to 400 yards, and islands and groves of cottonwood begin to appear all along the course of the river. The distance through Cleft Mountain Cañon is estimated at about 12 miles. After leaving the cañon we ran on down the valley about 21 miles, by river, coming nearly back to the outlet of the cañon we had just left. As it was rather rough work in there, we began to fear the river was going back on us, so we hauled in for the night under some large cottonwood trees, to take a sleep before we entered it again.

[J. W. POWELL, no entry for June 26]

[SUMNER] June 26th. — Made the portage and went a short distance when we came to another one, and had to make it in the rain; while the men were at work the Professor climbed up the side-hills looking for fossils; spent two hours to find one, and came back to find a peck that the men had picked up on the bank of the river; all ready by three o'clock, when we pulled out again; ran four miles at a rapid rate through the canyon, when all at once the great Uinta Valley spread out before us as far as the eye could reach. It was a welcome sight to us after two weeks of the hardest kind of work, in a canyon where we could not see half a mile, very often, in any direction except straight up. All hands pull with a will, except the Professor and Mr. Howland. The Professor being a one-armed man, he was set to watching the geese, while Howland was perched on a sack of flour in the middle of one of the large boats, mapping the river as we rowed along. Our sentinel soon signaled a flock of geese ahead, when we gave chase, and soon had ten of them in the boats. Summed up in the log, found we had run 23 miles since leaving the canyon, and camped for the night on the east side, under three large cottonwoods. Rested, eat supper, and turned in to be serenaded by the wolves, which kept up their howling until we dropped asleep, and I don't know how much longer, as I heard them the next morning at daybreak.

☀ Day #35

[BRADLEY] June 27. 69. We have had a hard day's work. Have run 63 miles and as the tide is not rapid, we have to row a little, which comes harder to us than running rappids. It is the same beautiful valley filled with green islands and contrasting strangely but pleasantly with the dry and barren bluffs which back them and which sometimes come down to the water's edge and entirely crowd out the valley for a short distance. Our camp tonight is alive with the meanest pest that pesters man, mosquitoes. Yet they will be as quiet as death in an hour or so for the night wind is too cool for them and they take shelter in the grove. We must be very near to the Uinta River which everybody said we could never reach but everybody will be mistaken for we are nearing it so fast and so easily that we are certain of success.

[O. G. HOWLAND, *ROCKY MOUNTAIN NEWS*, August 18, 1869, written in camp near mouths of Uinta and White rivers, on the Green, July 1, 1869.] June 27th — In looking around last evening among the bluffs, I found that the river had found out its mistake, for it turned reluctantly to the left when within sight of the cañon and went wandering around here and there towards all points of the compass for 50 or 60 miles, when we got pretty tired of that kind of thing and camped for the night.

The boys who have arms have had heaps of fun since we came out into the valley, running down and shooting a lot of poor geese unable to fly for want of full-fledged feathers. When run down too closely by the boats, they attempt to get away by raising themselves partially out of the water by their pin feathered wings, and by partly paddling with their feet and rowing with their wings, succeed in getting out of harm's way.

[J. W. POWELL, no entry for June 27]

[SUMNER] June 27th. — Off again at seven, down a river that cannot be surpassed for wild beauty of scenery, sweeping in great curves through magnificent groves of cottonwood. It has an average width of two hundred yards and a depth enough to float a new Orleans packet. Our easy stroke of eight miles an hour conveys us just fast enough to enjoy the scenery, as the view changes with kaleidescopic [sic] rapidity. Made 63 miles today, and camped on the west side, at the mouth of small, dirty creek. Killed eight wild geese on the way.

☀ Day #36

[BRADLEY] June 28. 69. Reached the desired point at last. And have camped close to the mouth of the Uinta River. The White River comes in about a mile below on the other side. Now for letters from home and friends for we shall here have an opportunity to send and receive those that have been forwarded through Col. Head. Hope to receive a good lot and think I shall. The musical little mosquitoes bite so badly that I can write no longer.

[O. G. HOWLAND, *ROCKY MOUNTAIN NEWS*, August 18, 1869, written in camp near mouths of Uinta and White rivers, on the Green, July 1, 1869.] On the twenty-eighth [of June] we ran down to this point and intend to remain in camp until the sixth. This gives time to get some supplies from the agency to replace those lost and other things necessary.

In footing up the estimated distance by river from Green River City to the head of this valley, we find it to amount to about two-hundred and twenty-five miles; from the head of the valley to this point, about one hundred and twenty-five miles. The first estimate is probably nearly correct, being almost all estimated from land points of view. But the latter is doubtless over-estimated, having all been guessed at from point to point while moving along in our boats. In making up our map from these last estimates, and then drawing a line from the mouth of the last cañon to this point, a distance nearly accurately known, we find our map exceeds that in the ratio of about five to three, this would make the distance from the head of the valley here only sixty-five miles, which is doubtless nearly correct. Our map shows the river runs from our starting point to the mouth of Henry's Fork, about 25° east of south; from there to the lower end of Brown's Hole, 25° south of east; from Brown's Hole to the mouth of Bear river, 25° west of south; Bear river to head of this valley southwest; from head of valley here 40° west of south.

This valley, as also the valleys of the White and Uintah for twenty-five or thirty miles, has the appearance of being very fine for agricultural purposes and for grazing. The Indians of Uintah Agency have fine looking crops of corn, wheat and potatoes, which they put in this spring, on the sod. They have also garden vegetables of all kinds, and are cultivating the red currant. Everything is said to look well. Most of the Indians are now from the Agency to see the railroad, while the rest stay to attend to their stock and keep their cattle from getting in and eating up their crops.

We have been nearly eaten up by mosquitoes since lying in camp here, our principal amusement having been fighting and smoking the pests.

Two of the Utes living at the Agency are here to take up our mail and some fossils we have collected, and will leave the morning. These are the only Indians we have seen since starting. It is scarcely sunrise yet, but anticipating an early start this morning I got up early to finish this letter and having done so will dry up. When or where you will hear from us again is hard to tell. Mr. Goodman, one of the wrecked party, leaves us here, being unable to raise a personal outfit for the remainder of the trip, so we now number only nine to finish up our work. — -O. G. Howland

[J. W. POWELL, no entry for June 28]

[SUMNER] June 28th. — Same character of country as yesterday. Saw four antelope, but failed to get any. Forty-eight miles brought us to the mouth of Uinta river, which place we reached about three o'clock, and camped on the west side of Green river, under a large cottonwood, at the crossing of the Denver City and Salt Lake wagon road, as it was located in 1865. There is not much of a road now, if any, as it has never been traveled since unless by wolves, antelope, and perhaps a straggling Indian at long intervals. Distance from the head of the valley by river, one hundred and thirty miles [actually 71.5 miles]; by land about fifty miles. General course of the river 10° west of south.

This part of the country has been written up so often by abler pens that I hesitate in adding anything more. As an agricultural valley it does not amount to much, as it is too dry on the uplands, and there are but few meadows on the river bottom, and they as a general rule are small — from fifty to two hundred acres in extent: The only exception that I know of is one opposite our present camp, lying between Green and White rivers. It is about two thousand five hundred acres in size, and overflows, though very seldom. At present it is clothed with a thick growth of grass, waist high. On the uplands there is the common bunch grass of the West — short but very rich. No part of the country that we have seen can be irrigated, except the river bottoms, as the uplands are rolling and cut up by ditches in almost every direction. But for a stock country it would be hard to excel, as almost all kinds would do well on the bunch grass throughout the entire year. There is plenty of timber for building purposes and fuel, and enough farming land to produce all that a settlement would require for home consumption. But there is one thing in the way. According to the treaty of 1868 between Gov. Hunt, of Colorado, and the Ute Indians, most, if not the whole of this valley belongs to the reservation, selected by the Indians themselves. Whether they will be permitted to keep it or not remains to be seen. Most likely they will, as one band of them have a permanently settled thing of it, and have a winter agency twenty-five miles from this point on the Uinta river.

What the country is below I know not. As far as the eye can reach there is a rolling prairie with a dark line through it that marks the course of the Green river. It is reasonable to suppose it to be the same character of country as that we have passed through in our last two days' travel. So far we have accomplished what we set out for. We were told by the frontiersmen while at Green river that we could not get to the mouth of White river. One man that filled the important office of policeman in Peitmont had the assurance to tell me that no boat could get as far down as Brown's Hole. We expect to remain here for a week to meet Col. Mead [Head?], and send off some specimens and all the notes and maps, to make sure of that much.

Total distance run 356 miles [actually 258 miles]; estimated distance to junction of Green and Grand rivers 300 miles [actually 245 miles] by river.

LIST OF ANIMALS LIVING IN THE COUNTRY THROUGH WHICH WE HAVE PASSED

Grizzly bear, cinamon [sic] bear, black bear, elk, mule deer, mountain sheep or bighorn, prong-horned antelope, gray wolf, prairie wolf [coyote], cougar, red fox, marten, mink, lynx, wild cat, prairie dog, beaver, otter, muskrat, badger, ground hog, mountain rat, gray squirrel, large striped ground squirrel, small do. do., small shrews and mice.

LIST OF BIRDS SEEN ON THE WAY

Wild geese, ducks of almost every kind, loon, stork, bittern, cormorant, rails, woodcock, snipes of many kinds, curlew, osprey, pelican, sand hill crane, bald eagle, golden eagle, colored raven, common crow, Clark's crow, sage grouse, black grouse, short-tailed grouse, magpie, long-crested jay, Canada jay, light blue jay, red-shafted flicker, small blackbirds, red-winged starling, Southern mocking bird, robin, brown thrush, crossbeak, wren, sparrows, sparrow hawk, sharp-shinned hawk, mouse hawk, pigeon hawk, mourning dove, meadow lark, woodpeckers of all kinds, and buzzards.

I write this at the request of Professor Powell, he urging me from the beginning to do so, while I, knowing there were many able pens in the party, as persistently declined, till I could no longer do so with any show of reason. I have written this with many misgivings, being more used to the rifle, lariat and trap, than the pen. Receiving no hints from any one, I have been compelled to write as I could. Were I to study grammar a little and sacrifice *truth* to flights of fancy, I might make a more interesting report, but I shall let it stand as it is. If it meets the approval of the public, well and good; if it does not, I will leave the report of the rest of the trip to other and abler hands, and return to my rifle and trap.

JACK SUMNER
Free Trapper

Indian lodge in the Uinta Valley (etching from *Canyons of the Colorado*).

Chapter 5.

INTERLUDE AT THE UINTA,
June 29 - July 5

*At the confluence of the Uinta River the expedition splits in half, five men —
Bradley, Dunn, the Howland brothers, and Sumner — staying with the boats, the other
half — Goodman, Hall, Hawkins, and the Powell brothers — hiking or riding to the
Uintah Agency twenty or so miles upstream. Back in camp the remaining men celebrate
yet grow nostalgic over the Fourth of July. Meanwhile they wage battle after battle against
swarms of mosquitos. Bradley, for one, tries to figure where it is that his life is going; he
has too much time on his hands. Major Powell sends off several letters from the agency,
offering progress reports on the Colorado River Exploring Expedition. In two of these
Powell brags about the boats' performances. But he also reveals that he still does not
understand that the crew of the No Name did see Powell's signal flag in time above
Disaster Falls, but, as O. G. Howland explained, the crew was unable to reach shore
due to the heavy load of water in their swamped — and ill-designed — boat. Powell
hobnobs with the Ute stay-at-homes.*

Day #37 [BRADLEY] June 29. 69. Have written a lot of letters and have
commenced to copy my notes but find the latter so great a job, fear unless
Major makes some change in his present design to go to the agency day
after tomorrow shan't be able to copy them. If not I will send originals
though it would puzzle a Philadelphia lawyer to read them. Camp is very
quiet for all are busy writing home. Built a huge fire last night to attract the
attention of any Indians that might be straggling in the bluffs. That they
might either come in themselves or report it to the agency, but no one has
come in today and fear it was not seen. Weather showery with hot sun when
it can get a chance to shine. Saw two pelican on the lake tonight but they are
on the opposite side out of reach of our rifles.

**[J. W. POWELL, *Chicago Tribune*, July 20, 1869, written at camp
at Mouth of the Uinta, June 29, 1869]**

Dr. Edwards:

My Dear Sir: The party has reached this point in safety, having run four cañons, of about 25 miles in length each, the walls of which were from 2,000 to 2,800 feet high. We have found falls and dangerous rapids, when we were compelled to make portages of rations, &c., and let the boats down with lines. We wrecked one of our boats, and lost about one third of our supplies and part of the instruments.

The instruments were duplicates, but the loss of the rations will compel us to shorten the time for the work. You will receive an account of our trip more in detail in *The Chicago Tribune*, as I shall send some letters to it for publication.

In the wreck I lost my papers, and have to use plant dryers for my letter paper.

I have not made a large general collection, but have some fine fossils, a grand geological section, and a good map.

Short walk to the Uintah Indian Agency, about twenty-five or thirty miles from camp, where I shall mail this letter, and hope to get letters and some news.

The boats seem to be a success; although filled with water by the waves many times, they never sink. The light cabins attached to the end act well as buoys. The wreck was due to misunderstanding the signal; the captain of the boat keeping it too far out in the river, and so was not able to land above the falls, but was drifted over.

We shall rest here for eight or ten days, make repairs and dry our rations, which have been wet so many times that they are almost in a spoiling condition. In fact we have lost nearly half now by one mishap and another.

Personally I have enjoyed myself much, the scenery being wild and grand beyond description. All in good health, all in good spirits, and all with high hopes of success. I shall hasten to the Grand and Green, as I am very anxious to make observations of the 7th of August of the eclipse.

With earnest wishes for your continued success and prosperity at Normal.

I am, with great respect,
yours cordially, J. W. Powell.

[J. W. POWELL/*The Missouri Republican--St. Louis*, July 22, 1869, written at camp at Mouth of the Uinta, June 29, 1869]

Dr. Henry Wing-My Dear Friend:

Your interest in our party, and desire for our success is so great that I take the first opportunity to report myself. I shall walk to the Uintah Indian Agency tomorrow, and hope to receive and mail letters there. The agency is twenty-five or thirty miles from camp.

Well, the boats seem to be a success. The closed cabins at each end work well as buoys, for although the boats have several times been filled with water, while loaded with men and rations, they still would float. Altogether, we have run about 100 miles of cañon, the water often plunging down twelve or fifteen feet in a hundred, among rocks that made the water rage.

The cañon walls have been from two thousand to twenty-eight hundred feet high; rarely perpendicular on both sides at once, and always footing to make portages, of which we have made a great many — one nearly a mile in length. We had one disaster. Howland failed to see or understand the signal to land, and so floated over a series of dangerous rapids, and the boat was at last wrecked. The three men in the boat managed to get to a little island, and were brought off in safety. By this we lost about one-third of the rations and the duplicate instruments. All the barometers were on the boat, but were removed from the wreck. A few candles and the case of records, barometer tubes and Howland's whiskey were all that was saved.

The men lost clothing, guns; everything but what they had on, and that was but little, shirts, drawers and socks.

The scenery was on a grand scale, and never before did I live in such ecstasy for an entire month.

Had good success in obtaining geological set (of specimens) through the cañons. Thirty-nine thousand feet of sandstone represented in one set. Made a good collection of fossils. Nothing else collected. All in good health and spirits, with high hopes of success.

With great respect, I am yours cordially, — J. W. Powell.

[SUMNER, no entry for June 29]

☀ **Day #38**

[BRADLEY] June 30. 69. Major has changed his mind and sent his brother & Andy to agency. Will go himself in two days. Have kept my letters and notes to send by him for I hope to get any mail before he goes. We carried the small boat about 100 yds. overland to the lake tonight but the pelicans are too shy. They hid in the tall reeds beside the water. Shot great quantities of geese & ducks. They can be counted by hundreds as they float on the lake or fly over our camp to their favorite feeding places — the mouth of the Uinta and White rivers below.

[O. G. HOWLAND, *ROCKY MOUNTAIN NEWS*, August 18, 1869, written in camp at mouth of Uintah River on the Green, June 30,

1869] As the Major and one of the boys are going to the Uintah Agency tomorrow, and I have not time to write you an account of our trip from Bear River here, having been employed upon the map of the river here since we got in, (the evening of the twenty-eighth,) I shall have to defer it a day or two, when, I presume, I can send it to the Agency by some Indians, who will probably be here when they know we have arrived at this point. Please save this, or a copy for me, as I have lost all my notes up to the time of the wreck, and they have been very meager for want of time to write, that time having been employed in making moccasins and replacing what I could of the map lost. — -HOWLAND [This letter is the final known writing by O. G. Howland on this expedition.]

[J. W. POWELL, Journal #1, no entry for June 30]

[SUMNER, no entry for June 30]

 Day #39

[BRADLEY] July 1. 69. Went out today with Major to find foccils which were reported to abound about three miles up White River. Think we were on the wrong side of the stream. They were found by an officer sent out by government with two companies of cavalry to lay out a stage road from Denver to Salt Lake City via White River in 1865. He had a train of 70 wagons camped just where we now lie. He built a ferry here and crossed over. According to the officer's notes which Major has, they sunk the ferry-boat under the tree where our boats are now lying but we have not sounded to see if she still remains. Presume she does. Across the river is a splendid meadow of the finest grass I ever saw growing naturally. It is without exception the finest mowing land I ever saw, as smoothe and level as a floor and no rocks. It would average two tons to the acre for four miles square. Talk of grazing land that beats even far-famed Texas.

[HALL, July 1, 1869]

Dear Brother;

It is with the greatest of pleasure that I now set down to write you a few lines to leet [sic] you know that I am all right yet. I wrote a letter to mother before I started with Major Powell to explore the Colorado. We had the greatest ride that ever was got up on the countenent [sic], the wals [sic] of the canone [sic] where the river runs through was 15 hundred feet in som [sic] places. i think we ar [sic] through the worst off the water now. I write from Unto [sic] reservation now but I will tell you more about it when i come home. The major is from Bloomington, Ill. I suppose you never herd [sic] of him and he is a Bully fellow you bett. if you can get the normal paper you can have the whole of the expedition. I have not time to write any more at present give my love to all and kiss Helen's baby fore me.

Be kind to our mother

No more at present

Yours affectionate
Brother Andrew Hall.

[J. W. POWELL, no entry for July 1]

[SUMNER, no entry for July 1]

☀ Day #40

[BRADLEY] July 2. 69. Major, Bill R. & Frank started for the agency early this morning. Sent letters, &c. Have had a very lazy day for there are but five of us left in camp and we feel lonesome. Since we came here I got enough currants for all hands and they were so good that I resolved to have some more and, as the mosquitoes drove me away before, I thought I would get ahead of them this time so I put a piece of mosquito bar over my hat and fastened it arround my waist and with gloves to protect my hands and a pair of boots coming to the knee to protect me from the rattle-snakes I set out and after hunting along the side of the Uinta River for more than a mile I succeeded in finding just one bush which I broke down and brought off in triumph.

The mosquitoes are perfectly frightful. As I went through the rank grass and wild sunflower sometimes higher than my head they would fairly scream arround me. I think I never saw them thicker even in Fla. [Florida] than at this place. I got more than three quarts of currants off the bush I brought in had an excellent supper of them. Our camp is on a little bluff only about ten or fifteen ft. above the river between the lake and the mouth of the Uinta, and strange to say the mosquitoes trouble us but little compared to what they do if we leave our camp. I keep a little smoke in front of my tent nearly all the time and that keeps them very quiet. One of the men says that while out on the shore of the lake a mosquito asked him for his pipe, knife, and tobacco and told him to hunt his old clothes for a match while he loaded the pipe — but I didn't hear the mosquito ask him, though there are some very large ones here.

[J. W. POWELL, Journal #1, very first entry] July 2. With Rhodes

[Hawkins] and Frank [Goodman] I started for the Uinta Indian Agency. At noon met Hall coming for me with pony. Had a long hard trip crossing and recrossing the river many times. Wrote letters at night.

[SUMNER, no entry for July 2]

☀ Day #41

[BRADLEY] July 3. 69. Another day of quiet rest. Have been cleaning rifle and pistols for constant wetting gets them in bad condition. Our cook being up to the agency, we have had a great time cooking today. I cooked some beans. Put on what I thought we could eat and set them to boiling. They boiled and swelled and I kept putting in hot water until I had a large bread-pan that will hold ten or twelve quarts solid full of beans. Cooked them as well as I could but their being so many they scorched a little for the pan wouldn't hold water enough to prevent burning. The rest took a boat and went up the Uinta River and got ducks and currants for tomorrow. We shall have a poor 4 of July anyway and we must make the best of it.

[J. W. POWELL, Journal #1, July] 3. Went with Lake to visit the Tsau-we-it and see the fields. This former chief is very old; his skin lies in wrinkles and deep folds on his limbs and body which were naked. Each Indian 1-3 acres (Indian the head of a lodge) of wheat, then turnips, beets, potatoes, &c., all doing well. Irrigation done by white men and some of the sowing the same. The Indians are learning fast, plough, sow, &c. Will not build houses, superstition. Their uncleanness probably a reason for it. I purchase certain articles. Beautiful place for reservation. Kindness of the people. Bishop wife of Tsau-we-it a great talk[er]. Has much influence, sits in council, often harangues the people. Indians gone to see the R.R. [railroad].

[SUMNER, no entry for July 3]

☀ Day #42

[BRADLEY] July 4. 69. No one has returned from the agency and we begin to feel some anxiety lest something has happened or they have failed to find it. Hope for the best. Have set our flag on the old and as we look upon it our thoughts wander back to other scenes and other days. Three successive 4ths I have been in the wilderness. Two years ago I was on Lodgepole Creek between Ft. Sedgwick and Ft. Sanders. Last year I was in the Uinta Mountains whose snow clad peaks loom to the west & north of our present camp. Where shall I be next 4th of July? Took a long walk tonight alone beside the lake and thought of home, contrasted its comforts & privileges with the privations we suffer here and asked myself why am I here? But those green flowery graves on a hillside far away seem to answer for me and with moistened eyes I seek again my tent where engaged with my own thoughts I pass hours with my friends at home, sometimes laughing, sometimes weeping, until sleep comes and dreams bring me into the apparent presence of those I love.

[J. W. POWELL, Journal #1, July] 4. Wrote letters. Lake went to city.

[SUMNER, no entry for July 4]

☀ Day #43

[BRADLEY] July 5. 69. All return today. Bill R., Andy & two Indians with pack ponies came in this morning, and Major & brother came in at night. The Indians are remarkably clean looking for Indians. They will take back a lot of stuff which the Major has traded off at the agency. He has got 300 lbs. flour which will make our rations last a little longer. Frank Goodman left while at the agency which will make our party one less. He is one of those that lost everything in the wreck.

[J. W. POWELL, Journal #1, July] 5. Wrote untill [sic] 10 A.M. and then came to camp with Walter.

[SUMNER, no entry for July 5]

George Y. Bradley rescues Major Powell (etching by A. Muller from *Canyons of The Colorado*).

Chapter 6.

DESOLATION, GRAY, LABYRINTH, &
STILLWATER CANYONS TO THE
COLORADO, July 6 - 15

Powell returns from the Uintah Agency with only 300 pounds of flour. The expedition relaunches into what now fairly passes for terra incognita *and begins this penetration of the unknown while operating on inadequate rations. The crew, already afflicted with wanderlust, promptly poisons itself with potato greens. Soon the men row into Desolation and Gray canyons, running most of the whitewater in "read-and-run" fashion. Even so, they are forced to line the boats a few times, improvising new ways to do so. The pre-monsoon July weather becomes so brutally hot that running rapids is the most desirable activity imaginable. But in Labyrinth and Stillwater canyons the river's gradient flattens to only about 3 feet per mile, forcing the men to row downstream for every foot gained. Still, the miles and the elevation unfold under the hulls of their Whitehalls satisfactorily, imbuing in the men a sense of river-running mastery which soon will be shattered on the Colorado in Cataract Canyon. The crew continues its mission of exploration and mapping. The Major focuses only on geology, and even then, cursorily.*

Day #44 [BRADLEY] July 6. 69. Started at about 10 A.M. and moved down the river once more. Was exceedingly glad to get away for I want to keep moving. Don't like long stoppings. Passed the mouth of White River about two miles below Uinta. Just above its mouth, in Green River, we passed a large island on which a man who used to be interpreter at Uinta had a garden. We had read that "stolen fruit is sweet" and thought we would try it. So got beets, carrots, turnips & potatoes all too small to eat the bottoms, so we did the next best thing, for Andy having cooked all together, we ate them as *greens*. I tried them but the potato tops tasted so badly I threw them away. Very fortunate for me for all the rest except Howland ate them and have been very sick all the P.M. All are vomiting freely now and begin to feel better though think we shan't eat any more potato tops this season. Made about 35 miles today. River smoothe but valley narrow.

[J. W. POWELL, Journal #1, July] 6. Started down river again. Got mess of greens on head of island. Made all hands sick. Camped on left bank of river, cottonwood grove, Camp No. 1. [For reasons no one quite understands, Powell began his true journal here, below the Uinta, hence his camp number system ignores all camps upstream of the Uinta confluence.]

[SUMNER] July 6, 1869. After 7 days of weary, useless waiting we are at last ready to cut loose from the last sign of civilization for many hundred miles — The "Emma Dean," now as before taking the lead, followed close by "Kitty's Sister" manned by Rhodes, Hall, and Howland. The "Maid" leaving last, manned by Bradley, Walter Powell, and Seneca Howland. Goodman being fonder of "bullwhacking" than rowing, left the party at the Agency. Dropped down to a large island (2 miles) to where some white men [Johnson] had planted a garden, landed and the Professor, Dunn and Hall stole their arms full of young beets, turnips and potatoes. Rowed down a few miles past some splendid cottonwood islands and camped for dinner under the shade of one. Cooked our stolen forage, ate it, and pulled out again, but had not rowed a mile when all hands were as sick as a landsman on their first voyage. The professor claimed that it was caused by some narcotic principle in the greens, but Hall decided the thing by swearing that they were not half cooked, as the first thing he pulled out of his neck was a potato vine a foot long and as hard as when it was growing. We all learned one lesson — never to rob gardens. 6th of July made 37 miles and camped on the east side in a cottonwood grove. Killed 4 wild geese on the way.

☀ Day #45

[BRADLEY] July 7. 69. Have had a pretty little run this morning but the hills beginning to get near and higher, we landed about 9 A.M. to measure them. I found on the one I climbed a pile of rocks placed as children call cob-house (they were long slatey sand stone rocks). Think it is the work of Indians for I could not find names or letters on any of the rocks. I repiled them and added a long rock, over seven feet, which I placed on end and made very secure. I also put my name on a flat stone with name of expedition & date and fastened it up very strong. Think it will stand many years. It is the first time I have left my name in this country for we have been in a part where white men may have been before, but we are now below their line of travel and we shall not probably see any more evidences of them until we get to White River No. 2 below here.

Major & Dunn found the mountain they climbed about 1,000 ft. above the river. The hills close into the river and we begin to call it a cañon, though it was nearly one yesterday with its banks set back from the river. In the A.M. we begin to find rappids. Run several good ones. Run all day 40 miles.

[J. W. POWELL made no further Journal #1 entries until July 20; instead he began his Journal #2, recording geology notes only].

[J. W. POWELL, Journal #2 Geology Notes] About the mouth of Uinta River chocolate Sds [sandstone] with gray and buff were noticed in the cliffs. Starting down the Green the rocks were seen to emerge from below along its banks chiefly gray Sds then buff gray and from there Sds, shaley then bituminous shales. At noon camp on the 7th a measurement was made. The lower half of the bluff was of bituminous shales interstratified with Sds. The shales and Sds of the upper half [were] not examined.

[SUMNER] July 7. Off again at 7 o'clock. Rowed down 10 miles when we came to a cañon and stopped to measure the walls. Height 1050 ft. Pulled out again at 10 o'clock and rowed until 6 o'clock through a channel that has no more current than a canal. It is cut through a sandstone plateau about 1500 ft. deep; there are also side cañons coming in every quarter of a mile, making the top of the plateau look like a vast field of honeycomb. Passed 2 rapids today; killed 2 otter and 4 wild geese, made 34 miles and camped on the east side. A few stunted cedars on the side of the cliffs, no timber on the river.

☀ **Day #46**

[BRADLEY] July 8. 69. Have made a run of 12 miles. Didn't start until 1 o'clock P.M. Climbed the mountain this morning, found it a very hard one to ascend, but we succeeded at last. In one place Major, having but one arm, could not get up; so I took off my drawers and they made an excellent substitute for rope, and with that assistance he got up safe. [note that J. W. Powell, in his 1875 report, says that this rescue by Bradley occurred on June 18, many miles upstream on the Yampa while climbing a cliff on that river, which the 1869 crew did not do.]

Found the mountain 1,500 ft. above the river. The scenery from its summit is wild and dessolate [sic]. A succession of craggy peaks like the one we were on was all we could see near us. We seemed to be in about the center of the range as we could look backwards or forwards and they looked about the same in extent, so judge we have got half way through the cañon — but not the worst half for since we started today we have had a succession of bad rappids but have run them all through. One, I think, was the worst we ever ran. Every boat was half full of water when we got through. It is a wild and exciting game, and aside from the danger of losing our provisions and having to walk out to civilization, I should like to run them all, for the danger to life is only trifling. We could almost sure get to land on one side or the other for the river generally narrows up considerably where the rapids are, so that we are near the shore.

We camp tonight at the head of one that Major has concluded we cannot run. So we shall have to make a short portage and let the boats over with ropes. I should run it if left to myself as the only trouble is sunken rocks, and in such swift water any rock that would injure us would show itself and we could avoid it. Major's way is safe but I as a lazy man look more to the ease of the thing. We have got the light boat and one of the heavy ones down tonight with one half the goods, so that in the morning we have but one boat and half the provisions to move which with our force is not a hard task. We have found foccil fishes' teeth in the rocks this morning and tonight Major has found foccils identical with those I found at Ft. Bridger so that we are still in the basin of an old lake which has now become a respectable mountain range. Run   miles. [Bradley left this mileage figure blank.]

[J. W. POWELL, Journal #2 Geology notes] At camp no. 2 the cliff was measured. Near the summit of this cliff were found shales with sands[tone] then sandstones gray and buff thickly bedded, at the base they were seamed with beds of red friable sandstones. After leaving the cliff measured at noon on the day we came to this point shales were seen to run up for 1 or 2 miles.

[SUMNER] July 8. Professor, Bradley, and Walter climbed the west wall with barometers; height 1598 ft. Pulled out at one o'clock and ran down 12 1/2 miles, passing 9 rapids. Camped on the east side on a sandbar. Small valley near camp covered with sage and greasewood.

☀ Day #47

[BRADLEY] July 9. 69. A terrible gale of dry hot wind swept over our camp and roared through the cañon mingling its sound with the mellow roar of the cataract making music fit for the infernal regions. We needed only a few flashes of lightning to meet Milton's most vivid conceptions of Hell. The sand from the beach buried our beds while that from an island below filled the air until the cañon was no comfortable place for repose, for one had to cover his head to get his breath. The barometer fell over 290 degrees. It moderated to an ordinary gale this morning, and we started on the wildest day's run of the trip thus far.

A succession of rappids, or rather a continuous rapid with a succession of cataracts, for 20 miles kept our nerves drawn up to their greatest tension.

We would dash through one with the speed of the wind, round too [sic] in the eddy, and pull for shore, sometimes with little water onboard but frequently half full. Bail out and having looked a moment to see the best channel through the next, repeat the same thing, dashing and dancing like so many furies. Twice we let down with ropes but we could have run them all if it had become a necessity to do so. We are quite careful now of our provisions as the hot blasts that sweep through these rocky gorges admonish us that a walk out to civilization is almost certain death, so better go a little slow and safe.

[J. W. POWELL, no Journal #1 nor Journal #2 Geology entries]

[SUMNER] July 9. Made a portage to begin our day's work, then ran 20 miles with that number of rapids, some of them very bad, and 2 that compelled us to let down with ropes. Passed the mouth of a small stream coming in from the west. Country worthless, though imposing, as there is some fine timber growing on the tops of the mountains. Camped on the east side in a cottonwood grove.

☀ Day #48

[BRADLEY] July 10. 69. Major, Dunn & Howland are gone out to climb the mountains. Didn't go as I want to do some washing and copy my notes. It is too much of a job to copy them all at once and I want to have them ready if any unexpected opportunity should offer, so as far as possible I shall copy whenever I get a sheet full. The walls begin to get lower and there are indications that this "Cañon of Dessolation" in which we have already passed for 45 miles is coming to a close. Those who climb the mountain will know more about it. Will wait until their return before writing more and probably until night for they can't get back much before noon and we shall start immediately after.

The men who climbed the mountain were gone until 5:00 P.M., found it 4,000 ft. high 4 miles back from the river. They report mountains below us so that the apparent coming out of the cañon is caused by the hills being low close to the river. I went out tonight and found a bad rapid about half a mile below our present camp. Think it can be run but don't know what the rest will think about it. The waves are very heavy but the water is deep on the left side and if run carefully, there is no trouble but our boats would not ride the waves if allowed to go through the worst of them.

Andy is singing for his own amusement and my edification a song that will no doubt someday rank with America's and other national anthems. All I can make out as he tears it out with a voice like a crosscut saw is the chorus - "When he put his arm arround her she *bustified* like a forty pounder, look away, look away, look away in Dixie's land."

[J. W. POWELL, Journal #2 Geology notes] At Camp No. 4 a section was made about 4000 ft. high (see observations var). From base to first obs dark red friable Sds aggregated in imperfect nodules from 1" to 2" dark and gray alternating the red Sds becoming thinner and often disappearing with a few rods or some yards of lateral extrusion. Fossils were seen in the upper beds of red. Some collected. Paludina melania. The upper part of this section exhibited slate-colored shales.

[SUMNER] July 10. In camp taking observation, repairing boats. Professor and Howland measure the east side of the cañon; height 4000 ft.

☀ Day #49

[BRADLEY] July 11. 69. Sunday again and Major has got his match, for in attempting to run a rapid his boat swamped [capsized], lost all of his bedding, one barometer, and two valuable rifles which we can ill afford to loose [sic] as it leaves but 7 rifles in the outfit and we may meet Indians who will think our rations worth a fight, though if they try it they will find them dear rations. The rapid is not so bad as some we have run but they shipped a heavy sea at the start which made their boat unmanageable and she rowled [sic] over and over turning everything out. Major had to leave the boat and swim to land as he has lost one arm and her constant turning over made it impossible for him to hold onto her with one hand. But the other two (Jack & Dunn) brought the boat in below safe with the losses stated and the loss of the oars [the last pair that remained on the boat]. We will have to make some oars so Major is compelled to keep Sunday, though against his will. Weather windy. Run 1/2 mile.

[J. W. POWELL, Journal #2 Geology notes] Coming down river there was found to be 200 ft. by estimation of additional dark red Sds in the bed mentioned above. The gray Sds & shales dip still N. but somewhat increased. One of these beds below the red a blue limestone was found to contain fossils.

[SUMNER] July 11. Pulled out early and ran 3/4 mile; swamped [capsized] the "Emma Dean." Lost $300 worth of arms, all the bedding of the crew and ruined $800 worth of watches. Got the boat ashore by vigorous kicking and camped on the east side to make oars and dry out. Rain in the afternoon.

Powell's 1871 boats moored across from Lighthouse Rock, Desolation Canyon. Photo by E. O. Beaman.

☀ Day #50

[BRADLEY] July 12. 69. Got a good start this morning and run several fine rappids with little difficulty. When we had just begun to think all of the worst ones were over when we came suddenly upon an old *roarer* and, in attempting to run it, my boat was swamped [but not capsized]. The little boat ran it by shipping considerable water but the first big wave swept right over our stearn [sic], nocking [sic] me over the side so that I held the boat by one hand and filling the boat. Before we could recover from the shock we had shipped several seas and all we [Bradley, Walter, and Seneca] could do was to cling to the boat and keep her from turning over. In this we were successful and, having collected our oars from the water as soon as we got below the rapid, we got the boat on shore without any loss or inconvenience except a glorious ducking and a slight cut on one of my legs which I got when I was nocked over board. All I fear is that the constant wetting and drying of my pictures will ruin them.

We let the other heavy boat over the rapid and since that we have run many more, and tonight we have just finished letting the boats down one where the walls are perpendicular. We let down by wading along and, where it was too deep, we would let the boats down ahead and then swim down until we could touch again. Made 15 miles.

[J. W. POWELL, Journal #2 Geology notes] At Noon of the 12th two beds of impure lignite were found and a stratum of rock intervening composed chiefly of fossils, some of which were collected. At Camp No. 6 the cliff is estimated at 1800 ft. and does not reach to the red above.

[SUMNER] July 12. Pulled out at 7 o'clock and ran 16 miles; passed 10 bad rapids and 20 [sic] portages, one very bad portage made under an overhanging cliff on the east side. Let the boats down by stages, the last man swimming after the boats had passed. [By "stages" Sumner meant that first boat was lined partway down the rapid, then the second boat let down by rope to join it, then ditto with the third; the next stage consisted of again moving one boat 130 feet farther down the shoreline, then of lining the second boat to join it, then the third to join them both again; this done, they may have moved boat number one yet a third time, then added boat number two, then three yet again, keeping the three boats as close to an intact fleet as possible at each stage, until all were moored at the foot of the rapid. The reason why they lowered the boats down in these stages of all three boats in steps instead of employing their normal technique of lining one boat all the way to the foot of the rapid then returning for the next one is: the men could not return back up the rapid because they would be forced to swim upstream to do so, as Bradley mentions in his entry for this date. Each trip for each man was a one-way, one-time affair.]

Saw a herd of sheep but failed to get any. Walls of cañon getting lower and more broken. Camped on the east side on a sandbar.

☀ Day #51

[BRADLEY] July 13. 69. We have had a fine run of 18 miles this A.M. and have run 19 roaring rappids without any accident. Have now come out of Coal Cañon (the name given to the last part of the Cañon of Dessolation because we found some coal beds) into a valley which seems very extensive, that is, it seems to be *long* but on each side is a barren parched dessert [sic]. The winds that sweep it are hot and sultry indicating that it is quite wide. It is so smoky that we can't see many miles but we are confident that the mountains are quite distant. We have come several miles in the valley and the water continues quite rapid. I hope it will for I am anxious to run down our altitude before we leave Green River so that we may have an easier time in the Colorado. We are prepared however to take it as it comes. We have run so many rappids we pay but little attention to them and the weather and water both being warm we rather enjoy getting wet and laugh at the one who gets wetest [sic].

We are now lying beneath the friendly shade of a cottonwood. Have eaten dinner and are now waiting for the 1 o'clock observation. Shall know more of the valley before night and will wright [sic] more. Ran 22 miles this P.M. with no difficulty. Current rapid but only occasionally very bad. Large mountains in sight on the left but the valley is continuous, that is, the plain still bounds the river but in many places the green valley is crouded [sic] out for a little while. Think we passed *White* River No. 2, but it is so small we doubt it a little. Grand River can't be very distant for it must flow to the right of the mountains we can see to the east of us. Think we must reach it this week if the river don't cañon badly between here and the confluence.

[J. W. POWELL, Journal #2 Geology notes] Dip still N. up to Camp No. 7 though less [?] than between the last two camps. After leaving Cañon the rocks were slate colored shales with gray Sds then red and chocolate with gray all thinly bed[d]ed. Then dark brown rocks not examined closely. A few miles above camp No. 7. 3/4 miles above rapids a bed of spar was found evidentally the site of an old mineral spring. Two specs. saved.

[SUMNER] July 13. Pulled out early and had an exciting ride of 18 miles, passing 19 rapids, when we came to an open valley and camped for dinner; passed the mouth of the "Little White River" (a stream 2 rods wide and a foot deep coming in from the west) down about 2 miles above noon camp. Pulled out about 1 o'clock and ran down about 2 miles when we came to the old Spanish Crossing of Green River; at the ford of the river is about 250 yards and very shallow. Saw a vast pile of Satin spar on the east side 10 miles below the ford. Came in sight of "Uncompahgre Mts."; they are a beautiful cluster of snow-capped cones in western Colorado, south of Green River. Made 40 miles and camped on the east side, near the head of another cañon. The valley, or rather desert, first passed is of little use to anyone; the upland is burned to death and on the river there are a few cottonwood trees, but not large enough for any purpose but fuel.

Powell's 1871 crew & boats at Gunnison Butte at foot of Gray (a.k.a. "Coal") Canyon. Photo by E. O. Beaman.

☀ Day #52

[BRADLEY] July 14. 69. Have run 33 1/2 miles today. Had to row much of the time for the river is very still. Cañon commenced again this A.M. and continues. The walls are perpendicular most of the way *on one side*, seldom on both. A man could leave the cañon in many places if it should become necessary to do so but with such still water there could be no necessity for doing so. The whole country is inceivably [sic] dessolate. As we float along on a muddy stream walled in by huge sandstone bluffs that echo back the slightest sound, hardly a bird save the ill-omened raven or an occasional eagle screaming over us, one feels a sence [sic] of loneliness as he looks on the little party, only three boats and nine men, hundreds of miles from civilization bound on an errand the issue of which everybody declares must be disastrous. Yet if he could enter our camp at night or our boats by day he could read the cool deliberate determination to persevere that possesses every man of the party and would at once predict that the issue of all would be success.

As we get farther south the weather gets hotter and the sun shining on the sandstone heats the whole cañon like an oven. We are nearly suffocated tonight and but for a breeze that occasionally draws in upon us, it would be intolerable. We expect it very hot when we come to the Colorado.

[J. W. POWELL, Journal #2 Geology notes] Below camp No. 7 Sds still N., the rock coming out from below but at a low angle three or four miles below. Camp a beautiful bluff and light red rock comes in sight. This noon rises so as to form the vertical walls of this canyon which are rather low. The buff which is above and left soon disappears and the light red only is seen. This I think is the same as the rock of "Flaming gorge."

[SUMNER] July 14. Pulled out early and ran 33 miles through as desolate a country as anyone need wish to see. The walls over the cañon about 1/4 mile apart, composed of a bluff [buff?] sandstone destitute of any strata. On the river there is in some places a small table that affords a footing for a few willows. At intervals of 4 or 5 miles there are also clumps of scrubby cottonwood trees. River about 125 yards wide with a current of 1 1/2 miles per hour.

☀ Day #53

[BRADLEY] July 15. 69. Made another hard run, for the sun was so hot we could scarcely indure [sic] it, and much of the time the cañon was so

Butte of the Cross (etching by Thomas Moran, from *Canyons of the Colorado*).

closely walled in that the breeze could not reach us. We have worked as hard as we could to get only 25 miles, and the river has been so crooked that in going 25 miles we have actually advanced less than 11 miles. We have almost lost our trees. We stopped for dinner today in the open sun with the thermometer over 100° close to the water. It is more comfortable to be out on the stream than to be on land for we can get a better breeze. The water is calm as a lake, hardly moves at all in some places. Camp tonight in a snug little nitch [sic] in the rocks but without any trees, yet at this time of the day the sun is so low that the walls of the cañon affoard [sic] ample shade. Most of us have been unwell today from eating sour beans for supper last night.

[J. W. POWELL, Journal #2 Geology notes] [The buff which is above and left soon disappears and the light red only is seen. This I think is the same as the rock of "Flaming gorge."] At Camp no. 8 it has a thickness of 300 ft. by estimate, and below is seen a [sic] fifty ft of a softer dark red Sds that might be discolored or breciated.

[SUMNER] July 15. Off again at 7 o'clock and a repetition of yesterday's work. Passed the mouth of the San Rafael 5 miles below camp. It is another dirty stream, 8 rods wide [1 rod = 16.5 feet] and a foot deep;

comes in from the west. River very crooked. Saw several beaver but got only one. Got one goose out of a flock that we have driven before us for 3 days. Walls of cañon 300 ft. perpendicular on both sides except at side cañons. Made 25 3/4 miles today by hard rowing. Camp on west side. Pulled dead willows to cook our scanty "grub."

1871 photo of Cataract Canyon. Photo by E. O. Beaman.

Chapter 7.

CATARACT, NARROW, & GLEN CANYONS TO THE PARIA, July 16 - August 4

At the confluence of the Grand and Green rivers the expedition reaches its approximate halfway point for mileage for the entire exploration — but the big whitewater is only beginning. Not knowing this yet, the men celebrate their progress, discover via their spoiled rations that they may soon face starvation, then hike the hot rock to the rim for some local exploring. The next 45 miles downriver in Cataract Canyon force a serious reappraisal of what is possible to accomplish in the crew's three surviving Whitehalls — and how long their rations might last — in what Sumner admits are "the worst rapids we have seen so far." Progress slows again to such a crawl that Bradley concurs: "So I conclude the Colorado is not a very easy stream to navigate." The crew lines and/or portages 18 times in Cataract. Meanwhile the monsoons begin. Finally breaking through to Narrow and Glen canyons, the men's spirits rise again and, with them, the urge blossoms anew to explore what becomes a true fairyland of stone hidden from the rest of the world. Here the infamous incident in which Major Powell names a northern tributary Dirty Devil creek — in an apparently reference to William H. Dunn's personal grooming habits — seems to foster a festering of morale. Sumner shoots three bighorn sheep, but these will constitute the last of the wild game or fish that the crew will harvest from the canyons during the expedition.

Day #54 [BRADLEY] July 16. 69. Hurra! Hurra! Hurra! Grand River came upon us, or rather we came upon that very suddenly and, to me, unexpectedly 5 1/2 P.M. Had been running all day through higher walls mostly vertical but the river was smoothe though in some places more rappid than for two days. The cañon looked dark and threatening but at last, without warning — no valley or even opening unusual — in broke the Grand with a calm strong tide very different from what it has been represented. We were led to expect that it was a rushing, roaring mountain torrent which when united with the Green would give us a grand promenade acrost the mountains. The rock is the same old sandstone underlaid for the last 20 miles with limestone containing marine foccils and at the junction of the two rivers strangely curved and broken. The river Colorado formed by the junction of these two is, as we can see it (1,000 yds.) calm and wide and very much unlike the impossible, impassible succession of foaming and raging waterfalls and cataracts which have been attributed to it. It is possible that we are allured into a dangerous and disastrous cañon of death by the placid waters of this cañon which may be no fair specimine [sic] of the whole, but this is what has been represented as inaccessable [sic] by any means yet devised, and one adventurer actually offered to explore it with a balloon if congress would furnish the needful greenbacks. And here we float in upon the scene never before beheld by white men and by all regarded as dangerous of approach from any quarter and especially so by water. And the last 75 miles of our journey through a dark calm cañon which a child might sail in perfect safety. Surely men do get frightened wonderfully at chained lyons [sic]. Trees have been very scarce all though this cañon (Green River cañon) and at last failed altogether.

We stopped at noon in a notch of the wall where the melting snow and rain have worn away the rocks until we could climb out. Major did so but could not see anything at any distance. We were so fortunate as to get two beaver today and they will afford us fresh meat which we need very much. They are quite decent eating and the tails make excellent soup. After eating bacon for some time we find any kind of fresh meat pallitable [sic], even the poor old geese, so poor they can't fly and just off the nest, go good to us when long fed on bacon.

[J. W. POWELL, Journal #2 Geology notes] Going down to Camp No. 9, still lower strata of this rock are seen. The cañon walls gradually rise. Dip N. but at low angle. Beds of gray and blue Sds are interstratified with the dark red. The whole formation having a thickness of 450 ft. by estimate at Camp No. 9. Of the light red compact upper rock, 300 ft. When this made the entire wall it was vertical. When the lower dark red set in, the walls had a slope up to it [them] and were then vertical. At Camp No. 9 there is also 50 ft. of Sds seen above the river, also compact.

Coming down the river on the morning of the 16th this bed was noticed to rise from below about 2 1/2 miles untill [sic] it had attained a thickness of 100 ft. Then a red Sds appeared which was softer. At noon of 16 [I] climbed cliff up to this gray and estimated the thickness of the lower arm [?] up to this gray above limestone at 600 ft. The limestone, or rather calciferous [sic] Sds, was seen to emerge from below water level 200 yds. below camp. This arm [?] of red is thinly bedded soft dark with a few beds of buff interstratified, some of which was non compact.

The light red compact rock mentioned as forming the low vertical walls of the cañon above was here seen to stand at the summit of the cliffs and between the lateral cañons forming conspicuous vertical monuments in every direction for miles.

Coming down to this junction of the Grand and the Green the

limestone formation was seen to come up more rapidly than did the Sds before.

A great abundance of ecrinite [crinoid] stems was seen 3/4 mile below noon camp. The upper calciferous beds have purple beds of Sds interstratified. Then beds of gray Sds were found interstratified down to the junction where fossils were found.

[SUMNER] July 16. Off at 7 o'clock again, and ran for 29 miles through a terrible desolate cañon with nearly continuous vertical walls on both sides. At 4:45 we came to the mouth of Grand River, pride of the Colorado. Camped on the point of land between Green and Grand. Distance from the mouth of Uinta River 344 miles. General course west of south. Number of rapids ran 64, portages 4....

Our enterprising edition [sic, should read "one enterprising editor"?] went so far as to claim that he had laid out a town and called it Junction City. Where he had his burgh is more than I can say, as it is an apparently endless cañon in 3 directions — up the Grand, up the Green, and down the Colorado, the walls 1250 ft. high, not timber enough within 10 miles to supply one family 6 months. There are a few scrubby hackberry trees on both sides of the Colorado for half a mile below the junction and 3 small ones on the point between the 2 branches. The Green is about 70 or 80 yards wide and 10 ft. deep. Grand about 125 yards wide, same depth and flow, but a clear stream and 6° colder than the Green. There is apparently an annual rise of 25 or 30 ft,. at the junction.

☀ Day #55

[BRADLEY] July 17. 69. Rained considerably last evening. A real southern thunder shower roared through the cañons lighting them for a while with fearful briliancy [sic] and shaking the old clifts with peals of thunder that seemed as if commissioned to make doubly dessolate this regeon [sic] set apart for dessolation. But it cleared off about 10 P.M. and we had a lovely night for sleep.

Have been overhauling the rations and find the flour in a very bad condition. Have sifted it all through a mosquito bar taking out the lumps and washed the sacks and put it up again. We have only about 600 lbs. left and shall be obliged to go on soon for we cannot think of being caught in a bad cañon short of provisions. It was the intention to remain at this point until Aug. 7 to observe the eclipse but shall not probably remain more than three or four days, just long enough to get Latitude and longitude as the junction of these rivers has never been surely known within one hundred miles.

[J. W. POWELL, no Journal #1 nor Journal #2 Geology entries for three days]

[SUMNER] July 17, 18, 19, and 20. In camp taking observations and repairing outfit. Examined our stores and found we were getting very short, as we were compelled to throw away 200 lbs. of flour that got wet so often it was completely spoiled.

☀ Day #56

[BRADLEY] July 18. 69. Sunday again and though a thousand spires point Heavenward all arround us yet not one sends forth this welcome peal of bells to wake the echoes of these ancient clifts and remind us of happier, if not grander, scenes. All has been quiet in camp today, no work, no firing of guns, no noise of any kind. Each seeks the shade of the stinted bushes that skirt the bank and engaged with his own thoughts or in conversation spends the time as suits him best. I, with blanket spread on a little bench of sand shaded by overhanging willows, have been sleeping off the effects of a heavy dose of beavertail soup. And now I sit upon the sand bench and write.

Our camp is pitched in the angle formed by the two rivers on a sand bank washed down from both of them. To our right, when looking south, comes the Green with a rappid muddy stream for it has been rising since we arrived and now sweeps the Grand back well towards the left bank. But when we came, the Grand was master of the field, and I think that is generally the case for now that it is a quite low water and is clear almost as the Merrimac yet it moves with a strong, deep tide and is wider than the Green though with its present swift currant [sic] the latter probably poars [sic] the most water. The Grand flows in from the left and its course is not so much changed by the union as the course of the Green, in fact it is properly the Colorado and the Green is its tributary.

Our boats swing lazily at the bank in the eddy. Everything has been taken out of them and they subjected to a thorough clenzing [sic]. We have not yet measured the clifts but estimate them at about 1,200 to 1,500 ft. above the river. Shall measure them before we leave, probably tomorrow, for I judge we shall not remain longer than the day after, for we, like Valandigham, "must arrise [sic] and go on or stay and die" as our rations are very limited.

☀ Day #57

[BRADLEY] July 19. 69. Washing day with us. Almost all of us have had a turn at it today, getting ready for what comes below. Grand River has been quite muddy today indicating rain in the mountains above. Hot weather continues and with our scanty shade our camp is not a very pleasant one. Since we left Uinta we have hardly seen a mosquito. so hot, dry & dessolate is it that it won't produce even that little pest. But the constant and not unwelcome churping [sic] of the large black cricket is never silent except where the cañon walls are so vertical as to utterly forbid him a foothold. We sometimes hear the harsh shriek of the locust but only in occasional localities. Have been but few since we came to this point.

☀ Day #58

[BRADLEY] July 20. 69. Started to climb the mountains on the east at noon. Thermometer at 95° in the shade. Climbed three hours and at last succeeded in reaching the top of the tallest cliff. The rocks were heated by the sun until the top, which is usually the coolest, was hotter than the cañon for the thermometer indicated 99° at the summit. The cliff is a strange one for the soft sandstone on top has worn out in caves and the top is all like honey-comb with them. We paced one of them 75 yds. in a straight line, so high we could walk anywhere in it and many thousand men could shelter in that single cliff. The senery [sic] from the top is the same old picture of wild dessolation we have seen for the last hundred miles. Curiously shaped spires and domes rise everywhere and the walls for two hundred feet at the top — are vertical giving one the impression that the river banks would be the same, but they are not so on the Colorado so far as we can see but may become so when we reach the hard rocks below the limestone. Shall start tomorrow morning.

[J. W. POWELL, Journal #1, July] 20. Climbed "Cave Cliff" with Bradey [sic]. Summit of cliff full of caves, hence name. Pinnacles in the rdsds. [red sandstone]. The terraces, the monuments of the stages of erosion. Found a cool spring in gulch on our way up. Our [One?] cave 75 paces long, dome skylight at each end connected by fissure 6 or 8 inches wide, from 10 to 40 ft. wide, 5-12 ft. high.

☀ Day #59

[BRADLEY] July 21. 69. Started this morning and by hard labor have made 8 1/2 miles today. Rappids commenced about 2 miles from the junction and have now become continuous. We can't run them, or rather we don't run many of them on account of our rations. We are afraid they will spoil and, if they do, we are in a bad fix. Have let down with ropes much of the way. Made four portages and camp tonight in a place where we can only find sleeping ground by piling up rocks along the edge of the water and then collecting the scant sand from between the huge bowlders, in that way we have made comfortable beds. Have made two portages within 100 yds. above, and there is another waiting not a hundred yds. below. So I conclude the Colorado is not a very easy stream to navigate.

[J. W. POWELL, Journal #1, July] 21. Came down River 8 1/4 miles, bad rapids, 3 portages, lost three oars from *Emma Dean.* The flood plains 18 to 20 feet higher than river is now. Camped among rocks on left bank. No. 11.

[J. W. POWELL, Journal #2 Geology notes] The river here seems to cut through an irregular anticlinal axis, the strata dip into the blufs [sic] on both sides. At a point on the east side 2 miles about below the junction the dip was 75° or 80° a little S. of E. Cave cliff was climbed and limestone found. 100 feet below its summit this light gray compact Sds in which were many brown [?] caves.

[SUMNER] July 21. Off again early and commenced real work of exploration. Rowed through a very smooth channel for 5 miles when we came to a very bad rapid, but ran it all right. But we came to a worse one 200 yards below...for 200 yards and got into a...made 8 1/2 miles, 4 portages and ran...rapids; swamped [capsized?] the small boat and lost...oars. Camped on south side among the rocks.

☀ Day #60

[BRADLEY] July 22. 69. Made but a short run today, only 1 1/2 miles for Major wanted to determine what has so disarranged the strata here and we, having lost a pair of oars lifting the little boat over a rappid, he determined to lay by a day and make oars and climb the mountain. He with his brother climbed the nearest cliff, which they found to be 1,200 ft. high. The strata all along here dips both ways from the river, which Major says is caused by sliding down of part of the mountains. Have looked below for 2 miles and we can run all the way for that distance though we can see rappids from there that think we can't run.

[J. W. POWELL, Journal #1, July] 22. One & three quarters [miles?] to confusions of rock. Boys commence to make oars. I examined the points of rock before dinner. After dinner Walter & I climbed Mt. over Camp. Easy found pitch. Unraveled the mystery of the rocks. Bar. Obs. camp scene. Supper poor. Rhodes [Hawkins] takes instruments to determine the lat. & long. of the nearest pie. Camp No. 12.

[J. W. POWELL, Journal #2 Geology notes] A half mile below camp No 11 the dip is shown on both sides of river quite well and is about 25°. The river to this point seems to have cut along an anticlinal axis which is very irregular. At Camp No 12 confusion of rocks. A careful examination was made to determine the cause of the strange dip which has usually from the river, especially at points and these would often overlap. It was found that the walls had broken off from 1/4 to 3/4 of a mile back. And in falling had tumbled back at top, the bottom pushing out toward the river. See diagram [no diagram included in either journal].

[SUMNER] July 22. Made a portage and ran a mile and camped on the south side to make oars and repair boats. Professor and Walter climbed the south wall, height 1000 ft., saw fresh moccasin tracks on the sand near camp.

☀ Day #61

[BRADLEY] July 23. 69. Another day of hard labor. Have made 5 1/2 miles with three good long portages and all the way rappids. Much of the last three miles we have let down with ropes. Rappids get worse as we advance and the walls get higher and nearly perpendicular. We camp tonight above a succession of furious cataracts. There are at least five in the next mile around which we shall have to make portages. Let it come. We know that we have got about 2,500 ft. to fall yet before we reach Ft. Mohava [sic], and if it comes all in the first hundred miles we shan't be dreading rappids afterwards, for if it should continue at this rate much more than a hundred miles, we should have to go the rest of the way *uphill*, which is *not often the case with rivers*. Major estimates that we shall fall fifty feet in the next mile, and he always underestimates. We have as yet found no place on the Colorado where we could not land on either side of the river, for though the walls come quite close to the water yet there has always been a strip of fallen rocks or a sand bank. Where we lay yesterday there was a sand beach half a mile long and much of the way more than a hundred yds. wide.

The heat is quite oppressive during the day. The thermometer indicates above 100° most of the time, and that heats the cañon like an oven which lasts nearly all night but usually gets quite cool by morning. The tide mark indicates that the water is sometimes the water is [sic] 15 to 20 ft. higher than now, and there must be fun here when it is at that hight. [No doubt true...]

[J. W. POWELL, Journal #1, July] 23. Difficult rapids. Three portages. Ran 5 1/2 miles. West wall of cañon vertical except 1/4 or 1/3 of height from base, which has a steep talus. Camp on left bank. No. 13.

[SUMNER] July 23. Ran 4 miles of good current, then rapids. Ran 5 bad ones and made 4 portages in 1/2 mile. Average width of river 80 yards; height of walls, 1800 feet; north wall nearly all perpendicular. Camped on south side on a sandbar.

☀ Day #62

[BRADLEY] July 24. 69. Well, we got over or arround three out of the five rappids. Had to take everything arround by hand, and arround the second we had to carry our boats over the huge bowlders which is very hard work as two of them are very heavy, being made of oak. We had to slide them out on the rocks at the third rappid but not so far or so hard work as at the second. Have made only 3/4 mile today and camp at another rappid which they tell me is not so bad as the others but I haven't been to look at it yet. They don't interest me much unless we can run them. That I like, but portage don't agree with my constitution.

We found part of the bones of what Major pronounces an aligator [sic] tonight. He must be on an independent exploring expedition, probably to discover the junction of Grand and the Green and failed, as many do, for want of breath. All I have to say is he was sensible to die before he attempted to assend [sic] the next rappid for it has an almost direct fall of from 15 to 20 feet. We have met nothing to compare with it before.

Weather is not quite so hot today. We are in good spirrits and we are glad to get down our altitude before the cañon gets narrower and higher, as it will do when we come to the harder rocks. In these rapid places the river narrows up unaccountably. Andy has been throwing stones acrost for amusement tonight.

[J. W. POWELL, Journal #1, July] 24. Only made 3/4 mile today. Three long portages where the river fell by estimate 42 ft. Huge rocks across the river. The camp among the large rocks. I sat for an hour watching the waves. Ridges at all angles to the direction of the river, mounds and even cones with crests of foam that falls back. No. 14.

[J. W. POWELL, Journal #2 Geology notes] Up to camp No 14 the rocks are to all appearances horizontal and for two miles the cliffs have not been broken off so as to show dip from the river as they had most of the way from the junction to that point.

[SUMNER] July 24. Hard at work early making a portage in the worst rapids we have seen so far. Make 4 portages in 1/2 mile. "Kitty's Sister" had another narrow escape today. While crossing between rapids Howland broke an oar in a very bad place and came near being drawn into a rapid that would smash any boat to pieces. Saw the tracks of an otter and mountain sheep on the sand. Walls...00 ft., 3/4 blue marble, the remainder grey sandstone, lightly touched with red by a thin bed of red shale on the top. Driftwood 30 ft. high on the rocks. God help the poor wretch that is caught in the cañon during high water. Camped on the south side among the rocks, 3 small hackberry bushes in sight of camp.

☀ Day #63

[BRADLEY] July 25. 69. Sunday brings no rest to us, no notice being taken of it. Have been working hard today to make 3 1/2 miles. Two of the boats come in tonight leaking badly. Mine is now the only tight one we have left and fear she will not long remain so if we continue to meet such severe rappids. The river is still one foaming torrent, yet I believe there is a slight improvement today. We can see from the bluff quite a long distance and it is all very rappid and covered with foam but we can't tell at this distance whether we can run it or not. We intended to remain here tomorrow and repair the boats but find we can't get out of the cañon to get pitch, so we shall move on in the morning — I hope for a longer run than we have had for the past few days.

[J. W. POWELL, Journal #1, July] 25. More rapids. Let down one long one in which the *Emma Dean* was suddenly turned round. Then ran 3 in a series before dinner where Jack made a heavy oar, then ran down half a mile, let down past one rock, and run between two others. Bad run half a mile more and let [down] a long rapid. Crossed over to right for camp No. 15.

[SUMNER] July 25. Made a portage of 200 yards to begin with, then ran a bad rapid to get to another portage, made it and camped for the night at the head of another portage, north side. Made 3-1/2 miles.

☀ Day #64

[BRADLEY] July 26. 69. Another day wasted foolishly. Run 1 1/2 miles and finding a latteral [sic] cañon, Major wished to land and climb the mountains, so five of us started on a wildgoose chase after pitch, but it was so hot we all backed out except the Major, who says he climbed the cliff, but I have my doubts. It is unaccountably hot on the mountains but being showery tonight the air feels a little cooler. Rappids continue. One below our present camp will give us another portage. Found the camp of an Indian today with meat bones that had been picked within two months.

[J. W. POWELL, Journal #1, July] 26. Ran a short distance after breakfast and then went into camp No. 16.

Tried Bars. [barometers]. Repaired boats. Made our lunch at 10 A.M. With Cap P., Bradley, Seneca, and Andy started up cañon on left. Soon found pools of water then brook, then amphitheater with deep pool, clear and green. Climbed to left on shelf, crept [to?] another amphitheater, deep pool. Cut off 3 miles from camp. Return one mile climb to North first on a slide [of?] large rocks. Then up an irregular amphitheater on points that form steps and give hand hold, then up a cleft will [wall?] fashion 20 or 30 feet, then up gorge along benches to left, away round point to left, still along benches up over grey sds. [sandstone] to summit.

Take obs., collect pitch, use shirt sleeve for sack. Hard rain, hail. Came down in mud, found Mt. Torrent rushing down over dry bed. Water red and thick. Reach camp about 10 minutes before creek. Little rain at camp. Camp 16.

[J. W. POWELL, Journal #2 Geology notes] At camp No 16 I climb and take obs. for alt. on thick gray Sds, under which are red and gray beds of Sds, the red sometimes chocolate. It must be 1500 ft. to summit of limestones which are gradually replaced by *Sds.* In lower part of limestone formation there are a lot of beds of black indurated clay which, near the river, are thickened and pressed out. This is the cause of the rock fall of the walls above.

[SUMNER] July 26. Pulled out and ran a bad rapid in 1 1/2 miles and camped on the south side to repair boats. 5 of the men tried to climb the cliff to get some rosin from the pine trees at the top but all failed but the professor, he being lucky enough to get about 2 lbs. Repaired our boats the best way we could and turned in. Rain this evening.

☀ Day #65

[BRADLEY] July 27. 69. Have made a good run today of 11 1/2 miles. Part of the way had very bad rappids. Made one portage and let down with ropes several times. The walls are getting nearer the water and in many places they meet the water on both sides so that if we meet an impassable rappid we shall have to run it with all the risk or abandon the expedition.

But if it is not a very bad *direct* fall we shall try to run it. For several miles above our present camp the walls were in that way, but we have a good little bank now on both sides as far as we can see. We were so lucky as to get two sheep today which, in the present reduced state of our ration, is hailed as the greatest event of the trip. Weather showery but not much rain.

[J. W. POWELL, Journal #1, July] 27. Let down boats over rapids with portage. Another let down before dinner. One after dinner then through narrow cañon with vertical walls for several hundred feet, above which the walls rise in steps 10 or 12 feet of the walls at the base was black with iron.
Camp 17.
At noon of 27, Capt. P. commenced with Bar. [barometer].

[J. W. POWELL, Journal #2 Geology notes] Shortly after leaving camp No 16, say two miles, the dip was seen to set in to the S. Up to this point it was slightly to the N. Only now and then could any dip be seen from the junction. But the finding of the limestone at a higher altitude proved it. At the end of Marble Cañon [now Cataract Canyon] the limestone disappeared under water. Toward the top of this formation beds of limestone grow gradually thinner and the Sds thickens and it runs out in seams.

[SUMNER] July 27. Made a portage of 200 yds. and ran 11/12 miles, passing 6 bad rapids. Killed 2 mountain sheep today — a Godsend to us, as sour bread and rotten bacon is poor diet for a hard work as we have to do. River today about 40 yards wide, walls 1000 ft. perpendicular except at side cañon. Camped on a sandbar.

☀ Day #66

[BRADLEY] July 28. 69. Had a very hard run this A.M. to make only two miles. Made two portages, the longest we have made on the Colorado but since noon we have had an excellent run of 12 1/2 miles. Most of the distance it was very rappid. The last few miles, however, it has been very still and we fear the rappids are going to quit us altogether for a while and then come on again as at this point the walls of the cañon are very low, not over 150 ft., and when they rise again we may have swifter water. We camp tonight upon a stream that is not down upon any of our maps. It is larger than White River No. 2 and quite muddy, indicating recent rains in the mountains which we can see S.W. of us. The mountains are quite high. Think they are not snow clad but it is so smoky we can't determine yet. We can tell in the morning. The creek comes in from the west and sweeps far out into the Colorado. It is not now much more than 30 to 50 yds. wide but has a channel much wider. Evidently at some seasons it is much larger and very noisy.

[J. W. POWELL, Journal #1, July] 28. Made two portages today, one very long at noon. After dinner ran a long chute about half mile, very narrow, very rapid, down the slope of the rocks. It had a marble floor. There the cañon was rapid, narrow, straight, the walls rising from the water's edge and running back with two grand steps that gradually came down to the water's edge between these smaller interrupted steps. Near the end of Marble Cañon on the right was the thousand crags. From the bend down to the mouth of Dirty Devil Creek was very dr--et [?], very narrow and very quiet (estimated at 25-75 yds. wide). Beautiful view of mts. through the cleft of the cañon to W. Walter and I climbed cliff. Had good view of Red Monuments and in creamy pink rock, bass [base?] gray sloping up to the far N.E. Beautiful rounded ridges running down from a long ridge seen S. of W. from night camp. No. 18.

[J. W. POWELL, Journal #2 Geology notes] Through Narrow Cañon the dip was to the West by nearly S.W. and quite rapid. By estimate we ran through 1000 ft. of gray Sds from the head of the Cañon to a point 2 1/2 miles below the mouth of D. D. ["Dirty Devil"] Creek when it disappears under water and the dark red noduliferous Sds sets in. Here a measurement was taken of the dark red up to thick bed of gray. There are several thinner beds of gray below.

[SUMNER] July 28. Row a mile of smooth water. We came to 100 yards portage, made it on the south side, then ran another mile of smooth water and got to a very bad rapid. Runs very narrow, with a fall of about 20 ft. in 200 yards; made a portage around it, ate dinner and pulled out again and ran 12 1/2 miles through a grand cañon with straight walls, average width 40 yards; current 4 miles per hour. Passed the mouth of an extensive dry gulch coming in from the south. Camped on the north side at the mouth of a stream 3 rods wide and 2 ft. deep. It is not laid down on any map. The water is about as filthy as the washing from the sewers of some large, dirty city, but stinks more than cologne ever did. It has been named "Dirty Creek" [Dirty Devil River]. From the mouth of San Rafael River to 10 miles below the junction, the walls gradually increase in height and decrease from that point to the mouth of Dirty Creek [Dirty Devil]. At the mouth of dry gulch the limestone disappears, leaving the blue sandstone cut into every conceivable shape.

☀ Day #67

[BRADLEY] July 29. 69. Run 20 miles with ease. Found many small rappids or what we call *small* ones now but which would pass for *full-grown cataracts* in the States. We like them much for they send us along fast and easy and lower our altitude very much.

Major named the new stream "Dirty Devil Creek" and as we are the only white men who have seen it, I for one feel quite highly complimented by the name, yet it is in keeping with his whole character, which needs only a short study to be read like a book.

Those mountains we saw last night are not snow clad. We passed them today, leaving them on our right. They have considerable wood on them and are quite grand in appearance as they contain harder rocks than any we have before seen on the trip. Bazalt [sic] Granite &c. which wears away slowly and gives them a very rough appearance. Hope we shan't meet any such right in our way but expect to do so before we get through for all its explorers of the lower Colorado predict that there are Bazaltic & Granite walls to the unknown cañon from 3,000 to 6,000 ft. high. If so we ought to meet them pretty soon for we are fast making distance into the unknown.

We found an old ruin of a Moqui house today. It was built in a dessolate place where they could find a little grass and a little low land in which to raise a few vegetables. It must be one or two hundred years since it was inhabited as every trace of path or roof timbers are blotted out. It was built of stone with a thick strong wall some of which is still standing, but most has fallen down. It contained four rooms of the following dimensions: 13 X 16 -- 13 X 18 -- 13 X 16 -- 13 X 28 [feet]. There was also another not so well preserved built under the bluff as if for a sort of kitchen or shelter for their cattle. We found many specimens of curiously marked fragments of crockery some of which I have saved but may not be able to even get them home. I would like very much to find one of their villages along the river for they are a hospitable people and retain more of the former customs of the old race than any other living tribe.

[J. W. POWELL, Journal #1, July] 29th. Climbed rock on right, going most of the day through cañon with low red walls. During the afternoon found ruins of house with fragments of pottery on rocky bluff to left. At foot of rock where it was overhanging, the remains of other walls were seen, perhaps three houses or compartments of one. Between the bluff and the river was a valley 1/3 mile long & 200-300 yds. wide.

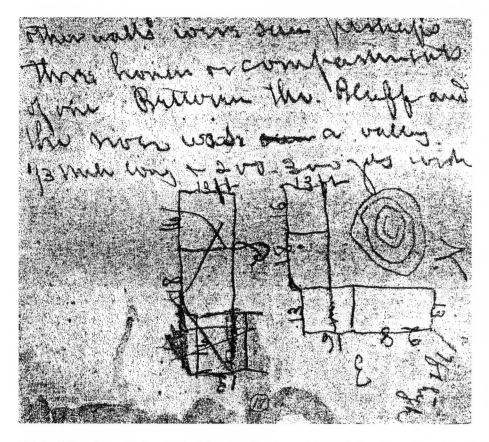

Original drawing of Moqui (Puebloan) ruins from John Wesley Powell's original journal #1, July 29, 1869.

Some mortar was yet left. Where the walls had not fallen there was an opening in the wall at the N. near corner. Everything old looking. May be two or more centuries. After leaving ruins we ran down to camp 3 or 4 miles and I climbed the right wall and went back a mile or two. This Monument formation is wonderfully rounded above into mounds and cones, deep holes are worn out. In one well I saw a tree well 25 ft. deep. Mts. to N.W. Returned by dark and took obs. for Lat. Camp No. 19.

[J. W. POWELL, Journal #2 Geology notes] Afternoon of July 29th: Have been most of the day in the red Sds that lies above the gray of Narrow Cañon. Below it is dark red often disintegrating into nodule like fragments sometimes a little shaly. A few thin beds of buff or light gray below these, thicker above. Some a slate gray, then a compact light red or deep orange bed from 750-800 ft. This rock seems to have been colored after deposition, the lower part sometimes being buff and mottled with orange as though an orange colored liquid had sunk down through deeper in some places than others. Still over this is a creamy pink rock. The whole I call the Still-Water Cañon Formation. The monuments are in this form. The compact upper rock protecting the lower silt [?] which washes out with fewer slopes and rounded ridge talus. The light red is often jointed, giving a columnar appearance to the upper parts of the monuments. The pinnacles and spires are in this. The creamy pink seems to be jointed but the joints [are] farther apart and, as it more easily disintegrates, the columns are rounded and often slope back to the crest of the wall. On the night of the 29th, I climbed the cliffs (see description of rocks).

[SUMNER] July 29.
Pulled out at 7 o'clock and ran down through a very crooked channel for 20 3/4 miles; passed 15 rapids, but none of them very bad. Passed an old Moqui ruin on a hill 30 ft. high, 200 yds. south of the river. One house or rather the remains of it, contained 4 rooms. Under the hill there are several more, but all have fallen to the ground leaving little but the foundation. How they contrived to live is a mystery to me, as the country around is as destitute of vegetation as a street. There is a small beach of a few acres between the hill and the river that might support half a dozen people if it was cleared of willow, cactus and horned toads. Passed 2

"A typical cliff dwelling" (etching from *Canyons of the Colorado*).

small creeks coming in from the south side. Camped on the north side near a clump of oak trees.

☀ Day #68

[BRADLEY] July 30. 69. Made another run of 21 miles though much of the way there was but little tide. The walls of the cañon are quite low though somewhat higher than for the last few days. We are expecting to come to the San Juan River, for by a Mormon map which we have it is only fifty miles from the junction and we have already come nearly twice that distance. By the official map from Washington it is put down as "probably" 100 miles, but as we have run farther west than they have marked the probable course of the Colorado, that will make the mouth of the San Juan farther down, though we shall probably strike it tomorrow. Begin to find occasional pieces of Granite which indicates that there are mountains of it near from where it has rolled down.

[J. W. POWELL, Journal #1] July 30. Rain today through cañon in monument forms. Where the walls are broken down there are many gently rounded mounds and slopes toward the river. In the middle of afternoon dip changed to a little N. of E. Cañon wall gradually higher, and a terrace on the points. At noon I walked back some distance from river. The country rises back in broken ledges. At night I went up gulch and collected beautiful ferns found in dense masses. Camp on right. No. 20.

[J. W. POWELL, Journal #2 Geology notes] About the middle of the afternoon of the 30th, we had run to 150 or 20[0] ft. of the summit of the monument form, the dip changed to E.N.E. about two miles below the camp of that night (No 20). The up axis was reached 200 ft. below the Homogeneous [sic] light red bed. Here there was more gray in the upper strata of the lower part of the form. This axis is at the point where the river makes the bend to the W. a little N. Maybe the walls are much broken down.

[SUMNER] July 30. Off again at 7 o'clock and made a good day. Ran through a grayish sandstone cañon, as destitute of vegetation (except where there is room on the river for walls) as the paper I write on. Passed 12 rapids, but none large enough to give us any trouble. Camp on the north side under a cliff 100 ft. high. Dunn killed a half-starved coyote near camp, the only sign of animal life we have seen for 3 days. Made 31 miles today.

☀ Day #69

[BRADLEY] July 31. 69. The last day of the month finds us at the mouth of the San Juan and we find it about the size of White River No. 1, though not so deep as that was when we passed it. It has a very rappid tide and is quite muddy. It will add considerably to the amount of water and probably increase the speed for a little while. There is not a tree at its mouth and the place is most dessolate and uninviting. Fear Major will conclude to remain here and observe the eclipse on the 7th but sincerely hope not for to find shade we have to crawl into the rocks and let the evelike projection of the cliff shelter us and the rocks are almost hissing hot. The thermometer seldom gets lower than 100° except just before sunrise when it falls a little. The air is so dry that there is generally over 41° difference between the wet and dry thermometers. Have run 19 1/4 miles today.

[J. W. POWELL, Journal #1] July 31. Cool pleasant ride today through this part of Mound Cañon [Glen Canyon]. The large boats racing. Still more cones and rounded points. After dinner soon found the mouth of San Juan. Then I climbed Mt. Failed on Obs. by reason of clouds but obtained alt. of B. Ceti [star Beta Ceti] in morning. Camp No. 21.

[J. W. POWELL, Journal #2 Geology notes] After passing this axis the strata soon dip down again untill the lower part of the Monument Form. is is [sic] below water. The San Juan is in the homogeneous red. There must be more than 800 feet of his light red.

[SUMNER] July 31. Pulled out at 7 o'clock and rowed 18 miles against a strong head wind when we camped for dinner on the south side under and oak tree 15 inches diameter and 15 ft. high. Found granite boulders at camp, the first on the trip. Pulled out at 1 o'clock and rowed 1 1/2 miles — that brought us to the mouth of the San Juan River, a stream 30 yds. wide and 15 inches deep, dirty as can well be, but not salty as most of the side streams are. Camped on the point between the 2 rivers and spent the whole of the afternoon in trying to find a place to get out, but failed to do so in any direction we wanted to. There is nothing growing at the junction but a few willows. One mile below on the south side of the Colorado River there is some scrubby oak. Cañon walls from 300 to 800 ft. all sandstone, so steep and smooth that it is next to impossible to get out. Distance from Grand River, 116 miles. General course, due southwest. Country worthless to anybody or anything. Number of rapids run, 45. Portages 18.

☀ Day #70

[BRADLEY] August 1st. 69. Sunday finds us again on the move. Major tried in vain to climb the low cliff on the south side of the San Juan. They are all so very smooth that they defy his efforts and he, becoming disgusted, has moved down the river a mile or so to find a better camp. We are on the left side of the Colorado in a little bunch of oaks and willows which, with a little fixing, will afford a tolerable shelter.

Just saw three sheep this A.M. but failed to get one of them. The rocks are so smoothe it is impossible to follow them for they can run right up the side of a cliff where man can get no foothold. Their feet are made cupping and the outer surface of the hoof is as sharp as a knife. They seem to have no fear of falling but will leap from rock to rock, never stumbling nor slipping, though they will be a thousand ft. above us and a single miss-step would dash them to atoms. They are very good eating and we need meat very much, not having over 15 lbs. of bacon in the whole outfit. We are short of everything but flour, coffee, and dried apples, and in a few days our rations will be reduced to that.

[J. W. POWELL, Journal #1] Aug. 1. Up early taking obs. Dropped down 1 3/4 miles and went into camp. Took obs. for time, by lunar. During afternoon I went up into "Music Temple," 100 yds. long, 50 yds. wide, cleft of rock above "Sky light" 25 ft. wide. Trickling cascade. Pool, a dozzen [sic] Poplars at entrance. Tufts of pines. Sang the old House at Home to: Geo., Bram & Harry. Rock above 300 ft. high, temple 200 ft. Camp 22.

[SUMNER] August 1. Ran down 1 3/4 miles and found a good camp in some oak and willow bushes. Camped on the south side to repair boats and take obs. Thermometer, 104° in the shade.

☀ Day #71

[BRADLEY] Aug. 2nd. 69. In the same camp, doomed to be here another day, perhaps more than that, for Major has been taking observations ever since we came here and seems no nearer done now than when he began. He ought to get the Latitude & Longitude of every mouth of a river not before known and we are willing to face starvation if necessary to do it but further than that he should not ask us to waite [sic] and he must go on soon or the consequences will be different from what he anticipates. If we could get game or fish we should be all right but we have not caught a single mess of fish since we left the junction. Major has now agreed to move on in the morning so we feel in good spirrits tonight.

[J. W. POWELL, Journal #1] Aug. 2. Still taking Obs. Spent several hours during afternoon in temple, good sleep. Jack and I went up after dark to sleep there on account of storm, hard time getting there. Same camp.

[SUMNER] August 2. In camp repairing and taking obs. Half a mile or less from camp there is a curious alcove worn in the sandstone by the rain water of a gulch. It is large enough to contain 2000 people. Wall 200 ft. high and nearly closed at the top. There are three cottonwood trees growing in the clear white sand floor and a little lake of pure water on one side. We christened it "Music Hall." Strong wind all day. Heavy shower at dark.

☀ Day #72

[BRADLEY] Aug. 3rd. 69. Have made an easy run of 33 miles. Passed several rappids but none that we could not run easily. Have lowered our altitude finely. Over 750 ft. [this figure was an error; it should have been more like 150 feet] since we left the San Juan. This A.M. Jack was so fortunate as to kill a sheep which sets us up again and as the hills are a little more covered with grass we begin to hope that we may get an occasional sheep. If so, we can live very well for they are very good eating and the one we got today is quite fat and will weigh about 80 lbs. dressed. There was another with it that we came near getting but it got away and perhaps it is well that it did for when we got two before, part spoiled and we had to throw it away. We have taken the precaution to dry part of this so there is little danger of its spoiling. [This would be the last big game animal taken during the expedition.] Fish were very plenty as we passed along today but they will not bite as they get plenty to eat; all along where the water is still we could see them catching small flies that the river seems covered with. The cañon continues low, and the sandstone through which the river now runs has a strange tendency to form mounds and monuments from which Major has concluded to call it "Monument Cañon" from the mouth of the San Juan. Where we camp tonight there are pony tracks and evidences that the Indians can get in here. We think it must be through a little stream that comes in at this point, but most such places become perpendicular if followed back a short distance. The weather continues very hot.

[J. W. POWELL, Journal #1] Aug 3. Ran down through upper part of Monument Cañon. Many high monts seen near river and back some distance, low walls giving a view. Stopped at night just below a small, clear creek where had been an Indian camp. Camp No. 23.

[J. W. POWELL, Journal #2 Geology notes] On the third of Aug., the light red slowly went down. Above was a gray and buff Sds interstratified with light red, the light red beds becoming thinner above. Then gray shales were seen in the cliffs back from the river. At camp No 22 the summit of the light red was but about 200 ft. above the water.

[SUMNER] **August 3.** Pulled out early, made a good run. Saw 2 mountain sheep in a little valley on the south side. How they got there I will leave others to judge, as there is no outlet to the valley that a man can climb. Killed one and chased the other through the natural pasture for an hour and pulled out again. Made 33 miles and camped on the north side at the old Ute crossing between Utah and western Colorado and New Mexico. The trail on the north side comes down a side cañon not more than 10 ft. wide with walls 200 ft. high. worn by a small, clear stream through the sandstone. On the north side it is broken and easy to get out with ponies. The river is about 200 yards wide and when we were there, about 7 ft. deep.

☀ Day #73

[BRADLEY] **Aug. 4. 69.** Another long run of 38 1/4 miles. Water very still all the way and a head wind which this P.M. has sometimes blown a perfect tornado with lightning and rain. The walls for the last twenty miles have been getting higher and the cañon narrower. Tonight, however, we came suddenly to a point where the strata is [are] very much broken and quite a basin is formed by the washing away of the upturned rocks, but just below a few miles the strata is again horrizontal [sic] so that probably the break is only local. Jack & Bill D. have just come in from a short hunt and report that there seems to be quite an extensive plain off to the south of us. Where we are now encamped are signs of Indians such as brush cut for beds, and old bones, but quite old. We are at or very near the Ute trail where the Indians cross the river [the Paria, Mile 0 of Grand Canyon]. Tomorrow or next day we ought to come to the Pah Rhear River. A small trail where the Mormons have a ferry. Have made but little altitude today as the river has been too still but just below our camp a fine rappid commences that is roaring pretty loud and I can see the white foam for quite half a mile so judge we make a little altitude while the rocks remain broken. We have all learned to like mild rappids better than we do still water, but some of the party want them *very mild*.

[J. W. POWELL, Journal #1] **Aug. 4.** Cañon walls grow higher to day, still monuments for 10 or 12 miles. As the walls are higher, the Cañon is narrower. Gradually the walls change from 200 ft. to 600 ft. Late in the afternoon we found the rocks disturbed with long, broken slopes where river bends to W., may be a little N. Camped at mouth of Ute Creek [actually the Paria]. I found a green sds [sandstone]. Camp No. 24.

[J. W. POWELL, Journal #2 Geology notes] On the 4th, dip changes, the light red coming up to more than 800 ft. alt. Just before going into camp No 24 the lower part of Monument Form. came up with a dip of 12° or 15°. Here with the upper gray there is a bed of green Sds 25 or 30 ft. thick. Dip E.

[SUMNER] August 4. Pulled out early and made a run of 38 miles, that brought us to the old Spanish Crossing between Salt Lake and New Mexico, called the Escalanta [sic] "El vade de los Padres." [note here that Sumner — and Powell — are confusing the "Crossing of the Fathers" roughly 30 miles upstream with their actual location, the future site of Lee's Ferry, which lies less than a mile upstream of the Paria River.] It is desolate enough to suit a lovesick poet. There is a small dirty stream coming in from the north called by the Mormons Pahria River. On a mound 600 ft. above the river there is an old Indian fort about 25 ft. in diameter, with a 3 ft. wall, or rather the remains of a wall, as the green sandstone is fast crumbling to pieces. Camped on the north side on a sandbar. Saw the remains of cattle probably stolen from the Mormons by the friendlys [Indians] and killed here.

"The Heart of Marble Canyon" (etching from *Canyons of the Colorado*).

Chapter 8.

MARBLE CANYON TO THE LITTLE COLORADO RIVER, August 5 - 10

Although none of the crew will know it until after the fact, on August 5 the expedition enters Grand Canyon. Unaware of their location, Powell decides to name this part, the first 61.5 miles of Grand Canyon, Marble Canyon, a name he had been hankering to use for Cataract Canyon. Here the men encounter serious rapids yet again, but ones that, relatively speaking. are minor league compared to what they will soon encounter in the Upper and Lower Granite Gorges (next chapter) *a week hence. Even so, these rapids are still nasty enough to demand lining — and even portaging — the boats in what Sumner calls "terrible hard work." Three days into Marble Canyon Bradley notes: "Have been in camp all day repairing boats for constant banging against rocks has begun to tell sadly on them and they are growing old faster, if possible, than we are." It is here in Marble Canyon that Fate will begin to shift the fortunes and futures of each man of the crew as each labors on starvation rations in brutally hot weather to line their beat-up Whitehalls around whitewater obstacles.*

Day #74 [BRADLEY] Aug. 5. 69. Well I said yesterday that we had learned to like rappids but we came to two of them [Badger and Soap Creek] today that *suit us too well.* They are furious cataracts. The first one we passed before we ate dinner, and after dinner we ran a few miles and came upon one that has lasted us all the P.M. But we are over it, or rather arround it, for we had to take the boats out in one place. We have lowered our altitude today very much for this A.M. we had a series of rappids which we could run and which let us down very fast. Am very tired tonight. Hope a good sleep will set me good but this constant wetting in fresh water and exposure to a parching sun begins to tell on all of us. Run 12 miles today.

[J. W. POWELL, Journal #1] Aug. 5. A very long rapid to start with, still more rapids, a portage, fall 14 ft. Dinner on right bank. Run of 2 or more miles. Another long portage. Camp on right bank [below Soap Creek and River Mile 11.5 in Marble/Grand Canyon] on sand. No. 25.

[J. W. POWELL, Journal #2 Geology notes] On the 5th, we soon ran through Monument [Glen Canyon] Form. into narrow canon form. There are beds of calciferous Sds in the upper part of this with many encrinite stems. Gradually the walls grow higher, about 400 ft. of grey Sds, rather homogeneous. The[n] about 4 or 500 ft. of red Sds and shales dark red, thin beds of hard rock between, then beds of soft andfriable Sds. Then 5 or 600 ft. of Sds more thickly beded [sic] with a few seams of soft shales. Like above, some of thick beds buff, others dark red buff stained dark red.

[SUMNER] August 5. Pulled out early and ran a long rapid to begin with, then 12 more in 8 miles; made 2 portages over rapid of 15 ft. fall in 25 yds.; stove a hole in the "Maid" while lifting her over the rocks. Heavy wind and rain at night. Made 15 miles. Very hard work; camped on the north side on a sandbar.

☀ Day #75

[BRADLEY] Aug. 6. 69. Another hard day for 10 3/4 miles. The cañon has lofty walls, much of the way perpendicular, and wherever the rocks have fallen in or there is a side cañon we have a rappid. Where we can run the currant is swift and we make good speed. This forenoon we came upon a dangerous rappid where we had to cling to the smoothe sides of the rocks until we could view the *situation* and, having discovered little footholds on the left at the top of the fall, we succeeded in landing all our boats safely. And climbing over the rocks that made the rappid, we carried our rations and then lowered our boats and were in and away again. Three times today we have had to carry everything arround rappids, but the last few miles we came tonight we found the rappids less furious, and I hope we are out of the worst of this series.

Tomorrow is the eclipse, so we have to stop and let Major climb the mountain to observe it. We have camped in a place where the rock is so much broken that possibly he may climb out but the chances are against him for if he succeeds in reaching a point where he can see out, the probability is that it will be cloudy and rain about the hour for the eclipse as it has done for the last three or four days.

The dip of the stratta [sic] changes here to the west and the limestone is just in sight; it is fortunate that it changes for it always has given us trouble when that old hard marble comes up. It was that which gave us frightful cataracts when we first came into the Colorado and if we have escaped it, we are lucky.

[J. W. POWELL, Journal #1] Aug. 6th. Walls still get higher as down we go to the limestone. Had a hard climb along benches and through cleft of rock to see rapids. Made portage, another after dinner, long. I went up lateral cañon, found fossils. Saw cascade of red mud. Camped at night on right bank. Cañon with high walls, narrow, walls terraced. The chief terrace about 350 ft. high with slope of 40° - 45°. Upper vertical wall with many projecting points like end of wall. Below rocks often projecting over water. Camp No. 26.

[SUMNER] **August 6.** Repaired the "Maid" and pulled out again into more rapids. Made 3 portages and ran 10 bad rapids in 10 1/2 miles. Walls of cañon 2000 ft. and increasing as we go. River about 50 yds. wide, rapids and whirlpools all the way. Camped on the north side on a sandbar at dark.

☀ Day #76

[BRADLEY] **Aug. 7. 69.** Have been in camp all day repairing boats for constant banging against rocks has begun to tell sadly on them and they are growing old faster, if possible, than we are. Have put four new ribs in mine today and calked her all arround until she is as tight again as a cup. Hope it is the last time she will need repairs on this trip.

Major & brother have climbed the mountain to observe the eclipse but think it almost or quite a total failure for it has rained almost or quite all the P.M. We could see the sun from camp when it was about half covered but it clouded immediately and before the cloud passed it was behind the bluffs. Major has not yet come in. Cannot tell whether he saw it or not. If he did we shall have our Longitude. The river is very red and rising some. Hope it is caused only by these little showers for we now have all the water we want and any more would make it harder for us. Have pitched our tent for the first time since we left Uinta.

[J. W. POWELL, Journal #1] **Aug. 7.** Took obs. in morning. Climbed mt. after dinner to observe eclypse [sic]. Failed, clouds. Slept on mt. side, to [sic] dark to get all the way down. Same camp.

[J. W. POWELL, Journal #2 Geology notes] On the 7th, I climbed right wall and found fossils at summit — Productus & Athyris [both Brachiopods]. The lower members of the Monument Form. could be seen two or three miles distant on either side of river with thin characteristic colors. There is some lime in this upper rock of the wall and some beds of Calciferous Sds.

At the foot here the limestone is seen 20 ft. above the water. The lower bar [bed?] stood at this point 20 ft. above river.

[SUMNER] **August 7.** In camp all day repairing boats and taking observations.

☀ Day #77

[BRADLEY] **Aug. 8. 69**. Major & brother were in the bluffs all last night. They looked at the eclipse and at the river and mountains until they could not get to camp before it got too dark, for one cannot come down perpendicular walls unless he has daylight for it. The sun clouded at the moment the eclipse passed off, so we know no more about our longitude now than when we came here.

Though it is Sunday it brings no rest to us. We have found five rappids today arround which we have had to make portages. Have run only 3 1/2 miles today. Never made so many portages in one day for we never had so little to carry arround them as now. The weather is more pleasant tonight and the river is clearer but it is very muddy yet. There is one good rappid at our camp that we can run and another about 500 yds. below that will require another portage but we can't get down to look at it for the walls come down to the water and it is too deep and swift too [sic] wade past it. We have always found some footing arround bad rappids so far, for the rock that makes the rappid makes also a chance to get arround it, and I apprehend that it will always be so for if there is no obstruction it is simply *swift*. And we like that for we can ride as fast as water can run if there are no rocks or heavy waves.

We begin to be a ragged looking set for our clothing is wearing out with such rough labor, and we wear scarce enough to cover our nakedness for it is very warm with a sun poaring down between sandstone walls 2,000 ft. high. They are that hight now and gradually rising, though Major says that 12 or 15 miles ahead seemed to be a slight valley or break probably where the Pah Rhear comes in and just beyond that are very high snow-clad mountains, but probably the snow is only what fell when we had the showers for they saw snow just back of the cliffs where they climbed yesterday.

The limestone is coming up again and there are some of the most beautiful marbles I ever saw, not excepting those in the Cap. at Washington. They are polished by the waves, many of them, and look very fine. Should like specimens of them but the uncertainty of adequate transportation makes it vain even to collect a foccil, not to speak of plain rocks.

We are interested now only in how we shall get through the cañon and once more to civilization. Though we are more than ever sanguine of success, still our slow progress and wasting rations admonish us that we have something to do. Fortunately we are a happy go lucky set of fellows and look more to our present comfort than our future damages and as the cook has a fine lot of beans cooking with every prospect that his sweating and swearing will issue us an ample breakfast in the morning, we shall make our beds tonight and nodoubts sleep as soundly as if surrounded with all the comforts of "happy home" instead of in a cave of the earth.

[J. W. POWELL, Journal #1] Aug. 8th. Five portages today. Beautiful marble, cream & pink & gray, purple with light red tints &c. Curious effect of the waters dashing against foot of pile of rocks. Alcoves and arches of water. A temple changing like a flame but by beets [beats?]. Camp in cave. Camp 27.

[J. W. POWELL, Journal #2 Geology notes] On the 8th, we ran down so as to get more than 200 ft. of this limestone. It is much flexed, the flexures being short, and shows much metamorphism as though thin beds had yielded, pressed out, and the great weight of the walls had changed it [them]. There is much beautiful marble in this cañon, some gray, drab cream, pink, purple, and brown and then mixtures of these. The purple beds mentioned before as the upper part of this form. have more lime here and I think would make a beautiful marble.

[SUMNER] August 8. Pulled out early and did a terrible hard work. Made 5 portages in 3 1/4 miles. Camped on the south side under a marble cliff; walls increasing in height. Gathered little twigs of driftwood to cook out bread and make coffee.

☀ Day #78

[BRADLEY] Aug. 9. 69. Have made but little distance on Sunday but today we have run 16 miles, made three portages, and passed 31 rappids, some of them very bad ones. Have had a little better running this P.M. Am in hopes that this series of heavy rappids is about ended. We have now run down our altitude until we are no longer apprehensive on that score. The limestone continues to rise fast. Think there is about one thousand ft. up now, but as the bottom part is softer than that which came up first, it wears faster and makes a better bed for the river.

We passed a beautiful cascade [Vasey's Paradise] today but the rappids were so furious and the walls so nearly vertical we could not stop to examine it. To me it was the prettiest sight of the whole trip. The green ferns arround it formed a pleasing contrast with the unending barrenness of the cañon.

[J. W. POWELL, Journal #1] Aug 9th. Scenery on a grand scale, marble walls polished by the waves. Walls 2000 - 2200 ft. high. 3 portages before dinner. This forenoon I had a walk of a mile on marble pavement [River Mile 27+] polished smooth in many places, in others embossed in a thousand fantastic patterns. Highly colored marble. Sun shining through cleft in the wall and the marble sending back the light in iridescence. At noon a cleft or cañon on left [Silver Grotto in Shinumo Wash?], quite narrow with a succession of pools, one above another, going back and connected by a little stream of clear water.

The pavement a little too wide for a Boston street - potholes filled with clear water. Banded marble at noon 20 ft. out of the water.

After dinner we found a spring gushing from an orafice [sic] in the marble as silvery foam glad to see the light, released from prison. A bank of luxuriant verdure (ferns chiefly) on the talus below. Many little springs this afternoon with patches of verdures below. A huge cave [Redwall Cavern] 1/2 mile below a spring. Vast no. of caves and domed alcoves in this region. Walls about 2,500 ft. high at 3 P.M.

Just below spring the high water mark comes down to 10 or 12 ft. and the first mezquit [mesquite] seen. Camp in mezquit grove. No. 28.

[SUMNER] August 9. Hard at work early. Made 4 portages and ran 27 bad rapids in 13 miles. Passed a beautiful spring pouring out of the cliff 100 ft. above the river. The white water over the blue marble made a pretty show. I would not advise anybody to go there to see it. The walls of the cañons are about 3000 ft. nearly perpendicular and it cannot be climbed from the river. Made 16 miles and camped on the south side on a sandbar.

☀ Day #79

[BRADLEY] Aug. 10. 69. About noon today Major concluded that our course south, our extreme southern latitude, and our continuous falling of Altitude all indicate that we had passed the Pah Rhear River and we're fast approaching some other, probably the Chiquito, or Little Colorado. He told us so at noon, and at 2 P.M. we came upon it. It is a lothesome [sic] little stream so filthy and muddy that it fairly stinks. Is only 30 to 50 yds. wide now and in many places a man can cross it on the rocks without going in to his knees.

There are signs of Indians here but quite old. Cannot tell whether they are Moquis or Apachies [sic]. I think more likely the latter for the Moquis keep close to their villages. We now conclude that we passed the Ute Trail Aug. 3. where we saw the pony tracks and that the lothsome [sic] little stream that comes in where we found the stratta so broken Aug. 4th. is no

"At the Mouth of the Little Colorado" (etching by C. Bogert in *Canyons of the Colorado*).

other than the Pah Rhear River [this conclusion is correct].

The Colorado continues very rappid. Indeed it seems more like an overgrown brook than it does like a large river. We have run 13 3/4 miles today in which we passed 35 rappids. We ran them all, though some of them were bad ones. One was the largest we have run in the Colorado for we have gone more cautiously in it than we did in the Green. I think we have had too much caution and made portages where to run would be quite as safe and much less injurious to the boats.

We shall have to stop here two or three days to get Latitude and Longitude as this point has not been determined, though it is said a man [James White] went through from here on a raft to Callville in eleven days. If so we have little to fear from waterfalls below, but I place little reliance on such reports, though his story has been published with much show of reason and Maj. has seen the man. We are sorry to be delayed, as we have had no meat for several days and not one sixth of a ration for more than a month. Yet we are willing to do all that we can to make the trip a success. Weather showery.

[J. W. POWELL, Journal #1] Aug. 10. Walls still higher. Water very swift, falling rapidly (altitude). Timber clad ridges seen to right. Reach Flax River at 2 P.M. Camp No. 29.

[J. W. POWELL, Journal #2 Geology notes] About 5 or 6 miles above mouth of Flax [Little Colorado] gray and purple Sds appear and rise rapidly to that point. Dip, I think, a little E. of N. These Sds [Tapeats Sandstone] are coarse, sometimes a conglomerate, and rather hard, wearing out in shelves and overhanging rocks as they did near mouth of Bear R. [Yampa].

[SUMNER] August 10. Pulled out at 7 o'clock and ran 14 miles, passing 20 rapids many of them bad. Came to mouth of the Flax or Little Colorado River, as disgusting a stream as there is on the continent; 3 rods wide and about 3 ft. deep, half of its volume and 2/3 of it weight is mud and silt. There are a few mesquite bushes growing on the south side of Flax River, nothing on the Colorado. Walls about 4000 ft. high, inaccessible except on a very few points. Camped under a ledge of rocks, 100 yards below Flax River, and 1/4 of a mile from the Colorado.

"The Inner Gorge" [actually Lava Falls] (etching by Thomas Moran in *Canyons of the Colorado*).

Chapter 9.

THROUGH THE GREAT UNKNOWN OF GRAND CANYON, August 11 - 28

As Fate would have it, in Grand Canyon downstream of the Little Colorado, the 1869 crew meets its most serious challenges in a seemingly endless gauntlet of huge rapids which must be lined, portaged, and sometimes rowed while the men's last reserves of strength and will ebb. On August 14, Bradley notes: "Well this is emphatically the wildest day of the trip so far." Here too the first words are penned which severely criticize Major Powell's leadership and also hint at mutiny. Meanwhile the monsoons rage on with a vengeance, drenching the starving and weakened explorers, creating ribbons of muddy falls shooting off the rims of the inner gorge and loading the swelling river with silt. Still the men run dozens of rapids in this race against starvation on 215 miles of wild river. Ironically, 239 miles into Grand Canyon and only 38 miles from its foot, the most notorious incident in perhaps all of Western exploration unfolds tragically as the Howland brothers and William Dunn decide to abandon Powell, the river, and the expedition and instead hike north to Mormon settlements. Bradley confides to his journal: "This is decidedly the darkest day of the trip..." Bradley, it would turn out, was all too correct. The expedition splits into two factions divided by a sharp diversion of opinions but a near commonality of high emotions about separating from one another. The six men who continue downriver run two of the very biggest rapids on the Colorado system between Wyoming and Mexico, arguably the two biggest — Separation Rapid and Lava Cliff Rapid (River Mile 246). Bradley and Sumner pen remarkably detailed and enthusiastic accounts of the runs of **Kitty Clyde's Sister** *and* **Maid of the Cañon** *through Separation and Lava Cliff.*

Day #80 [BRADLEY] Aug 11. 69. Have been in camp all day for I have nothing to wear on my feet but an old pair of boots in which I cannot climb the mountains and which are my only reliance for making portages. In the boat and much of the time in camp I go bare-foot. But I have a pair of camp moccasins to slip on when the rocks are bad or the sand is too hot. I have given away my clothing until I am reduced to the same condition of those who lost by the shipwreck of our boat. I cannot see a man of the party more destitute than I am. Thank God the trip is nearly ended for it is no place for a man in my circumstances, but it will let me out of the Army and for that I would almost agree to explore the River Styx.

I have rigged a stone table and chair and have commenced again to copy my notes. Have copied some from time to time and find it much easier than to do it all at once. Shall get them copied to date if we stay here tomorrow and I fear we shall have to stay several days, though Jack got one set of observations today which gives us time once more. And if it is not cloudy, Major will get Latitude on the North Star tonight, but it is generally cloudy at night. He is going to get Longitude by the sun & moon, which he can probably get tomorrow as it don't cloud up generally until two or three P.M.

Our camp is under the shelving edge of a cliff on the south side of the Chiquito and is protected from both sun and rain by overhanging rocks, though it is filthy with dust and alive with insects. If this is a specimine of Arrazona [sic] a very little of it will do for me. The men are uneasy and discontented and anxious to move on. If Major does not do something soon I fear the consequences. But he is contented and seems to think that biscuit made of sour and musty flour and a few dried apples is ample to sustain a laboring man. If he can only study geology he will be happy without food or shelter, but the rest of us are not afflicted with it to such an alarming extent.

[J. W. POWELL, Journal #1] Aug. 11. Capt. & Sumner take Obs. I walk up Flax 5 miles. Old Indian camps seen, trails, foot paths. Flax tumbling down over many falls. Water very muddy, salty.

P.M. Walter and I walk down river. Old path, well worn.

No lunar on account of clouds. Same camp, under rocks.

[SUMNER] August 11 and 12. In camp taking observations and measuring walls. The reason is plain to us why Lt. Ives and Dr. Newberry did not get to the junction.

☀ Day #81

[BRADLEY] Aug. 12. 69. Have copied my notes to date and now am anxious to be on the move. Major got Latitude last night by which we find ourselves as far south as Callville so that what we run now must be west from this point. Major's brother is out on the mountains with the barometer so we shall know their height when he comes in. There remains nothing more to be done that is absolutely necessary, for Lat. & Long. are sufficient and we ought to be away in the morning. Don't know whether we shall or not. It is looking like a shower tonight. I am surprised to find it raining nearly every night in a country where they say rain seldom falls.

[J. W. POWELL, Journal #1] Aug. 12. Take Obs. Capt. climbed mt.

☀ Day #82

[BRADLEY] Aug. 13. 69. Started about 9 A.M. and have made 15 miles. The rappids are almost innumerable, some of them very heavy ones full of treacherous rocks. Three times today we have let down with ropes but without making a portage. Our rations are so much reduced now that they make but little difference to the boats. We camp tonight at the head of the worst rappid [Hance Rapid] we have found today and the longest we have seen on the Colorado. The rocks are seen nearly all over it for half a mile or more. Indeed the river runs through a vast pile of rocks. I am convinced that no man had ever run such rappids on a raft, though it is possible that he might pass along the shore and build another raft below and so work his way out, but I pay little heed to the whole story.

Major has just come in and says the granite is coming up less than a mile down the river. We are now in the red sandstone of Lodore Cañon [called Shinumo Quartzite in Grand Canyon but Uinta Mountain Group in Lodore, this more than one-billion-year old rock looks very similar but is not the same age formation] but which we have run through very quickly this time for the strata has a great dip here, but if our course changes as it now seems inclined to the west and N.W., we may clear most of the granite. One thing is pretty certain. No rocks ever made can make much worse rappids than we now have.

[J. W. POWELL, Journal #1, August] 13. Fifteen miles of very rapid river. Walls much broken. Come to granite at night. Ind. camp nearby. I climb wall, still more rapids before us. Camp 30 [Red Canyon/Hance Rapid].

[J. W. POWELL, Journal #2 Geology notes] Coming down the river below the mouth of the Flax rusty gray Sdss [Sic] untill there is 600 ft. below the lowest limestones found. Then we come to the "Old Red" when the region is much broken up for 3 or four miles. The old red seems turned [?] into short folds but the dip N. predominates and is much greater than the dip of the marble, say 18° or 20°. The upturned edges have been much eroded, some deep gulches. After erosion a great out-pouring of "lava" [pillow basalts], then the deposition of the marble nearly or quite horizontal.

At Camp No 30 come to Granite, having run 12 miles through upturned old red. Dikes are seen in this region for 6 or 8 miles. Old patches are seen above the granite, there the rusty gray is always next to granite.

[SUMNER] August 13. Pulled out at 8 o'clock and enter into another nest of rapids. Ran 30 and let down with ropes; passed three more in 15 miles of travel. Ran the old red sandstone about 4 miles below the mouth of the Flax River; 6 miles below there are the remains of an old volcano. Camped on the north side at the head of a rapid about 1 mile long with a fall of 50 or 60 ft. that has about 100 rocks in the upper half of it [Hance Rapid, which drops 30 feet]. How anyone can ride that on a raft is more than I can see. Mr. White may have done so but I don't believe it. At the lower end of the rapid the granite rises for the first time. There is no granite whatever (except boulders) from Green River City to the head of this rapid.

☀ Day #83

[BRADLEY] Aug. 14. 69. Well this is emphatically the wildest day of the trip so far. We let down the first rappid this morning, ran the one at its foot, a very heavy one, and then a succession of very rough ones until near noon when we came to the worst one [Sockdolager] we had seen on the river and, the walls being vertical, or rather coming to the water on both sides, we had to run it and, all being ready, away we went each boat following close to the one next before. The little boat, being too small for such a frightful sea, filled soon after starting and swung around head up river almost unmanageable, but on she went, and by the good cool sence of those onboard, she was kept right side up through the whole of it (more than half a mile). My boat came next and the first wave dashed partly over us with fearful force striking one oar from the hand of Major's brother but did not fill the boat. She rose to battle with the next one. And by good luck we kept her head to the waves and rode them all, taking less water than we sometimes do on much smaller rappids. Bill R. came next and, quite as lucky as we were, he escaped with a good shaking up and a slight ducking. The waves were frightful beyond anything we have yet met and it seemed for a time that our chance to save the boats was very slim, but we are a lucky set and our good luck did not go back on us then.

This P.M. we have kept up the game until tonight we find ourselves six miles from where we started and in about the middle of a tremendous rappid [Grapevine Rapid] fully half a mile long. We have lowered the boats to this point by clinging to the side of the granite cliff and working them along as best we could. It injures them very much and if I could have my say we should run it, for the risk is no greater and we can run it in a few moments, while this will take us nearly another half day.

We have but poor accommodations for sleeping tonight. No two except Major & Jack can find space wide enough to make a double bed, and if they don't lie still we shall "hear something drop" and find one of them in the river before morning. I sleep in a wide seam of the rocks where I can't roll out. Andy has his bed just above the water on a fragment at the water's edge scarce wide enough to hold him. The rest are tucked arround like eve-swallows wherever the cliff offers sufficient space to stretch themselves with any degree of comfort or safety.

[J. W. POWELL, Journal #1] Aug. 14th. Made a portage from camp, then ran two miles to bad falls [Sockdolager] in narrow chute. No talus, no foothold of any kind. Must run it or abandon the enterprise. Good Luck! Little boat fills with water twice. Chute 1/2 mile long, fall 30 ft., probably. Huge waves. Then run of two or three rapids then a long portage.

Dinner in a cave. Camp on right on rocks in middle of long portage [Grapevine Rapid] on right bank. No. 31.

[SUMNER] August 14. Made a portage of half the rapid and ran the rest to get into a half dozen more bad ones in...when we came to a fearful looking...a long rapid with a fall of 30 ft. and no foothold to make a portage [Sockdolager Rapid, drops 19 feet at River Mile 79]. Climbed up the side of the cañon wall as far as we could to get a partial view of the thing. Returned to the boat. Fastened down the hatches of the cabins and pulled out into the waves. The two large boats went through without getting more than half full of water. But the small boat filled in the first waves and drifted 3/4 of a mile through a perfect hell of waves, but came out all right. Bailed out our boats, laughed over the scrape and pulled out again in some more, one of which filled "Kitty's Sister."

At 2 o'clock came to a rapid that cannot be run by any boat, half a mile long, 75 yds. wide, fall of 50 ft. [Grapevine Rapid, a drop of about 20 feet] and full of rocks. Landed on the north side and worked hard till sunset to get halfway down. Ate our supper of some bread and coffee and went to sleep on the bare, rough granite rock. Made 7 miles; 12 rapids, all bad. River very narrow. Granite 1000 ft high.

☀ Day #84

[BRADLEY] Aug. 15. 69. This morning (Sunday) we lowered the little boat with great labor and it nearly stove her. So we volunteered to run my boat through and, putting in the rations, away we went. "2.40" was no name for it. We went like the wind and as luck would have it took in but little water. Only one sea which was not quite quick enough to get onboard but swept our stearn with terrible force. Caught by the whirlpools below we whirled round and round until out of them and then rowed into the eddy and laid on our oars to have the fun of seeing Bill R. row it, which he did after a while. But not getting out quite far enough from shore, his boat nearly filled and he broke one oar. We have already (12 M.) made 4 miles and after we let down past the rappid at which we now lie we may make a good run yet. We don't expect it, however, for the granite raises Cain with this river.

Have run only 3 1/4 miles this P.M. for Howland had the misfortune to loose [sic] his notes and map of the river from Little Colorado down to this point, so we have camped at the first landing, which happens to be an excellent camping ground shaded by a fine weeping willow which throws a greatful [sic] shadoww [sic] over a wide circle. There is also a fine creek or river as they would call it in this country [Bright Angel Creek at River Mile 88] coming in from the north clear as crystal and quite swift and wide. There are fish in it. But Howland had tried in vain to catch them so they can't be trout. Think they are only whitefish. The boys have just come in from a walk up the creek and report good oar timber a few miles up the creek which had drifted down, so we shall probably stay a day or two and make oars.

The little boat had her cut-water broken this A.M. while running a rappid. There was only about fifteen feet between the rocks and the shore and, being caught suddenly by the eddy, she sheared against the rocks. She does not leak badly but it weakens her badly. My boat came within four feet of doing the same trick but we saved her just in time. We are all willing to stay here a day or two for we are quite worn out by the constant running of rappids and climbing over the granite cliffs letting down boats. It is very wearing, especially to me, for I have done so little rough work that it comes hard.

[J. W. POWELL, Journal #1] Aug. 15. Finish portage and make a short one where Billy [Hawkins] runs his boat to opposite shore, failing to reach us. After dinner, short run and portage and camp early at mouth of Silver Creek. I have a long walk up creek, find oar timber. Camp No. 32.

[SUMNER] August 15. Finished the portage and ran 12 more bad rapids and made 2 portages in 8 miles travel. Camped about 4 miles at the mouth of a clear trout stream coming in from the north. There is a large willow growing on a sand bar a few rods above the creek that affords a splendid camp. Stretched our weary bodies on the sand under the willow and rested the remainder of the day.

 Day #85

[BRADLEY] Aug. 16. 69. Have been at work hard getting out oars, for the stick we found was large and we have but poor tools to work with. Have got out three but mine is left until last and is not finished. They have come to think that my boat should carry all the rations, go into all dangerous places first, and get along with least. So be it. The trip is nearly ended and when it is up perhaps I shall be just as well off, but one can't help minding an imposition even in a wilderness so far from civilization.

There is another old Moqui ruin where we are camped tonight. Have found the same little fragments of broken crockery as we did before. Have saved a few little specimens. An unpleasant little accident occurred today which we shall feel keenly all the rest of the trip. The cook, having spread all the rations to dry, was engaged making oars when the boat swung around by the eddy tide, the roap [sic] caught the box of soda and drew it all into the river so we must eat "*un-leavened bread*" all the rest of the trip. Major has called the stream coming in at this point Silver Creek [a.k.a. Bright Angel Creek].

[J. W. POWELL, Journal #1] Aug. 16. Make oars and take obs. Same camp.

[SUMNER] August 16. In camp today and repair and rest. Made some oars from a pine log we found half a mile up the creek. The Professor named the stream "Silver Creek" [but renamed it in Washington, D.C. "Bright Angel Creek"]. Very hot all day.

☀ Day #86

[BRADLEY] Aug. 17. 69. We have run a succession of rappids and made three portages today. One portage lasted us nearly all the P.M. and as soon as we had finished it we came upon another very bad one and, knowing we could not pass it tonight, we have not tackled it at all but some of the boys have gone out hunting as we begin to see signs of sheep again. The granite peaks begin to get gradually lower but they are very irregular, for we sometimes see them only about 300 ft. and immediately come to another almost or quite 1,000 ft. The old red sandstone rests on the granite and then the marble above so that a little way back from the river the hills rise to from 4,000 to 5,000 feet and are covered with pines. We can see mountains to our right but probably the river will go arround them as it generally has all the others. Ran 9 3/4 miles today.

[J. W. POWELL, Journal #1] Aug. 17. Make run of 10 1/4 miles today with two bad portages. Camp at night just above one. Walk up creek 3 miles. Grand scenery, old Ind. camps. Through this cañon the limestone overlies the granite and runs down near the river in sharp, wall-like points. To the summit of this, the highest rocks that can be seen at any point, I estimate the height at 4000 ft., may be only 3500. Camp No. 33.

Granite Falls (etching by Thomas Moran in *Canyons of the Colorado*).

[J. W. POWELL, Journal #2 Geology notes] At camp No 33 I went up creek and had a good view of the rocks for more than a 1,000 ft., rusty gray Sds found with brown beds then shaley Sds gray and green then Shaley limestone, thin compact limestone stained red by the shaley Sds above. Here the Carboniferous must be 3,500 ft., about the same as it was 3 miles below [the] Flax. Above the compact marble is [are] found the same beds of red Sdss and limestones and then gray and buff up to summit [canyon rim].

The "granite" has been from 400 to 800 ft. Some garnetiferous shists [sic], much feldspar, some talcum shists.

[SUMNER] August 17. Pulled out at 8 o'clock and ran a continuous rapid for 3 miles; then came to a portage; while letting the "Maid" down with a line she struck a rock and loosened her head block badly. Repaired damages and pulled out again into more rapids. Made 2 heavy portages and ran 12 bad rapids in traveling 9 3/4 miles. Camped on south side at the head of another portage. Supper of unleavened bread. **[Original version]** Left Silver creek at 8 o'clock and ran a continuous Rapid for 3 miles then came to a portage. Made it and ran 1 more during the day's run of 9 3/4 and ran 10 Rapids. Camped on south side.

☀ Day #87

[BRADLEY] Aug. 18. 69. Hard work and little distance seem to be the characteristic of this cañon. Have worked very hard today and have advanced but four miles. Rappids very numerous and very large. A great many lateral [sic] cañons come in almost as large as the one in which the river runs and they sweep down immense quantities of huge rocks which at places literally dam up the river making the worst kind of a rappid because you can see rocks rising all over them with no channel in which to run them. If we could, we would run more of them because our rations are not sufficient to anything more than just to sustain life. Coffee and *heavy* bread cannot be called *light* rations, but one feels quite light about the stomache [sic] after living on it a while. We have just lowered our boats over a very treacherous rappid and camped at its foot, for just below us is another all ready to start on in the morning with a fine chance for a man to see what strength he has gained by a night's rest.

This P.M. we have had a terrible thunder-shower. We had to fasten our boats to the rocks and seek shelter from the wind behind the bowlders. The rain poared down in torrents and the thunder peals echoed through the cañon from crag to crag making wild music for the lightning to dance to. After a shower it is grand to see the cascades leap from the cliffs and turn to vapor before they reach the rocks below. There are thousands of them of all sizes, pure and white as molten silver. The water of the river is now very muddy from the continued showers which we have. It is not fit to drink but fortunately we find better among the rocks most of the time. The river at this point runs 25° North of West.

[J. W. POWELL, Journal #1] Aug. 18th. Bad rapids, portages and rain. Camp on right bank among the rocks. Wagon sheet makes but poor cover. Camp 34.

[SUMNER] August 18. Made 3 portages in 4 miles; camped on the north side on account of a terrible storm. Rained all night. **[Original version]** Made 3 heavy portages in 4 miles. camped on north side.

☀ Day #88

[BRADLEY] Aug. 19. 69. The rappid we started with this morning gave us to understand the character of the day's run. It was a wild one. The boats labored hard but came out all right. The waves were frightful and, had any of the boats shipped a sea, it would have been her last for there was no still water below. We ran a wild race for about two miles, first pulling right, then left, now to avoid the waves and now to escape the bowlders, sometimes half full of water and as soon as a little could be thrown out it was replaced by double the quantity. Our heavy boat ran past the lead boat and we dashed on alone, whirling and rushing like the wind. Looking for a place to land, at length we succeeded in checking her and landed in an eddy where we bailed the boat and waited for the others to come up.

Coming to one we could not run, we were forced to make a short portage and lower with ropes for 1/4 of a mile, which took us until after 12 o'clock. We took dinner on the side of a cliff where the cook could scarsely [sic] find a place large enough to hold his fire. For if there happens to be sufficient wood to cook with we don't dare look farther for we should be quite likely to come to another rappid where we should not be able to find wood.

It commenced raining last night and has hardly abated until 4 o'clock this P.M. Doubt if we don't have more before morning. All our clothing and bedding is wet and I expect a miserable night of it. Hardly had we started after dinner before we came to a furious rappid which seemed to have but few rocks, and we resolved to run it. The little boat took the lead but was not equal to the task, for she swamped at once [capsized] and we rushed on to her assistance hardly heeding the danger we ourselves were in. The whirlpools below caught us and our furious speed threw us against the rocks with terrible force. Fortunately we struck with the cut-water, which is the strongest part of our boat. We cleared the shore and reached the little boat, which by this time was nearly sunk, and the crew were all in the water holding her up. We took them in and towed them into an eddy below where we built a fire and have been lying ever since, drying the instruments, &c. Fortunately nothing was lost but a pair of oars. Have run only 5 3/4 miles.

[J. W. POWELL, Journal #1] Aug. 19th. Run bad rapid and two more below. Make portage. Dinner in rain among the rocks. After dinner, little boat swamped [capsized]. Bradey [sic] comes up with boat in good time. Camp on left bank, dig out a sleeping place, dry out by fire. Camp No. 35.

[SUMNER] August 19. Made 3 heavy portages and ran 3 very dangerous rapids; in one the small boat was swamped again [capsized for the third time]. Made 5 3/4 miles. Camped on the south side. Rain all day and most of the night. **[Original version]** Made two heavy Portages and Ran 3 very dangerous Rapids in 5 1/2 miles. Camped on south side.

☀ Day #89

[BRADLEY] Aug. 20. 69. We did not have rain last night, nor have we had any today, though last night our bedding was so wet that before morning we got very cold and uncomfortable. The sun came up clear this A.M., reached us about 8 1/2 o'clock, and as all was wet we concluded it was best to stay where we were and dry out. So we staid [sic] until noon, had dinner, and then loaded up our boats, having dried everything nicely. We have had a good little run this P.M. of 8 1/4 miles. Made one portage and lowered the boats with ropes twice. Rappids continued heavy but this P.M. seem a little farther apart. We must be getting near where the Mormons run the river, for they have run it 15 miles above Callville and one would think we had run rappids enough to be allowed a respite soon.

[J. W. POWELL, Journal #1] Aug. 20. Remained in camp untill noon. Made two portages in afternoon. Came at night to the "old red." Found remains of old Moquis village on bank [lower Bass Camp?], stone houses and pottery. (Found same remains at Silver Creek and Mill [mano & metate?]). Country broken up. Camp No. 36.

[J. W. POWELL, Journal #2 Geology notes] At camp No 36 we had ran [sic] so far N. so as to be almost out of the granite (50 ft.). Here the "old Red" reappears dipping to the N.E. or N.N.E. at 20°. The granite here

"The Grand Canyon" Upper Granite Gorge (etching by W. J. Linton in *Canyons of the Colorado*).

shows much erosion before the formation of the "Old Red." The Carboniferous is horizontal. This "Old Red" is here often gray, more gray than red. The red dark all hard. A cliff of trachyte was seen one mile below camp in the old red.

[SUMNER] August 20. Laid over till noon to dry out what little we had left. Pulled out at noon and ran one dangerous rapid to begin with, then 3 portages in 8 1/4 miles. Camped on the north side near a lot of Moqui ruins [River Mile 108, Lower Bass Camp?]. Course of river 25° north of west. **[Original version]** Made 3 portages and ran one bad rapid in 8 1/2 miles. Camped on north side. Course of River - 25 N of W.

☀ Day #90

[BRADLEY] Aug. 21. 69. Have run 21 miles today and it stands first for dashing wildness of any day have seen *or will see* if I guess rightly, for we have been all day among rappids furious and long but we have managed to run all but one of them which was, I think, the roughest looking one we have met [likely Waltenberg]. The granite rose up in huge slabs running far out into the river and the fall was furious. The granite disappeared this P.M. but to my surprise we had no fall or even bad rappid where the sandstone commenced. I thought that running out of hard rock into sandstone would make a fall where the two met but it made nothing of the sort. I feel more unwell tonight than I have felt on the trip. I have been wet so much lately that I am ripe for any disease, and our scanty food has reduced me to poor condition, but I am still in good spirrits and am threatening all sorts of revenge when I get to decent food once more.

[J. W. POWELL, Journal #1] Aug. 21. Good run today. Many bad rapids. Let down one near camp in morning. Made about 20 miles. The rocks near the river after leaving the granite were shelving and vertical then a sloping terrace. The marble walls with terraces. Camp on left bank, No. 37.

[J. W. POWELL, Journal #2 Geology notes] Two miles below camp No 36 ran out of the granite [at River Mile 117]. Old red seen on both sides of river for still a mile below. From time to time for 16 miles the granite reappearing sometimes 50 ft. high; no doubt forms the floor [bed] of the river all of the distance.

[SUMNER] August 21. Made a portage with half a mile of camp then ran 6 bad rapids in 7 miles when we came to a perfect hell — a rapid with a fall of 30 ft. in 300 yds. Made a portage on the south side, then pulled out again and ran 14 miles, passing 20 rapids, but ran them all without trouble. Ran the granite up and down again. Made 22 miles. Camped on the south side on a sand bar; a few willows, the first since leaving Silver Creek and second since Flax River. Near camp average width of river 60 yds.; height of walls 4000 ft. but getting less. Course of river northwest. **[Original version]** Made one portage to begin with then ran six rapids then came to a very dangerous Rapid fall of 20 feet in 300 yards. Made portage on south side. Made 14 miles today. passed 27 rapids, average width of river 60 yds. Course [?] river [?] north west, walls 4000 feet. Camped on south side.

☀ Day #91

[BRADLEY] Aug. 22. 69. It rained some last night and as we had no tent set up I took my overcoat and went into the cliff where I found good quarters for the night. Has been raining considerably today and we have pitched the tent which may perhaps *prevent rain tonight*. We have found about five miles of granite today for the river has been running within five degrees of east much of the time [River Mile 132]. What it means I don't know but if it keeps on in this way we shall be back where we started from, which would make us feel very much as I imagine the old hog felt when he moved the hollow log so that both ends came on the out-side of the fence. Fortunately we can see below our present camp where it turns again to the west & south. We have made 11 1/4 miles today if it is Sunday. Have been running rappids all the time we ran at all. Have found one very bad one which it took us several hours to make a portage arround [Dubendorff?]. That was the only one we did not run. Our camp tonight was a necessity, not our choice, for we have come to another rocky shallow rappid which has a great fall and we can't find any way to run it, so we must make a portage which will be a long hard job for us tomorrow morning. I feel very much better tonight than I did last night.

[J. W. POWELL, Journal #1, August] 22nd. Today made a long detour to N.E. Ran back again into the granite. Camp on right bank early on account of rain — at the head of a long portage. No. 38.

[J. W. POWELL, Journal #2 Geology notes] From last mentioned point no more granite seen untill we are 5 miles from camp No 38. Where it is seen getting thicker, say to 300 ft. for 4 miles, when it is suddenly disappears under Old red one mile above camp 38. This old red has a bed of Igneous rock, Sds above and below it, 125 ft. thick.
At camp No 38 Dip N.E. 28° 20° [sic].

[SUMNER] August 22. Made 11 1/4 miles — nearly all rapids, one heavy portage. Course of river northeast. Camped on north side on some lava [an intrusive igneous rock called diabese]. Ran the granite up and down today. Rain all day. **[Original version]** Made 11 1/4 miles. One very bad portage. Course north east. Camped on North side.

☀ Day #92

[BRADLEY] Aug. 23. 69. Have had another hard day of it. Made only two miles this A.M., but this P.M. we got out of the granite rock and have made 10 1/4 miles making 12 1/4 miles for the day which is somewhat encouraging seeing that the river has now got back to its proper direction again. Just below our camp tonight is another rapid arround which they talk of making another portage. Hope they will feel better about it in the morning and run it, for it is an easy and safe one.

[J. W. POWELL, Journal #1, August] 23. After portage ran short distance to dinner camp. In afternoon found beautiful fall from a curiously worn hole in lateral cañon 100 ft. high [Deer Creek Falls at River Mile 136.5]. When we ran into the marble, wall almost vertical. Cañon still grand. Very bad portage on right bank this afternoon. Camp on left, No. 39.

[J. W. POWELL, Journal #2 Geology notes] 1 1/2 miles below camp 38 the Igneous rock is lost. Granite walls near the water soon set in, sometimes 100 ft. high showing much erosion of the country before the deposition of the old red, as it has everywhere done. This granite constructed [?] as the floor of the river up to 2 miles of camp 39.

[SUMNER] August 23. Made 3 portages and ran 20 bad rapids in 12 1/2 miles. Passed 2 cold streams coming in from the north, one of them pouring off a cliff 200 feet high [Deer Creek Falls]. Camped on the south side between perpendicular walls 2000 ft. high, all marble [limestone & dolomite]. **[Original version]** Made 3 Portages and ran 20 Rapids in 12 1/2 miles. Camp on [?] south side. Passed 2 streams North.

☀ Day #93

[BRADLEY] Aug. 24. 69. Have run 22 3/4 miles today after making a bad portage this morning and letting down with ropes this noon. This A.M. we run only one hour and made over seven miles. Our boats are getting so very leaky that we have to calk them very often. We are still running a succession of rappids, but this P.M. have run all we came to except the one at our present camp, which we shall run in the morning. Did not run it tonight for just above it is a singular recess or alcove in the rock about 100 ft. long and 50 ft. wide forming a fine shelter and it was fast commencing to rain when we arrived so Major camped here where all can find shelter without pitching tents. We are now in the marble rock again so tonight it will not be strange if we *"dream we dwelt in marble halls."*

We are much surprised to find the distance to Grand Wash lengthened out so much beyond the Mormon estimate, for we have now run over 120 miles and they estimate it from 70 to 80 miles. The reason probably is that ours is a distance by river while theirs is the actual distance by land. For the river has run very crooked since we left the Little Colorado. We cannot now be very far from it unless the river turns back again, which it shows no sign of doing. As we advance the river widens and the tide slackens.

[J. W. POWELL, Journal #1, August] 24. Good run today of 22 miles. Many rapids. High water mark coming down. River widening. Camp under rock, No. 40.

[J. W. POWELL, Journal #2 Geology notes] To camp 40 we ran through the lower members of the carboniferous one or two hundred ft. disappearing under water. There is more limestone among these lower Carboniferous.

[SUMNER] August 24. Made a portage on the start. Ran a few miles to get to another — made it. Ate dinner of unleavened bread and pulled out again and ran 15 miles through a narrow gorge, between walls 1500 ft. high — all marble. Passed 12 rapids, 4 bad ones, but ran them all, as they were clear of rocks. Made 22 1/4 miles and camped on the south side under a ledge of rocks on a bed of lime and magnesia. **[Original version]** Made Portages and passed a dozen rapids in 22 1/4 miles, camped on south side in a lime cave.

☀ Day #94

[BRADLEY] Aug. 25. 69. Have run 35 miles today, all the way rappid. About 10 o'clock A.M. came to volcanic lava which had been poared out since the river had reached its present bed. It had at sometime filled up the channel as high as 1,500 ft. but was worn down so as only to leave a cataract, yet it was a bad one and we had to slide our boats out arround it. The country begins to look a little more open and the river still improves. Came very near having an unpleasant accident today, for as we were letting one of the heavy boats down the iron strap on the bow that holds the rope gave way. Fortunately there were four of us in the water holding and guiding the boat and we succeeded in getting a line to the ring-bolt in the stearn and turning her without accident. We commenced our last sack of flour tonight.

View of Lava Falls from Toroweap region. Photo by 1872 Powell Expedition.

[J. W. POWELL, Journal #1, August] 25. Good run in forenoon, 14 miles. Cañon still with marble walls. Sds. seen in distance now and then. Came to lava monument in middle of river, then to lava falls. These falls must have been very great at one time. Lava comes down to high water mark, may be lower, and is 1,500 ft. high on either side. The cañon was filled. Vast piles of gravel below point where lava crossed 100 ft. high. Limestone and sds. in lava. The falls now are among boulders some distance below the ancient fall. Coming on after dinner, it was seen that the lava had filled the cañon far below noon camp. The lateral cañons on the right were filled far out and to a great hight for about 5 miles. The same true on left side but fewer gulches filled. Great patches of rock were seen on both sides along the walls, sometimes as a thin lining, sometimes filling up old amphitheaters and alcoves, often little patches up on the shelves of the limestone, places were seen where it had rolled down on the sand and gravel.

In many places it was down below the water now. Much of it was collumnar [sic] in structure, which was best seen looking at a mass. These columns were seen to start from concentric points and shoot out untill they met like concentric masses. Sometimes the columns were curved. Two instances were noticed of the the [sic] filling of deep narrow gulches. The cooling commenced next the walls, giving two vertical plates composed of horizontal columns. Usually these columns were small, say four to six inches, but occasionally they were much larger, being from one to two feet square. Two of these instances was [sic] when the lava had run down on the sand and gravel.

After coming 5 or 6 miles, the lava was found to be lower in the cañon and still slowly to lower up to camp at night. Up to this point large or small patches were seen at small intervals on both sides of the cañon. T'was never out of sight. I think Lava came from right.

35 miles today. Camp 41.

[J. W. POWELL, Journal #2 Geology notes] At noon on the 25th, we came to a bed of Igneous rock that had at some time dammed the river. I estimated that it [was] 1500 ft. [in] hight [sic]. Could not see back, might be higher [2,200 feet]. Have some specs. Lower member of Carboniferous up to this point along the water, slowly coming up today as they went down yesterday. Still through lower members of Carboniferous. Granite reappeared about 5 miles above camp on the 25th. See journal for Description of Lava. [Here ends Powell's Journal #2 and his Geology notes.]

[SUMNER] August 25. Ran a bad rapid to begin our day's work, then a dozen more in 14 1/2 miles, when we came to a fall, or the nearest approach to it of any on the river; about 5 miles above the fall the cañon has been completely filled up with lava when it was as deep as it is now, and has all been cut out the second time except at the falls, where there is a large lot of basalt still in the river making a fall of about 15 ft. in 40 yds. On the south side of the river, 1/4 mile below the falls, there are a number of springs that flow more water combined than the Flax River does, but they are so strongly impregnated with lime as to scald the mouth when drank. Made a portage on the south side, had dinner and pulled out again and ran a dozen more rapids, some bad ones 3......and camped [in the lava cave at River Mile 190?] out of sight and hearing of [the river?].......first time in ten weeks...... ["...." = unreadable] **[Original version]** Ran 13th Rapids in 14 1/2 miles then came to a lava falls where portage on south side, then ran a continuous string of Rapids for 20 1/2 miles [?] made 35 1/2 miles, camped on North side. Walls getting lower and more broken.

☀ Day #95

[BRADLEY] Aug. 26. 69. Another 35 miles run with but one let down which was more choice than necessity. We happened to land on the wrong side to run it, so we let the boats over it. This A.M. we ran out of the lava which flowed down the river for many miles and which made or helped to make many rappids. We are now in the granite again and I anticipate trouble if it continues for we never strike it without trouble. The country which has been very broken for some miles begins to close in upon us and the river narrows and shoots through the granite like a brook in some places.

We found an Indian Camp today with gardens made with considerable care. The Indians are probably out in the mountains hunting and have left the gardens to take care of themselves until they return. They had corn, mellons [sic] & squashes growing. We took several squashes, some of them very large, and tonight have cooked one and found it very nice. Wish we had taken more of them. The corn and mellons were not quite ripe enough to be eatable [sic]. There were two curious rugs hung up under the cliff made of wildcat skins and sewed like a mat. They were quite neat looking and very soft, probably used for beds. They have no regular lodges but seemed to live in booths covered with brush and corn-stalks. From signs and scraps of baskets we judge they are Utes, probably Pah-Utes.

[J. W. POWELL, Journal #1, August] 26. Found Indian camp to day. Gardens. Good run of 35 miles. Camp 42.

[SUMNER] August 26. Pulled out early and ran 35 miles....portage. Passed an Indian garden....large dry gulch but not......pumpkins and a few...little use to us, but......[camp on north side]. **[Original version]** Made 35 miles ran 3 Rapids and made one Portage. Passed melon garden [?]. Camped on North side.

☀ Day #96

[BRADLEY] Aug. 27. 69. Run 12 miles today but at noon we came to the worst rappid yet seen. The water dashes against the left bank and then is thrown furiously back against the right. The billows are huge and I fear our boats could not ride them if we could keep them off the rocks. The spectical [sic] is appalling to us. We have only subsistance [sic] for about five days and have been trying half a day to get arround this one rappid while there are three others in sight below. What they are we cannot tell, only that they are huge ones. If we could get on the cliff about a hundred yards below the head of this one, we could let our boats down to that point and then have foothold all the rest of the way, but we have tried all the P.M. without success. Shall keep trying tomorrow and I hope that by going farther back in the mountains and then coming down opposite we may succeed. Think Major now gone to try it.

There is discontent in camp tonight and I fear some of the party will take to the mountains but hope not. This is decidedly the darkest day of the trip but I don't dispair [sic] yet. I shall be one to try to run it rather than take to the mountains. "Tis darkest just before the day" and I trust our day is about to dawn.

[J. W. POWELL, Journal #1, August]

5 - 24 - 28 = 119° - 42' - 40" [not written in Powell's pemmanship]

27. Run 12 miles. At noon came to bad rapids. Spent afternoon in exploration.

Camp on left bank in gulch. 43.

[SUMNER] August 27. Made 12 miles. Ran dozen bad rapids then came to cross gulches where Howland Senior [, Seneca?] and Dunn left 169 3/4 miles [178 miles downstream of the Little Colorado]. **[Original version]** Made 12 miles, passed a dozen bad Rapids, then came to cross gulchs [sic] where Howland, Seneca and Dunn left.

189 3/4 miles. [no further entry on remaining three quarters of blank journal page.]

Separation Rapid. Photo by the Kolb brothers.

☀ Day #97

[BRADLEY] Aug. 28. 69. Tried in vain to get arround or down the cliff and come to the determination to run the rappid or perish in the attempt. Three men refused to go farther (two Howlands & Wm. Dunn), and we had to let them take to the mountains. They left us with good feelings though we deeply regret their loss for they are as fine fellows as I ever had the good fortune to meet.

We crossed the river and carried our boats arround one bad point with great labor. And leaving the "Emma Dean" tied to shore, all the remainder of the party (six all told) got into the two large boats and dashed out into the boiling tide with all the courage we could muster. We rowed with all our might until the billows became too large to do anything but hold on to the boats, and by good fortune both boats came out at the bottom of the rappid, well soaked with water of course but right side up and not even an oar was lost. The three boys stood on the cliff looking at us and, having waved them adieu, we dashed through the next rappid and then into an eddy where we stopped *to catch our breath* and bail out the water from our now nearly sunken boats. We had never [run] such a rappid before but we have run a worse one since that, this P.M.

We got a good little run over almost continuous rappid until about the middle of the P.M. we came to some more of the lava and a tremendous rappid [Lava Cliff]. Thinking it possible to let our boats arround by the cliff, I got into mine to keep her off the rocks, and the men took the rope (130 ft. long) and went up on the cliff to let her down, not dreaming but what it was a comparatively easy task. For a time it worked finely, but the cliff rising higher as they advanced and the tide getting stronger as we neared the rappid, the task became more difficult until the rope was no longer long enough and they were obliged to hold it just where it was and go back to the other boat for more rope.

The water roared so furiously that I could not make them hear and they could not see me. I was so far under the cliff but where they held me was just on a point of the cragg where the tide was strongest. With four feet more of rope I could have got in below the point and kept the boat steady, but where I was she would shear out into the tide and then come in with terrible force against the rocks. I got out my knife to cut the rope but hoped relief would come soon, and one look at the foaming cataract below kept me from cutting it, and there I was suffering all the tortures of the rack but having sufficient sence left to look out the best channel through — if anything should give way. And it was lucky I did so for after what seemed like quite half an hour, and just as they were uniting the two ropes, the boat gave a furious shoot out into the stream. The cutwater, rope and all, flew

Lava Cliff Rapid. Photo by the Kolb brothers.

full thirty ft. in [the] air and the loosened boat dashed out like a war-horse eager for the fray.

On I went and, sooner than I can write it, was in the breakers. But just as I always am, afraid while danger is approaching but cool in the midst of it, I could steer the boat as well as if the water was smoothe. By putting an oar first on one side then on the other, I could swing her round and guide her very well. And having passed the worst part of it and finding that the boat was eaquel [sic] to the task, I swung my hat to the boys on the cliff in token of all's well.

Major says nothing ever gave him more joy than to see me swing my hat, for they all thought that the boat and I too were gone to the "Happy hunting grounds" until then.

The Major's bro. & Jack climbed along the cliff with rope to come to my assistance, but Major, not thinking I should ever be able to land the boat or hold her if I did, got into the other boat with Bill & Andy and came through after me. Their boat got turned around and they came very near going against the rocks. They found me safely stowed away in an eddy bailing out the boat when they came. It stands A-No. 1 of the trip. Run 14 miles.

[J. W. POWELL, Journal #1, August] 28th.
Boys left us.
Run rapids.
Bradey boat broke.
Camp on left bank.
Camp 44.
[This is the final known writing by John Wesley Powell on this expedition.]

[SUMNER] August 28. O. G. Howland and W. H. Dunn decided to abandon the outfit and try to reach the settlements on the head of Virgin River. Each took a gun and all the ammunition he wanted and some provisions and left us to go it or swamp. The remaining 6 men lifted the two large boats over the rock past some of the rapids, abandoning the small boat as useless property, and pulled out and ran the rest of the damned rapid with a ringing cheer, though at great risk, as the boats shipped nearly half full in a perfect hell of foam. Bailed out and pulled out again and ran 10 more rapids in 6 miles, when we came to another hell. There is a.......pouring in from the south.....of large rocks that.....to make a very bad......"Maid" down with.....[end of Sumner's entry for this date]

Towers on the Rio Virgin (etching by H. H. Nichols in *Canyons of the Colorado*).

Chapter 10.

BELOW THE GRAND WASH CLIFFS,
August 29 - September 10(?)

Once the crew realizes that they have rowed beyond the Grand Wash Cliffs, everything changes. There seems no possibility that the six remaining expeditionaries can encounter anything monstrous or menacing; after all, starving or not, they have successfully exited Grand Canyon into the rolling country of the Sonoran desert. Now it is simply a question of when and where they will reconnect with food again — and with those first letters from home. And, though hundreds of miles of river face some of the men before they hit the tidal bore at the mouth of the Colorado in Mexico at the Sea of Cortez, they also face the vexing question of what to do with the rest of their lives. Underneath all of this simmers the question of how the Howland brothers and Dunn are faring in their bid to reach the Mormon settlements by hiking overland through Indian country.

Day #98 [BRADLEY] Aug. 29. 69. This is the first Sunday that I have felt justified in running but it has now become a race for life. We have only enough flour to last us five days and we do not know how long we may be winding arround among these hills, but we are much incouraged [sic] by the constant improvement in the looks of the country. We run down the granite about 10 A.M., and then the country began to open, and we expect that we are now in the vacinity [sic] of Grand Wash, though we may pass it without knowing it. Indeed we may have passed it before this for we have worked hard today and have run 42 1/2 miles. We are quite worn out tonight, but with a good night's rest we shall, I trust, be able to renew the race in the morning. We have run all the rappids we have found today without stopping to look at them, for we have no time to waste in looking. The rappids grow less as we advance and we hope and expect that the worst of the trip is over.

All we regret now is that the three boys who took to the mountains are not here to share our joy and triumph. We have run some distance north today which will drive them far from their course for if the river runs north, the cañons running into it must run east and their proper course from where they left us is about N.W.

[SUMNER] August 29. We came out into a low rolling desert, and saw plainly that our work of danger was done — gave three cheers and pulled away steady strokes till 5 o'clock when we camped on the south side and summed up the log and found we had run 42 1/2 miles.

☀️Day #99

[BRADLEY] Aug. 30. 69. We got started at sunrise this morning expecting a long hard pull of it and worked hard until a little past noon, making 26 miles. The country all the while improving and opening when we came somewhat unexpectedly to the mouth of the Virgin River, a quite large but muddy stream coming in from Utah along which the Mormons have many settlements. We found three men and a boy (Mormons) fishing just below and immediately landed to learn where we were for we could hardly credit that all our trials were over until they assured us that we were within 20 miles of Callville and all right.

They immediately took us to their cabbin [sic] (they are fishermen) and cooked all they could for us of fish, squashes, &c., and we ate until I am now very much like the darkey preacher, too full for utterence [sic].

As soon as we got here we sent an Indian up to St. Thomas (about 25 miles) where we are assured Col. Head has sent our mail to, for none of us have had a letter since leaving Green River City, almost 3 1/2 months. I wrote a line and sent it to Lucy to assure Mother I was all-right, but I was so intoxicated with joy at getting through so soon and so well that I don't know what I wrote to her. [This is the final known writing by George Y. Bradley on this expedition.]

[SUMNER] August 30. Pulled out at sunrise, and made 24 miles by noon, seeing nothing but smooth water and rolling desert till 10 o'clock when we came to the palatial residence of a Piute [sic] Indian; found the paternal head of a large family without even the fig leaf wallowing in the hot sand and ashes under some weeds thrown over 2 poles. Her ladyship's costume was nice and light and cool. It consisted of half a yard of dirty buckskin and a brass ring. She was as disgusting a hag as ever rode a broomstick. Camped for dinner on the north side. Pulled out at 1 o'clock and rowed about 7 miles, when we came to the mouth of Virgin River, where we found 3 white men and a boy fishing with a net. Stopped, and dispatched a Piute [sic] Indian after the mail at St. Thomas, 25 miles up the Virgin; set the men cooking fish, settled back on our dignity till the fish was cooked, when we laid our dignified manners aside and assumed the manner of so many hogs. Ate as long as we could and went to sleep to wake hungry.

Lava Cliff Rapid. Photo by the Kolb brothers.

☀Day #100

[SUMNER] August 31 [-September ?]. Laid over to fill up and rest all. Our mail carrier came in at noon with word that the Mormon bishop [James Leithead] was on his way down with mail, flour and melons for us. He did not make his appearance till dark when we talked and ate melons till the morning star could be seen.

The Prof. and Walter concluded to leave and go to Salt Lake City rather than to go to Yuma and take the stage to San Franzisco [sic].

Distance from mouth of the Uinta River to junction of Green and Grand Rivers 248 miles. General course 10° west of south. Rapids run 61 — portages — 4--9/10 of the distance. Cañon and all worthless.

From junction to the mouth of the San Juan River 116 miles course 5° — south of west. Rapids run 45 — portages made 18 — all Cañon. From San Juan River to Flax, or Little Colorado River, 127 miles. Rapids run 45 — portages made 14 — Course southwest — all cañon. From mouth of the Flax River to mouth of Virgin River 290 miles course about 10° north of west. Rapids run 234 — Portages made 26 — all Cañon, but about 3 miles at the last end of route.

Total distance from Uinta River to Virgin River 877 miles — rapids ran

414 — portages made 62 — making 276 bad rapids, which it would be practically out of the question to go up. If any one thinks it can, go in, I say. I never want to see it again anywhere. Near the Grand Cañon it will probably remain unvisited for many years again, as it has nothing to recommend it, but its general desolation as a study for the geologist. The Cañon from the mouth of the Virgin to Cottonwood Valley is but little bedder [sic] as it is burned to a cinder. At Eldorado Cañon (80 miles from the Virgin River) there is a quartz mill running on ores for a mine 6 miles up the cañon. Wheter [sic] it pays or not is more than I can say, as I could get no satisfaction out of the "Dutch Boss." There are mines all the way down and the owners have the old story; some trifling thing stopped them for a short time. What I have seen of Arizona I do not consider worth settling. As a disgusted woodchopper expressed it, "The whole damned Territory is a Bilk." In Mojave Valley there is some good land but it must be all overflown or it yields no crops — It is so......it cannot be irrigated unless pumped up — and that happens to belong to the Mojave Indians. They are at peace now but it is hard to tell how long they will remain so. They are the largest Indians I have ever seen and differ from the rest. The dress of the men is much less than the Georgia uniform. The women wear a girdle of cottonwood willow bark around the loins and reaching nearly to the knees; all have a hankering after *"Agua,"* and when drunk the squaws can out talk a "Billingsgate fisherwoman."

The Chemohereis [Chemehuevi] Indians are a different class and I think altogether better as they work more and dress much better. They raise pumpkins, beans, and melons and cut cord wood to supply the smaller steamers plying between Yuma and Mojava. They are a smaller race — in fact a branch of Utes, as also are the Yumas and Mojaves, one tribe with two names. The country bordering the lower Colorado is some better than the upper, but still nothing to brag of as it is a desert off from the river bottoms. The bottom is moderately well wooded with cottonwood, mesquite and willows but none large enough to make lumber — at least I have not seen any that was. The soil when well cultivated yields well of corn and pumpkins, but I have not heard of its raising anything else to good advantage. A few words more and my weary work is done.

After two years of hard work of exploration of the Colorado and it tributaries, I find myself penniless and disgusted with the whole thing, sitting under a Mesquite bush in the sand. I write this journal hoping that it will give a faint idea of the country at large. If anybody disbelieves any of this or wants to know more of the cañons of the Colorado — go and see it. Before we started I was called a damned fool for embarking in such an enterprise, for nobody possibly gets through. Since I have got through, I have been called a damned fool for the same thing, because there has been many men long since that have proved that there was nothing to go for as they have it all. But of all reports I can find, that describes any part of the river.

To Col. Stacey and the Surgeon (whose name I have forgotten) at Fort Mojave, I am deeply indebted for many courtesies and much help; to Maj. Ponde and brother officers at Camp Colorado I feel very grateful for like favors. All that I can do is to return my hearty thanks, as I cannot get work in these parts of the country to earn my bread by the sweat of my brow. I shoulder my gun and bidding all adieu I go again to the wilderness, where I will have a chance to earn it.

J. C. Sumner
Fort Yuma, California

[This is the final known writing by John Colton Sumner on this expedition.]

☀ Day #110

[HALL, September 10, 1869] Fort Mojava   Friday the 10th

Dear Brother,

It is with the greatest of pleasure that I once more sit down to write to you to let you know that I am still alive and well after coming through hard and perilous voyage. I turned up all rite at last. We had reported all drowned by some lying scoundrel by the name of John Risdon from Illinois and he reported he was the last survivor of the party. There was no such man ever was with the party. Who ever he is he is a liar and a scoundrel and it wont do for him to let any of us see him.

We came through in from Greene river City in one hundred and eleven days to Vagus Wash when the exploration finished. The Major left us [on day #100] at a Mormon camp 25 miles above the wash and his brother Walter went with him. Of the 10 men that started from Greene river only six came through. Just before we came out of the canyon three of the men left us on the head of rapids. They were afraid to run it so they left us in a bad place. We were then short of hands and we had to abandon the Major's boat. The name of it was the "Emma Deene." Then we still had one left for each three men. The first boat that run the rapid was the "Sister" as we called her. It is the boat that Bill Rhoads and I started from Greene river with.

The Major was in the boat with us. We ran the rapid all right and gave a loud cheer. Next came "The Maid of the Canyon" named by J. Y. Bradley and the Major's brother. Now I will give you the names of all the boats. "The No Name" wrecked on the Green river, the "Emma Deene" abandoned in the Canyon, the "Maid of the Canyon" and "Kitty Clyde's Sister" that was given to Bill Rhoads and me. The other was given to Bradley and Sumnar [sic].

We are now at Fort Majova [sic]. We start today for Fort Yuma, John Sumnar and I. The other two boys think of going to Los Angeles by land. Write to me at Fort Yuma, California. Must close. Give my best respects to all. Write soon.

Yours till death,
Andrew Hall

The Chicago Tribune.

VOL. XXIII.   CHICAGO, SATURDAY, JULY 3, 1869.   NUMBER 3.

VOL. XXIII.

FEARFUL DISASTER.

Reported Loss of the Powell Exploring Expedition Confirmed.

Twenty-one Men Engulfed in a Moment.

Arrival of the Only Survivor at Springfield.

His Statement of the Manner of the Accident

Special Despatch to The Chicago Tribune.
SPRINGFIELD, July 2.

The fate of the Powell expedition has caused a feeling of intense anxiety among his friends and the public generally, and is now determined by the report, as brought by the only survivor of the ill-fated party, and I send you the story as told to me to-day by him, which settles the fate of Major Powell and party

The survivor's name is John A. Risdon, and was a member of the Powell expedition. Joined Major Powell's party on the 18th day of July, 1868, at La Salle. His duties were to assist as chainman, and whatever he could do to be made useful. He has been with the party every day since it left Illinois, and, of course, is well acquainted with all who composed it.

On the 7th or 8th day of May the party reached

Inscription ("Dunn 1869" in lower left corner of photo), apparently by William H. Dunn, atop Mount Dellenbaugh, along the route from Separation Canyon to southern Utah. Photo by Eli Butler.

Chapter 11.

THE REST OF THE STORY:

The Fates of the Nine Who Dared

After struggling to survive and succeed on an expedition of such harrowing high adventure as the 1869 first descent of the Green and Colorado river canyons, men change. No doubt the horizons of every man expanded farther into the distance after finally abandoning the last two weatherbeaten, waterlogged Whitehalls on the banks of the Lower Colorado. Amazingly, despite the teamwork required to succeed on the river, every surviving man went his own way. Only the Howland brothers and William Dunn remained together. What follows are the stories of the fates of each of the nine men who rowed (or rode) the *Maid of the Cañon*, *Kitty Clyde's Sister*, and *Emma Dean* downstream from the confluence of the Uinta and Green rivers to ultimately explore Grand Canyon.

William H. Dunn

Oramel G. Howland

Seneca B. Howland

The biggest mystery — though certainly not the only mystery — concerning the fates of Powell and his crew is: What happened to William H. Dunn, Oramel G. Howland and Seneca B. Howland once they hiked away from the river at Separation Canyon?

To unravel this tragic mystery we must look first to Powell's ability in 1869 to lead men when the chips were down. John Wesley Powell, the evidence shows, possessed many skills. But he lacked the leadership skills of a Captain Meriwether Lewis or a Captain William Clark. These two men commanded and orchestrated the most famous exploration of unknown

wilderness on North America — struggling up the Missouri over horren-
dous portages then running whitewater on the Pacific side — without losing
a single man to accident or to violence during their two-year epic
expedition. Instead, in just a few months, the self-absorbed J. W. Powell lost
six men of his potential eleven to desertion and three of these to murder.

The mystery lies in how and why?

The first clue lies in the events which occurred only sixteen days
downstream from Green River, in the Canyon of Lodore. Here the
Howland brothers and Frank Valentine Goodman missed pulling into shore
along side the *Emma Dean* and instead rode the 21-foot *No Name*, swamped
and out of control, into Disaster Falls. As described in several of the
journals on June 8, the *No Name* smashed into midstream boulders and
disintegrated in successive collisions. The men aboard her barely escaped to
a midstream island alive.

After a daring rescue by John Sumner, who rowed the *Emma Dean*
across to the midstream island to scoop up the three men stranded on a
large island shrinking due to rising water, the expedition reunited. The
Howland brothers and Goodman were alive. Otherwise everything aboard
the *No Name* except the barometers, thermometers, and a keg of whiskey
was lost. Vanished to the bottom of the Green was one-third of the
expedition's ten-month supply of food and equipment. And with this went
the three men's rifles, revolvers, clothes, bedrolls, and other personal gear.

Understandably, Major Powell was upset about this huge loss.
Goodman, now destitute, quit the trip afterward at his first opportunity.
This occurred two weeks later at the Uinta. Worse than this one desertion,
as Sumner would later write, "From this wreck commenced the many
quarrels between Major Powell and O. G. Howland and Bill Dunn which
caused so much trouble and finally terminated in their leaving the party and
the murder of the Howland brothers and Bill Dunn. As soon as O. G.
Howland got out of the boat [the *Emma Dean*] after the rescue, Major
Powell angrily demanded of him to know why he did not land [but instead
ran downstream of the *Emma Dean*]."

Seventy-four days later (August 5) and seven hundred miles out of
Green River, Wyoming, Powell and his eight remaining stalwarts rowed
their three beat-up boats past the future site of Lee's Ferry. Here they
entered Grand Canyon. Five days of rowing carried Powell's crew to the
Little Colorado (River Mile 61.5). By now the men were reduced to
starvation rations of flour balls, lots of dried and moldy apples, a few beans,
and plenty of black coffee. Deer and bighorn sheep seemed to have long
since vanished from the Inner Canyon. Even the fish had refused to bite for
Bradley, a consummate fisherman. Worse, the monsoons had begun, and
the men were reduced to one blanket for every two of them and two or
three wagon-tarp tents for all of them.

The explorers camped for three days at the Little Colorado River while the Powell brothers geologised and to determine latitude and longitude. This, Bradley wrote, was "a lothesome [sic] little stream, so filthy and muddy that it fairly stinks." It frothed with mud from the Painted Desert. Sumner called it "as disgusting a stream as there is on the continent....Half its volume and 2/3 of its weight is mud and silt."

Discontentment too seethed here beneath the surface of most of the men's attitudes about lingering on less than half rations among the dust and hordes of insects next to this cesspool of a stream. "The men are uneasy and discontented," Bradley confided to his journal here on August 11, "and anxious to move on. If Major does not do something soon I fear the consequences, but he is contented and seems to think that biscuit made of sour & musty flour and a few dried apples is ample to sustain a laboring man."

Eventually the expedition did shove off downstream into what Powell would later refer to as the "Great Unknown." Strangely, posterity knows less than one might guess about how this expedition proceeded from here. As we've seen, the journals cover specific hardships, but with ever decreasing detail about the feelings of the crew.

Sumner would later describe the grim side of this journey's final leg:

"And if any men ever did penance for their sins we did a plenty for the next two hundred miles. To add to our troubles, there was a nearly continuous rain, and a great rise in the river, that created such a current and turmoil that it tried our strength to the limit. Starvation stared us in the face, weakened by hardships and ceaseless toil twenty out of twenty-four hours of the day. I felt like Job....A ceaseless grind of running or letting down rapids with lines, varied in places by making portages of boats and contents. The contents were a small item, but the boats were water logged, and very heavy, and taxed our strength to the limit....[and while heading downstream in general] there was not much talk indulged in by the grim, clenched teeth squad of half starved men, with faces wearing the peculiar, stern look always noticed on the faces of men when forming for a charge in battle."

In Powell's very brief journal he wrote little to nothing about this part of the journey in the Canyon. What he did write about at length was geology, specifically the lava bracketing the Toroweap region around Lava Falls. Only much later, back East, would Powell compose via dictation what would be published as his "journal" of running the river itself. Meanwhile the only other surviving journals — the official one of Sumner and the secret journal, mostly optimistic, that Bradley wrote — do express undisguised disgust and impatience at their predicament with Powell in the Canyon. Interviews, by letter, of Sumner and of Hawkins conducted later by Robert Brewster Stanton and William Wallace Bass revealed the ambience described above and even worse dynamics described below.

So what went wrong in Grand Canyon?

It seems that the conflict of wills and attitudes that had begun at Disaster Falls between Powell and Oramel G. Howland continued to fester. Powell had held Howland most responsible for the wreck of the *No Name*, and possibly was finding fault with his map-making as well. Howland, in turn, found fault in Powell's decision-making regarding food resupplies at the Uinta in repeated, tit-for-tat spats. Nor were these disputes trivial. Sumner explains:

> "Major Powell was gone five days, and brought back a shirt tail full of supplies. I thought at the time it was a damned stingy or foolish scheme, as there was plenty of supplies to be had, to bring back such a meagre mess for nine to make a thousand mile voyage through an unknown and dangerous cañon, but as I wasn't boss I suppose I ought to keep still about it."

A bit later yet another, parallel, bad relationship allegedly began between Major Powell and William Dunn, the long-haired mountain man who rowed Powell's *Emma Dean*. This relationship too grew worse in Grand Canyon.

What we know most about this issue of deterioration of leadership and near mutiny comes from Hawkins' and Sumner's letters, thousands of words in length, to Stanton and Hawkins' 1919 long letter to Bass. Hawkins' explained his motive for writing to Stanton: "I do not wish to cast any discredit on Major Powell's report or upon his memory of the Colorado expedition; but — in honor to Dunn and the Howland brothers — the account in the report, which accuses them of cowardice, I shall say that it is entirely wrong, and was perhaps made to cover up the real cause of their leaving. The state of Ohio never turned out a man that had more nerve than William Dunn."

This deterioration occurred with Dunn in part because Dunn, apparently the best (or most willing) swimmer of the crew, took the more risky posts perched on boulders in the river as the crew lined the boats along the edges of scores of rapids. During one of these episodes, apparently in early August, notes Hawkins, "the ropes happened to catch Bill Dunn under the arms and came near drowning him, but he managed to catch the ropes and come out." Still in Dunn's pocket from some previous chore with the barometer was one of Powell's watches — among the last that worked. It was ruined.

At dinner Sumner remarked that Dunn had come close to drowning. Then (Sumner and Hawkins agree on this) Walter Powell "made the remark that it would have but little loss." Major Powell was so angry at Dunn that he ordered him to pay $30 for the ruined watch then and there or else leave the trip and hike out of the Canyon. Depending on where this episode occurred, Dunn's easiest exit (to the south) could have demanded that he climb 4,600 feet up cliffs to the middle of a waterless nowhere. The closest escape would have been to the uninhabited and unexplored Coconino Plateau, many miles even from Indian villages, let alone white settlements. Indeed nothing had changed on this plateau since eleven years earlier when Lieutenant Joseph Christmas Ives explored it in the spring of 1858. After months of exploring upriver by steamboat to Black Canyon, Ives had struck across overland to the "Big Canyon" with a train of more than 100 mules plus soldiers and his invaluable Mojave guide, Ireteba. Ives had reached the river in Western Grand Canyon at Diamond Creek (River Mile 226) and had almost made it into Supai as well. Next he had forged farther east to make sense of the confusing — and arid — terrain. After losing several mules due to dehydration, he finally turned south and concluded:

> "The positions of the main water-courses have been determined with considerable accuracy. The region last explored is, of course, altogether valueless. It can be approached only from the south, and after entering it there is nothing to do but to leave. Ours has been the first, and will doubtless be the last, party of whites to visit this profitless locality. It seems intended by nature that the Colorado river, along the greater portion of its lonely and majestic way, shall be forever unvisited and undisturbed. The handful of Indians [Hualapai and Havasupai] that inhabit the sequestered retreats where we discovered them have probably remained in the same condition, and of the same number, for centuries. The country could not support a large population, and by some provision of nature they have ceased to multiply. The deer, the antelope, the birds, even the smaller reptiles, all of which frequent the adjacent territory, have deserted this uninhabitable district....We start for the south with some anxiety, not knowing how long it may be before water will be met with again."

Not only was this the terrain that William H. Dunn would have had to face had he succeeded in hiking out of the Canyon, it was also the terrain that Major Powell *knew* Dunn would face. Powell, of course, had read Ives' 1861 *Report* — virtually the only modern exploration ever done in the region up to Powell's own trip — and he intended to go Ives one better in the annals of exploration, and, as time would prove, turn a profit on Ives' profitless locality.

Dunn responded to Powell's weird tantrum with, "A bird could not get out of that place."

Although the men at first thought that Powell was joking, he soon convinced them that he was serious.

As Hawkins tells it, Dunn told the Major that, "he could not leave then, but that he would go as soon as he could get out."

Hawkins soon informed Powell that if Dunn were to leave, they would take a boat, and that he, Hall, and Bradley would accompany Dunn downriver. This allegedly sobered Powell, who relented slightly. For as long as Dunn were to delay his departure from the trip, Powell allegedly demanded, he must pay a boarding fee of $30 (or $50) per month (Hawkins' and Sumner's letters disagreed over Powell's stipulated fee). Later Powell decided that Dunn could pay the $30 for the ruined watch after the trip.

Powell's tantrum may seem merely high-handed and morale-busting, but still forgivable. Sumner interceded and told Powell that he could neither order Dunn off the trip nor compel him to pay for rations. Even so, relationships apparently spiraled downward. For example, not much farther downstream, Hawkins noted in a far more serious allegation (made in 1919, to William Wallace Bass), that while lining a rapid Powell "saw his chance to drown Dunn:"

> " — as Dunn was a fine swimmer, the Major asked him to swim out to a rock so the boat could swing in below. He made the rock all O.K. and was ready to catch the rope which was supposed to be thrown to him, so he could swing in the boat below, but the Major saw his chance to drown Dunn, as he thought, and he held the rope. That was the first time he had interfered in the letting of the boats around bad places, and the rope caught Dunn around the legs and pulled him into the current and came near losing the boat.
>
> But Dunn held on to the rope and finally stopped in water up to his hips. We were all in the water but the Major and the Captain. Dunn told the Major that if he had not been a good swimmer he and the boat both would have been lost. The Major said as to Dunn that there would have been but little loss. One word brought on another, and the Major called Dunn a bad name and Dunn said that if the Major was not a cripple he would not be called such names.
>
> Then Captain Powell said he was not crippled, and

started for Dunn with an oath, and the remark he would finish Dunn. He had to pass right by me and I knew he would soon drown Dunn, as he, so much larger could easily do. He was swearing and his eyes looked like fire. Just as he passed I caught him by the hair of his head and pulled him over back into the water. Howland saw us scuffling and he was afraid Cap would get hold of my legs. But Dunn got to me first and said, 'For God's sake, Bill, you will drown him!' By that time Howland was there and Cap had been in the water long enough and Dunn and Howland dragged him out onto the sand bar in the rocks. After I got my hold in Cap's hair I was afraid to let go, for he was a very strong man. He was up in a short time, and mad! I guess he *was* mad! He cursed me to everything, even to being a 'Missouri puke.' I wasn't afraid of him when I got on dry ground. I could out-knock him after he was picked up twice.

He made for his gun and swore he would kill me and Dunn. But this talk did not excite me. As he was taking his gun from the deck of the boat, Andy Hall gave him a punch behind the ear and told him to put it back or off would go his head. Cap looked around and saw who had the gun, and he sure dropped his. This all happened before the Major got around to where we were. He soon took in the situation and came to me and made the remark that he would have never thought I would go back on him. I told him that he had gone back on himself, and that he had better help Cap get the sand out of his eyes, and that if he monkeyed with me any more, I would keep him down next time..."

Of this argument between Dunn and the Major, Sumner admitted, "I think the Major's one arm only saved him from a broken head, if nothing worse."

The expedition at this juncture had stretched its thin thread of solidarity to the breaking point. As Hawkins continues to tell it:

"...Sumner and I had all we could do to keep down mutiny. There was bad feeling from that time on for a few days. We began not to recognize any authority from the Major. We began to run races with the boats, as the loads were almost gone. It was fun for the first two days but then the water began to get rough. Hall, Howland, and myself were in my boat. I had become an expert in bad rapids. We ran several that the other two boats were let over with ropes."

Sumner adds: "Major Powell did not run the outfit in the same overbearing manner after that. At a portage or a bad let-down he took his geological hammer and kept out of the way."

Many historians and biographers over the years — Darrah, Stegner, and David Lavender, to offer just a few examples — who have wanted to preserve Major Powell's image unblemished have either ignored Sumner's and Hawkins' testimonies disparaging Major Powell's leadership and accusing the Powell brothers of attempted murder or else they have discounted Sumner's and Hawkins' words as lies. William Culp Darrah, for example, in his *Powell of the Colorado* (page 141) utterly discounts what Hawkins and Sumner said after 1869, basically accusing both men of lying and being motivated by bitterness toward Powell. Lavender, in his *River Runners of the Grand Canyon*, explains away Sumner's and Hawkins' lengthy testimonies with a facile rhetorical question and an even more facile assertion of mental incompetency:

> "If they [the events that Hawkins and Sumner wrote about] did not occur, why did the two men invent them? Spleen perhaps. Though Powell gave the men the expedition's boats and what money he had at the end of the trip neither Hawkins nor Sumner felt he had received his due. The neglect festered, to find relief in wild tales to Stanton when the men were old and their memories fading."

If "spleen" had given birth to Hawkins' and Sumner's multiple and consistent disclosures of Powell's decisions leading up to the Separation incident, did some bone of contention for Sumner or Hawkins exist to provide this facile excuse for so many previous "historians" who had fallen in love with Powell to have so arrogantly labelled Sumner and Hawkins — men both loyal to Powell and courageous beyond these historians' abilities to comprehend — as liars?

The hand-written copy of Powell's original contract (the "AGREEMENT") for this trip, you might remember, hired only three of the nine men present for $75 each for the duration of the expedition, anticipated to last up to a year. The men were also to be allowed time on their own to trap and prospect. All three of these hired men were to run the boats and work in all general capacities on the expedition from June 1, 1869, until, if needed, May 31, 1870. Dunn was also supposed to take twice-daily barometric readings and also determine elevations of cliffs, et cetera. Sumner was to take readings with the sextant. Oramel G. Howland was contracted as the expedition cartographer to draw maps of the river canyons as the men traversed them.

Apparently no other known written record or contract written in 1868 or 1869 survives regarding what anyone else on the 1869 trip was to expect as payment. Hawkins, however, was the expedition's cook. He prepared every meal. He even washed Major Powell's one hand for him prior to meals and then served him his meals. No Powell scholar believes Hawkins did this gratis. Indeed, Hawkins wrote the following in 1907 to explain the arrangements Major Powell had made with him back in 1868 at Hot Sulphur Spring:

> "I told the Major that Sumner was thinking of selling his trading post, and in company with Dunn and myself, we were going to try the cañons as far as Cottonwood Island. That I had already packed my year's supplies in from Denver, to which the Major replied, 'Those things are just what I want, also your mules and horses, I will buy them and pay you just what you can sell them for elsewhere.' I told him I would think the matter over and let him know in the evening. In the meantime, he and Sumner arranged a trade for Sumner's supplies at his post. Later I went to the Major's camp and told him if we could arrange things and agree on a price for my animals, I would join his party. I showed him my bills and everything I had in stock, and he allowed me the price of the goods, and for packing them over the range, and he allowed me a fair price for three of my animals, but, for the other one, we could not agree upon a price, so I kept it, as it was a favorite of mine and had safely carried me through several Indian fights. After all was counted up, outside of 36 steel traps, it amounted to $960.00. The traps, he said, could be used that winter and, when we got to Cottonwood Island, we would replace them. He also offered me $1.50 per day for cooking for the outfit, and, when we got through our journey down the Colorado Cañon, he would pay our transportation back to where we were then, at Sumner's place. The Major added, 'Now, as to the money you are to receive for your goods and horses, I expect to get it from the Government, and also to pay your transportation back,' saying that he had money with him and that he would let me have what I needed during the trip, and that he would be responsible to me for the remainder, and he gave me a receipt for the amount due me at that time.
>
> Sumner told me that he was to receive good prices for

his supplies and stores, and good pay for his work, and that he would have several thousand dollars coming to him when he got through, and that he was to receive it all when he got to the end of the river journey. Later in the fall, Major Powell told me that if he could get the Government to appropriate $12,000., there would be $1,000 for each of us and $2,000 for himself for the trip.

When we got to the mouth of the Virgin River, the Major and his brother left us. I cannot tell how much money he paid to each one, but he gave each man some. He gave me $60. and Hall $60., and said that he would send us a government voucher for the rest, and also for what he was to pay me for the provisions and animals I sold him. As we had not come to Cottonwood Island, I asked him how about my traps, that he was to make good — there were 36 of them, and I had paid $3.00 apiece for them. 'Well,' says the Major, 'they got lost on Green River.' 'Yes,' I said, 'but you agreed to make them good when we got to Cottonwood Island.' Then he said he would allow me $2.50 for each trap, and would find out what the transportation was and send me a voucher for the whole amount — **the voucher is still coming**. " [bold mine, and note the irony here that this was written four years after Powell had died.]

Hawkins did work for Powell again during the 1870s — though never again on a river — and Powell reassured Hawkins that he was still expecting government appropriations (which Powell *did* receive every year after 1870) and that he would pay Hawkins then. But Powell never did pay him.

Sumner's account mirrors Hawkins'. Sumner says that he too was out more than $1,000 on equipment and supplies lost or used on the 1869 expedition for which Powell said he would reimburse Sumner after the expedition and after Congress issued him the money. At the Rio Virgin, Powell paid Sumner his $75 as originally contracted. But, as with Hawkins, Sumner mentions that Powell never reimbursed him that $1,000. Indeed Powell asked Sumner to accompany Powell on his second Colorado Expedition. Sumner, however, sent Powell word that he could not make it. Both Sumner and Hawkins likely felt to their dying days that Powell had welshed on his debts to them despite their loyalty to him and despite Powell having access to government funds. So maybe "spleen" is one way of expressing Hawkins' and Sumner's disappointment in Major Powell's capacity for keeping his alleged promises. Even so, none of this means that either Sumner or Hawkins would therefore fabricate lies about what happened during the 1869 expedition. Indeed, the only member of the expedition whom we *know* did fabricate lies about it was Major Powell himself, and in print.

Critics of Sumner's and Hawkins' accounts, such as Darrah and Lavender, point out further that Sumner's journal mentioned no such attempted expulsion of Dunn, nor did it mention fights. But Sumner was writing his journal at Powell's behest to supplement Powell's own very weak one. Under such conditions Sumner could not have been expected to spell out in it any mistreatment by Powell of his crew — any more than Powell himself would have penned such admissions. Sergeant George Y. Bradley's secret journal, however, also reveals no specifics about Powell vs. Dunn. At first glance this lack seems to carry more weight. Bradley does say, as we've seen, that Powell was oblivious to the true feelings of his crew toward him, and that these feelings were often unfavorable. He also mentions, on August 25, a boating accident that might have gotten worse had certain things happened differently. On a slightly different tack, despite Bradley's alleged (by some authors) "complaining" in his journal, Bradley obviously did *not* write about what most troubled him. He did not, for example, even mention that the *No-Name* was smashed to splinters; yet all historians consider this an extremely significant event during the expedition.

To see this quirk of Bradley's better, remember how, in all of the 22,200 words that Bradley wrote, he never wrote the name "Walter" or otherwise said much of anything about Walter Powell, the demented man with whom Bradley spent three months in the same boat? As a man who wanted to retain his sanity, Bradley never confided even to his secret journal the experience of traveling with Walter. Nor, I suspect, did he want to record any tantrums and abuses of Walter Powell's older brother, John Wesley.

Hawkins' and Sumner's interviews late in life were conducted independently hundreds of miles apart, months apart, years apart, and by different interviewers. Sumner's and Hawkins' accounts, despite being independent, agreed on Powell's mistreatment of Dunn, et cetera. In short, if these two separated men — both brave, capable, and *loyal* to Powell during the 1869 expedition — were lying to vent their spleen, they would have been doing so with a phenomenal coincidence of specific detail — and also would have been doing so very out of character. And, as historian Martin J. Anderson reminds us, "It is important to note there was no collusion between Sumner and Hawkins. They wrote their versions at different times from different places."

The upshot? By the time Powell's first trip entered the Great Unknown, it had begun to disintegrate. Somewhere in mid-Grand Canyon Hawkins and Hall began running *Kitty Clyde's Sister* independently of Powell's decisions. Until River Mile 239.5. At this point even Hawkins knew that he should wait for Powell to catch up in the *Emma Dean*.

The rapid here looked bad. The river narrowed to fifty yards wide, as

Sumner remembers, where twin side canyons, mouth to mouth along a transverse fault, had doubly choked the Colorado and partially dammed it with flash-flood-generated debris flows. Worse, cliffs on both sides appeared to preclude a portage, or even a lining of the Z-shaped rapid at the water level that the crew faced. River Mile 239.5 is now called Separation Rapid because, after many hours of scouting it, Oramel Howland and William Dunn decided here to exit the expedition by hiking up the north side canyon to seek the Mormon settlements many miles farther north. As Hawkins remembers it:.

> "When we came to the rapid where the Howland boys and Dunn left the party, we all looked at it, and Hall and I had our course picked out on that rapid for the morning. The Major and some of the other boys went across the river to look to see if there was any chance to let the boats over it by ropes...[the next morning] Bradley came up to the fire and I asked him if it was not coming to a show down. He said he could not understand the Major, but there was something going to happen. I did not know, or care, what happened, as I was sure Andy and Bradley would stand by me in any thing that was reasonable....
>
> [After dividing the flour balls Hawkins had cooked] The Major, the Howland brothers, Dunn and Sumner went off to one side to hold another council. Bradley came over to where Andy Hall and I were standing and completely broke down and shed tears, and said such actions made him feel like a child again. By that time the Major came up to where we were standing and said, 'Well, Billy, we have concluded to abandon the river for the present.' Stating that on account of the scarcity of provisions, and as the rapids were getting more severe, he thought the better thing to do was to abandon the river, as it could not be more than one hundred miles to some settlement in Utah, and that we could get a new supply of grub and return and complete our journey. By that time all the boys were standing and listening to him. When he finished his say, I asked him if he would sell the boat to Andy and me, and he said if we would come back and finish the trip he would give us the boat. I told him I proposed to finish my part of it then, I said, 'Major, you have always looked on Hall and me as being too young to have anything to say in your council, but Hall and I are going to go down this river whether you or any of the rest go or not,' and I told him that if he left the

river I would not think of following him one foot on land, that my mind was set. Then the Major said, 'Well, Billy, if I have one man that will stay with me, I will continue my journey or be drowned in the attempt.' I told him that Bradley, Hall and I had made up our minds to continue....

Sumner spoke up and said, 'Stay with it, Billy, and I will be with you,' and it did not take long to settle the rest of it. The Howland brothers and Dunn had made up their minds and would not change them. Of course we knew what was the reason Dunn left: as for fear, he did not possess it. As for the other two boys, they never showed any signs of fear. The older of the Howlands was in the boat with me since his boat [the *No Name*] was wrecked.

We all crossed over to the north side, hid our supplies and instruments [Sumner identified these as two barometers and some beaver traps], and left one boat for the boys. It is my opinion that if the Howland boys had not agreed to leave the river in the council I referred to, that they would have come with us, but they were sore the way Dunn had been treated...."

Sumner recalls this incident from a different perspective that first afternoon.

"I talked with Major Powell quietly on the subject. He seemed dazed by the proposition confronting us. I then declared that I was going on by the river route, and explained my plans to him how to surmount the difficulty, which plans were carried out the next morning. I explained to the boys — the Howlands and Dunn — how we could pass the rapid in which they agreed — but what was below? We knew that we were less than seventy miles from the mouth of the cañon, but had no idea what kind of river we had to encounter below where we were.

As O. G. Howland appeared to be the leader of the three, and had fully made up his mind to quit as the rapids had become a holy terror to him, I saw that further talk was useless and so informed Major Powell, and suggested we make duplicate copies of field notes, and give the men latitude and longitude and a draft of the location of the Mormon settlements as far as we knew. Major Powell and I were up most of the night to get an observation, and he worked out the calculations while I kept a light burning for him with mesquite brush. At daylight we crossed back to the north side of the river and commenced to make the portage...."

On the morning of August 28, 1869, the trip split their guns, cash, food, and copies of the field notes, as Sumner said (in haste, some parts of these accounts may have been split unequally, with duplicate copies of some sections going by land while no copies went by water) between the three hikers and the six boaters. It is unclear whether or not Powell paid O. G. Howland and William Dunn their $75 each in wages, but it seems that he may have. Powell did ask the hikers to tote a $650 barometer (or chronometer — accounts of this vary). The three also carried a batch of personal letters to be mailed, and Sumner's watch — to go to his sister in Denver in the event that Sumner drowned. Here too Major Powell abandoned his 16-foot *Emma Dean* tied on the north bank; it was damaged yet may have been useful had the three hikers changed their minds.

That morning the three hikers helped the other six men line and portage the two oak boats a fraction of the way down the rapid to a little eddy about forty feet long adjacent to the roaring rapid. Once both oak boats wobbled in this eddy, several of the men asked Dunn and the Howlands to reconsider. Hawkins explains:

> "Dunn held me by the hand and tears came into his eyes when he said he hated to leave Sumner and me; that we had had many a hard and daring time together before we ever saw the Colorado River. 'But,' he said, 'Billy, you cannot blame me.' I could not answer; I, for one time in my life, was hurt to the very heart, and in silence I shook his hand for the last time in this world. All this time Sumner and Hall were talking to the Howland boys.
>
> The Major came into my boat [*Kitty Clyde's Sister*], and we started first, but when we struck the main current it was so swift that it sent us back in the eddy in the little cove. By this time things were getting interesting, and again Dunn and the Howland brothers said we would never make it. I said, 'Watch my smoke this time.' I told Hall to put all his strength in the oars and I would do the rest. The Major got a firm hold with his left hand and sat in the bottom of the boat. I headed for the lower side of the cove so as to strike the main current more on a downstream course than before. It was perhaps thirty feet from the mouth of the cove to the middle of the high waves which were over fifteen feet in height, but Hall had the boat under such

headway that I could manage it with my steering oar [whether this "steering oar" refers to a running oar in a lock or instead to one braced against the stern remains unknown], so I caught the side of the main waves, then cut them for the other side, which we made all right, and landed below. Then came Bradley and Sumner and Captain Powell in the other boat.

We only took in, perhaps, thirty gallons of water in my boat; the other boat did not fare so well, as it struck the rapid too high up, but we got through all right, and we all landed and halloed to the other boys that we left on the rock to come, but they would not.

It was here that Major Powell took off his life preserver and handed it to me, saying he would have no more use for it and would make me a present of it. I told him he had better keep it on, but he said that any man who could come through the way I did between the rocks he felt safe with, and that he would make me a present of it. I thanked him, and said I would keep it to remember the Major and the daring trip and hardships through the entire length of the Colorado River cañons. I have the life preserver now in my possession, although it is unfit for use [38 years later] by reason of age.

Peace and good will to all men. W. R. Hawkins"

Sumner watched Hawkins and Hall row Powell in *Kitty Clyde's Sister*. Here is his account.

"The first start was not successful, but the second time away they went as the current took hold of the bow and whirled the boat round in a flash, but shot her nearly across the river, and cleared the dangerous rock and fountain waves below. We watched them till they passed the two falls farther down, *and we saw them turn in and land* on a sandy beach a half mile beyond.

We repeated the same tactics with the other boat and rounded in beside them. We waited for about two hours, fired guns, and motioned for the men [the Howlands and Dunn] to come on, *as they could have done by climbing along the cliffs.* The last thing *we saw of them* they were standing on the reef, *motioning us to go on*, which we did. If I remember rightly, Major Powell states it was not as bad as it looked and we had run worse. I flatly dispute that statement. *At the stage of water we struck it,* I don't think there is one chance in a thousand to make it by running the whole rapid." (italics either Stanton's or Sumner's)

Clearly, while it may have been fear of the river at this point that drove the Howlands and Dunn to hike out and to emphatically refuse to rejoin the other six below Separation Rapid, it was no longer fear of this rapid itself (Andy Hall's letter suggests he felt certain that Dunn and O. G. Howland were indeed afraid of Separation Rapid) which they now could have hiked around. Downstream some smaller rapids were visible, but these were minor league threats.

Interestingly, Powell would later write — in his 1875 report (p. 100) and in *Canyons of the Colorado* — somewhat differently of the aftermath of running Separation Rapid:

"We land at the first practicable point below, and fire our guns, as a signal to the men above that we have come over in safety. Here we remain for a couple of hours, hoping that they will take the smaller boat and follow us. *We are behind a curve in the canyon and cannot see up to where we left them, and so we wait until their coming seems hopeless, and then push on.*" [italics mine]

In reality, the river corridor immediately downstream of Separation Rapid runs phenomenally straight for two miles. Bradley's and Sumner's and Hawkins' accounts of the men's final separation as being visible to one another seem more accurate (and perhaps less self-serving) than Powell's 1875 report. Powell's actual *entire* journal entry for that fateful day reads: "Boys left us. Ran rapid. Bradey [sic] boat Broke. Camp on left bank. Camp 44."

Was this brevity merely the result of Powell's awkwardness in the mechanics of writing due to having lost his right arm? Maybe. But, on August 25, only three days before the Separation incident, the Major had penned 365 words in his journal #1 describing the new geology at the Toroweap/Lava Falls region. These 365 words, his longest entry during the entire trip, constitute 12.5 percent, or one-eighth, of Powell's entire two-month journal #1 from the Uinta to the Virgin River. Powell's average journal entry for the 45 days on which he wrote anything at all held 65 words. Hence his Lava entry was a record six-fold increase over his average, while his Separation entry three days later was only one fifth of his average. Or, looked at another way, Powell wrote 28 times more words to describe Lava than to describe the fateful events leading to the separation of the

Howlands and Dunn from the expedition. Perhaps Powell was simply apportioning his words according to the subjects which he found most interesting or important. Perhaps, instead, he was too stunned by events to write. Either way, Powell's "Boys left us" entry would be his final entry for the 1869 expedition. How and what he actually felt about this event we can only guess (more on this below, in the section covering the fate of John Wesley Powell).

The six remaining river runners in the two boats ran six more miles of fast river. Then, mostly out of control, they survived a truly hair-raising, willy-nilly run down what Bradley considered the worst rapid of the entire trip, Lava Cliff. Ironically, the next day, Powell and his surviving five men rowed past the Grand Wash Cliffs, thus exiting Grand Canyon and escaping the last whitewater dangers. Yet another day later, 99 days and a thousand miles out of Green River, they rowed into the mouth of the Rio Virgin.

Here the Powell brothers decided to go north overland and catch a train back East. The other four men would row downriver to continue surveying a few more miles and beyond that, just for the hell of it. Before they separated, Major Powell asked the small Mormon community up the Rio Virgin to pass the word to help the Howland brothers and Dunn, were they discovered. Unfortunately, he did not take the time or use the money (even if this meant not paying Sumner?) to ask for, organize, accompany, and/or pay for a genuine search party. As time would reveal, this decision may have been the fatal one, and arguably the greatest single mistake Powell would make in his life.

On September 8, twelve days after the morning of the Separation incident, the *Deseret Evening News* reported that the Howlands and Dunn had been helped by friendly Indians "almost five days ago," who "put them on a trail leading to Washington, in Southern Utah. On their journey they saw a squaw gathering seeds and shot her; whereupon they were followed by three Shebetts [sic] and killed."

Powell read this and also received a telegraph message in Salt Lake City, Utah, informing him that the Howlands and Dunn had been killed by Indians. No evidence exists to indicate that Major Powell, while still in Salt Lake City where he stayed until at least September 18, attempted to make an earnest effort to investigate these murders or identify the bodies. Tellingly also, in Powell's 400-page *Canyons of the Colorado* he expresses no words of regret that Dunn and the Howlands had been murdered (more on this under Powell's "fate").

In 1870, however, Powell did return to southern Utah for more exploring. He visited the Uinkaret Indians, neighbors to the Shivwits Indians whose territory straddles the route the Howlands and Dunn would have taken. The Uinkarets requested for Powell an interview with the Shivwits. Jacob Hamblin, Mormon scout and proselytizer assigned by

Brigham Young to guide Powell, interpreted for him the Shivwits' explanation of the fate of his three men. As Powell would later write, the Shivwits, Hamblin said, had met the three as they were trying to exit the Canyon. The Shivwits had helped them with food and directions. But after the three continued on, Indians from the south side of the Colorado arrived and told the Shivwits that they were chasing some drunken miners who had abused and murdered a squaw. At this information, Hamblin explained, a few of the Shivwits pursued, then ambushed the Howlands and Dunn, murdering them in retribution and in sympathy with these other Indians.

Hamblin gave a slightly different account than Powell's. The Shivwits, Hamblin said, had told him that:

> " — some of their friends from the other side of the river crossed on a raft and told them that miners on their side of the river abused their women.
>
> They advised them to kill the three white men who had gone back from the river, for if any mines were found in their country, it would bring great evil among them. The three men were then followed, and killed when asleep."

This same basic story of how and why Powell's three men who hiked out were killed by the Shivwits exists in every book that discusses Powell's full journey. But even on cursory examination, it makes little sense. The full story itself — of miners killing a squaw and Powell's three men being misidentified as these miners — did not seem to surface until nearly a year after the Howlands and Dunn had been killed. This late breaking of this story is strange in light of the Mormons having reported for a year that the Shivwits had killed the Howlands and Dunn over a murdered woman. If the Mormons knew that these Indians had killed these three whites for such a reason, why had they never during a year of opportunity asked all the details of *exactly* why? This lack was not because relations between the Shivwits and Mormons were too weak. The Mormons had baptized the tribe en masse into the LDS church seven years earlier, in 1862.

Indeed, this "We-killed-them-by-mistake-because-other-Indians-who-had-rafted-the-Canyon-came-and-told-us-that-they-were-bad-miners-who-shot-a-squaw" story is improbable on many levels. The Howlands and Dunn were well-armed and experienced with Indians, while their adversaries were few and had only bows and arrows. On top of this, the two Indians who "confessed" were never arrested by the Mormons. Nor were any of the items carried by Powell's three men — their guns, Powell's chronometer and barometer, Sumner's watch, or the expedition's records — ever mentioned as having been recovered from this tribe by the Mormons.

Besides, who *were* those bad miners who had allegedly perpetrated the rape-murder? Where did they come from and where did they go? This is even weaker. There exist virtually no written records of mining or prospecting activity for this region of Western Grand Canyon — which indeed was terra incognita for whites, including Jacob Hamblin himself — in 1869. Claim records found by George Billingsley, E. E. Spamer, and D. Menkes in their exhaustive history of Canyon mining *Quest for the Pillar of Gold: The Mines & Miners of the Grand Canyon* postdate Powell's 1869 trip. Indeed it was *this* trip that gave the green light to pursuing riches in Grand Canyon.

Moreover, during the years 1867 to 1869, the Hualapai Indians living in the Western Grand Canyon south of the Colorado were locked in a brutal war against the U.S. Cavalry. Lengthy scorched-earth campaigns by the army against the Hualapais finally fizzled out during 1869-1870. In short, 1869 was not a likely year for miners to have been prospecting in this region. As local historian Michael Belshaw — who followed on foot the Howlands' and Dunn's hike out Separation and noted a "Dunn inscription atop Mount Dellenbaugh" — explains:

> "That a small group of Indians or a solitary Indian from the South would be motivated to cross the river and carry the news to unrelated tribes is on the thin edge of probability. The story is less plausible because no mining had been carried out within a hundred miles of Shivwit territory [until 1872 in Kanab Canyon and in Grand Gulch] and should have been of little interest to them. Frederick S. Dellenbaugh reports that the Indians were incited by members of their own band, who reported outrages to the north....It is also most unlikely that the [Powell's] three men wantonly killed an Indian woman as reported in the *Deseret News*."

Is it impossible that there could have been any miners in this region at the end of August in 1869? No, but there have been few worse years in known history for a miner to survive — let alone prospect — in Western Grand Canyon. Even so, note anthropologists Henry F. Dobyns and Robert C. Euler, mining *had* been taking place since 1864, 60 air-miles south-southwest of the edge of Shivwits territory (about 100 miles by an overland route), and hence may not have been unknown in concept to the Shivwits. More to the point, Dobyns and Euler add, some Shivwits had moved south of the river to Pine Spring near camps of their trading partners, the Hualapai, and thus *could* have been the "friends" who crossed the river to the north as Jacob Hamblin reported. On top of all this, because the Hualapais had been very badly treated by the U.S. Cavalry, the Shivwits too may have looked upon *any* white men — including the Howlands and Dunn — as enemies. Hence the Shivwits remain likely suspects with plausible motives.

A few stories from southern Utah attempt to pinpoint not merely the Shivwits but also the specific scene of the crime and even the identities of the individual killers.

The earliest "sleuth" was Frederick S. Dellenbaugh. In his otherwise exhaustive history, *The Romance of the Colorado River: The Story of its Discovery in 1540, with an Account of the Later Explorations, and with Special Reference to the Voyages of Powell through the Great Line of Canyons*, he recounts a mere scanty hybrid of Hamblin's and Powell's versions of the murders. Dellenbaugh then pinpoints a *tinaja*, a bedrock pool, in an intermittent stream atop the Shivwits Plateau and southeast of Mount Dellenbaugh that he visited around 1875 as the murder site and from his imagination, it seems, paints the men's demise:

> "The trail to the water leads down under a basaltic cliff perhaps thirty to forty feet high, as I remember the spot, which I visited six years later. As the unfortunate men turned to come up from filling their canteens, they were shot down from ambush. In consequence I have called this Ambush Water-pocket. The guns, clothing, etc. were appropriated by the Shewits [sic], and I believe it was through one of the watches that the facts first leaked out."

Dellenbaugh, however, offers no clues and cites no evidence whatsoever (spent cartridge cases, broken arrowheads, bones, etc.) to support his conclusion that Ambush Water-pocket was the scene of the crime or, indeed, that any ambush actually happened; he simply cites proximity to the route he believes that the Howlands and Dunn hiked and then relies on his intuition.

Several years after 1869, Anthony W. Ivins "surmised," based on what he admitted were "somewhat obscure facts," that "soon" after the Howlands and Dunn were killed, a party of Shivwits arrived in St. George to trade several 19th century articles, including a watch. They said they had found these at an abandoned camp. Unfortunately, none of these articles have even been found or identified. Nor were the Indians themselves.

An unspecified number of years after 1869, Ivins bought the Mojave Land and Cattle Company, which had bought water hole rights from the Shivwits. But when Ivins brought in his herds, the Shivwits began hunting his stock as wild game. This led to the Shivwits being "relocated," at Ivins' request, on a reservation on the Santa Clara River. Among those who gathered there "was one man who was a constant source of trouble. He was obstinate, uncontrollable, a constant mischief maker," Ivins writes. "He pretended to be possessed of supernatural power, was a medicine man, and pretended to see, in dreams and visions, the past, present and future. His name was Toab. We called him John."

Toab later murdered a fellow Shivwit, "George," in a dispute over water, by beating him to death with a hoe. Toab was tried for this murder, Ivins writes, convicted, and sent to prison. The warden, however, asked Ivins to return him to his people. Because Toab was such a trouble maker, Ivins suspected that Toab had had something to do with the murder of the Howlands and Dunn, though Ivins offers no reasons or evidence for his concluding this, other than his own intuition.

In conflict with Ivins' story is, as historian LaVan Martineau notes, Utah State Prison records show no record for Toab having been tried or convicted of murder. Instead they only show that Toab spent six days in prison, from September 14-19, 1907, for stealing a horse.

Ivins writes further that, twenty years after the 1869 murders, he was riding the range a little east and north of the Parashant Ranch House and happened upon a small camp site. Although apparently nothing existed at this location to tie it to the Howlands and Dunn, Ivins felt his intuition at work again: "Like a bolt from the blue the thought came---This is the spot where Powell's men were killed."

Much later, in 1923, after Toab had died, Ivins interviewed Old Simon--"the only man [Shivwit] remaining, who would have personal knowledge of the details of the tragedy." Old Simon allegedly told Ivins when "he was a big boy three white men came up from the river which flows through the Grand Canyon, and were killed by the Indians on Shivwit Mountain." Strangely, Ivins does not say that, 54 years after the crime, Simon said anything about which Indians had committed the murder or about their motive. Nor did Simon even refer to the "three bad miners" story.

Even so, Ivins concludes that Powell's three men had followed an old Shivwits trail east of Green Spring Canyon. "It appears that," Ivins writes, filling in innumerable gaps in evidence by using his imagination, the three men were met by friendly Shivwits whose attitudes were turned sour because "Toab insisted that they be dealt with as enemies. Persuading two young Indians to go with him, he followed the men a short distance north east of the Para-shont [sic] Ranch House, which was built many years after, where they attacked them from ambush, and killed them." Although Ivins never offers any evidence at all for his ultimate "solving of the crime," not even testimony by Simon---and certainly no confession by Toab---Ivins, who besides having run cattle was a mayor of Saint George, had been appointed one of the high Council of Twelve Apostles by Joseph Smith and was counselor to the First LDS Presidency, ends his report with the following amazing summation:

"It is interesting to know that the point marked by Simon as the spot where the tragedy occurred, is the exact locality where some invisible influence caused the writer to stop his horse and reflect, as before stated, and it was at that time that the resolve came to him some day to fix the responsibility for this needless and unjustifiable murder, where he always believed it belonged, on John To-ab [sic]."

In 2002, Frank M. Barrios, writing without citing his sources of information, tells a somewhat different story of Toab. Toab, he writes, was living near the Wildcat Ranch on the plateau during the early part of the 20th century:

"and claimed to be a small boy in 1869 when the incident occurred. He once pointed to a nearby landmark [vaguely near Mount Dellenbaugh] and told local cowboy Jimmy Guerrero that this was the location where his people killed the men from the Powell expedition, claiming they begged and pleaded for mercy as his people killed them. Toab was said to be a scoundrel and the stated location where he says the ambush occurred may or may not be the place."

For that matter, one might conclude, the rest of Toab's stated 'history" may not be true as well. Clearly it is difficult, if not ludicrous, to conclude anything firm from either Ivins' or Barrios' or even Dellenbaugh's accounts – yet some historians apparently do. In short, concluding that Toab ever laid eyes on the Howlands or Dunn, or whether any Shivwits, with or without Toab, killed them, remains precarious.

Which brings us back to Jacob Hamblin's story of bad miners abusing Indian women, as translated from the Shivwits. Even with Toab's rumored report, it still seems a concoction made up post hoc by the Indians to justify their killing and robbing innocent men – or instead made up by someone else to cover their own unjustified murder of the Howlands and Dunn.

Interestingly, despite the Shivwits' (a.k.a. Hamblin's) or Ivins' stories, the concept of Indians having killed the Howlands and Dunn seemed flimsy to Jack Sumner even in 1869. Sumner doubted from the beginning that the Indians could have killed his three comrades. He later wrote to Stanton that, even while Powell's six were still inside Grand Canyon on their final day:

"The boys discussed the conduct and fate of the three men left above. They all seemed to think the red bellies would get them sure; but I could not believe that the reds would get them, as I had trained Dunn for two years in how to

Plaque bolted to bedrock at foot of Separation Canyon commemorating the heroic performances of William H. Dunn, Oramel G. Howland, and Seneca Howland. Photo by R. D. Quartaroli.

avoid a surprise, and I did not think the red devils would make an open attack on three armed men. But I did have some misgiving that they would not escape the white double dyed devils that infested that part of the country. Grape vine reports convinced me later that that was their fate....

....I heard about two months afterwards, while at Fort Yuma, California, that they [Mormon searchers] brought in the report that the Howland brothers and Dunn came to an Indian camp, shot an Indian, and ravished and shot three squaws. The Indians then collected a force and killed all three of the men. But I am positive I saw some years afterwards the silver watch that I had given Howland [to pass on to Sumner's sister]. I was with some men in a carousal and one of them had a watch and boasted how he came by it. I tried to get hold of it so as to identify it by a certain screw that I had made and put in myself, but it was spirited away and I never afterwards could get sight of it. Such evidence is not conclusive, but all of it was enough to convince me that the Indians were not at the head of the murder, if they had anything to do with it."

Not only was Sumner "positive" about the watch being his, but back on August 30, 1869, when he, Hawkins, Hall, Bradley, and the Powell brothers arrived at the Rio Virgin, he was also suspicious about the motives of at least one of the local whites they met there. This being only two days after the Howland brothers and Dunn had started their hike up Separation Canyon, Powell and the others explained to these friendly Mormons the three men's predicament and location, asking that help be sent if possible. During this request, as Sumner later complained in disgust:

" — but when Major Powell made the foolish break of telling them the amount of valuables the boys had, I noticed a complete change in the action of a certain one of the men. From a listless demeanor, he instantly changed to a wide-awake, intensely interested listener, and his eyes snapped and burned like a rattlesnake's eyes, particularly so as Major Powell told him of an especially valuable chronometer that he had paid six hundred and fifty dollars for."

Aside from this insight into which of Powell's priorities might be served by asking these Mormons to render assistance to Dunn and the Howlands, Sumner's observation also clarifies how a significant monetary motive could quickly have developed for a robbery-murder of the missing three men. It also offers a possible explanation for why nothing at all that was carried by the Howlands and Dunn was ever visibly recovered from the Mormons' friends, the baptized Shivwits, who had little use for chronometers, watches, or notes of river expeditions.

In 1919, Billy Hawkins, seventy years old, mentioned to William Wallace Bass, also old, that "some years afterwards [after 1869] I, with a party of some others, buried their bones [the Howlands' and Dunn's] on the Shewits Mountains, below Kanab Wash." No more has been said on this burial. Nor has anyone found its location or that of the murders since. Nor, again, has any item the Howlands or Dunn carried been found — other than that watch Sumner was positive was his.

Could the Howlands and Dunn have been murdered by Mormons for a simple robbery? Or was it something more?

That something more would likely be the same set of conditions that prompted the September 7, 1857, Mountain Meadows Massacre perpetrated by Indians and whites in southern Utah. Indeed, without understanding this massacre, the murders of the Howlands and Dunn make little sense.

In late summer of 1857, a wagon train of about 140 people from Arkansas crossed Utah from northeast to southwest. This train was led by one of the three Baker brothers — Captain John T., George W., and Abel Baker — but has been identified historically as the "Fancher party" after Alexander Fancher, its outspoken member. Within weeks rumors would spread that the Fancher train trampled Mormon crops, shot a Kanosh Indian, stole Indian cattle, and may have poisoned a water hole that killed more cattle and more Indians. Historian Will Bagley, however, notes that no evidence exists that members of the Fancher train committed any of those alleged offenses. Instead, he notes, the allegations are all mere rumors, folklore, and deliberate anti-Gentile propaganda. Next, before leaving Utah, the Bakers and Fancher made the decision to camp at Mountain Meadows in southwestern Utah to fatten their oxen and hundreds of head of livestock before crossing the bleak Nevada deserts.

As is told in detail by Juanita Brooks in her *Mountain Meadows Massacre* and half a century later more accurately by Will Bagley in *Blood of the Prophets*, Brigham Young's war stance against the U.S. and his religious stance of vengeance against Gentiles for the murders of Joseph Smith, Parley Pratt, and other Prophets let to a combined attack by southern Utah Mormons aided by Paiutes on the Fancher train. Young's tactics were to eliminate it and steal all its possessions. Brigham Young's larger strategy goal, however, being to stop all passage of emigrant trains westward through Utah. Despite absolutely fierce fighting for five days the well-armed Fancher party continued to withstand the combined siege.

To break this stalemate, the combination of Mormons and Indians,

Brooks writes, enlisted John Doyle Lee, a prominent Mormon and the local Indian Agent, to act as intermediary. But Lee was subordinate to Major John M. Higbee of the Mormon militia, who had orders from Isaac C. Haight to kill "all the immigrants who could talk."

So Lee convinced the train to surrender their weapons.

If their surrender seems to make no sense, the Arkansans by now were low on ammunition, many had been wounded, including women and children, and their prospects for escape looked bleak in the extreme. Their draft oxen had been shot dead. Perhaps the Fancher party also worried that they might not reach the southern Sierra in time for a safe crossing unless they left Utah soon. Besides, the besieged wagon train had been isolated from their only source of water, a nearby spring. For whatever reasons, now unknowable, the Fancher party agreed to Lee's conditions.

The Mormons, Brooks and Bagley continue, convinced the fifty men of the train to separate from the wagons by a few hundred yards and then formally surrender their arms. Then, as soon as each man handed his gun over, his Mormon counterpart shot him dead (some Mormons of this militia refused to commit murder, but others nearby did it for them). Meanwhile the Paiutes spent the next half hour murdering all the women and most of the children with knives and hatchets. They spared the eighteen youngest for adoption into Mormon families. After killing 120 people, the murderers stole everything the victims had owned, including $4,000 in gold held in a strong box. Indeed, this theft may have been a prime motive; as Mark Twain noted in his appendix in *Roughing It*, the Fancher Train was wealthy enough in goods, livestock, and even cash to have excited the envy of many locals in Utah, both Indian and white. Significantly, subsequent research and interviews with the surviving little children revealed that many of the "Paiutes" who murdered the women and children were actually Mormons painted and dressed as Indians, and they used guns and knives.

Most accounts, including Brooks' and Bagley's, however, pay only selective attention to the first successful investigation of the crime by Brevet Major James H. Carleton, U.S. Army, Captain 1st Dragoons. In 1859, Carleton received orders to investigate the loss, somewhere in Utah, of what was then known as the "Perkins" train, named because Perkins was the guide for the Baker and Fancher brothers. Local whites, Carleton found as he attempted interviews, were less than coherent and very unhelpful. He did learn that Jacob Hamblin, Indian sub-agent for the Paiutes, had advised the train to camp at Mountain Meadows, which Hamblin owned (as a gift from the Mormon Church), to "recruit" (rest and fatten) the train's at least five hundred head of livestock.

Hamblin told Carleton that soon afterwards, during Hamblin's absence, the wagon train had been wiped out. Hamblin returned to his summer ranch four miles from Mountain Meadows on September 18, 1857, to find "three little white girls [sisters Rebecca, Louisa, and Sarah Dunlap rescued by John D. Lee and for whom Mrs. Hamblin felt pity] in the care of my wife; the oldest six or seven years of age, the next about three, and the next about one. The youngest had been shot through one of her arms, below the elbow, by a large ball, breaking both bones and cutting the arm half off." Hamblin next told Carleton:

> "The *Indians* have often told me that they made an attack on the emigrants between daylight and sunrise as the men were standing around their campfires, killing and wounding fifteen at the first discharge, which was delivered from the ravine near the spring close to the wagons and from a hill to the west....The *Indians* say they then run [sic] off the stock but kept parties at the spring to prevent the emigrants from getting to the water, the emigrants firing upon them every time they showed themselves, and they returning the fire. This was kept up for six or seven days. The *Indians* say they lost but one man killed and three or four wounded. At the end of six or seven days they say a man among them who could talk English called to the emigrants and told them if they would go back to the settlements and leave their property, *especially their arms*, they would spare their lives; but if they did not do so, they would kill the whole of them. The emigrants agreed to this and started back on the road towards my ranch. About a mile from the spring there are some scrub oak bushes and tall sage growing on each side of the road and close to it. Here a large body of Indians lay in ambush, who, when the emigrants approached, fell upon them in their defenseless condition, and with bows and arrows, and stones and guns and knives, murdered all, without regard to sex or age, except a few infant children, seventeen of which have been since recovered. This is what the Indians told me nine days after the massacre took place....When I buried the bones last summer, I observed that about one third of the skulls were shot through with bullets, and about one third seemed to be broken with stones....These are the all facts, within my knowledge, connected with the destruction of one, and the passing along of the other, of those two trains [the second train, several days behind the Perkins-Baker-Fancher train, having been protected by Dudley Leavitt at Hamblin's urging]."

When Carleton next interviewed Hamblin's 45-year-old wife, Carleton was impressed that Hamblin insisted on being present during the interview and he often prompted his wife on the events of the massacre, even though she had been present at Mountain Meadows during the murders and he had been absent. She heard all the shooting, she said, for day after day, and watched the Indians pass and re-pass her house. She also saw John D. Lee several times, saying that he was trying to stop the hostilities. Carleton considered her a simple-minded woman who saw the world through the eyes of her husband. And Carleton seriously doubted the honesty of that husband.

Next, Albert, Hamblin's Crow Indian helper and adopted son, told Carleton that he saw the Paiutes lying in ambush as Hamblin had described, with the emigrants *walking, women first, men second,* without wagons, toward them. The Indians then massacred all but a few children, Albert said, over the next half hour. Carleton later learned that two of the surviving children identified Albert as the man who murdered their two sisters. Carleton found so many holes and inaccuracies in Albert's story that he considered him a liar and his account a worthless fiction.

Interestingly, Carleton found a Paiute of the Santa Clara band named Jackson who admitted that he was one of the attackers, but who also said that John D. Lee had led a group of sixty Mormons, all painted and disguised as Indians (the costuming being done one mile from the spring at which the train was camped), and that "Lee and Haight led and directed the combined force of Mormons and Indians in the first attack---throughout the siege---and at the last massacre."

On May 25, 1859, Carleton finished his report. He noted that some of the local Mormons had a feud with anyone from Arkansas. The locals, he added, expressed no regret that 120 people had been murdered. More intriguing, Carleton found that several Cedar City Mormons said they held no doubt that Lee, Haight, and Higby "were the leaders who organized a party of fifty or sixty Mormons to attack this train," with many Indians as helpers. "The Mormons say," Carleton added, "the emigrants fought 'like lions' and that thy [sic] could not whip them by any fair fighting." Carleton heard from locals plus a dentist named Whitelock (at Camp Floyd who had interviewed a self-admitted Mormon participant in the massacre who fled to California and was suffering from obvious post-traumatic stress disorder) that hostilities ended in the following way:

> "After some days fighting, the Mormons had a council among themselves to arrange a plan to destroy the immigrants. They concluded finally, that they would send some few down and pretend to be friends and try to get the emigrants to surrender. John D. Lee and three or four

others, head men from Washington, Cedar and Parowan, (Haight and Higby from Cedar) had their paint washed off, and dressing in their usual dress, took their wagons and drove towards the emigrants' corral as if they were just travelling on the road on their ordinary business. The emigrants held out a little girl toward them. She was dressed in white. Had a white handkerchief in her hand which she waved in a token of peace. The Mormons with the wagons waved one in reply and then moved on to the corral. The emigrants then came out---no *Indians or others being in sight at this time*; and talked with these leading Mormons with the three wagons. They talked with the emigrants an hour, or an hour and a half, and told them that the Indians were hostile, and that if *they gave up their arms, it* would show that they did not want to fight; and if they, the emigrants would do this, they would pilot them back to the settlements. The immigrants had horses which had remained near their wagons, the loose stock, mostly cattle, had been driven off, not the horses. Finally the emigrants agreed to these terms, and delivered up their arms to the Mormons with whom they had counselled. The women and children then started back toward Hamblin's house, the men following with a few wagons that they had hitched up. On arriving at the scrub oaks, &c., where the other Mormons and Indians lay concealed, Higby, who had been one of those who had inveigled the emigrants from their defenses, *himself gave the signal to fire*, when a volley was poured in from each side and the butchery commenced and was continued until it was consummated."

The property from the Fancher train was then sold in Cedar City at public auction and called "Property taken at the siege of Sabastopol." When Carleton questioned the Paiutes along the Muddy River, whom the Mormons had said were the Mountain Meadows culprits, The Indians responded with, if we did it, then "Where are the wagons, the cattle, the clothing, the rifles, and other property belonging to the train? We don't have them. You will find these things in the hands of the Mormons." Carleton added that Hamblin had told him that in 1855 the entire tribe possessed only three guns. How, Carleton asked rhetorically, could they then, in 1857, have beaten fifty well-armed male emigrants?

Carleton and his men gathered up the bones of thirty-four victims at Mountain Meadows. He buried them in a mass grave, then had built a rude conical monument fifty feet in circumference of loose granite. Atop this he placed a cross of cedar twenty-four feet high and inscribed it with the facts of the mass murder (which Brigham Young ordered destroyed in 1861). How did these victims — the women and children 600 yards closer to Hamblin's cabin than the men — die?

> "I observed that nearly every skull I saw had been shot through with rifle or revolver bullets. I did not see one that had been 'broken with stones'....The scene of the massacre, even at this late day, was horrible to look upon. Women's hair in detached locks and in masses, hung in the sage bushes and was strewn over the ground..."

Carleton was so disturbed by this mass murder and the devious means by which it had been committed that he characterized the Mormons as "Latter Day Devils" and concluded:

> "Crime is found in the footsteps of the Mormons wherever they go, and so the evil must always exist as long as the Mormons themselves may exist...They are an ulcer on the body-politic. An ulcer which it needs more than cautery to cure. It must have excision; complete and thorough extirpation before we can ever hope for safety or tranquility."

On August 23, 1999, however, a backhoe's claw excavating for the construction of a new monument on site accidentally disinterred 2,602 bone fragments in a mass grave of at least 28 victims of the massacre. Due to strange political machinations, forensic biologist Shannon Novak at the University of Utah's Medical School was restricted in her analysis of the original damage inflicted on the cranial fragments of 18 victims to one single 25-hour marathon of forensic examination. She carried this out from September 9 to 10, 1999, before being required to return the bones to Shane Baker, archeologist at Brigham Young University. What Novak discovered during those mere 25 hours of study opened a Pandora's Box.

For starters, she found that at least five of the men had been shot in the head while facing their executioners. More troubling, Novak found that one child between the ages of ten and fifteen had also been shot through the top of the head. Two children, age four and seven, had been beaten to death. Most revealing, however, was the following: Novak found *no* evidence whatsoever of any Indian-specific attacks on any of the victims — no arrow wounds, no knife or hatchet wounds, and no evidence of scalping.

This lack not only corroborates the Indians' own stories, as told in 1859 to U.S. Army Major James H. Carleton, that the Indians had not been principals in the massacre but instead local whites had painted their faces and done most of the killing themselves. It also helps explain why local whites would have been even more highly motivated to keep all details about this massacre absolutely secretCforever.

Hence it is no surprise that, after the massacre, everyone involved swore a "Covenant of Silence." The entire wagon train and the Fancher party simply ceased to exist.

Interestingly, within the first few months following the Mountain Meadows Massacre, Lieutenant Joseph Christmas Ives led an expedition of exploration *up* the Colorado River hundreds of miles from its mouth to the Virgin River. Beginning on December 30, 1857, Ives and his crew steamed upriver — in some sections they also were forced to tow the fifty-foot iron boat — until reaching the foot of Black Canyon (now submerged by Lake Mead) on March 19, 1858. From there Ives plus a few crew members rowed, towed, and sailed, using a blanket as a sail, one of their skiffs thirty miles upstream into and beyond the head of Black Canyon. They arrived at what Ives judged to be the mouth of the Virgin on March 12. After poking around a bit to take in the lay of the land — meanwhile worrying about the hostile Paiutes against whom the very friendly Mojave Indians had warned him — Ives and his stalwarts rowed back downstream. After a blissfully speedy trip to rejoin the *Explorer*, Ives' crew was reunited. They steamed downstream into the valley of the friendly Mojaves.

Only now they were no longer friendly.

Ives was nonplussed. What the hell had gone wrong, he wondered, during the few days while he and all of his men had been upstream? The first inkling came from a solitary white man they met on shore on March 16. He proved evasive about identifying himself. But he did tell Ives a story that a wagon train traveling southwest through Utah was headed into trouble with a thousand or more Indians lying ahead. One of Ives' crew had been in Utah and recognized the man as a Mormon bishop. The bishop's story was so garbled, inconsistent, and vague that Ives noted, "This and several similar discrepancies did not argue well for the bishop's sanctity."

Besides, this wagon train story still failed to explain the suddenly hostile posture among the Mojaves. Soon, however, some of Ives' Indian friends arrived at the *Explorer* to recount recent events to him. As Ives' tells it, one Indian, Mariano, explained to him that, "the Mormons have created a prejudice against us by informing the already suspicious Mojaves that we have come to take away their lands. Mariano further states that they have proposed to these Indians to commence hostilities, promising the assistance of themselves and the Pai-utes, and that they bribed Ireteba [one of Ives' Mojave friends] this morning, by offer of a mule, to conduct the scouting party to the Mojave villages, the visit being intended for our especial disadvantage."

Lieutenant Joseph Christmas Ives' *Explorer* in Mojave Canyon, along the lower Colorado (from Joseph Christmas Ives' 1861 *Report Upon The Colorado River of the West*).

Ives' relations among the Mojaves now seemed suddenly more sinister. Fortunately for Ives, many of the Mojaves already suspected that the Mormons themselves were "already looking with a covetous eye on the beautiful Mojave valley." Meanwhile, a Lieutenant Tipton had been leading a re-supply mule train to Ives in Mojave valley. Tipton's Yuman scouts also learned from local Mojaves "that the Mormons had been endeavoring in every way to excite the hostility of the last mentioned Indians against the expedition, and had urged them to commence an attack by stampeding the animals." Ives explains:

> "This statement coincides entirely with what Ireteba and Mariano have repeatedly told me. I have found these two Indians invariably truthful, and know not what object they could have had in manufacturing a story. Corroborated as it is by the Yumas and by many circumstances that have occurred, I hardly know how to credit it, though I feel reluctant to believe that any white men could be guilty of such unprovoked rascality."

The question of how any white men could be guilty of such "rascality" is an interesting one. This question can perhaps be rephrased to: Was the "wagon train" referred to the Fancher Train? Was the bishop's inconsistent story to Ives an attempt to create a credible rumor or alibi to explain how and where the Fancher Train vanished — namely along the Nevada-California border due to an attack by a thousand Mojaves, instead of by Mormons and possibly Paiutes in Mountain Meadows in Utah? Or was he covering up for yet another train attacked along the Utah-Nevada border?

Ives next learned that Mormons had waylaid his Indian letter carrier traveling overland to Lieutenant Tipton. The Mormons had ripped his letters to shreds. Ives rose to the challenge. To prevent this mess from getting any messier — or bloodier — Ives had a long palaver with one of the well-respected Mojave chiefs, Cairook. Ives had been so friendly with the Mojaves on his upstream run that patching things up now proved fairly easy. Within hours the hundreds of Mojave men had put away their bows, war arrows, and warclubs, and the Mojave women and children were now clustered again in a jolly horde in Ives' camp. The crisis was over.

Despite several federal investigations over the years after 1858, by 1869 no one had been arrested, tried, or punished for the mass murder at Mountain Meadows. But the U.S. government still wanted answers.

Knowing all of this, the additional question immediately arises: Was Jacob Hamblin's explanation of the Shivwits having killed Powell's three men a cover-up to hoodwink Powell? Was Hamblin reliable? John D. Lee, who worked with and around Hamblin for years, later referred to him as "Dirty-Fingered Jake" and as an habitual liar. These disparaging remarks were made in the context of Hamblin having testified against Lee during Lee's trial regarding his role in the Mountain Meadows Massacre. Lee found Hamblin's testimony ironic in that it was at Hamblin's cabin, with Hamblin's first wife, that the Mormon militia stayed the night before murdering those fifty men of the Fancher train at Mountain Meadows, which also, by the way, was on Hamblin's land. Lee's "dirty fingers" allegation may have been in reference to Hamblin having ended up with a share of the loot from that massacred train stowed safely in that same cabin. John Doyle Lee was found guilty during this trial and was executed in 1877 by firing squad. As the only person ever arrested or tried for the Mountain Meadows Massacre, Lee had obviously been sacrificed as a scapegoat. "Scapegoat" does not mean "innocent. " Indeed, Lee's 19th wife Ann Gordge reported that later, when one of the Fancher train's surviving children saw Emma Lee all dressed up, she said Emma was wearing her mother's dress. J.D. Lee "reached down, took the child by the head and bent her back and cut her throat from ear to ear, then threw her body in a well nearby. This I saw with my own eyes. "

The larger question regarding the fates of the Howland brothers and Dunn remains: But what might Hamblin have been covering up, if anything, with his Shivwits story?

And what *really* happened to the Howland brothers and Dunn?

One might guess that if we did not know by now, we never will. But this could be wrong. "New" information surfaced recently via a fluke discovery made by Wesley P. Larsen, professor emeritus and former dean of the College of Science at Southern Utah University. In the early 1980s, Larsen purchased the old historic house built by John Steele in Toquerville. Steele, born in Ireland in 1821, was an unpublished but accomplished explorer of the plateaus of southern Utah and northern Arizona. Steele was also a Parowan judge, a mayor, and a county recorder.

Larsen, also a Mormon, had sifted through a trunk of old documents and letters that John Steele's great grandson, Gary Callister, had turned up. Larsen found among them a letter, verified as authentic, written to John Steele in 1883 by William Leany, apparently in response to a letter that Steele — by then an old man — had written to him suggesting that it was time for them both to confess to and repent their sins.

William Leany, born in 1815, was a Parowan city council member and Harrisburg water master. He had fallen from the church's graces, however, in 1857 when he gave food to William Aiden, one of the members of the doomed Fancher party soon to be massacred at Mountain Meadows. Leany had given William Aiden food because he was the son of Dr. S. R. Aiden, who had saved Leany's life earlier in Tennessee from an anti-Mormon mob while Leany was on a church mission. For this minor repayment for saving Leany's life — by giving food to an "enemy," as Fancher's wagon train was dubbed — local Mormon Barney Carter ambushed Leany at night on his own front porch. He broke a picket-like club over Leany's head, fractured his skull, and left him for dead. Leany failed to die, though years passed before he recovered.

Leany's 1883 letter back to Steele was anything but repentant. He had nothing to repent, he said, adding that his accusers were "drunken, adulterous, murderous wretches." Leany continued, as Larsen interprets, to "spill his guts" to his old friend Steele:

> " — God shall bear me witness that I am clean of all of which they [President Erastus Snow and others] accuse me & they guilty of all that I accuse them & much more....And I cannot see that for me to confess to a lie would make me more worthy or they less guilty & here let me say that my object is & has been to stay the overwhelming tide of thieving whoredom murder and Suicide & like abominations that threaten to desolate the land & you are far from ignorant of those deeds of blood from the day the picket was broken on my head *to the day those three were murdered in our ward & the murderer killed to stop the shedding of*

*more blood....*As the old Prophets said of the blood & violence in the city & blood tondreth blood if that was not fulfilled in *the killing of the three in one room of our ward* please say what it was & for all this & much more unrighteous dominion shall we be cast out of the land....Be assured that I will, God being my helper, clear my skirts of the mobbing, raking, stealing, whoredom, murder, suicide, lying, slander & all wickedness & abominations even in high places." (italics mine)

Larsen admitted to writer Scott Thybony that Leany's letter led him to suspect that Powell's three men had succeeded in their hike through Shivwits country. The three must have been seen, Larsen concluded, and then brought to Toquerville, the county seat and local center of Church authority. Only weeks earlier in 1869 — Larsen also found out — Brigham Young had ridden circuit through southern Utah to warn faithful Mormons that there would soon come yet another attempt by Gentiles to invade Utah. The coming "war," Young had warned, would be so hellacious that blood would flow as deep as the bridles of their horses. To avoid being attacked by surprise in this war, the Latter Day Saints posted sentries at all passes leading into southern Utah.

Hence, the Howland brothers and Dunn *were* likely spotted as they hiked north. And, once spotted, they would have been brought to Toquerville.

Leany's letter mentioned to Steele, "*our ward.*" Larsen looked into this and found that the only time that Leany and Steele had shared a ward was in 1869–1874. On top of this, Leany mentioned "*in one room of our ward.*" The only ward of that time, Larsen found, with more than one room was the one in Toquerville, the one Larsen had purchased from John Steele's heirs (and since then repurchased back by the community of Toquerville).

Larsen next wondered if all of this could refer to some other three people murdered or killed somehow. So he searched the records of 1869 for the local region of southern Utah. Only one trio had been killed in that year, the Howland brothers and Dunn.

But why would they have been murdered?

1869 was another year of prejudice against Mormons, of federal investigation concerning the as-yet-unsolved Mountain Meadows Massacre, of Mormon paranoia about being punished, and of Mormon vigilance against federal spies. Into this climate of paranoia and fear wandered three very beat-up river runners from a river that not only had never been run before, but whose name was synonymous with impossibility — almost with death itself. In this climate, when most strangers were suspected to be federal spies, the Howlands and Dunn would have been doubly suspect given their improbable story about having boated down the impossible Colorado in Grand Canyon. In short, to some inquisitors, they would have been unbelievable. Hence, they were lying. Hence they must have been covering up something. Something like being federal spies. The three, Larsen suspected, might have been killed outright — and robbed of their valuables — once they were brought from somewhere along the trail route from Separation Canyon to Mount Trumbull and then past the Hurricane Cliffs to Toquerville even without sanction from higher church authorities.

If this did happen, then word of their execution would soon have reached Salt Lake City, some message to the effect that "we just executed three federal spies whose cover story was that they had just boated Grand Canyon." Such a message would have arrived at virtually the same time as word from John Wesley Powell at the Rio Virgin reached Salt Lake saying that his expedition had been successful, but three of his men had hiked north from Western Grand Canyon and would need assistance. Together these two messages would have caused instant turmoil — if not panic.

Larsen suspects that church authorities quickly sent word back to Toquerville commanding that the executioner himself must be executed and the entire crime itself be covered up completely to avoid further bloodshed. Leany's passage in his 1883 letter, "*& the murderer killed to stop the shedding of more blood*," suggests too that this is what happened. Larsen suspects further that the blame for the three killings was officially placed on the Mormons' Indian allies (who also took the blame for the Mountain Meadows Massacre and for other deeds committed by Mormon militias who dressed up like Indians to assassinate enemies). As with the booty looted from the Fancher Train, nothing that the Howlands and Dunn had been carrying has surfaced except Sumner's watch, which very likely was pocketed by accomplices at the scene of the crime, perhaps in downtown Toquerville.

Indeed, the discovery that the Indians had killed the Howlands and Dunn was announced by Mormons only about ten days after the killings actually happened. How would they have known this so soon from the isolated Shivwits who had so little contact with whites? Was it via Anthony Ivins' vague rumor of Indians trying to sell booty, or instead by other Indians simply showing up to report a murder, a report that would seriously screw up their lives? No, says Larsen, it was Mormons. And after the Mormon cover-up that Larsen suspects actually explains the "Indian" story, everyone involved was sworn to a blood oath "covenant of silence" similar to that sworn after the Mountain Meadows Massacre.

In Hurricane, Utah, Wes Larsen told Flagstaff author Scott Thybony that, while this scenario was the only one that seemed to add up to account for all the facts, he wanted to corroborate his hypothesis with more evidence. Larsen had a friend who submitted for him a request to examine documents of that era in the Mormon Archives.

Larsen waited for an hour. The chief archivist demanded to know on whose authority Larsen could view such documents. Larsen said, "Well, I'm a Mormon." The archivist denied Larsen access and told him to leave.

"I guess you have to be a *good* Mormon," Larsen said wryly to Thybony, the irony being that earlier, during the heat of that day, Larsen had steadfastly refused a cold beer because of his religion.

Thybony asked Larsen if he was worried about repercussions from the church if he published what he had put together.

"Hell yes, I'm worried."

But Larsen did not give up. One of the most important missing pieces to this puzzle was who, specifically, had murdered the Howlands and Dunn and then was executed himself. As Larsen dug deeper it seemed clear to him that the murderer was Eli N. Pace. Pace was a son-in-law of John D. Lee and had killed all three, Larsen reckoned, to protect Lee from the three armed federal men coming out of "nowhere." Pace died on January 29, 1870 (five months after the Howlands and Dunn) under mysterious — and suspicious — circumstances, shot with a Remington or Colt's revolver positioned to suggest that he had done it by his own hand.

Soon after the Howlands and Dunn were murdered, Brigham Young would send John D. Lee himself to the confluence of the Paria and Colorado rivers to build and run a ferry — Lee's Ferry. Not only was the ferry necessary to colonize northern Arizona, its desolate location would keep Lee isolated from federal marshals.

Just before Larsen and Thybony parted company, Larsen answered Thybony's question of why he had gone to all the trouble he had to investigate the killings of the Howland brothers and Dunn.

"If these were Mormons who did it," Larsen answered, "and the Paiutes got the damn blame for everything, it's...it's...." He stopped. Later he admitted, "I only wish I'd felt this way fifty years ago."

Wes Larsen, Scott Thybony, and other historians are still seeking additional clues on the Shivwits Plateau and in the settlements of Utah to firmly pin down, without the shadow of a doubt, the fates of Dunn and the Howlands. To further complicate matters, in 2003, historian Don Lago noted how Richard Fryer murdered his estranged wife Theresa, their infant son, and Thomas Batty in 1875 in Toquerville. A sheriff's posse shot Fryer. These four killings may, Lago suggests, instead be the murders that William Leany referred to in his letter to John Steele. Each of us now must simply weigh the existing evidence and arrive at our own conclusion. Did the Shivwits murder the Howlands and Dunn? Or did whites? You decide.

As you've read, John Colton Sumner had already decided a century ago. What I've held back until now is that Sumner also knew why. While Wes Larsen has been the main detective trying for more than a decade to solve this crime, Sumner had somehow "known" the culprits almost all along, indeed for a century. In 1906, Sumner wrote a long letter to his old friend Lewis Keplinger (this letter, discovered by historian Don Lago, is reproduced below in full under the fate of *John "Jack" Colton Sumner*. In it Sumner answered Keplinger's question as to what had happened to the members of the 1869 crew. Sumner explained what he knew of each man's fate. Then he dropped the big bombshell (one with a long-delayed detonation fuse because the letter has remained hidden and unread for so long in the Kansas State Historical Society's Keplinger Collection). In it Sumner tells Keplinger: "the two howlands [sic] and Dunn were killed. Powell states by Indians & I Say Killed by the Mormons, Part of the Same old 'Mountains Meadows' massacre gang."

Andrew Hall

Hall and Hawkins were the only two men of Powell's original 1869 crew who afterward settled in Arizona. Hall moved to Prescott in 1874. But whereas Hawkins eventually became a part of Arizona's landed Mormon "gentry" in southeastern Arizona, Hall gravitated back to his profession of staying on the move; specifically by "riding shotgun." Hall moved to Florence where he worked as an express messenger for Wells Fargo on the route from Casa Grande to Globe.

For several decades up to 2001, Andy Hall's death has been erroneously reported by historians to having occurred in something like the following way. In 1882, Andy Hall was riding shotgun on a stagecoach near Globe, Arizona, and carrying a strongbox of gold. The stage was ambushed, the story goes, by desperados who killed the driver, wounded Hall, then made off with the gold. Hall, wounded, tracked them down and tried to arrest them but was filled full of lead for his troubles and died.

Again, many details of this story are wrong. The reality is far more interesting and more tragic. And it provides far more insight into the character of one of the first two, and nearly the only, men in history — Sumner was the other — who boated from Green River City, Wyoming, all the way to the Sea of Cortez just for the hell of it.

First, there was no stage coach. And no riding shotgun. And, tragically perhaps, no shotgun either.

On Sunday, August 20, 1882, 32-year-old Andy Hall watched with one eye as Frank Porter loaded his mule train at Pioneer Pass. In those days, the stage road from Casa Grande ended at the top of Pioneer Pass; from this tiny settlement a pack trail descended the final ten miles to Globe. Porter's mules regularly carried the mail and express goods that Wells Fargo shipped, once the Wells Fargo buckboard reached the end of the road at Pioneer Pass.

On this particular day, Cicero Grime, a local, poverty-stricken photographer from Globe, was leaning against the Wells Fargo shack. He offered to lend Porter a hand. Grime lifted the heaviest express box to the back of the strongest mule in Porter's train. Meanwhile Andy Hall tried to figure out what was wrong with his shotgun. It obstinately refused to fire. Hall had accompanied the Wells Fargo shipment from Casa Grande by buckboard to here and would continue with Porter, now by mule, into Globe. But Hall knew he would be happier on the narrow trail ahead if his shotgun were working.

After helping Porter, Cicero Grime, unarmed, mounted his horse and cantered down the trail well ahead of the mule train.

In that heavy express box nestled $5,000 in gold intended as payroll for the workers at the Mack Morris Mine in the foothills of the Sierra Apache beyond Globe.

About four miles from Pioneer Pass, just before Sixshooter Canyon, a gully crossed the trail. On the left side of the trail here the hill rose steeply. And on the right side stood a huge white boulder which obscured the view. Here Grime pulled in the reins of his horse and told an accomplice, Curtis F. Hawley:

> "The pack train will be along shortly. I helped lift the box onto the pack saddle, and it is heavy. Porter is unarmed and Hall has only a small revolver. He had a shotgun, but it was out of order and he said he would leave it in the shack." Grime hesitated, then added, "I think we had better give this up and forget it."

Hawley, a big, dark complected man, stepped out from hiding and said, "No! We came out here to get this box and we are going to get it."

A much smaller man, Lafayette (a.k.a. Fate) Grime also had cold feet. He stepped out onto the trail to follow his brother Cicero Grime to Globe. But Hawley turned his gun on Fate and said, "You stay, or else..."

Minutes later, Andy Hall, riding lead, passed this same white boulder. Behind him the mules plodded dutifully. Porter brought up the rear. As the mules entered the gully, rifle fire whizzed over their heads, then a bullet struck the lead mule carrying the strong box. The other mules panicked and galloped down the trail half a mile.

Finally getting them under control again, Andy Hall dropped to the ground. A bullet had wounded him in the thigh. Ignoring the pain, he told Porter to ride ahead into Globe and round up a posse, while he tried to track the robbers. Then Hall crept back up to the white boulder.

The robbers, arguing, had already shifted the gold from the strongbox into two canvas saddle bags called "catinas." Hawley and Fate, large and tiny, now escaped on foot along the east slope of the Pinals before Hall arrived.

Soon they met a local prospector and druggist, Dr. F. W. Vail, riding and leading a pack horse en route to El Capitan Mine. Vail asked the pair, why all the shooting?

Hawley told Vail that Indians were raiding again.

Vail nodded, then asked Hawley and Fate to help him unload his pack horse and hide the goods. "We can ride and tie with these two horses into Globe quicker than you two fellows can walk in."

Hawley took Vail up on his offer by riding his horse. But after only a mile Hawley dismounted and told Vail it was his turn to ride. Once Vail remounted, Hawley shot him off his horse. Then Hawley commanded Fate to also shoot Vail two more times. "We are in this thing together and you have got to go as far as I do." Fate then shot Vail twice.

The two robbers then rode off with their loot, leaving Vail for dead.

A mile farther, the two stopped to argue yet again. They stopped here long enough for Andy Hall to catch up with them. At first Hall trained his gun on them. But when he saw that they were familiar white men, he lowered his revolver. "I thought you were Indians," Hall said, surprised. "We had all better get into Globe. There are robbers in these hills."

As Hall talked, he rolled something in his other hand. It was a small caliber bullet that he had pried from his thigh after that barrage during the ambush. Hall's grit in continuing to track robbers on foot for this many miles for Wells Fargo despite a bullet wound in his leg speaks volumes about his tenacity to duty, a firm sense of resolution that likely was instrumental in creating the success of Powell's 1869 expedition.

The two robbers acted as if Hall's arrival was lucky for them. The three men now continued toward Globe. But soon Hawley and Grime became suspicious of Hall's staring at their heavy catinas. At that point, Hawley dropped to the rear. At the top of the hill overlooking Russell's Gulch, Hawley shot Andy Hall in the back.

Hall hit the dirt badly wounded. He drew and tried to aim his own pistol. But Hawley emptied his six-shooter into him. Andy Hall died with one eye closed and with his finger on the trigger, a split second too late to avert the ring of bullets now encircling his heart.

The robbers now abandoned Doc Vail's horses and continued on foot. Then they stopped to split up the gold. Soon they saw two riders below. The two desperados dived into the brush and fled with their loot.

In Globe, Mack Allison, the telegraph operator, noticed Cicero Grime hunched up against the wall of the *Arizona Silver Belt* building. Grime seemed inordinately nervous to Allison as he stood watching the trail entering town.

Porter finally arrived in Globe after having followed a roundabout route. Minutes after hearing his report of the ambush of his mule train, a posse raced back up the trail. At dusk, they found the original ambush site. Behind the big white boulder they saw boot prints scarring the soil. Tiny, size-four boot prints.

The posse also found where Andy Hall had blazed his trail away from the ambush site by dragging one boot heel in the dirt at intervals, and then by breaking off small branches and scattering them on his trail. Farther on, where no bushes grew and no soil lay, the posse found tiny bits of Hall's handkerchief torn and dropped to mark his trail.

Just a few miles beyond these, the posse found Doc Vail. Andy Hall, they now discovered, had also happened upon Vail and, seeing him in such critical condition, had taken off his own coat, rolled it up, and placed under Vail's head as a pillow. The prospector/druggist was still breathing, but unconscious. As the men worked on him, Vail awakened and mumbled to posse member Dan Lacey:

> "Two men from Globe. One was a big dark complected man, the other a small light complected man."

After uttering these words, Vail lapsed into unconsciousness again, then died.

At the head of Russell's Gulch the posse found Andy Hall dead with eight bullets in him. Beside Hall stood Vail's two horses. The posse took Hall's and Vail's bodies to the Wells Fargo Express Company office in Globe.

Come daylight on Monday morning, Pima County Sheriff W. W. Lowther carefully studied the feet of every citizen he saw. When he saw the feet of Fate Grime, a local dancing instructor, he knew he had a suspect. The small man's feet were the tiniest of anyone in town. Indeed, it was well known that Fate's feet were so small that he had trouble finding boots to fit him at all. Fate wore size four. But how, the sheriff wondered, could such a mild-mannered young man have murdered Hall or Vail?

Fate left Globe that afternoon to seek work at the Mac Morris mill in Wheatfields. At the end of his shift, Pete Gabriel, deputy U.S. Marshall and Sheriff of Pinal County, in Florence, having been alerted by Dan Lacey, who did not trust Sheriff Lowther, arrested Fate Grime.

At stake was justice — and a $6,000 reward. Lacey and Gabriel wanted some of the former and all of the latter. Under their questioning, Fate broke down and confessed, implicating Curtis E. Hawley and Fate's own brother, Cicero.

Hawley did not seem a likely suspect either. He ran a small general contracting business supplying timber for mines; he was neither penniless nor desperate. Even so, Lacey and Gabriel, with Norman Slater, rode through the dark that Monday night to Hawley's cabin.

Hawley answered Slater's knock with a gun in his hand. Then, seeing Slater, he explained, "The Mexicans have been bothering me a great deal and I have concluded to stop it."

Marshall Gabriel shoved the muzzle of his Winchester through Hawley's rear window and commanded, "Hands up!"

Hawley submitted to arrest. By Wednesday morning, after some chases by Gila County Sheriff Lowther after Marshall Gabriel and his prisoners back and forth through a saguaro-studded landscape with the issues of custody, jurisdiction, and that $6,000 reward at stake, Hawley and the Grime brothers, both of whom had now confessed, found themselves back in Globe. In jail.

At sundown on Wednesday an angry mob of citizens gathered at the one-room adobe jail. The mob offered the sheriff two options: 1. give up all three prisoners, or, 2. they would overpower the sheriff and take all three prisoners anyway.

The sheriff countered by saying he would take all three to stand before Justice of the Peace George Allen if the mob would allow a hearing. Soon Hawley and the Grime Brothers stood before Justice Allen in an overflowing Stallo's Hall.

All three prisoners confessed. Then they signed their confessions. Justice Allen bound the three over to Superior Court for trial. By the way, the three were asked, where had they hidden the $5,000 in stolen gold?

One share, it turned out, was hidden in Hawley's cabin. Two shares had been sequestered in Fate's, suggesting that Cicero was not at all innocent.

Hawley asked Justice Allen if he could make a will to leave his own personal property, worth $5,000, to be sent to his wife.

Late that night, now early Thursday morning, August 24, the lynch mob took control. They led Hawley and both Grime brothers through the light of a full moon to the big sycamore tree growing in front of the Saint Elmo Saloon. This tree had a stout horizontal branch growing about fifteen feet above the dusty street. The hangmen dropped nooses over the heads of all three. Volunteers then hauled the three murderers off the ground and tied the ropes to the sycamore's trunk.

Hawley's noose had been set too loose when the volunteers yanked him off the ground. The mob could hear him for several minutes, even from a block away, strangling.

Andy Hall, the good-hearted prankster on the 1869 expedition who named Lodore Canyon after a poem he'd heard as an orphaned child in his native Scotland, had been avenged.

Even so, I find myself wishing that his humorous yells still echoed off that wall of sandstone at the confluence of the Green and Yampa and that he had lived to toss stones again across the Colorado in Cataract Canyon.

Walter Powell

Walter Powell continued living after 1869, but with his uncontrolled emotional handicaps, he never functioned in a productive way. Debate continues over the organic cause of Walter's mental illness. Thomas M. Myers, M.D. suspects that Walter was bipolar and continued to degenerate. Just how serious Walter's condition was even *before* the 1869 expedition is revealed by a letter discovered by historian Ardian Gill and written by Lieutenant Xavier Picquet, Walter's fellow P.O.W. at Camp Sorghum. As Picquet notes:

> Capt W.H. Powell was taken down sick, and sent to the Hospital so called because it consisted of a tent. We neither saw nor heard any more of him until thanksgiving day, on that day our mess was assembled in our humble cabin speculating on what was probably still in reserve for us, when what was our astonishment he suddenly appeared amongst us, he stood, His tall form dominating all of us, his head towards the heavens, his arms held aloft in supplication as it were, and out of his lips there poured forth an eloquent but solemn and sad prayer, for an instant we stood confounded, and instead of a general and hearty peal of laughter the tears stood in our eyes, we perceived that our comrade was out of his mind.
>
> We gently took him to the Dead line & called the officer of the day to whom we consigned him, we then learned that our comrade in his delirium had escaped from the Hospital and at the peril of his life rushed across the Dead line to see his comrades. That is the last time I saw him. During the time I knew him, that is about a year of army life Capt W.H. Powell enjoyed good health. Written with my own hand without dictation. Xavier Picquet
> Late 2d Lieut Co K 32d Regt Ill (illegible)
> A.A. Ordn officer 4th Div 17th A.C.

Again, Walter Powell lived another 45 years after the 1869 expedition but never accomplished much of anything. His sisters took care of him in their homes. Eventually, Walter Powell was committed to an insane asylum in Washington, D.C., where he died on March 10, 1915, at age 72.

William Robert Wesley (a.k.a. "Missouri Rhodes") Hawkins

Hawkins and Bradley floated to Fort Mojave. From there they went their separate ways, Bradley toward San Francisco and Hawkins to the north. Hawkins returned to Utah and also worked briefly for Powell again, but never on a river trip. Hawkins also remained loyal to Powell, both during the 1869 expedition and long afterward. Hawkins settled first in Pine Valley, Utah, but later moved to Gila Valley in Arizona.

Hawkins married in 1873 and ultimately settled in Eden, Graham County, Arizona, where he lived for 35 years and farmed and ran livestock. Hawkins raised a family of six sons. Eventually he served as a Justice of the Peace. Hawkins outlived all other expedition members; dying at 71 years old, in September, 1919, in St. Joseph's Hospital in Phoenix — but not before penning his two accounts — to Robert Brewster Stanton and to William Wallace Bass — of the dark side of John Wesley Powell's 1869 first descent of the Green and Colorado rivers and of the positive and worthy characters of his fellow boatmen, Oramel and Seneca Howland and William Dunn.

John Wesley Powell

As mentioned earlier, for Major John Wesley Powell the 1869 Colorado River Exploring Expedition ended at the Rio Virgin because it was here that Lieutenant Joseph Christmas Ives had ended the upriver portion of his exploration in 1858. Powell knew that, due to the rigors of dragging, sailing, and rowing their skiff upstream on short rations, Ives had managed very few cartographical measurements from the mouth of Black Canyon (where now Hoover Dam is situated) up to the Virgin. So Powell apparently asked Sumner to take yet more measurements and readings as he, Bradley, Hall, and Hawkins continued down the Colorado. Meanwhile the Major and his brother would abandon the expedition to travel north to Salt Lake City.

Powell historians have uniformly taken Powell at his word as to what happened here at the Rio Virgin; Powell's implication (from his 1875 report and his book *Canyons*) is that Brigham Young had somehow alerted southern Mormons to be on the watch for Powell and to render him assistance when he arrived at the Virgin. This, apparently, is another Powell fiction.

The reality of what happened at the Virgin has been hidden from the world until this book. The man who met the 1869 expedition with food and many other forms of critical assistance for Major Powell was Bishop James Leithead. Bishop Leithead wrote up his experiences with Powell in a short autobiography that was included in a longer, unpublished collection of Leithead family histories. I owe the discovery of Leithead's illuminating report to historian Don Lago's indefatigable inquisitiveness — and also to his generosity. Don knew that Leithead's little gem of revelation would add even greater insight to what the 1869 expedition might have been like in reality, and Lago decided that it belonged in this book. So, with characteristic magnanimity, Don just handed me this — and other — vital new discoveries and said, "This will be a real coup."

Here is what Bishop James Leithead had to say about his experience with Powell at the Rio Virgin — and beyond.

"When Major Powell made his first trip down the Colorado River he landed at the mouth of the Rio Virgin twenty five miles from St. Thomas. He sent an Indian with a note directed to the postmaster, stating that he had landed and would stay a few days before proceeding farther and to send any letters or papers for him and his men. He also intimated that they were short of everything at that time.

I was postmaster at St. Thomas. The Indian arrived in the night. I wrote a note stating that I would be down the next morning and would bring his mail with me. In the morning I got Brother Gibbons to go with me, taking one hundred pounds of flour, some tea, coffee, sugar, tobacco, and about twenty-five very nice melons. It was after night before reaching his camp, but he was expecting us and met us a short distance from camp bare headed, having lost his hat during the perilous trip down the river. They had a blazing fire burning when we drove up and when we tumbled out the melons they went into them with a will after being for months running the fearful rapids of the river wet day after day, it was a treat unlooked for. After talking until after midnight we made our bed to take some rest. In a short time the Major came and asked us if we were asleep. When we told him no, he said ["]you might as well get up. I want to talk and want to hear the news.["] We got up and after satisfying him he gave us some account of his trip down the river. He had one of his boats smashed all to pieces and its occupants thrown into the raging rapids, but escaped with their lives. Another boat they left at the head of the last rapids: two of his men refused to run the rapids and he left the boat with the hope that after seeing him thru safe would follow in the boat. He also left them a part of the bedding, food, guns, and ammunition and they attempted to cross the country to St. George or some of the settlements in southern Utah, were killed by the Indians.

When I afterwards learned of their fate I wrote Major Powell and acquainted him of the fact. He was very much concerned about them, feared they would perish and so they did in that way.

In the morning before Brother Gibbons and I were ready to start, the Major had concluded to go with us to St. Thomas, him and his brother and let his other men have the boats and everything else left from the ravages of the river and pursue their way to Ft. Mojave. He gave them an order on the commandment [commandant?] there for sixty days rations. And we returned to St. Thomas, arriving there before night, we learned that Brother Henry Nebeker had started that morning with a four horse and wagon for Payson. I furnished the Major a hat, his brother a pair of shoes and some other articles which I do not remember now. We prepared food to last them to St. George, got some young men to overtake Nebeker during the night and he would give them passage to Payson. All of this I furnished myself as well as what I took to the river; and in the Major's book he gave all credit to Brigham Young, so I have been told. He did not even send me a copy of his book."

Ironically — but consistent with Powell's modus operandi — Major Powell not only never thanked or reimbursed Leithead, Powell mentioned him only cursorily in his 1875 report and in *Canyons*. Even then, he spelled Leithead's name wrong.

Regardless of who was left in Powell's wake unthanked, unreimbursed, or unpaid, his 1869 expedition down the canyons of the Green and Colorado rivers worked wonders for his own career. The drama of the expedition — wrecks, deaths, frightful dangers that no man had ever seen before, let alone surmounted — all positioned Powell on an exploration pedestal (one which he never invited any of his crew to share). Better yet, from a congressman's perspective, Powell had accomplished the seemingly impossible with no federal funds beyond a few paltry rations from a western Army fort. This was a man who got things done. Big things, and with little expense. On top of this, it was clear that Major Powell was the genuine article, an ambitious and capable man who saw the uncharted West as a national as well as personal quest.

Nor did it hurt that Major Powell was consumed by geological curiosity, by fascination for the customs and beliefs of the last unspoiled Indians in America, and that he had, at every challenge, seemed to have shown physical courage that proved more than equal to the task.

On July 12, 1870, Congress voted an appropriation for Powell of $12,000, one he had requested to "prosecute to completion the geographical and topographical exploration of the Colorado River and its tributaries, and to establish, by astronomical observations, four of the most important points, viz: the junction of the Grand and Green rivers, the mouth of the San Juan, the mouth of the Little Colorado, and the mouth of the Virgin River." In March of 1871, Congress renewed Powell's $12,000 grant for year number two "for completing the survey of the Colorado of the West and its tributaries."

Powell would launch yet another Green-Colorado trip with re-designed boats a foot longer and with a crew drastically different in character from that of 1869. For his 1871-72 expedition Powell chose relatives, friends, and acquaintances from the civilized regions east of the Hundredth Meridian. He pointedly ignored his tried and true boatmen of 1869, those independently-minded and self-sufficient Westerners with combat experience whose labor, acumen, and skill originally carried Powell to fame. One guesses that the tragic denouement of that expedition prompted Powell to seek men more malleable and susceptible to his command. Powell did ask Jack Sumner to return to row a new *Emma Dean*, but Sumner sent word back that the heavy snow pack would not allow him to make it. (Of course sending word in those days meant that someone *did* make it and that Sumner had tacitly decided that working for Powell again was against Sumner's best interests and/or perhaps stood in conflict with his self-respect.)

In 1871-72, most of Powell's actual field work would progress under the command of his brother-in-law, Almon H. Thompson, not Powell himself.

And, tellingly, of Powell's new, 1871-72, ten-man crew, equipped with life jackets, half of the men quit — or "deserted" — the 1871-72 expedition before ever departing from Lee's Ferry, a worse record than the four men who quit during the 1869 expedition. Then, at River Mile 144, Powell himself got cold feet after a dangerous swim due to a capsize of the *Emma Dean (II)*; when he announced that the expedition would end here, halfway through Grand Canyon (133 miles short of the Grand Wash Cliffs). His remaining crew, their journals reveal, all quit with him with profound feelings of relief and, in some cases, enthusiasm. And not with disappointment – as Bradley, Hall, Hawkins, and Sumner, even without life jackets, would have felt.

Did the Major actually have an attack of cold feet (not until 1890 would a second expedition – Robert Brewster Stanton's – again run as far as Separation Rapid and beyond)? The commonly stated reason for Powell's decision is Jacob Hamblin's having sent a warning to Powell that the Shivwits were upset over several of their band having been killed near Mount Turnbull. But Dellenbaugh, Powell's boatman there at the confluence with Kanab Creek on September 7, 1872, would later write: "but Powell, instead of directing this course [of continuing downstream], announced that he had decided to end the river work at this point on account of the extreme high water, which would render impassable the rapid where the Howlands and Dunn had left."

In 1872, Powell resigned his position as curator of Illinois Normal University, leaving much of the museum and its collected specimens in disarray. Powell's exodus hinged on Congress having voted him another $20,000 for his survey. The Major moved to Washington, D.C. to buy the house in which he would live for nearly thirty years. Again, none of his funds seemed to have gone to pay even a fraction of his alleged debts to Hawkins or Sumner.

In 1874, Representative Garfield told Powell to write a report on his Colorado discoveries or else forget further federal funding. Powell's 1875 report, *Exploration of the Colorado River of the West and Its Tributaries, Explored in 1869, 1870, 1871, and 1872*, soon appeared. It worked funding wonders, despite the many liberties with fact that Powell took that alienated his crew of 1869 and, even more, that of 1871-72. Indeed, by 1878, Congress had awarded Powell yearly appropriations totalling $209,000.

Meanwhile, Powell vastly increased his survey of geology and geography to encompass ethnology. He fostered an expanded effort to photograph the tribes of the Colorado Plateau. Often, however, he dressed up his subjects in Plains Indian garb purchased from the buffalo tribes on the prairie near the railroad. Many of his bogus ethnological photos were taken with commercial sales in mind. And these made enough "soft" money to pay off Powell's mortgage in Washington, D.C., though the photos of the Indians apparently did not earn enough money, notes Powell biographer Donald Worster, to pay his Indian "models" any cash to help avert their imminent starvation. These photos also nudged Powell into an entirely new scientific arena, one that he expanded not only into a second career, but into an institution in itself. In the 1870s Powell shifted his work to the auspices of the Smithsonian Institution; in 1879 he "created" a new bureau within it, the Bureau of Ethnology. Powell became its first director, a position he held — despite all other jobs he would hold and despite his own diminishing interest in American Indians — until shortly before his death in 1902.

In the 1870s, Major Powell had felt, rightly it proved, that he could travel with a mere one or two men into Indian Country and safely conduct his ethnological inquiries and photo sessions. Powell's stance on the Indians was emphatically anti-missionary, but it was very pro-reservation. One of his arguments for confining tribes on reservations was that the Indians must be separated from resources such as timber, or else they would destroy forests by burning them. "Only the white hunters of the region," Powell wrote, "properly understand why these fires are set, it usually being attributed to a wanton desire on the part of the Indians to destroy that which is of value to the white man. The fires can, then, be very greatly curtailed by the removal of the Indians."

Powell's preoccupation with the Plateau's several thousand Indians, including the redoubtable Hopis (among whom Powell allegedly claimed to have spent two months, when, in fact, he had spent only two weeks), included his avid promoting of their own protection and survival — at least until they could be uplifted into a farming life and then civilized.

Back on the geological front, Powell had warned Congress in the 1870s that 40 percent of the USA "has a climate so arid that agriculture cannot be pursued without irrigation." He also informed them of the extremely unwelcome news that only 1 to 3 percent of those vast lands in the arid West lay within the realm of possible "redeeming" via irrigation. A decade later, in 1888, he revised this drastically upward to 15 percent. Yet even this "fantasy" re-estimate would win limited friends in political circles. Later, in 1893, a failing Powell would sink back into the real world and warn the First Irrigation Congress, in Salt Lake City, that a mere four percent of the West was irrigable due to limited water. In this last figure, as with his first, he was fairly accurate.

Significantly, Powell's experience among the Mormon settlers of Utah prompted him to propose an entirely new and revolutionary set of standards to revise the Homestead Act. Instead of the standard 160-acre, quarter- (of a square mile) section granted to homesteaders in the green East, Powell recommended that Western homesteads for pasturage be sized *at least* 16 times bigger, at four square miles (2,560 acres). Irrigation homesteads, he added, on the other hand, might be adequately sized as small as a mere 20 acres, provided that their access to a stream be firmly guaranteed. In this same vein, Powell pointed out, irrigation homesteads should not be surveyed in the right-angled, Euclidean manner of the East, but instead as nature dictates, clustered along large, perennial water courses in irregular shapes best suited to the limits of the topography, as determined by trained engineers, and according to the needs of the farmers and their community. Developing such water resources, he added, should be limited to the cooperative labor, industry, and capital of the farmers themselves who homesteaded along these large streams. These homesteaders, he added further, should also "have the right to make their own regulations for the division of the lands, the use of the water for irrigation and for watering the stock, and for the pasturage of the lands in common or in severalty."

While Powell's new ideas did fit the harsh realities of the arid West far better than the existing Homestead Act's simple, wet climate guidelines did, especially in Powell's additional stipulation that the water rights of a land parcel should not be sellable separately from the land itself, Powell's ideas were not in concert with the desires of politicians of that era or of its big businessmen (these very wealthy businessmen often were those same politicians). Hence when Powell's recommendations were presented as a revision bill to congress, the revisions died before ever getting out of committee.

Even so, in 1878, after congress had spent $23 million on various independent land surveys of the West, including Powell's, the National Academy of Sciences recommended combining all of the surveys under a new Coast and Geodetic Office as the U.S. Geological Survey (the USGS). In 1881, Powell, upon the retirement of geologist Clarence King after only one year at the helm, became the second director of the USGS.

During the late 1880s, Powell again went to war. Not a military one this time, but one of politics and economics. His enemy was epitomized by William "Big Bill" Stewart of Nevada, architect of the still extant 1872 Mining Law, among other things. One of those other things was Stewart's avid promotion of federal irrigation of arid Western lands.

Yet even by 1890, Powell's USGS was still not yet ready with its maps of the arid lands beyond the 100th Meridian. What was irrigable and what was not of these vast public lands remained undesignated. Hence, until Powell finished his work, the Homestead Act would be somewhat in limbo in the West. There would be no irrigation, settlers, development, economic growth, rising tax base, and their attendant agricultural business opportunities for entrepreneurs. All would remain on hold until Powell's USGS has finished its survey of where the water was, where the good soil was, and what might be the best combinations of both for development. Besides, Powell added, no matter where the survey might reveal such propitious combinations to be located, the development of each region of prosperity should be accomplished via local self-government in each hydrologic basin, each one "a commonwealth within itself."

While well intended and well informed, Powell's ideals were a recipe for stalling into immobility a nation which had been expanding aggressively west for a century. Indeed, Powell rather suicidally warned: "I say to the Government: Hands off! Furnish the people with institutions of justice, and let them to the work (of dam-building, water management, and of forest and rangeland management) themselves."

With Powell saying "hands off!" until he finished the survey, but then not finishing the survey, the irrigation-hungry Senator Stewart became incensed. In 1890, Stewart launched his campaign to remove Powell from the USGS. The Major fought back. But for the first time in his life, it seems, he had run up against a man with far greater will, resources, and determination than himself.

Powell, Stewart said, "was drunk with power and deaf to reason....his greed for office and power unsurpassed." Stewart next wrote, "I have never met so unscrupulous and extraordinary a man, ambitious to the last degree, and the most artful, insinuating, and persevering lobbyist known in the annals of this country."

Stewart and several other Western senators were so intent on deposing Powell that they were willing to risk losing Western irrigation as a whole to do so. They combined their votes with those of Eastern senators who did not want to spend federal money at all on any kind of Western irrigation, period. That summer the Senate killed Powell's irrigation survey.

The House complied with the Senate. Next, as the 1890s unfolded, congress began slashing at the USGS budget as well.

Perhaps surprisingly, but also tellingly, as historian Donald Worster notes, no fellow scientist came firmly to Powell's defense in this crisis. This was despite John Wesley Powell's recent presidency of the American Association for the Advancement of Science (the AAAS). Although it may seem insensitive to mention this possibility, this lack of loyalty among fellow scientists for Powell may be indicative of his loyalty for his associates during his career. Perhaps the small-mindedness which Powell exhibited at the Virgin River in not leading a search party for the Howland brothers and William Dunn north of Separation Canyon — which well might have saved their lives — or in his decision to not even attempt to identify these men's bodies once they had been reported to him as having been murdered, had finally come home to roost.

In 1894, Powell resigned as director of the USGS. His successor, Charles Walcott, battled successfully to re-establish and re-fund the USGS. Meanwhile, William John McGee took over the actual work of the renamed Bureau of American Ethnology, but with poor success. As a sign of how weak "science" had become at the Bureau, Powell accepted a bet from McGee as to which of them had the bigger brain. Ironically, this bet was to be settled posthumously.

Possibly in an attempt to re-establish his fame or popularity — or simply to write his swan's song — Powell next decided to re-publish his 1875 report as the expanded and lavishly illustrated 1895 book *Canyons of the Colorado*. As mentioned earlier, the mere 1,000 copies printed failed to sell. Even so, the quarter century since the expedition went its separate ways below the Grand Wash Cliffs may have given Powell sufficient pause to realize how lucky he had been in his choice of crews in 1869. In his Preface to *Canyons* Powell wrote:

> "Many years have passed since the exploration, and those who were the boys with me in the enterprise are — ah, most of them are dead, and the living are gray with age. Their bronzed, hardy, brave faces come before me as they appeared in the vigor of life; their lithe but powerful forms seem to move around me; and the memory of the men and

their heroic deeds, the men and their generous acts, overwhelm me with a joy that seems almost a grief, for it starts a fountain of tears. I was a maimed man; my right arm was gone; and these brave men, these good men, never forgot it. In every danger my safety was their first care, and in every waking hour some kind of service was rendered me, and they transfigured my misfortune into a boon.

To you — J. C. Sumner, William H. Dunn, W. H. Powell, G. Y. Bradley, O. G. Howland, Seneca Howland, Frank Goodman, W. R. Hawkins, and Andrew Hall — my noble and generous companions, dead and alive, I dedicate this book."

One can conjecture many motivations for such a grateful and gracious dedication to the men who either died or were rendered nearly bankrupt to build for Powell his fame. One of these motivations might be simply that the Major was truly grateful for men whose superlative performances in the face of hardship, starvation, and terrifying dangers outshone the exploits of all those who would follow their path for generations to come. But, on perusing the revised text itself of *Canyons of the Colorado*, one comes away haunted by the question: why, *still*, did Powell fail to state in at least a few simple words that the murders of William H. Dunn, Oramel G. Howland, and young Seneca B. Howland were heartfelt tragedies whose echoes still seared his heart?

Instead, in 400 pages, he tells us in just a few dozen words only that the Shivwits admitted that they killed the three (as Hamblin interprets to Powell) in a case of error, the Indians having been egged on by a "bad" man from south of the Colorado (pp. 322-323 of *Canyons*) who had lied to them. Then Powell explains to his readers what this tragedy means to him with only the following: "That night I slept in peace, although the murderers of my men, and their friends, the Uinkarets, were sleeping not 500 yards away."

That's it. Really. In fact, in Powell's amazingly inconsequential farewell to the Howlands and Dunn, he never even mentions either "Howland" or "Dunn." The men remain nameless. Nor does Powell add anything more later to explain their fates or what they meant to him. Space in his book was not an issue. Just before mentioning this tragic and controversial incident he spent seven pages of *Canyons* recounting an Indian myth of very little point. This micro-mention of nameless murder was Powell's entire story of three men's violent deaths, their obituary, and their eulogy. Very telling, Powell expressed no grief, no heartfelt regrets, and no thanks for their sacrifice. He instead gives us a mere fraction of an anonymous page ending pathetically with "That night I slept in peace."

Many readers of Powell's *Canyons* have concluded that Powell's true message lay in what was missing. By Powell's omission of regret, they say, he tells us — shouts at us — that he regretted nothing. Instead he is telling us that William Dunn and Oramel and Seneca Howland were deserters. Deserters who deserved their fate.

Here the words of Powell's brother-in-law and long time associate A. H. Thomspon echo more loudly, "He wasn't all Saint," Thompson insisted. "He could lie on occasion — be generous one minute and contemptible the next."

Powell's treatment of the Howland brothers and William Dunn — in life and in *Canyons* — was, at the very least, a vindication of Thompson's assertion; in this Powell was indeed contemptible.

Meanwhile, on the home front during Major Powell's political and professional decline, his wife and second cousin, Emma Dean, allegedly became something of an unpleasant marital partner. The two had one child only, Mary, who would neither marry nor develop a career, and would die childless.

So, after all, what *was* John Wesley Powell's true legacy? First, he did lead, however fatally, the first descent of the Green and Colorado rivers. But, as can be seen in this book, Powell's success in reaching the Grand Wash Cliffs relied heavily on being blessed with good luck and with the high capabilities and mostly even temperaments of his surviving crew. And despite Sumner's and Hawkins' plans to prospect and trap the river from Wyoming southward, without Powell this expedition might not have occurred for several more years or might not have gone as far as it did — for Hall and Sumner, all the way to the Sea of Cortez. A long hidden treasure, recently discovered by historian Don Lago, however, provides perhaps the most pertinent insight on who should receive major credit for the success of the 1869 expedition. Lewis Keplinger wrote to a friend in 1912: "The success of that expedition was largely due to Mr. Sumner. Major Powell himself has told me since that but for Sumner he never would have got through the canyon alive."

Beyond the exploration of the Green and Colorado, the accomplishment that was indisputably the launch pad that would catapult Powell to fame, to Washington, D.C., and to his claims of being a "scientist," however, what did Major John Wesley Powell accomplish?

Despite his character faults, Powell *was* visionary. His realistic appraisal of the limits of potential water development in the West and his warnings to congress of the tragic and destructive consequences of exceeding these limits via over-optimistic and excessive federal, instead of local, water projects would prove prophetic. This should not be misread, however, to say that Powell was the original Colorado River conservationist. He was not. As historian Donald Worster notes, Powell was in no way a conservationist in the modern, or even the old, sense: "I cannot find in Powell anywhere," notes Worster, "not even in his commonwealth idea, any room for this awareness....[that the West] holds treasures of natural beauty and biological diversity that should be preserved against all threats of development or use." In short, John Wesley Powell was neither John Muir nor Henry David Thoreau nor Aldo Leopold. Instead Powell stood firmly in the "man over nature" camp — but only if that ascendancy was done right (i.e., locally, Powell's way).

Hence Powell's legacy remains complicated. This is because, despite Powell's ideas about appropriate land use, his attempts to revise the Homestead Act to make it better fit the arid realities of the West failed. On the other hand, despite Powell's proposed land revisions and water appraisals having failed to change anything or to convince the right people, Powell was personally responsible for originating the Bureau of Ethnology in the Smithsonian and for fostering an effort to record the customs and languages of many North American tribes before they were lost. This was not only vital to posterity but important as time passed to the descendants of these Indians themselves, who were being acculturated into white society and belief systems. It is too bad, one realizes now, that Powell was not more interested in the spiritual beliefs and mythic cosmology of these Indians whom he proposed to study. Even so, Powell was ahead of his time in at least defending their right to continue living. Yet even this held a price tag. Powell, remember, advocated concentrating these Western tribes on restricted reservations distant from forests and, in some cases, also distant from these bands' traditional lands. In hindsight, perhaps he was advocating the wisest course; without protecting these Native Americans on reservations, however desolate, many more of them might have died to war, disease, alcohol, and starvation. So part of Powell's legacy must lie in his emphasis that Indian customs deserve to be recorded and Indians themselves deserve to survive — even if many of these customs survived only in the Smithsonian's valuable two-volume *Handbook of North American Indians*.

J.W. Powell also "fathered" the Bureau of Reclamation, a highly notable achievement despite the ultimately rampant ecologically devastating damage caused by the big dams that the Bureau would build. Powell also tried in other ways to inject his brand of "science" into the exploration and exploitation of the West. But his rather glaring lack of success in actually effecting progressive change away from the steamroller "colonization" of the Southwest makes Powell's legacy one more of tragedy than of triumph. In short, Powell's legacy intermixes tragic high adventure in a romantic landscape unlike any other on Earth, failure in land policy revisions, compromise in his ethnological studies, personal character flaws leaving human casualties in his career wake, and missed potential of grand proportions. No wonder biographers flock to him.

In January of 1902, Major Powell suffered a stroke. On 23 September of that year he died, at age 68, of a cerebral hemorrhage.

As ordered, the Major's brain was surgically excised to then be measured for its size (cranial volume). About a decade later W. J. McGee's brain was removed as well. Who "won" the bet over owning the bigger brain?

Powell did.

John ("Jack") Colton Sumner

As is evident from the men's letters and journals, John Colton Sumner was Powell's "head boatman," whether hired as such or not. Sumner's competence was the catapult that would send the Major flying into focus for historians of the future. Oddly, few, if any, historians have seen this with clarity. Sumner, again, was a man of honor, ideals, and a sense of fairness that seemed a separate symbiotic organism living within him. Sumner's idealism occasionally took control of him, transforming him to a hot-tempered, judgmental man of action who was willing to burn bridges — if not cities — in the cause of justice. Sumner, remember, was not just a combat veteran but a sharpshooting sniper who held few illusions about the sanctity of human life — especially if that human had transgressed according to Sumner's book of rules. Even more, Sumner was a man for whom self-responsibility, competency, and paying his own way constituted a religion. Men of Sumner's exacting convictions have been few in any age. And throughout history men of lesser conviction who surrounded such men have often found themselves at a loss to explain what they were seeing.

We have no one to better describe what happened to Sumner in the four decades after 1869 than Sumner himself. Luckily, he did this in a newly discovered 1906 letter to Lewis W. Keplinger. Keplinger was a fellow Civil War veteran (and college student) with whom Sumner and Powell had spent much of the summer of 1868 in the Rocky Mountains. Yet again, I owe thanks for this letter to historian Don Lago, who dug it out of obscurity and generously offered it to me as a scoop. Here is what Sumner had to say:

Paradox, Colorado September 14, 1906
Mr. L. W. Keplinger
Kansas City, Kansas

"Dear Old Friend, It seems that after 38 years you Remember your old Friend "Jack." Well I am greatly Pleased to get a letter from you and will try to answer it. things have not went as well with me as they have with you. I will try to give you an Idea of the ups and downs since you parted with us on oak Creek. I Remember the Long's

Peak Episode very well. After you left us we proceeded on to White River where we Built cabins and Spent the winter hunting and Exploring the Country. in March we left that camp and proceeded to old Fort Bridger where we sold our stock and came back to Green River Wyoming where we took Boats for the great unknown and we had a Hell of a time of it getting through.

After you left I had to take charge of the Sextant so it kept me Pretty Busy for 20 hours out of the 24. Must catch a Star as you can for about 800 miles. lost a boat and lots of Supplies in Green River. at the Mouth of uinta river Powell neglected to get Supplies and we were nearly Starved in consequence. we were 111 days from Green River Wyoming to the Mouth of the Virgin River [actually 99 days] where the Powells left us and went to Salt Lake and I have seen neither of them Since.

I took the two Boats left and with Bradley, Hawkins and Hall proceeded on down the Colorado River. Bradley and Hawkins stopped at EhrenBurg Arizona. Hall and I went on down to the head of the Gulf of California then came back up the River about Old Fort Yuma and Being Level Broke we commenced Killing a few Deer to Sell to the Mexicans and what few whites were there. one day while hunting the Apaches Jumped me and I had to kill two of them. as they appeared to be Government pets I had to walk from the Colorado River to owen's valley--500 miles--California. as you probably know I am a little too Hot-headed to Submit to an arrest under such trivial pretexts.

When I struck Owen's valley I found a job and went to work cutting cord wood for a Mining Company. After working two months I wanted my money so I could Start back to the Rocky mts. the Boss Refused to give me my money or a horse he owned. Which of course caused a row. there was nothing left for me to do but adopt drastic measures. So I took Horse saddle and Bridle away from him and his Pet henchman who happen[ed] to be the Sheriff at the time. I Rode the Horse alone across that Sink of Hell, Death Valley; across Nevada Desert; Utah and Back to Green River Wyoming. lived on my Gun the entire distance.

After that went onto the plains and Hunted Buffalo, Wolves, and occasionally a Damned Sioux to vary the monotony of my life. for the last 25 years I have lived west of the range Engaged most of my time in Mining with various ups and downs. Mostly downs. I have a wife and three grown Sons all Doing for themselves, two of them Publishing Newspapers and one a farmer. I am the same old wanderer that I always was and will Probably wind up under a cedar tree fit Subject for Wolf Bait. this is a great Copper Country and I have some pretty fair prospects and if I have good luck with them I may be able to make you a visit a [at] K.C. [Kansas City] when we can smoke a pipe and perhaps Boost a bottle.

You ask about the Colorado River party. here is the list as far as I know and Believe Correct. ten started from Green River. J. W. Powell. Walter Powell. O. G. Howland. Seneca Howland. George Bradley. Frank Goodman. and Jack Sumner. Andrew Hall. Bill Dunn. Goodman quit us at uinta river. the two howlands and Dunn were killed. Powell states by Indians & I Say Killed by the Mormons, Part of the Same old "Mountains Meadows" massacre gang.

Of course you know J. W. Powell is Dead. Walter Powell is in the Bug House. Bradley Killed accidentally at San Diego California. Hall Killed by Road agents in Arizona. all that are left are Wm. R. Hawkins and myself. Hawkins joined the Mormons and has two or more women and had when I saw down on the Gila River three years ago a good sized Kindergarten of his own which he has doubtless increased since.

I presume you remember A. C. Lankin, the fellow that stole the mule and grub on your first trip to Bear River. Well he Scrimped and Saved until he had accumulated $30,000 then went into his room in Rawlins Wyoming, whrote [sic] on a card "life is not worth living" and Sent a Bullet through his head.

So J. W. Powell Says I Saved his Bacon a time or two did he? Well from Reading his Report one would think there was no one in the Party but Capt Powell and himself. he Evidently didn't tell you of the row in Cataract Canyon when I got so damned mad at his abuse of howland and Dunn that I had to "Speak out in meeting," which culminated in my taking full command of the Expedition and Keep it to the end. Poor Walter was crazy when he was in the Park [Middle Park, Rocky Mountains] and got worse. Peticoat [sic] dementia [syphilis?] or a plain case of rats in the Garret I don't Know which.

Well I Guess I have written enough to tire you, so I will close. hoping to hear from you again soon. If you know of anyone wanting Copper prospects tell them to drop me a line. If you want Specimens of the copper, will send them.
Yours most truly   Jack Sumner
Paradox Montrose Co. Colorado

In September of 1869 Sumner continued surveying for Powell below the Virgin River to "link up" with the scientific work that Joseph Christmas Ives had conducted up to 1858 upriver from the Gulf of California in his fifty-foot, steel stern-wheeler, the *Explorer*. Sumner continued downriver, far beyond the call of duty — instead listening now to the Siren of curiosity — into Mexico and then 90 miles to the gulf with Andy Hall. The pair felt unimpressed with the prospects in this desolate location atop the Sea of Cortez. After a few hours of sight-seeing the two rigged a wagon tarp as a sail and sailed on the upstream winds back to Fort Yuma, California. There the last pair of boatmen on this historic expedition separated, Hall traveling into Prescott, Arizona, then to Florence, Sumner making that truly epic trek west, then east, then much farther northeast to the Rockies.

Major Powell requested that Sumner work again for him on the 1871-72 expedition which ultimately aborted near River Mile 144, Kanab Canyon in Grand Canyon. Sumner vacillated in agreeing to accompany Powell. Again, he eventually sent word to Powell that he could not make the trip.

Only four years after the first descent, on June 30, 1873, Sumner married Alcinda Jane [Jennie] Norris in Muscatine, Iowa. The couple had three sons. Sumner moved back to Colorado, where he had met Major Powell. Sumner first lived at Julesburg, then in Denver, where his sister lived. Restless, he next moved to Rawlins, Wyoming, then to Grand Junction. He supervised the Hawarden Placer Mines on the Dolores River. Next he helped build Mesa County's Big Ditch. Sumner was a truly restless man who tried his hand at many opportunities, frequently seeking gold along rivers of the Colorado system. Indeed, as mentioned in the introduction, Robert Brewster Stanton met Sumner in Glen Canyon while Sumner was placer mining in late 1889. These placer mining operations would eventually vastly disappoint Sumner, Stanton, and financier Julius F. Stone as well.

Sumner's second son, Edward, settled in Vernal, Utah, and set up a livery business. After the turn of the century Sumner often lived in Vernal. Like Bradley, Sumner was originally from a Massachusetts family. He was also a grandson of Governor Robert Lucas of Ohio. Sumner spent his last years plagued by illnesses, poverty, and depression. The latter proved to severe, notes historian Don Lago, that on May 24, 1902, near Green River, Utah Sumner castrated himself with a knife. In 1903, he began his lengthy correspondences with Stanton. In 1907, Sumner completed his account of the 1869 first descent.

It is fortunate for posterity that he decided to do so; the sands in Sumner's hourglass had ebbed to a few specks of dust. He died on July 5, 1907, at age 67, in Vernal or Fort Duchesne, Utah. His sons and wife buried him in the family plot in Denver next to his mother. Sumner's widow survived him by 27 years. But unlike Bradley's sister — or even Powell's wife, Emma — Jennie Sumner wanted posterity to recognize her husband's heroic qualities in 1869.

The *Rocky Mountain News* published John Colton Sumner's obituary. But unlike Bradley's obituary, which never happened at all (until now), and even Major Powell's weak one, the lengthy and heroic (and occasionally inaccurate) obituary of Sumner in the *News* stated:

> " — Without dwelling at length on the incidents of this thrilling and perilous journey — and there were many — it may be truthfully asserted that it was due almost wholly to Sumner's cool nerve, calm judgement and quick and ready resourcefulness in all circumstances and in the face of every trying situation that the party completed the journey. He was always in the lead boat, and approached each of the numerous falls and rapids apparently unconcerned whether the descent was five feet or 500 feet, but ready for any emergency.
>
> Twice when the boats were wrecked he saved Major Powell's life by pulling him from the seething flood by the hair. When everything seemed lost, Sumner was ready with some new expedient for assuring the completion and success of the expedition. He was its real leader, and to him alone is due the fact that the entire party did not go down in the awful currents of the mighty cañon.

POWELL'S SCURVY TRICK

The trip complete, Powell left the six men who had accompanied him at Fort Yuma, on the lower river, and returned East to become famous as an explorer. To Sumner he gave sufficient money to return home, but left the other five penniless. Sumner promptly divided the money [from Powell at the Rio Virgin] with his companions, and from that day had no use for the man whose life he had twice saved, and who owed so much to him for the services he had rendered.

Sumner finally started Westward on foot with nothing

but his gun as a means of subsistence, and for weeks lived on nothing but fish and game. He was frequently fired at by Indians, but he bore the charm of life, and his assailants seldom lived to attack another white man.

Sumner crossed Death Valley on foot, and kept himself supplied with water by following rabbit tracks in the early morning. Reaching a telegraph office at last, he wired W. N. Byers and was supplied with funds, which once more brought him home to his friends.

....Death was the only foe to which he ever surrendered.

George Young Bradley

Bradley continued downriver from the Virgin in company with William Hawkins, Andy Hall, and Jack Sumner. Major Powell knew from Lieutenant Joseph C. Ives' 1861 *Report* that Ives' upriver exploration had ended at the Virgin River confluence in 1858. He also guessed, however, that Ives' had been in a hurry in the stretch of the Colorado between the Virgin and the Mojave valley. So Powell apparently asked Sumner, if not Bradley, Hall, and Hawkins, to continue his observations and journal entries — even as Major Powell and Walter headed north to Salt Lake City, where Powell would regale the locals with his lectures describing his conquest of the Colorado.

The Colorado downstream of the Grand Wash Cliffs and the Virgin does contain rapids, but nothing remotely like the big water and technical rapids of Grand Canyon, Cataract Canyon, or Lodore. Hence the downstream float for the final four expeditionaries was a bit of a holiday, though very likely one plagued by a growing disillusionment over the significance of their 1,000-mile accomplishment and a growing sense of anticlimax because no one they met seemed to fully understand the nature of their immense triumph. The four had become a very elite fraternity of the world's first professional Grand Canyon river guides, yet, ironically, none of them ever wanted to see the place again. My guess is these next few days of drifting set each man to seriously contemplating his future and what he now needed to do to have one.

Bradley and Hawkins stopped at Fort Yuma and went separate ways, Hawkins north, Bradley northwest to San Francisco by stage coach. Ten months later, on July 29, 1870, the California Census listed a George Y. Bradley from New England living alone, without owning real estate, in the El Monte township of Los Angeles County where he was working as a laborer. Because the land around El Monte was limited for agriculture, many workers and farmers began drifting south.

Possibly near San Diego, California, Bradley became something of a rancher. Many years later (in the 1940s), Bradley's great nephew E. L. Morss noted that his mother could not recall whether Bradley's property was simply a small ranch or instead an orchard. Nor could she recall where in California this property was. My own searches via the resources of the San Diego Historical Society turned up no record whatsoever of a George Y. Bradley. The city and county directories from 1870-1921 failed to list him, as did biographical files, homestead records, deed books, 1880 census records, and the *San Diego Union*. In short, I, as did Darrah fifty-odd years before me, found nothing to indicate that George Y. Bradley ever lived in San Diego County. The records do show a George Bradley who filed there in 1882 and 1884 for 160 acres. This sounds promising but this may be the same George Bradley who already resided in Ballena on April 17, 1869, five weeks *before* the 1869 expedition shoved their boats onto the Green River. Hence, George Y. Bradley's whereabouts in the Golden State after 1875 remain a mystery.

At any rate, sabotaging several years of Bradley's modest success as a rancher, was some sort of accident, the nature of which is still a mystery. Whatever this accident, Bradley had been seriously injured enough to suffer increasing paralysis.

In the summer of 1885, he wrote to his nephew, George E. Morss, who lived in Haverhill, asking him to come to California to help Bradley home to Newbury, Massachusetts. His nephew did so. Bradley sold his land interests and, with Morss, returned to New England. With him Bradley carried his secret journal of the 1869 expedition. Sadly, Bradley did not have long to live. But at least he was back with his family, possibly in West Newbury, with his sister, Lucy A. Bradley (who had married a Watson).

On November 13, 1885, a Friday, Bradley died of medical complications from his injury at an age of approximately 50 years old. His family buried him in the family plot in the Bridge Street Cemetery in West Newbury. Apparently Bradley's sisters, Elizabeth (Mrs. Jacob C.) Morss and Lucy A. Watson, did not understand the significance of Bradley's epic journey of exploration down the canyons of the Green and the Colorado 16 years earlier, a journey of daring, courage, and intelligence that would kill many who attempted to follow. Neither sister notified the local papers with the news or the seeds of a fitting obituary. When Bradley died, he did so silently.

I, for one, am thankful that this silence was broken by Bradley's nephew, Charles H. Morss, who possessed the presence of mind thirty years later to offer Bradley's journal to the Library of Congress stipulating no restrictions as to its publication. His son, E. L. Morss, also granted permission for its publication in the 1947 *Utah Historical Quarterly*, noting that no restrictions existed and no permission was necessary. In my opinion, Bradley's journal, newly transcribed for this book, is a priceless document due to the quality of light it sheds on America's quintessential river exploration. Maybe its appearance here will finally break the silence of his death and gain for Bradley that long delayed obituary:

George Y. Bradley
Soldier, Patriot, Geologist, Explorer, & Boatman
A Key Member of the First Explorers to Traverse The Great Unknown
of the Canyons of the Green and Colorado Rivers
of the American Southwest in 1869
And Chief Chronicler of the Expedition.

"As we float along on a muddy stream walled in by huge sandstone bluffs that echo back the slightest sound, hardly a bird save the ill-omened raven or an occasional eagle screaming over us, one feels a sense of loneliness as he looks on the little party, only three boats and nine men, hundreds of miles from civilization bound on an errand the issue of which everybody declares must be disastrous. Yet if he could enter our camp at night or our boats by day he could read the cool deliberate determination to persevere that possesses every man of the party and would at once predict that the issue of all would be success."

George Y. Bradley was not merely a witness to this success, he was a primary reason for it.

Thus passed the crew members of the North America's most infamous exploring expedition into unknown terrain, one that continues to generate awe, controversy, and emulators to the tune of nearly 25,000 people per year through Grand Canyon via the Colorado River. And, yes, there are still a handful of us who would give almost anything to have accompanied that original 1869 trip.

I guess what we need to pull this off is a reliable time machine....

EPILOGUE

A BOATMAN'S FANTASY

Imagine that our river trip is floating on the upper reach of Lake Mead, the Colorado River impounded behind Hoover Dam, at River Mile 239 plus a bit. We are nearing the foot of Lower Granite Gorge. The Precambrian rock juts above us on both sides in vertical but undulating foliations caused by an extreme metamorphosis during the era when the mini-continent containing the future states of California, Nevada, Oregon, Washington, plus part of British Columbia and Alaska slammed into the main continent of North America to create what geologist Paul Hoffman called the "United Plates of America." This was a whopping 1.78 billion years ago. A leap in time of this magnitude would melt the singularity generator in our time machine into slag. Besides, we don't really want to jump that far into the past. At least I don't.

The time and place where I would aim our time machine — and our entire river trip — would be August 27, 1869, evening, Western Grand Canyon, River Mile 239.6, Separation Rapid.

Imagine that our field generator induces a cosmic singularity distorting the relationship of cause and effect. In a blinding flash and a disconcerting yank through an instantaneous wormhole we find ourselves and our five boats rowing to shore at Mile 239.6. But it is now a strangely altered Mile 239.6. There's a rapid here now. A big one.

Our laser perfect composite oar blades whip across the smooth silt-laden water above the rapid to propel our bright yellow inflatable boats rigged with heavy aluminum frames, decking, and boxes. In these boxes and in the drop bags beneath our decks and in our 172-quart Gott coolers is still more food than we can eat. In fact, the greatest single curse on these commercial river expeditions is gaining weight due to over-eating the rich food — despite the many hikes and all the rowing. Too much beer. Cold beer.

On the north shoreline are tied three wooden boats, faded, gouged, scratched, cracked, splintered, patched with repairs, leaky, but strangely buoyant — they are virtually empty of cargo. The oars are crude, hand-sawed, rough hewn from driftwood poles. The decks are innocent of equipment except for Walter Powell's Winchester on the deck of the *Maid*. The bowlines of hemp look as frayed as if they had been dragged over a hundred miles of sandstone.

Most stark and telling is the crew. The nine men are short, gaunt, sun-baked, silt-hewed, unshaven, and wearing nearly nothing in the 100-degree heat but a ragged tatter of shirt and a belt securing a Bowie knife. Here and there a revolver is visible. What no one at all is wearing is a pair of britches.

The bearded, one-armed man down by the rapid is hatless and naked but for a rubber horse-collar life jacket. The universal scowls and calloused fists rubbing bearded chins on the shore line reveal that this rapid has these men worried. The roar of the rapid forces each man to yell whatever comment he wishes to communicate. But they are mostly silent. Again, their body language, however, shouts that this rapid has spooked at least a couple of them.

We row to shore and leap out to tie nylon bowlines to boulders.

"Who the hell are you?" William Hawkins asks, looking up from a cluster of unbaked baseball-like biscuits of unleavened dough lined up near his campfire. Nearby is a stained flour sack reading "Property of U.S. Army." It is now nearly empty. It appears that Hawkins is about to bake most of this sack's entire supply of flour.

Instead of a pitched camp, all this crew has set in place here is this camp fire, biscuits, a battered pot of coffee, and a couple of bedrolls propped against a slab of schist.

Startled, but still a man who knows that hospitality is the ultimate propriety in the West, Hawkins offers a rough hand in greeting. I take it. Crumbs of dough grind between us to drop onto the fine sand.

"We're river runners...from the future," I say, knowing it sounds absurd. "I have an important message for you. Life or death. But only a few minutes to tell you what you need to hear. Take me to your leader."

Hawkins stares into my face, then looks hard at our boats, and then at the people dressed in Hot Chilly's T-shirts, nylon shorts, and sunglasses milling in disbelief around them. Cameras are popping out everywhere. Then he looks back at me. "You're *what?*"

"Commercial river runners," I tell him. "My name's Michael Ghiglieri. I'm leading this trip. It's...it's hard to explain in any way so you'll not think me a liar. People these days go on these trips for fun, for sport. They hire us to guide them safely. I've rowed this river more than a hundred times myself. We're from the twentieth-first century," I add. "I know this is hard to believe. By the way, I've got some food I can give you. Even cold beer."

Hawkins stares at me and tries to process my apparent insanity. Then he glances at the rest of us. He shakes his head as if admitting to himself the fact that this encounter is all just a hunger-induced hallucination. Then, yielding to the hallucination, he takes me to Powell.

If Hawkins was unbelieving, Powell is astounded. Dumbfounded. He shakes my left hand as if sleep-walking. He now looks even more worried than moments ago when he was staring at the rapid.

"I've got a problem," Powell finally admits later, after I have convinced him that we are real. "Three of my boys are deserting the expedition. They want to hike out."

"Why?" I ask. I think I had this mystery solved, but if I am wrong, I want to know now. And I want to know badly. I might be able to help. But the right words, the ones that would constitute help, depended on what was really going on here.

The knowledge that Oramel and Seneca Howland and William Dunn will certainly die if I don't utter the right words — and knowing that I'd better blurt them out fast before this cosmic singularity that we've artificially generated untangles itself and whips me and my crew and passengers back to the age of National Park Service helicopter evacuations and DVDs of Powell reinactments — tortures me with indecision.

Before it's too late, what should I say to these heroic and starving explorers who are now so unsuccessfully battling the tension between themselves?

Should I say to Powell, "Try harder to keep the Howland brothers and Dunn with you? Apologize to them? Be a leader. Explain how important they are to the expedition — tell them how much you owe them, that you appreciate them, that you *need* them?"

And to the Howlands and Dunn? "Don't quit this expedition. In thirty hours by boat you'll escape Grand Canyon and win a place in history. If you hike out instead, you will be treacherously murdered. No matter what, go *downriver*. Even if you have to crawl on your hands and knees."

Would they listen to a stranger? Would I have time to explain anything? It's only a fantasy. But I still wonder, what else should I tell them?

I can see from Powell's uncomprehending face that what I am saying is not working. I need some help here.

What would you tell them?

Separation Canyon (drawing by Bernard Black, 2001).

APPENDIX

J. W. POWELL'S ASTRONOMICAL OBSERVATIONS
1869

The following astronomical observations were painstakingly transcribed by Richard D. Quartaroli, Special Collections Librarian, Northern Arizona University, Cline Library. These observations are from J. W. Powell's original astronomical journal and include all calculations made while on the expedition. Even so, no one thus far has been able to convert these observations to actual measures of latitude and longtitude. If you wish to attempt this, good luck.

(NAA p.11)

Obs for Alt. July 7th at noon
Camp cliff on right of the river
9.30 a.m.

D	W	At	Bar
74	54.8	74.5	25.540
81	57	81	24.426

Upper Bar against rocks exposed
to the sun lower in shade

Obs for alt July 8 Cliff on
right of River at Camp No 2

D	W	At	Bar
89.5 -	54 -	89	25.428
83	52	83	23.914

(NAA p.12)

Obs for Alt July 10 at
Camp No 4

base	D	W	At	Bar
	75.8	54	75	25.680

summit of
dark red 74   44   74   25.172
Sds thick
    bed

Summit of red beds & base
75 − 52 − 75 − 23.738
84.5 − 54.8 − 85 − 25.686

Two red beds ??? found above about 275 ft.

Mt. 4 ½ miles E. of Camp

88	55	88.5	25.654	12:30
70	49	70	22.150	
87	55	90	22.150	1 P.M.
69	48	69	22.142	

Cliffs much more ????
Estimates 150 ft higher

(NAA p.10)

Obs for lat at camp
No 7   July 13   69

Alt Saturn double
61° 6' 40"
Index Error +3' 55"

Obs for Lat Camp 8
July 14ᵗʰ   69
61° - 47' - 50"   Alt Double of Saturn
Index Error 0

(NAA p.13)

Lunar at Junction of
Grand & Green July 18ᵗʰ 1869
Index Error - 2° - 20'

		h
Al Spica	55° - 10'	8 – 19' – 32"

Up. L. 70° - 18' – 50"   8 - 23' – 23" (h)

nearest limit
		h
41° - 39' – 30"	=	8 – 36' – 17"
41 - 39 – 50	=	8 – 38 – 49
41 - 41 – 10	=	8 – 42 – 35
41 - 41 – 35	=	8 – 44 – 43
41 - 42 – 20	=	8 – 46 – 50
41 - 43 – 00	=	8 – 49 – 19
41 - 44 – 10	=	8 – 52 – 29
41 - 45 – 30	=	8 – 54 – 09
41 - 47 – 00	=	8 – 58 – 10
41 - 48 – 50	=	9 – 02 – 26
41 - 49 – 50	=	9 – 04 – 44

(NAA p.14)

h
Al ? Up L. 64° - 50' – 00"9 – 10' – 59"
"   38 – 04 – 00   9 – 22 – 02

Index Error – 2' 00"

(NAA p.15)
                    Obs for Lat at Junction
            Grand & Green July 18th
                Polar Star
                    Index Error – 2' – 00"
            Double Altitudes   h
            75° - 14' – 40" = 9   – 45' – 14"
            75 - 15 - 00   = 9   – 47   – 08
            75 - 16 - 30   = 9   – 48   – 30
            75 - 18 - 30   = 9   – 51   – 32
            75 - 19 - 40   = 9   – 53   – 00
            75 - 21 - 00   = 9   – 54   – 18
            75 - 22 - 20   = 9   – 56   – 34
            75 - 24 - 00   = 9   – 59   – 00
            75 - 25 - 00   = 10 – 00   – 52
            75 - 26 - 10   = 10 – 02   – 55
            Index Error – 1' 51"

(NAA p.17)
                        Obs for time E.A. Sun
            July 18th 69   Junction Gr & Grn.
        111° 30 =   9 – 51 – 33 = 2 – 23 – 30
            40 =   9 – 52 – 02 = 2 – 23 – 02
            50 =   9 – 52 – 26 = 2 – 23 – 02
        112° 00 =   9 – 52 – 54 = 2 – 23 – 30
            10 =   9 – 53 – 24 = 2 – 23 – 02
            20 =   9 – 53 – 48 = 2 – 23 – 02
            30 =   9 – 54 – 16 = 2 – 23 – 02
            40 =   9 – 54 – 44 = 2 – 23 – 02
            50 =   9 – 55 – 11 = 2 – 23 – 02
        113 00 =   9 – 55 – 39 = 2 – 23 – 30
            10 =   9 – 56 – 06 = 2 – 23 – 02
            20 =   9 – 56 – 34 = 2 – 23 – 02
            30 =   9 – 57 – 04 = 2 – 23 – 02
            40 =   9 – 57 – 30 = 2 – 23 – 02
            50 =   9 – 57 – 56 = 2 – 23 – 02
        114 00 =   9 – 58 – 23 = 2 – 23 – 30
            10 =   9 – 58 – 53 = 2 – 23 – 02
            20 =   9 – 59 – 19 = 2 – 23 – 02
            30 =   9 – 59 – 46 = 2 – 23 – 02
            40 = 10 – 00 – 14 = 2 – 23 – 02
            50 = 10 – 00 – 42 = 2 – 23 – 02
        106.00 = 10 – 01 – 12 = 2 – 23 – 02

            9 – 56 – 15,272 = 2 – 18 – 35,681

(NAA p.16)
                    Cor of Elgin July 18th
                obs on last page
                        h
                    12 – 7' - 25".476
                dif 4 - 22 – 20.409
            Dec. 20° 56" 23.58
            Eq of ?   5' – 56".4

H Dif   26".87

9.4299	9.3546
1.4292	1.4292
<u>9.8964</u>	<u>9.5827</u>
.7555	3665

$+$ 5".713   - 2".861

<u>2 861</u>

2 . 852

```
                    12 – 7 – 25 476
                              2 852
                    ────────────────
                    12 – 7 –28 –328
                         5  56 – 400
                    ────────────────
                    12 – 1  31 – 928
```

(NAA p.19)

Obs for time July 19ᵗʰ Sun
for Elgin rate at Noon

102°	0' = 9	25	53	= 2	47	53.5
	10 = 9	26	20	= 2	47	30
	20 = 9	26	41.5	= 2	47	03
	30 = 9	27	13	= 2	46	37
	40 = 9	27	38.5	= 2	46	10.5
	50 = 9	28	05	= 2	45	44
103°	0' = 9	28	34	= 2	45	18
	10 = 9	29	0	= 2	44	51.5
	20 = 9	29	28	= 2	44	25.5
	30 = 9	29	55.5	= 2	44	0
	40 = 9	30	18	= 2	43	32
	50 = 9	30	55.5	= 2	43	05
104	0' = 9	31	12	= 2	42	38.5
	10 = 9	31	38.5	= 2	42	12.5
	20 = 9	32	07	= 2	41	45
	30 = 9	32	32	= 2	41	18.5
	40 = 9	33	00	= 2	40	51.5
	50 = 9	33	24	= 2	40	27
105	0' = 9	33	48.5	= 2	39	58
	10 = 9	34	18	= 2	39	35
	20 = 9	34	43	= 2	39	06
	30 = 9	35	11	= 2	38	40
	40 = 9	35	37	= 2	38	12
	50 = 9	36	24	= 2	37	47
106	0' = 9	36	31	= 2	37	21
	9ʺ	31ˑ 21.52			2.43.024	

(NAA p.18)

Obs for Lat July 19 69
Junc. Grand & Green
Meridian Al double Saturn
Index Error
---- 1
62° -- 40' – 20"

(NAA p.1)

Lunar July 19ᵗʰ
A & A Aquilar
h m s

```
Al        9   2   49 = 64°. 56'. 30"
Al        9 . 6 . 06 = 84° 29' 30"
Index error =  + 50'
          h     m      s        °     '      "
          9. – 15. – 52 = 48 – 19 – 50            fathest limit
          9  -  18  -   3 = 48 – 18 – 50
          9  -  19  - 31 = 48 – 18 – 20
          9  -  20  - 54 = 48 – 17 – 30
          9  -  22  -   8 = 48 – 17 – 20
          9  -  23  - 46 = 48 – 17 – 10
          9  -  24  -  57= 48 – 17 –  0
          9  -  25  -  57= 48 – 16 – 45
          9  -  27  -  19= 48 – 16 – 25
          9  -  28  -  43= 48 – 16 –  0
          9  -  29  -  50= 48 – 15 – 30
          9  -  31  -   0= 48 – 15 – 10
          9  -  31  - 56 = 48 – 15 –  0
          9  -  33  -   7= 48 – 14 – 40
          9  -  34  -  21 = 48 –14 – 25
          9  -  35  -  20= 48 – 14 – 15
          9  -  36  -  27= 48 – 14 – 05
```

(NAA p.2)

over

```
          h     m      s        °     '      "
          9  -  34  - 30 = 48 – 13 – 55
          9  -  38  - 42 = 48 – 13 – 45
          9  -  39  - 47 = 48 – 13 – 30
          9  -  41  - 13 = 48 – 13 – 20
          9  -  42  - 12 = 48 – 13 – 10
          9  -  43  - 22 = 48 – 12 – 40
          9  -  44  - 39 = 48 – 12 – 20
                    Index error =  + 1' 10"
          h     m      s        °     '      "
Al.       9 – 52 – 18 = 99 – 29 – 40
Alt       9 – 55 – 12 = 62 – 21 – 30
                    Index  error =  + 1'
```

(NAA p.3)

```
                    h   m     s         h   m     s
96° - 10' = 9 – 10 – 49    = 3 –   1 – 59
       20 = 9 – 11 – 15    = 3 -   1 – 35
       30 = 9 – 11 – 40    = 3 -   1 – 07.5
       40 = 9 – 12 – 06    = 3 -   0 – 42
       50 = 9 – 12 – 32    = 3 -   0 – 16
97° -   0' = 9 – 12 – 59   = 2 – 59 – 49
       10 = 9 – 13 – 25    = 2 -  59 – 20
       20 = 9 – 13 – 52    = 2 -  58 – 59
       30 = 9 – 14 – 19    = 2 -  58 – 32
       40 = 9 – 14 – 44    = 2 -  58 – 05.5
       50 = 9 – 15 – 10    = 2 -  57 – 40
98° -   0' = 9 – 15 – 37   = 2 – 57 – 13
       10 = 9 – 16 – 03    = 2 -  56 – 46
       20 = 9 – 16 – 30    = 2 -  56 – 21.5
       30 = 9 – 16 – 33.5 = 2 -  55 – 53
       40 = 9 – 17 – 20.5 = 2 -  55 – 28.5
       50 = 9 – 17 – 47    = 2 -  55 – 02
99° -   0' = 9 – 18 – 13.5 = 2 – 54 – 37
```

```
            10 = 9 – 18 – 40    = 2 -  54 – 09.5
            20 = 9 – 19 – 06.5 = 2 -  53 – 43
            30 = 9 – 19 – 31    = 2 -  53 – 16
            40 = 9 – 19 – 57    = 2 -  52 – 51.5
            50 = 9 – 20 – 26.5 = 2 -  52 – 26
100° -  0' = 9 – 20 – 52    = 2 – 52 – 00
            10 = 9 – 21 – 17    = 2 -  51 – 33
```

Obs for time July 20th for rate
Of Elgin Sun

(NAA p.4)

Lunar July 20. Junction G.&G.
Saturn

```
            h
Al      8 – 21' – 27 = 62° - 12' – 50"
Al      8 – 25  – 29 = 52  – 17  – 10
     Index Error   00
            h
        8 – 39" – 56 = 18° - 57' – 50"
        8 – 42  – 36 = 18  – 58  – 50
        8 – 44  – 26 = 18  – 59  – 30
        8 – 45  – 46 = 19  – 00  – 00
        8 – 47  – 33 = 19  – 00  – 20
        8 – 49  – 03 = 19  – 01  – 00
        8 – 51  – 28 = 19  – 01  – 0
        8 – 52  – 04 = 19  – 02  – 20
        8 – 53  – 25 = 19  – 02  – 50
        8 – 54  – 51 = 19  – 03  – 20
        8 – 55  – 56 = 19  – 04  – 15
        8 – 57  – 32 = 19  – 04  – 40
        8 – 58  – 52 = 19  – 05  – 00
        8 – 00  – 02 = 19  – 05  – 30
        9 – 01  – 15 = 19  – 05  – 45
        9 – 02  – 37 = 19  – 06  – 20
     Index Error –  10
Al      9 – 12' – 33" = 58° - 26" – 00
 "      9 – 16  – 30 = 61  – 36  – 20
```

(NAA p.5)

Obs Alt. July 20th Cave Cliff

D	W	At	Bar
99	63	99	25.164"
94	60	96	26.134

Upper Bar in Sun

Obs Alt. July 22 /69
   At Camp No 12   confusion of
Rocks

D	W	At	Bar
99 -	64 -	97.6 -	26.240
100 -	63 -	100 -	25.334

Upper Bar. in Shade

(NAA p. 6)

Obs. For Alt July 26, 69
Camp No 16 and cliff up the
Canon to the N.E. marked "A" on
Map

D	W.	At	Bar
96 -	65 -	96 -	24.136
103 -	67	103.4	26 324

Upper Bar in Shade   The lower
Always is in shade

(NAA p.7)

Obs for Alt July
29th Cliff on right bank
for thickness of red rocks
uniform Sds up to thick bed of gray
97 – 63   – 97 – 26.600
96 – 62.5 – 96 – 26.370

Obs for Lat on Star
in leg of Ophici 3 July 29
camp No 19 below ruins
2 Al.   64° 5' 50"
Index Error + 11' 20"

(NAA p.8)

Obs Lat Mouth San Juan [July 31]
☐ Citi 2 Alt. = 68° - 6' – 20"
I.E. + 9' 20"

Lat 37° - 11' – 47" approx.

	Lunar at Camp 21 Sun	
Al	9 – 13 – 16 =	96 – 20 – 00
"	9 – 24 – 28 =	88 – 22 – 20
	9 – 33 – 26 =	78 – 36 – 30
	9 – 36 – 16 =	78 – 35 – 30
	9 – 37 – 34 =	78 – 33 – 40
	9 – 38 – 34 =	78 – 33 – 10
	9 – 45 – 10 =	78 – 31 – 10
	h	
Al.	9 – 49 – 44 =	99 – 5 – 20
"	9 – 54 – 16 =	111 – 26 – 20

I.E. + 11' – 20"

Music T.
Aug 1st

(NAA p.22)

Obs for Lat Polaris
Aug 1ˢᵗ   Music Hall
h
8 – 41 – 36 = 72° - 52 – 30
8 – 45 – 38 = 72   - 55 – 00
8 – 48 – 34 = 72   - 57 –
I.E. + 10' – 40"

Lunar Aug 2ⁿᵈ Sun Music Temple
h
Al   9 – 06 – 50 = 89° - 00 – 00
A   9 – 16 – 35 = 117° - 04 – 30
I.E. + 11" – 30"
9 – 34 – 42 = 66 – 55 – 50
9 – 37 – 42 = 66 – 53 – 00
9 – 40 – 12 = 66 – 52 – 10
9 – 41 – 21 = 66 – 51 – 00
9 – 42 – 54 = 66 – 50 – 10
High Wind intervening between
this and next

(NAA p.21)

Lunar Continuum
2ⁿᵈ Series
9 – 48 – 41 = 66 – 50 – 00
9 – 50 – 37 = 66 – 49 – 50
9 – 52 – 10 = 66 – 49 – 30
9 – 53 – 34 = 66 – 48 – 50
9 – 54 – 31 = 66 – 48 – 30
9 – 56 – 04 = 66 – 47 – 50
9 – 57 – 30 = 66 – 47 – 10
9 – 58 – 47 = 66 – 46 – 50
9 – 59 – 56 = 66 – 46 – 30
10 – 00 – 51 = 66 – 46 – 00
I.E. + 11' – 50"
h
Al   10   11 – 00 = 98° - 40' – 00"
"   10 – 13 – 55 = 113 – 51 – 20

(NAA p.20)

Obs for time Aug 1
at Music Temple for rate of Elgin

92° - 20' = 9 – 02 – 42   = 3 – 03 – 05
92 - 30   = 9 – 03 – 11.5 = 3 – 02 – 38
92 - 40   = 9 – 03 – 35   = 3 – 02 – 15
92 - 50   = 9 – 04 – 00.5 = 3 – 01 – 47
93 - 00   = 9 – 04 – 29   = 3 – 01 – 22
93 - 10   = 9 – 04 – 54   = 3 – 01 – 56
93 - 20   = 9 – 05 – 22   = 3 – 01 – 31
93 - 30   = 9 – 05 – 46   = 3 – 01 – 05

```
93 - 40  = 9 – 06 – 15  = 2 – 59 – 39
93 - 50  = 9 – 06 – 41  = 2 – 59 – 12
94 - 00  = 9 – 07 – 08  = 2 – 58 – 46
94 - 10  = 9 – 07 – 36  = 2 – 58 – 21
94 - 20  = 9 – 08 – 02  = 2 – 57 – 54
94 - 30  = 9 – 08 – 28  = 2 – 57 – 26
94 - 40  = 9 – 08 – 51  = 2 – 57 – 02
94 - 50  = 9 – 09 – 18  = 2 – 56 – 36
95 - 00  = 9 – 09 – 46  = 2 – 56 – 09
95 - 10  = 9 – 10 – 12  = 2 – 55 – 41
95 - 20  = 9 – 10 – 38  = 2 – 55 – 13
95 - 30  = 9 – 10 – 04  = 2 – 54 – 49
```

(NAA p.23)

Time Aug 2nd for rate of Elgin
```
84° - 40’ = 8 – 55 – 43 =  3 – 39 – 39
        50’ = 8 – 56 – 43 =  3 – 39 – 13
85° - 40’ = 8 – 56 – 43 =  3 – 38 – 46
        10’ = 8 – 56 – 43 =  3 – 38 – 20
        20’ = 8 – 57 – 43 =  3 – 37 – 55
        30’ = 8 – 57 – 43 =  3 – 37 – 30
        40’ = 8 – 58 – 43 =  3 – 37 – 03
        50’ = 8 – 58 – 43 =  3 – 36 – 37
86° - 00’ = 8 – 59 – 43 =  3 – 36 – 11
        10’ = 8 – 59 – 43 =  3 – 35 – 45
        20’ = 8 – 59 – 43 =  3 – 35 – 22
        30’ = 9 – 00 – 43 =  3 – 34 – 55
        40’ = 9 – 00 – 43 =  3 – 34 – 27
        50’ = 9 – 01 – 43 =  3 – 34 – 03
87° - 00’ = 9 – 01 – 43 =  3 – 33 – 36
        10’ = 9 – 02 – 43 =  3 – 33 – 10
        20’ = 9 – 02 – 43 =  3 – 32 – 45
        30’ = 9 – 03 – 43 =  3 – 32 – 20
        40’ = 9 – 03 – 43 =  3 – 31 – 53
        50’ = 9 – 03 – 43 =  3 – 31 – 27
```

(NAA p.24)

Pah Reah
Lat   Ute Creek Aug 4
2   Alt Saturn   65 – 00 – 30
I.E. + 10’ – 30” (ç) (¿)

Alt of Wall | right | Aug. 7
Lower bar carried to upper station
obs 1h 20’ apart
below 2 – 40 PM 27 094   79372o
above 4 . 00   "   25.234   - 74 – 66

(NAA p.25)

Lat. 2 Alt Polaris Aug 11th Astr. Date
                                  12th Common date

I.E. + 10' – 00
4ʰ – 46' – 30" = 75° - 00' – 00"
4 - 49 - 18   = 75 – 00   - 30
4 - 53 - 11   = 75 – 00   - 00
4 - 54 - 45   = 74 – 59   - 50
4 - 57 - 15   = 74 – 59   - 30
I.E. + 11' – 40"

              Alt Cliff in angle of Col. R.
& Flax   Aug. 12ᵗʰ 69
              At   W
              101 – 78 – 25.128
              81.8 – 66 – 27.270

              lower Bar. came up

(NAA p.26)
              Time Elgin Aug 11ᵗʰ Mouth of Flax
109° - 30 = 10 – 34 – 40   = 2 – 52 –51
        40 = 10 – 35 – 09   = 2 – 52 – 24
        50 = 10 – 35 – 39   = 2 – 51 – 54
110 - 00 = 10 – 36 – 07   = 2 – 51 – 27
        10 = 10 – 36 – 34.5 = 2 – 50 – 59
        20 = 10 – 37 – 04   = 2 – 50 – 28
        30 = 10 – 37 – 31.5 = 2 – 50 – 00.5
        40 = 10 – 38 – 01   = 2 – 49 – 31
        50 = 10 – 38 – 29   = 2 – 49 – 03
111 - 00 = 10 – 38 – 57   = 2 – 48 – 33.5
        10 = 10 – 39 – 26   = 2 – 48 – 07
        20 = 10 – 39 – 55   = 2 – 47 – 37
        30 = 10 – 40 – 24   = 2 – 47 – 09
        40 = 10 – 40 – 51   = 2 – 46 – 40.5
        50 = 10 – 41 – 22   = 2 – 46 – 12
112 - 00 = 10 – 41 – 49   = 2 – 45 – 42
        10 = 10 – 42 – 18   = 2 – 45 – 13.5
        20 = 10 – 42 – 48   = 2 – 44 – 45
        30 = 10 – 43 – 18.5 = 2 – 44 – 17
        40 = 10 – 43 – 45   = 2 – 43 – 47

(NAA p.27)
          Time. Aug 12ᵗʰ Flax River Elgin

120 – 10 = 11 – 19 – 05 = 2 – 30 – 14
       20 = 11 – 19 – 37 = 2 – 29 – 42
       30 = 11 – 20 – 07 = 2 – 29 – 09
       40 = 11 – 20 – 40 = 2 – 28 – 37
       50 = 11 – 21 – 15 = 2 – 28 – 06
120 – 00 = 11 – 21 – 46 = 2 – 37 – 32
       10 = 11 – 22 – 18 = 2 – 27 – 00
       20 = 11 – 22 – 50 = 2 – 26 – 27
       30 = 11 – 23 – 24 = 2 – 25 – 54
       40 = 11 – 23 – 56 = 2 – 25 – 20

$$50 = 11 - 24 - 31 = 2 - 24 - 47$$
$$120 - 00 = 11 - 25 - 04 = 2 - 34 - 15$$
$$10 = 11 - 25 - 37 = 2 - 23 - 43$$
$$20 = 11 - 26 - 11 = 2 - 23 - 08$$
$$30 = 11 - 26 - 44 = 2 - 22 - 33$$

A.M. $+ 41 - 00$ PM $+ 41$ 30
$- 20 - 40$ $- 20 - 00$

(NAA p.28)

Lunar Aug 11th 69 Sun   Flax R.
Al $2^h - 52' - 51" = 109° - 30'$ Sun
" $3 - 12 - 48 = 97 - 54$

$$3 - 18 - 30 = 55 - 17 - 10$$
$$3 - 20 - 25 = 55 - 17 - 50$$
$$3 - 23 - 15 = 55 - 18 - 00$$
$$3 - 24 - 30 = 55 - 18 - 20$$

I.E. I.E. $+ 9'$ 15

(NAA p.29)

Lunar Mouth Flax Aug 12
A. Aquillar

I.E. $+ 10' - 10"$
Al $= 8^h - 30 - 52 = 57 - 23 - 30$
" $= 8 - 35 - 26 = 89 - 57 - 40$
$$8 - 42 - 30 = 86 - 14 - 10$$
$$8 - 44 - 23 = 86 - 13 - 20$$
$$8 - 46 - 12 = 86 - 11 - 30$$
$$8 - 48 - 33 = 86 - 10 - 40$$
$$8 - 50 - 20 = 86 - 09 - 50$$
$$8 - 51 - 57 = 86 - 09 - 00$$
$$9 - 19 - 28 = 86 - 32 - 30$$
$$9 - 23 - 11 = 86 - 56 - 10$$

I.E. $10 - 20$

(NAA p.30)

Lunar Altair   Aug 15
Silver Creek

Al $8 - 27 - 47 = 104 - 24 - 30$
$$8 - 31 - 39 = 64 - 55 - 50$$
I.E. $= + 11' 50"$
$$8 - 47 - 11 = 50 - 55 - 10$$
$$8 - 47 - 11 = 50 - 55 - 50$$
$$8 - 47 - 11 = 50 - 55 - 50$$
$$8 - 47 - 11 = 50 - 55 - 50$$
$$8 - 47 - 11 = 50 - 55 - 50$$
$$8 - 47 - 11 = 50 - 55 - 50$$
I.E. $+ 11' - 50"$
Al $= 9 - 55 - 57 = 59 - 41 - 50$
$$= 9 - 18 - 40 = 116 - 00 - 00$$

Meridian Alt of Altair same
night by Sumner
123° - 45' – 20"
I.E. + 11' – 50"

(NAA p.31)

Time Aug 16   69 Elgin

```
112 – 50 = 10 – 23 – 58   =  2    09 – 52
113 – 00 = 10 – 24 – 26   =  2 – 09 – 20
        10 = 10 – 24 – 55   =  2 – 08 – 48.5
        20 = 10 – 25 – 26   =  2 – 08 – 18
        30 = 10 – 25 – 59.5 =  2 – 07 – 50
        40 = 10 – 26 – 31   =  2 – 07 – 23
        50 = 10 – 27 – 02   =  2 – 06 – 48
114 – 00 = 10 – 27 – 33   =  2 – 06 – 15
        10 = 10 – 28 – 06   =  2 – 05 – 49
        20 = 10 – 28 – 33   =  2 – 05 – 14
```

I.E. A.M. + 42' – 00
                - 18 – 00

(NAA p.32)

Al. Alair Aug. 27 for Lat
Separation Camp
125° 13' 00"   I.E. 12.20

Al Alair Aug 29 for Lat
124° - 45' – 50"   I.E. + 10' – 10"

Al. Saturn for time Aug 29
51° - 43' – 50" = 8ʰ – 54' – 00"
Polaris for Lat
11° - 41 – 40 = 8 – 58 – 18
                    I.E. + 10' – 00

(NAA p.33)

Lat Atlair Sep. 4ᵗʰ St George

122 – 29 – 00
I.E. + 24 – 30

AUTHOR PROFILE

MICHAEL P. GHIGLIERI grew up at Lake Tahoe, Nevada. An honorably discharged Vietnam Era veteran, he earned his Ph.D. in Biological Ecology from the University of California at Davis for his pioneering research project on wild chimpanzees in Kibale Forest, Uganda. In addition to teaching university level courses in primate behavior and ecology and in human evolution, he has directed overseas university semesters in sustainable resource management in Kenya, the Turks and Caicos Islands, Palau,  Australia, and in British Columbia. President of Grand Canyon River Guides Association (2002-2003), Ghiglieri has worked as a wilderness river guide since 1974, running commercial whitewater trips (plus treks) in Canada, Ethiopia, Java, Kenya, Papua New Guinea, Peru, Rwanda, Sumatra, Tanzania, Turkey, Uganda, and the U.S.A. His expeditions include 154 two-week trips in Grand Canyon as a rowing or paddling guide/trip leader plus a few as an NPS River Ranger. He has also rowed the other canyons explored by the 1869 expedition: Lodore, Whirlpool, Split Mountain, Desolation, Gray, Labyrinth, Stillwater, Cataract, and Narrow. Ghiglieri has spent more than 2,000 days inside Grand Canyon as a professional and worked 660 river trips overall, rowing or paddling more than 46,000 miles on 3 dozen river runs. A Flagstaff resident, married and father of three children, Ghiglieri is the author of six other books. Three of these deal with wild chimpanzees and/or the violent natural history of men (*The Dark Side of Man*). Three others focus on international river-running and/or Grand Canyon. Ghiglieri also wrote the award-winning documentary screenplays "River of Stone" and "Artists of the West." His previous books on Grand Canyon include *CANYON*, which was hailed by the *Library Journal* as **"the single best introduction to a myriad of aspects of this 'most impressive place' this reviewer has seen. Recommended for all — "** and, with Tom Myers, *Over the Edge: Death in Grand Canyon*, the bestseller hailed by award-winning, Southwestern mystery author Tony Hillerman as follows: **"If you believe that everything interesting about the Grand Canyon has already been written, you're dead wrong."**

TO ORDER COPIES of PUMA PRESS BOOKS:

Photocopy this page and fill out your order. Please print legibly.

Please send_____ copies of OVER THE EDGE: DEATH IN GRAND CANYON, $22.95 softcover (if being shipped to an Arizona address, please add $1.88 sales tax per copy)   subtotal =

Please send_____copies of OFF THE WALL: DEATH IN YOSEMITE, $24.95 softcover (if being shipped to an Arizona address, please add $2.03 sales tax per copy)   subtotal =

Please send_____copies of FIRST THROUGH GRAND CANYON: The Secret Journals and Letters of the 1869 Crew Who Explored the Green and Colorado Rivers, $19.95 softcover (if being shipped to an Arizona address, please add $1.62 sales tax per copy)   subtotal =

Please send_____copies of GRAND OBSESSION: Harvey Butchart and the Exploration of Grand Canyon, $19.95 softcover (if being shipped to an Arizona address, please add $1.62 sales tax per copy)   subtotal =

Shipping & Handling: please add $3.00 for the first book, $1.00 for each additional book.   shipping subtotal =

TOTAL = $ _____

Order via our website: pumapress.org or

Enclose your check or money order for the total above payable to:
Puma Press P.O. Box 30998, Flagstaff, AZ 86003 USA
Thank you for your order. Please allow 3 weeks for delivery.

ADDRESS TO WHICH YOU WISH YOUR ORDER TO BE SHIPPED
(please print)

NAME _____

ADDRESS _____

CITY _____

STATE _____   ZIP CODE _____

SOURCES for INTRODUCTION

Page:
1.   "Powell's journey down the legendary river of the West was one of the greatest events": Worster, D. 2001. *A River Running West: The Life of John Wesley Powell*. New York: Oxford. p. 200.

2.   Bradley's secret journal emerges from obscurity: Darrah, W. C. 1947. The Powell Colorado River Expedition of 1869. *Utah Historical Quarterly* 15:16.

2.   "Indeed, Bradley is harshest when he speaks of the Major": Darrah, W. C. 1947. George Young Bradley 1836-1885. *Utah Historical Quarterly* 15. p. 30.

3.   Bradley was "a man of nerve and staying qualities, as he proved later on": Hawkins, W. W. [sic]. 1920. in W. W. Bass (ed.) *Adventures in the Canyons of the Colorado By two of its earliest explorers, James White and W. W. Hawkins with introduction and notes*. Grand Canyon, Arizona. W. W. Bass. pp. 19 & 20.

5.   Powell's 1895 book, *Canyons of the Colorado*, was published in 1,000 copies by Flood and Vincent but never sold out; Flood and Vincent went bankrupt: Worster, D. 2001. *A River Running West: The Life of John Wesley Powell*. New York: Oxford. p. 545.

5.   " – the account given by the Major is a literary composition rather than a scientific document": Darrah, W.C. 1947. The Powell Colorado River Expedition of 1869. *Utah Historical Quarterly* 15:9 – 18, p.16.

5.   Powell's literary efforts were spurred by the pointed warning of Representative Garfield: Anderson, M. J. no date. John Wesley Powell's Reporting of History: Fact? Fiction? or Fantasy? undated manuscript. In the Northern Arizona University Cline Library Special Collections, MS 77, Box 1, p. 2. Martin J. Anderson Collection.

5.   Major Powell's book is problematic on several fronts: Powell, J. W. 1895 [1964]. *Canyons of the Colorado*. New York: Argosy-Antiquarian Ltd.

5.   On Powell's inaccuracies: W. W. Bass (ed.). 1920. *Adventures in the Canyons of the Colorado By two of its earliest explorers, James White and W. W. Hawkins with introduction and notes*. Grand Canyon, Arizona. W. W. Bass. pp. 8 & 9.

6.   "At last we find ourselves": Powell, J. W. 1975. *Exploration of the Colorado River of the West and Its Tributaries Explored in 1869, 1870, 1871, and 1872, Under the Direction of the Secretary of the Smithsonian Institution*. Washington: Government Printing Office. p. 82.

6.   " — At about 2 PM was hailed by a man on shore....There's lots in that book besides the truth": Stanton, R. B. 1932. [1982] *Colorado River Controversies*. Boulder City: Westwater Books, p. 104. *see also* Anderson, M. J. (undated ms.) John Wesley Powell's Reporting of History: Fact? Fiction? or Fantasy?. In the Northern Arizona University Cline Library Special Collections, MS 77, Box 1, pp. 10-11. Martin J. Anderson Collection.

7.   "Major Powell's work and that of his companions in 1869, to my mind, stands out as one of the bravest exploits ever known anywhere" [but] "the Major was undoubtedly guilty of suppression of the truth and unblushing exaggeration": Stanton, R. B. 1932 [1982]. Major Powell as Historian. in *Colorado River Controversies*, pp. 97-137. Boulder City: Westwater. pp. 97. 100, 102, 107, 111, 122, 137.

7. "The Major was not blameless when it comes to deliberate inaccuracy." and Powell's Report and book were "a literary composition rather than a scientific document": Darrah, W. C. 1947. The Powell Colorado River Expedition of 1869. *Utah Historical Quarterly* 15:9-18. p. 16.

7. On J. W. Powell's deliberate changing of the history of the 1869 expedition: Anderson, M. J. (undated ms.) John Wesley Powell's Reporting of History: Fact? Fiction? or Fantasy?. In the Northern Arizona University Cline Library Special Collections, MS 77, Box 1, Martin J. Anderson Collection.

8. A flawed attempt to publish the original journals as a book: Cooley, J. 1988. *The Great Unknown: The Journals of the Historic First Expedition Down the Colorado River.* Flagstaff: Northland Publishing.

12. George Y. Bradley's origin: Darrah, W. C. 1947. George Young Bradley 1836-1885. *Utah Historical Quarterly* 15:29-30.

12. "He was something of a geologist and, in my eyes far more important, he had been raised in the Maine codfishery school, and was a good boatman, and a brave man, not very strong but tough as a badger": Sumner, J. C. 1907 [1982]. Jack Sumner's account. in Stanton. R. B. [1932] *Colorado River Controversies.* pp. 167-213. Boulder City: Westwater. p. 174.

13. Powell wrote of Bradley: "He is scrupulously careful, and a little mishap works him into a passion, but when labor is needed": Powell, J. W. 1895 in R. B. Stanton, A.M., C.C.B.A. no date (written in 1906-1909). The River and the Canon: The Colorado River of the West, and the Exploration, Navigation, and Survey of its Canons, from the Standpoint of an Engineer. (unpublished manuscript). p. 441. Loaned to Cline Library Special Collections by New York Public Library, Manuscripts and Archives Division.

14. Bradley as "petulant" and an "inveterate worrier": Worster, D. 2001. *A River Running West: The Life of John Wesley Powell.* New York: Oxford. p. 159.

15. Charles H. Morss donated George Y. Bradley's journal to the Library of Congress as an "unrestricted" gift: Sibussat, St. G. L., Chief, Division of Manuscripts, Library of Congress. 1947. letter to W. C. Darrah, February 7. *see also* Darrah, W. C. 1970. letter to Charles Eggert. January 23. in William Culp Darrah Collection, Utah State Historical Society. Salt Lake City.

16. William H. Dunn's sketchy origin: Darrah, W. C. 1947. The Howland Brothers and William Dunn. *Utah Historical Quarterly* 15:93-94.

16. "The state of Ohio never turned out a man that had more nerve than William Dunn.": Hawkins, W. R. in R. B. Stanton, A.M., C.C.B.A. no date (written in 1906-1909). The River and the Canon: The Colorado River of the West, and the Exploration, Navigation, and Survey of its Canons, from the Standpoint of an Engineer. (unpublished manuscript). pp. 434.

17. Andy Hall's young life: Account related by Mamie Hall Laughlin (642 Poplar, Topeka, Kansas) and recorded by H. S. Bryant, Grand Canyon, August 30, 1941. This short letter is from the Cline Library Special Collections archives, MS 77, Box 1, of the Martin J. Anderson Collection.

18. Hall was "nineteen years old, with what seems to us a 'secondhand head'": Powell, J. W. 1895 in R. B. Stanton, A.M., C.C.B.A. no date (written in 1906-1909). The River and the Canon: The Colorado River of the

West, and the Exploration, Navigation, and Survey of its Canons, from the Standpoint of an Engineer. (unpublished manuscript). p. 441. Loaned to Cline Library Special Collections by New York Public Library, Manuscripts and Archives Division.

19.   William Hawkins' origin: Lago, D. 2001. Billy Hawkins: abducted by Alias! *boatman's quarterly review* Fall, 2001, 14(3):10-11. *see also* Darrah, W. C. 1947. Hawkins, Hall, and Goodman. *Utah Historical Quarterly* 15:106-108.

20.   Hawkins, Dunn, and Sumner meet and "sign on" with Major Powell: Hawkins, W. R. in R. B. Stanton, A.M., C.C.B.A. no date (written in 1906-1909). The River and the Canon: The Colorado River of the West, and the Exploration, Navigation, and Survey of its Canons, from the Standpoint of an Engineer. (unpublished manuscript). pp. 428-430. Loaned to Cline Library Special Collections by the New York Public Library, Manuscripts and Archives Division. *see also* Hawkins, W. R. 1932 [1982]. William Hawkins' Story, in Stanton, R. B. (ed.) *Colorado River Controversies*, pp. 140-153. Boulder City: Westwater. pp. 141-142.

21.   Hawkins "is an athlete and a jovial good fellow, who hardly seems to know his own strength": Powell, J. W. 1895. in R. B. Stanton, A.M., C.C.B.A. no date (written in 1906-1909). The River and the Canon: The Colorado River of the West, and the Exploration, Navigation, and Survey of its Canons, from the Standpoint of an Engineer. (unpublished manuscript). p. 441. Loaned to Cline Library Special Collections by the New York Public Library, Manuscripts and Archives Division.

21.   there was no collusion between Hawkins and Sumner: Anderson, M. J. 1982. Commentary on Part Two: The Affair at Separation Rapids. in Stanton, R. B. [1932] *Colorado River Controversies*, pp. 253-259. Boulder City: Westwater. p. 257.

23.   Oramel and Seneca Howland's origins: Darrah, W. C. 1947. The Howland Brothers and William Dunn. *Utah Historical Quarterly* 15:93-94.

24.   Seneca "suffered a minor wound at the battle at Gettysburg and was temporarily incapacitated for further action": Darrah. W. C. 1947. The Howland Brothers and William Dunn. *Utah Historical Quarterly* 15, pp. 93-94. p. 93.

24.   on William Culp Darrah's early history and on discrepancies between Darrah's account of Seneca Howland versus reality: Lago, D. 2002 [in press]. Seneca Howland: The Unsung Hero. *boatman's quarterly review*. 6 ms. pages.

24.   the battle of Gettysburg: Millett, A. R. & P. Maslowski. 1984. *For the Common Defense A Military History of the United States of America*. New York: The Free Press. pp. 205-208

25.   Abner Doubleday shouted, "Glory to God! See the Vermonters go it!": Steward, G. R. 1963. *Pickett's Charge: A Microhistory of the Final Attack at Gettysburg. July 3, 1863*. Greenwich, Conn: Fawcett.

26.   On William Culp Darrah's professional history: 1991. Lyons, P. C. and E. Darrah Morey. 1993. A Tribute to an American Paleobotanist: William Culp Darrah (1909-1989). *Douzieme Congres International de la Stratigraphie et Geologie du Carbonifere et Permian, Comptes Rendus, Vol. 2*, pp. 117-126. Buenos Aires, 22-27 Septembre.

26.   "Major Powell was truly the young Darrah's hero, a role model for outstanding accomplishment in the face of adversity and great obstacles": 1991.

Lyons, P. C. and E. Darrah Morey. 1993. A Tribute to an American Paleobotanist: William Culp Darrah (1909-1989). *Douzieme Congres International de la Stratigraphie et Geologie du Carbonifere et Permian, Comptes Rendus, Vol. 2*, pp. 117-126. Buenos Aires, 22-27 Septembre. p. 118.

27.   "Yet the simple fact is they [the Howlands and Dunn] were afraid to go farther and deserted": Darrah, W. C. 1951. *Powell of the Colorado*. Princeton: Princeton University Press. page 141.

27.   "Of course we knew what was the reason Dunn left: as for fear, he did not possess it": Hawkins, W. R. in R. B. Stanton, A.M., C.C.B.A. no date (written in 1906-1909). The River and the Canon: The Colorado River of the West, and the Exploration, Navigation, and Survey of its Canons, from the Standpoint of an Engineer. (unpublished manuscript). pp. 437.

28.   John Colton Sumner writes very well of Seneca, describing him as: "as good and true a man as can be found in any place": Sumner, J. C. 1869. J. C. Sumner's Journal, June 8.

28.   John Wesley Powell as a saint: Stegner, W. 1953, 1954 [1962]. *Beyond the Hundredth Meridian: John Wesley Powell and the Second Opening of the West*. Boston: Houghton Mifflin Co./ Cambridge: The Riverside Press. *note that*: Stegner allegedly deliberately avoided writing in this biography of Powell any of the decisions Powell made via weak character. Stegner's quote being, "I know Powell did some bad things, but he's not going to do them in *my* book": Bruce Babbitt. 1988. Personal communication to M. P. Ghiglieri on Colorado River, October 31.

29.   John Wesley Powell's early life: Darrah, W. C. 1951. *Powell of the Colorado*. Princeton: Princeton University Press.

30.   Powell as a facile scientist: Worster, D. 2001. *A River Running West: The Life of John Wesley Powell*. New York: Oxford. p. 320.

31.   "It was a great thing to destroy slavery:" Worster, D. 2001. *A River Running West: The Life of John Wesley Powell*. New York: Oxford. p. 96.

31.   John Wesley Powell's military experience: U.S. Army records, Powell, J. W. # 360400, Batt'y F, 2 Illinois L. Art'y, Book Mark 5519-U.S. '86. 17663-U.S. '83: card numbers 28164047, 28164188, 28164345, 28164503, 28164664, 28164823, 28164973, 28165098, 28165244, 28145245, 28165387, 28165533, 28165682, 28165826, 28165958, 28166090, 28166224, 28166364, 28166559, 28166752, 28166938, 28149524, 28145245, 28167242, 28167654, 28167890, 28150711, 31920799, 34351082, 34351117, 34351159, 34834318, 42581394, 42581510, 42606397, 42606442, 42872932, 42872942, 42872959, 42872974, 42872987, 42873006, 42873091, 42873774, 42873775, 42873776, 42873777, 42873778, 42874488, 42978995, 42979078.

31.   "About four o'clock:" Worster, D. 2001. *A River Running West: The Life of John Wesley Powell*. New York: Oxford. pp. 92-93.

33.   Sumner says he suggested to Powell the idea of running the Colorado: Sumner, J. C. 1932 [1982]. Jack Sumner's account. in Stanton. R. B. [1932] *Colorado River Controversies*. pp. 167-213. Boulder City: Westwater. p. 169.

33.   Whose idea was the 1869 river expedition? "The result of the summer's study was to kindle a desire to explore the cañons of the Grand, Green, and Colorado Rivers": Powell, J. W. 1875. *Exploration of the Colorado River of the West and Its Tributaries Explored in 1869, 1870, 1871, and 1872*. Washington, D.C.: Government Printing Office. p. *ix*.

33.   "The major is from Bloomington, Ill. I suppose you never herd [sic] of him
          and he is a Bully fellow you bett": Hall, A. 1869 (1948-1949). Three
          letters by Andrew Hall. edited by W. C. Darrah. *Utah Historical
          Quarterly* 16-17:505-508. p. 507.

33.   "We had a fine lot of men on that expedition": Dellenbaugh, F. S. 1934. letter
          to Mrs. Whittemore, December 6. the William Culp Darrah
          Collection. Utah State Historical Society. Salt Lake City.

34.   "I can say one thing truthfully about the Major": Hawkins, W. R. 1932 [1982].
          William Hawkins' Story, in Stanton, R. B. (ed.) *Colorado River
          Controversies*, pp. 140-163. Boulder City: Westwater. p. 146.

34.   "As I shared the blankets with Major J. W. Powell for two years, I believe I
          knew him": Sumner, J. C. 1907. in R. B. Stanton, A.M., C.C.B.A. no
          date (written in 1906-1909). The River and the Canon: The Colorado
          River of the West, and the Exploration, Navigation, and Survey of its
          Canons, from the Standpoint of an Engineer. (unpublished
          manuscript). p. 424.

35.   —"you will notice neither you nor I speak of his justice or loyalty": Anderson,
          M. J. no date. John Wesley Powell's Reporting of History: Fact?
          Fiction? or Fantasy? undated manuscript. In the Northern Arizona
          University Cline Library Special Collections, MS 77, Box 1, pp.14-15,
          16. Martin J. Anderson Collection.

35.   "The whole party is disgusted with the way the expedition is run": Powell, W.
          C. 1948. Journal of Walter Clement Powell. *Utah Historical Quarterly*:
          *The Exploration of the Colorado River and the High Plateaus of Utah in
          1871-72,* Vols. XVI-XVII:257-478. pp. 288, 365, 367, 369, 371, 373,
          388.

36.   "no business motive should lead a man to be unjust": Steward, J. F. 1903
          [1948]. John F. Steward (profile by William Culp Darrah). *Utah
          Historical Quarterly*: *The Exploration of the Colorado River and the High
          Plateaus of Utah in 1871-72,* Vols. XVI-XVII:175-179. pp. 176; *see also*
          pp. 236, 246.

36.   Major Powell's life jacket: Hawkins, W. R. 1932 [1982]. William Hawkins'
          Story, in Stanton, R. B. (ed.) *Colorado River Controversies*, pp. 140-163.
          Boulder City: Westwater. p. 153. *see also* Stanton, R. B. 1982 [1932].
          Major Powell as Historian. in *Colorado River Controversies*, pp. 97-137.
          Boulder City: Westwater. pp. 130-135.

36.   "Major Powell said he was dressed when he had his life preserver on, and he
          always had it on when the water was bad": Hawkins, W. R. in R. B.
          Stanton, A.M., C.C.B.A. no date (written in 1906-1909). The River
          and the Canon: The Colorado River of the West, and the
          Exploration, Navigation, and Survey of its Canons, from the
          Standpoint of an Engineer. (unpublished manuscript). p. 433. Loaned
          to Cline Library Special Collections by the New York Public Library,
          Manuscripts and Archives Division.

38.   In 1867 Powell was entertaining the idea of traveling the river *upstream* - :
          Darrah, W.C. 1947. The Powell Colorado River Expedition of 1869.
          Utah Historical Quarterly 15:9-18, p.9.

38.   Walter Powell's origin: Darrah, W. C. 1947. Walter Henry Powell 1842-1915.
          Utah Historical Quarterly 15:89.

39.   "Captain Walter Powell was about as worthless a piece of furniture as could be
          found in a day's journey": Sumner, J. C. 1932 [1982]. Jack Sumner's
          account. in Stanton. R. B. [1932] *Colorado River Controversies*. pp. 167-

213. Boulder City: Westwater. p. 211.

39. Bradley's perspective on Walter Powell: Bradley, G. Y. 1947. George Y. Bradley's Journal. *Utah Historical Quarterly* 15:31-72. Also a copy of original journal in script.

39. "None of the party except the Major liked Capt. Powell. He had a bull-dozing way that was not then practiced in the West. He threatened to slap me several times for trying to sing like he did, but he never did slap anyone in the party": Hawkins, W. R. 1932 [1982]. William Hawkins' Story, in Stanton, R. B. (ed.) *Colorado River Controversies*, pp. 140-163. Boulder City: Westwater. p. 157.

40. "[Walter Powell refused Hall] which so angered Hall that he wanted to blow the top of his damn head off": Anderson, M. J. 1982. Commentary on Part Two: The Affair at Separation Rapids. in Stanton, R. B. 1932 [1982] *Colorado River Controversies*, pp. 253-259. Boulder City: Westwater. p. 256.

41. Sumner's origin: 1907. Jack Sumner, Borderman, is Buried in Riverside: Colorado Pioneer Ends Life of Activity. Noted Scout, Soldier, Explorer and Frontiersman Dies at Vernal, Utah. *Rocky Mountain News, The Daily News: Denver, Colorado* July 10. p. 5. *see also* Sumner, J. C. 1947. J. C. Sumner's Journal, July 6-August 31, 1869. *Utah Historical Quarterly* 15:113-124.

41. Sumner's origin: Darrah, W. C. 1947. John C. Sumner 1840-1907. *Utah Historical Quarterly* 15:109-112.

41. Sumner threatens to blow the cabin full of Indians to hell: Stanton, R. B. 1932 [1982]. *Colorado River Controversies*. Boulder City: Westwater. p. 165.

42. Robert Brewster Stanton described Sumner as "a true frontiersman, with a kind, gentle, loving heart": R. B. Stanton, A.M., C.C.B.A. no date (written in 1906-1909). The River and the Cañon: The Colorado River of the West, and the Exploration, Navigation, and Survey of its Cañons, from the Standpoint of an Engineer. (unpublished manuscript). p. 348. Loaned to Cline Library Special Collections by the New York Public Library, Manuscripts and Archives Division.

42. Sumner "fired back at him the counter-proposition — *the exploration of the Colorado River of the West*, from the junction of the Green and Grand Rivers to the Gulf": Stanton, A.M., C.C.B.A. no date (written in 1906-1909). The River and the Cañon: The Colorado River of the West, and the Exploration, Navigation, and Survey of its Cañons, from the Standpoint of an Engineer. (unpublished manuscript). p. 388. Cline Library Special Collections.

42-43. "The result of the summer's study [in 1867 in Middle Park] was to kindle a desire to explore the canyons of the Grand, Green, and Colorado rivers": Powell, J. W. 1875. *Exploration of the Colorado River of the West and Its Tributaries Explored in 1869, 1870, 1871, and 1872*. Washington, D.C.: Government Printing Office. p. *ix*. *see also* Powell, J. W. 1895 [1964]. *Canyons of the Colorado*. New York: Argosy-Antiquarian Ltd. p. 17.

45. the tenderfoot who didn't dare: Powell, J. W. 1947 [1870]. Major J. W. Powell's Report on His Exploration of the Rio Colorado in 1869. in W. A. Bell (ed.) *New Tracks in North America*, reprinted in the *Utah Historical Quarterly* 15:21-27. p. 26.

46. the tenderfoot who didn't dare: Hawkins, W. R. in R. B. Stanton, A.M., C.C.B.A. no date (written in 1906-1909). The River and the Canon:

The Colorado River of the West, and the Exploration, Navigation, and Survey of its Canons, from the Standpoint of an Engineer. (unpublished manuscript). pp. 431-432. Loaned to Cline Library Special Collections by the New York Public Library, Manuscripts and Archives Division. *see also* Hawkins, W. R. 1932 [1982]. William Hawkins' Story, in Stanton, R. B. (ed.) *Colorado River Controversies*, pp. 140-153. Boulder City: Westwater. pp. 144-145.

47.   W. H. Bishop decides not to accompany Powell downriver: Worster, D. 2001. *A River Running West: The Life of John Wesley Powell.* New York: Oxford. pp. 147-150.

48-49.   the contract between Powell and Sumner, Dunn, and Howland: Powell, J. W. 1869. Copy of unpublished "agreement" between J. W. Powell, party of the 1st part and parties of the 2nd part: J. C. Sumner, William H. Dunn, and O. G. Howland. In University of Arizona Dellenbaugh Collection, Box 5, folder 9.

50.   Powell's contract with Hawkins: Hawkins, W. R. 1932 [1982]. William Hawkins' Story, in Stanton, R. B. (ed.) *Colorado River Controversies*, pp. 140-153. Boulder City: Westwater. p. 142.

52.   on Powell's 1869 boats: Anderson, M. J. undated ms. Who designed Powell's boats? Cline Library Special Collections archives, MS 77, Box 2, of the Martin J. Anderson collection.

52.   In 1871-72, Powell's crew sawed their running oars down to eight feet long: Dellenbaugh, F. S. 1922. *A Canyon Voyage The Narrative of the Second Powell Expedition down the Green-Colorado River from Wyoming, and the Explorations on Land, in the Years 1871 and 1872.* New Haven: Yale University Press. P. 14.

57.   "*the oarsmen back water*": Powell, J. W. 1895 [1964]. *Canyons of the Colorado.* New York: Argosy-Antiquarian Ltd. facsimile edition. p. 151.

60.   "The boat at times will be wedged in between the rocks while we are tugging and pullng away; suddenly away she will go, dragging us after her, holding on for dear life, and woe to the unlucky one who does not keep his legs in his pockets at such a time. 'Tis a wonder that some of us have not had a leg or two broken. All of us wear horrible scars from our knees downward to remind us of the days when we made portages": Powell, W. C. 1948. Journal of Walter Clement Powell. *Utah Historical Quarterly: The Exploration of the Colorado River and the High Plateaus of Utah in 1871-72,* Vols. XVI-XVII:257-478. pp. 328-329.

60.   Fifty years later Hawkins remembers this as 22 feet: Hawkins, W. W. [sic]. 1920. in W. W. Bass (ed.) *Adventures in the Canyons of the Colorado By two of its earliest explorers, James White and W. W. Hawkins with introduction and notes.* Grand Canyon, Arizona. W. W. Bass. p. 19.

61.   on the origin of the *No Name*: Lago, D. in press. Call me *No Name. boatman's quarterly review.*

62.   on Kitty Clyde's Sister: Gill, A. 2001. Who was Kitty Clyde anyway? *boatman's quarterly review,* Summer, 14(2):44-45.

64.   38 and 50 years later, Hawkins twice mentions doing something like this: Hawkins, W. R. in R. B. Stanton, A.M., C.C.B.A. no date (written in 1906-1909). The River and the Canon: The Colorado River of the West, and the Exploration, Navigation, and Survey of its Canons, from the Standpoint of an Engineer. (unpublished manuscript). p. 438. *see also* Hawkins, W. W. [sic]. 1920. in W. W. Bass (ed.) *Adventures*

in the Canyons of the Colorado By two of its earliest explorers, James White and W. W. Hawkins with introduction and notes. Grand Canyon, Arizona. W. W. Bass. p. 19.

65-66.   mishaps and losses in 1871: Steward, J. F. 1948. Journal of John F. Steward. *Utah Historical Quarterly: The Exploration of the Colorado River and the High Plateaus of Utah in 1871-72,* Vols. XVI-XVII:181-252. p. 249.

65-66.   mishaps and losses in 1871-72: Powell, W. C. 1948. Journal of Walter Clement Powell. *Utah Historical Quarterly: The Exploration of the Colorado River and the High Plateaus of Utah in 1871-72,* Vols. XVI-XVII:257-478. pp. 268, 322, 443, 444, 445, 446.

66.   *Kitty Clyde's Sister* would "neither gee nor haw nor whoa worth a damn": Sumner, J. C. 1932 [1982]. Jack Sumner's account. in Stanton. R. B. *Colorado River Controversies.* pp. 167-213. Boulder City: Westwater. p. 175.

68.   the significance of the transcontinental railroad: Arrington, L. J. 1969. The Transcontinental Railroad and the development of the West. *Utah Historical Quarterly* 37(1):3-15.

68.   finishing the transcontinental railroad: Best, G. M. 1969. Rendezvous at Promontory: The "Jupiter" and No. 119. *Utah Historical Quarterly* 37(1):69-75.

68.   driving the golden spike: Bowman, J. N. 1969. Driving the last spike at Promontory, 1869. *Utah Historical Quarterly* 37(1):76-101.

68.   the building of the transcontinental railroad and the Indians' resistance to it: Ambrose, S. E. 2000. *Nothing Like It in the World: The Men Who Built the Transcontinental railroad 1863-1869.* New York: Simon and Schuster.

69.   Denis Julien's river running & inscriptions: Knipmeyer, J. H. 1996. The Denis Julien inscriptions. *Utah Historical Society* 64(1):52-69. *see also* Kelly, C. 1933. The mysterious "D. Julien." *Utah Historical Quarterly* 6(3):82-88.

70-71.   James White's story of rafting Grand Canyon: W. W. Bass (ed.). 1920. *Adventures in the Canyons of the Colorado By two of its earliest explorers, James White and W. W. Hawkins with introduction and notes.* Grand Canyon, Arizona. W. W. Bass. *see also* Adams E. 2001. *Hell or High Water: James White's Disputed Passage Through Grand Canyon 1867.* Logan: Utah State University Press.

71.   As noted by William Culp Darrah: "Powell was determined to descend the Grand River to its junction with the Colorado in the following summer [of 1868] "; Darrah, W.C. 1951. *Powell of the Colorado.* Princeton: Princeton University Press. p. 89.

73.   The strong possibility exists that Powell secretly believed that James White *did* raft through Grand Canyon...: Adams E. 2001. *Hell or High Water: James White's Disputed Passage Through Grand Canyon 1867.* Logan: Utah State University Press. pp. 91-100.

75.   drowning and life jackets: Ghiglieri, M. P. and T. M. Myers. 2001. *Over The Edge: Death in Grand Canyon.* Flagstaff: Puma Press. pp. 208-209.

SOURCES on CHAPTER 11. FATES:

237-238. On the triumph of Lewis and Clark: Ambrose, S. E. 1996. *Undaunted Courage: Meriwether Lewis, Thomas Jefferson, and the Opening of the American West.* New York: Simon and Schuster.

238.   "From this wreck commenced the many quarrels between Major Powell and O. G. Howland and Bill Dunn which caused so much trouble":

Sumner, J. C. in R. B. Stanton, A.M., C.C.B.A. no date (written in 1906-1909). The River and the Canon: The Colorado River of the West, and the Exploration, Navigation, and Survey of its Canons, from the Standpoint of an Engineer. (unpublished manuscript). p. 395.

239.   "And if any men ever penance for their sins we did a plenty for the next two hundred miles": Sumner, J. C. in R. B. Stanton, A.M., C.C.B.A. no date (written in 1906-1909). The River and the Canon: The Colorado River of the West, and the Exploration, Navigation, and Survey of its Canons, from the Standpoint of an Engineer. (unpublished manuscript). p. 409, 410 & 413.

239.   Sumner's journal did not express all of his feelings freely because it was written *for* Powell: Sumner, J. C. 1947. J. C. Sumner's Journal, July 6-August 31, 1869. *Utah Historical Quarterly* 15:113-124.

240.   "Major Powell was gone five days, and brought back a shirt tail full of supplies": Sumner, J. C. in R. B. Stanton, A.M., C.C.B.A. no date (written in 1906-1909). The River and the Canon: The Colorado River of the West, and the Exploration, Navigation, and Survey of its Canons, from the Standpoint of an Engineer. (unpublished manuscript). pp. 399-400.

240.   "I do not wish to cast any discredit on Major Powell's Report or upon his memory of": Hawkins, W. R. in R. B. Stanton, A.M., C.C.B.A. no date (written in 1906-1909). The River and the Canon: The Colorado River of the West, and the Exploration, Navigation, and Survey of its Canons, from the Standpoint of an Engineer. (unpublished manuscript). p. 434.

240.   "the ropes happened to catch Bill Dunn under the arms and came near drowning him": Hawkins, W. W. [sic]. 1920. in W. W. Bass (ed.) *Adventures in the Canyons of the Colorado By two of its earliest explorers, James White and W. W. Hawkins with introduction and notes.* Grand Canyon, Arizona. W. W. Bass. pp. 23-27.

241.   "The positions of the main water-courses have been determined": Ives. J. C. 1861. *Report upon the Colorado River of the West, Explored in 1857 and 1858 by Lieutenant Joseph C. Ives. Corps of Engineers, Under the Direction of the Office of Explorations and Surveys, A. A. Humphreys, Captain Topographical Engineers, in Charge, by Order of the Secretary of War.* Washington, D. C.: Government Printing Office. p. 110.

242.   " — as Dunn was a fine swimmer, the Major asked him to swim out to a rock so the boat could swing in below": Hawkins, W. R. 1919. in Stanton, R. B. 1932 [1982]. *Colorado River Controversies.* Boulder City, Nevada: Westwater. pp. 158-160.

243.   "I think that only the fact that the Major had but one arm saved him from a broken head, if nothing worse." Sumner, J. C. 1907. in R. B. Stanton, A.M., C.C.B.A. no date (written in 1906-1909). The River and the Canon: The Colorado River of the West, and the Exploration, Navigation, and Survey of its Canons, from the Standpoint of an Engineer. (unpublished manuscript). p. 415.

244.   "Major Powell did not run the outfit in the same overbearing manner after that": Sumner, J. C. 1907. in R. B. Stanton, A.M., C.C.B.A. no date (written in 1906-1909). The River and the Canon: The Colorado River of the West, and the Exploration, Navigation, and Survey of its Canons, from the Standpoint of an Engineer. (unpublished

manuscript). p. 416.

244.	"If they did not occur, why did the two men invent them? Spleen perhaps....The neglect festered, to find relief in wild tales to Stanton when the men were old and their memories fading": Lavender, D. 1985. *River Runners of the Grand Canyon*. Grand Canyon: Grand Canyon Natural History Association. p. 17.

244-245. wages that Sumner, Howland, and Dunn were to be paid: Powell, J. W. 1869. Copy of unpublished "agreement" between J. W. Powell, party of the 1st part and parties of the 2nd part: J. C. Sumner, William H. Dunn, and O. G. Howland. In University of Arizona Dellenbaugh Collection, Box 5, folder 9.

245.	What Hawkins was to be paid for the 1868-1869 expedition: Hawkins, W. R. 1907. in R. B. Stanton, A.M., C.C.B.A. no date (written in 1906-1909). The River and the Canon: The Colorado River of the West, and the Exploration, Navigation, and Survey of its Canons, from the Standpoint of an Engineer. (unpublished manuscript). pp. 429-431.

247.	"It is important to note there was no collusion between Sumner and Hawkins. They wrote their versions at different times from different places": Anderson, M. J. 1982. Commentary on Part Two: The Affair at Separation Rapids. in Stanton, R. B. 1932 [1982]. *Colorado River Controversies*. Boulder City, Nevada: Westwater. p. 257.

247-248. The scene at Separation Rapid: Ghiglieri, M. P. 1992. *Canyon*. Tucson, Arizona: The University of Arizona Press.

250.	Hawkins' version of the episode at Separation Rapid: Hawkins, W. R. in R. B. Stanton, A.M., C.C.B.A. no date (written in 1906-1909). The River and the Canon: The Colorado River of the West, and the Exploration, Navigation, and Survey of its Canons, from the Standpoint of an Engineer. (unpublished manuscript). pp. 434-439.

249, 251. "I talked with Major Powell quietly on the subject. He seemed dazed": Sumner, J. C. 1907. in R. B. Stanton, A.M., C.C.B.A. no date (written in 1906-1909). The River and the Canon: The Colorado River of the West, and the Exploration, Navigation, and Survey of its Canons, from the Standpoint of an Engineer. (unpublished manuscript). pp. 417-419.

252.	Andrew Hall was certain that Dunn and O. G. Howland were afraid of Separation Rapid: Hall, A. 1869 (1948-1949). Three letters by Andrew Hall. edited by W. C. Darrah *Utah Historical Quarterly* 16-17:505-508.

253.	"They [the Howlands and Dunn] were followed by three Shebetts and were killed": staff. 1869. Three of the Powell Expedition Killed by Indians. *Deseret Evening News,* September 8.

254.	" — some of their friends from the other side of the river crossed on a raft": Little, James A. 1881. *Jacob Hamblin: A Narrative of His Personal Experience, as a Frontiersman, Missionary to the Indians and Explorer.* Salt Lake City: Juvenile Instructor Office. p. 97.

254.	All previous histories of Powell's 1869 trip has the Shivwits killing the Howlands and Dunn: Dellenbaugh, F. S. 1902 [1962]. *The Romance of the Colorado*. Chicago: Rio Grande Press. pp. 227-230. *see also* Darrah, W. C. 1951, *ibid.* & Worster, D. D. 2001. *ibid.*

255.	the history and timing of mining claims in Western Grand Canyon: Billingsley, G. H., E. E. Spamer and D. Menkes. 1998. *Quest for the Pillar of Gold: The Mines & Miners of the Grand Canyon*. Grand Canyon: Grand

Canyon Association. *also* George H. Billingsley. 2000. Personal interview by M. P. Ghiglieri, February 4.

255.   gold prospecting on the Colorado in 1872: Powell, W. C. 1948-49. Journal of Walter Clement Powell: April 21, 1871--December 7, 1872 (edited by Charles Kelly) *Utah Historical Quarterly* 16-17:257-478. pp. 397-406, 410.

255.   The Hualapai war with the U.S. Army: McGuire, T. R. 1983. Walapai. in *Handbook of North American Indians Volume 10 Southwest,* pp. 25-37. Washington, D.C.: Smithsonian Institution.

255.   "That a small group of Indians or a solitary Indian from the South would be motivated to cross the river": Belshaw, M. 1979. The Dunn-Howland killings: A reconstruction. *The Journal of Arizona History* 20(4):409-423.

255-256. mining *had* been taking place since 1864, 60 air-miles south-southwest of the edge of Shivwits territory: Dobyns, H. F. and R. C. Euler. 1980. The Dunn-Howland killings: additional insights. *The Journal of Arizona History* 21(1):87-95.

256.   "The trail to the water leads down under a basaltic cliff": Dellenbaugh, F. S. 1904 [1965]. *The Romance of the Colorado River: The Story of its Discovery in 1540, with an Account of the Later Explorations, and with Special Reference to the Voyages of Powell through the Great Line of Canyons.* Chicago: Rio Grande Press. pp. 229-230.

256-258. the identification of Toab as the killer of the Howlands and Dunn: Ivins, A. W. 1944. A mystery of the Grand Canyon solved. in Nibley, P. (ed.) 1944. *Pioneer Stories Compiled under the Direction of the Presiding Bishopric for the Youth of the Church.* (fourth printing). Salt Lake City: Deseret News Press. pp. 199-210.

257.   Toab's prison record only lists horse theft; Toab murdered a fellow Shivwit, "George": Martineau, L. 1992. *Southern Paiutes, Legend, Lore, Language, & Lineage.* p. 66.

258.   Toab was merely a small boy, not the Howlands & Dunn killer: Barrios, F. M. 2002. An 1869 appointment with death. *The Ol' Pioneer A magazine of the Grand Canyon Pioneers Society,* January/March 2002, 13(1):3-6.

261-262. "They all seemed to think the red bellies would get them sure": Sumner, J. C. 1907. in R. B. Stanton, A.M., C.C.B.A. no date (written in 1906-1909). The River and the Canon: The Colorado River of the West, and the Exploration, Navigation, and Survey of its Canons, from the Standpoint of an Engineer. (unpublished manuscript). p. 419 & 422.

260.   "but when Major Powell made the foolish break of telling them the amount of valuables the boys had": Sumner, J. C. 1907. in R. B. Stanton, A.M., C.C.B.A. no date (written in 1906-1909). The River and the Canon: The Colorado River of the West, and the Exploration, Navigation, and Survey of its Canons, from the Standpoint of an Engineer. (unpublished manuscript).pp. 421-422.

261-262. details of the Mountain Meadows massacre: Brooks, J. 1950 [1991]. *The Mountain Meadows Massacre.* Norman: University of Oklahoma Press. see also Logan, R.V., Jr. 1992. New light on the Mountain Meadows caravan. *Utah Historical Quarterly* 60(3): 224-237. and Bagley, W. 2002. *Blood of the Prophets: Brigham Young and the Massacre at Mountain Meadows.* Norman: University of Oklahoma Press.

262-266. on the details of the 1859 investigation of the Mountain Meadows Massacre: Carleton, J. H. 1859 [1995]. *The Mountain Meadows Massacre: A Special Report by J. H. Carleton, Bvt. Major U.S.A.* Captain 1st Dragoons.

Spokane, Washington: Arthur H. Clark.

266-267. New revelations about the culprits of the Mountain Meadows Massacre based on forensics performed on 28 victims' bones disinterred in 1999: Vaughan, K. 2002. Utah's Killing Field: A remote valley's soil yields secrets to famed 1857 massacre that some aren't ready to hear. *Rocky Mountain News,* February 25.

267.   "This and several similar discrepancies did not argue well for the bishop's sanctity.": Ives. J. C. 1861. *Report upon the Colorado River of the West, Explored in 1857 and 1858 by Lieutenant Joseph C. Ives. Corps of Engineers, Under the Direction of the Office of Explorations and Surveys, A. A. Humphreys, Captain Topographical Engineers, in Charge, by Order of the Secretary of War.* Washington, D. C.: Government Printing Office. pp. 86-92.

269.   details of John D. Lee's relationship with Jacob Hamblin and of Wesley P. Larsen's personal experiences while researching the William Leany letter: Thybony, Scott. Many personal communications with M. P. Ghiglieri over the years from 1990-2002. Flagstaff, Arizona.

270-271. William Leany's letter to John Steele: Larsen, W. P. 1993. The "letter" Or were the Powell men really killed by Indians? *Canyon Legacy* #17, Spring, pp. 12-19.

271.   Anderson, V. 1993. Did murders happen in Mormon Ward? 1883 letter may solve mystery of trio. *The Salt Lake Tribune.* November 28, p. B3.

274.   'the two howlands and Dunn were killed. Powell states by Indians & I Say Killed by the Mormons, Part of the Same old "Mountains Meadows" massacre gang': Sumner, Jack. 1906. letter written to L. W. Keplinger, Paradox, Colorado. September 14. In the Keplinger Collection, Kansas State Historical Society. *See also* Lago, D. 2002. Jack Sumner looks back. *boatman's quarterly review* 15(2):40-41.

274.   the violent demise of Andy Hall: Woody, C. T. and M. L. Schwartz. 1977. *Globe, Arizona.* The Arizona Historical Society. pp. 65-77.

278.   "Capt W.H. Powell was taken down sick": Gill, A. 2002. Regarding *Jack Sumner looks back* by Don Lago, BQR 14:2. *boatman's quarterly review* 15(3):7.

279.   Walter Henry Powell's post 1869 experiences: Worster, D. 2001. *A River Running West: The Life of John Wesley Powell.* New York: Oxford. *see also* Darrah, W. C. 1947. Walter Henry Powell 1842-1915. *Utah Historical Quarterly* 15:89.

280.   William Robert Wesley Hawkins' post 1869 experiences: W. W. Bass (ed.) 1920. *Adventures in the Canyons of the Colorado By two of its earliest explorers, James White and W. W. Hawkins with introduction and notes.* Grand Canyon, Arizona. W. W. Bass. pp. 13-14. *see also* Darrah, W. C. 1947. Hawkins, Hall, and Goodman. *Utah Historical Quarterly* 15:105-108. p. 108. *see also* Worster, D. 2001. *A River Running West: The Life of John Wesley Powell.* New York: Oxford. pp. 195, 372. *and* Lago, D. 2001. Billy Hawkins: abducted by Alias! *boatman's quarterly review* Fall, 2001, 14(3):10-11.

281-282. "I was postmaster at St. Thomas": Leithead, J., Bishop. undated. "Autobiography." in Special Collections, Harold B. Lee Library. Brigham Young University.

282.   Major Powell not only never thanked or reimbursed Leithead, Powell mentioned him only cursorily in *Canyons* — and, even then, spelled his name wrong: Powell, J. W. 1895. [1964]. *Canyons of the Colorado.* New York: Argosy-Antiquarian Ltd. facsimile edition. p. 287.

283-291. On Major Powell's post-1869 career: Worster, D. 2001. *A River Running West: The Life of John Wesley Powell.* New York: Oxford. pp. 209, 218, 244, 246, 344, 304-305, 270-271, 286-87, 292, 284-285, 349, 495-573.

284.   "Powell...announced that he had decided to end the river work at this point:" Dellenbaugh, F. S. 1904. [1965]. *The Romance of the Colorado.* Chicago: Rio Grande Press. p. 341. quoted by R. B. Stanton, A.M., C.C.B.A. no date (written in 1906-1909). The River and the Canon: The Colorado River of the West, and the Exploration, Navigation, and Survey of its Canons, from the Standpoint of an Engineer. (unpublished manuscript). p. 36. Loaned to Cline Library Special Collections by New York Public Library, Manuscripts and Archives Division.

285.   "The fires can, then, be very greatly curtailed by the removal of the Indians.": Powell, J. W. 1878. [1983]. *Report on the Lands of the Arid Region of the United States with a More Detailed Account of the Lands of Utah.* (Facsimile of the 1879 Edition). Boston: The Harvard Common Press. pp. 17-18.

285.   Powell's proposed revisions of the Homestead Act for the arid West: Powell, J. W. 878. [1983]. *Report on the Lands of the Arid Region of the United States with a More Detailed Account of the Lands of Utah.* (Facsimile of the 1879 Edition). Boston: The Harvard Common Press. pp. 21-22, 23, 28-45.

289.   Powell was lucky in his 1869 crew and in the expedition itself: Anderson, M. 1979. First through the Canyon: Powell's lucky voyage in 1869. *The Journal of Arizona History* 20(4): 391-408.

289.   "The success of that expedition": Lago, D. 2002. Jack Sumner Looks Back. *boatmen's quarterly review* 14(2):40-41. Summer 2002.

289.   "I cannot find in Powell anywhere, not even in his commonwealth idea, any room for this awareness: Worster, D. 1994. *An Unsettled Country: Changing Landscapes of the American West.* Albuquerque: University of New Mexico Press. p. 29.

290.   On Powell's "almost" legacy: Powell, J. W. 1879 [1983]. *Report on the Lands of the Arid Regions of the United States with a More Detailed Account of the Lands of Utah.* (Facsimile of the 1879 Edition). Harvard and Boston, MA: The Harvard Common Press.

291-294. "Dear Old Friend, It seems that after 38 years you Remember your old Friend "Jack.": Sumner, Jack. 1906. letter written to L. W. Keplinger, Paradox, Colorado. September 14. In the Keplinger Collection, Kansas State Historical Society.

294-295. John Colton Sumner's post-1869 history: 1907. Jack Sumner, Borderman, is Buried in Riverside: Colorado Pioneer Ends Life of Activity. Noted Scout, Soldier, Explorer and Frontiersman Dies at Vernal, Utah. *Rocky Mountain News, The Daily News: Denver, Colorado* July 10. p. 5. *see also* Darrah, W. C. 1947. John C. Sumner 1840-1907. *Utah Historical Quarterly* 15:109-112. *see also* Worster, D. 2001. *A River Running West: The Life of John Wesley Powell.* New York: Oxford. pp. 195, 214, 222, 515.

295.   " — it may be truthfully asserted that it was due almost wholly to Sumner's cool nerve": 1907. Jack Sumner, Borderman, is Buried in Riverside: Colorado Pioneer Ends Life of Activity. Noted Scout, Soldier, Explorer and Frontiersman Dies at Vernal, Utah. *Rocky Mountain News, The Daily News: Denver, Colorado* July 10. p. 5.

296.   where did Bradley settle in California and what did he do there?: E. L. Morss.

1947. letter to W. C. Darrah, February 11. in the William Culp
Darrah Collection, Utah State Historical Society. Salt Lake City.

297.   Darrah had no luck in locating George Y. Bradley in San Diego County:
Owen, A. G. 1947. letter to W. C. Darrah from Supervising
Reference Librarian, the City of San Diego, July 22. *see also* Darrah,
W. C. 1947. letters to Louise Bradley, July 3, July 25. *see also* Bradley,
L. 1947. letter to W. C. Darrah, July 12. July 21, August ?. in the
William Culp Darrah Collection, Utah State Historical Society. Salt
Lake City.

297.   Darrah's search for George Y. Bradley's final month: Darrah, W. C. 1946,
1957. letters to E. L. Morss, January 23 & June 18. *see also* Morss, E.
L. 1946, 1947. multiple letters to W. C. Darrah, November 27,
February 11, March 21, June 30. in the William Culp Darrah
Collection, Utah State Historical Society. Salt Lake City.

Addendum to second edition

16.   Goodman's biography: Welch, V. 2004. Frank's early exit and long goodbye.
boatman's quarterly review 17(3): 14–17, pp. 15–16.

38.   William N. Byers as trip leader in 1869: Lago, D. 2008. New evidence on the
origins and disintegration of the Powell expedition in T. R. Berger
(ed.) *Reflections of Grand Canyon Historians. Ideas, Arguments, and First
Person Accounts.* Grand Canyon Association. pp. 119–122.

64.   To complicate matters: Hawkins, W. R. W. 1919. Letter to W. W. Bass (ed.) in
Adventures in the Canyons of the Colorado. 1920. Grand Canyon. W. W.
Bass. p.20.

261.   No evidence exists that Fancher train committed wrongs: Bagley, W. 2002.
Blood of the Prophets: Brigham Young and the Massacre at Mountain Meadows.
Univ. of Oklahoma, p. 117.

264.   J. D. Lee slit the girl's throat: Bagley, W. 2002. *Blood of the Prophets: Brigham
Young and the Massacre at Mountain Meadows.* Univ. of Oklahoma, p.
263.

273.   Three other murder victims in Toquerville in 1875: Lago, D. 2003. The
Toquerville myth. *boatman's quarterly review* 16(3): 32–33.

294.   Jack Sumner self castrates: Lago, D. 2003. The madness of Jack Sumner.
boatman's quarterly review 16(2): 42–43.

INDEX